ISBN 978-0-483-22347-9
PIBN 10179559

THE
UNPOPULAR
REVIEW

PUBLISHED QUARTERLY

VOL. II

JULY—DECEMBER

1914

NEW YORK
HENRY HOLT AND COMPANY

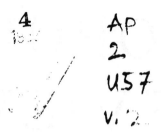

Contents

VOLUME II

No. 3. JULY–SEPTEMBER, 1914

No. 4. OCTOBER–DECEMBER, 1914

The Unpopular Review

No. 3   JULY—SEPTEMBER, 1914   Vol. II

UNSOCIAL INVESTMENTS

THE "new social conscience" is essentially a class phenomenon. While it pretends to the rôle of inner monitor and guide to conduct for all mankind, it interprets good and evil in class terms. It manifests a special solicitude for the welfare of one social group, and a mute hostility toward another. Labor is its Esau, Capital its Jacob. Let strife arise between workingmen and their employers, and you will see the new social conscience aligning itself with the former, accepting at face value all the claims of labor, reiterating all labor's formulæ. The suggestion that judgment should be suspended until the facts at issue are established is repudiated as the prompting of a secret sin. For, to paraphrase a recent utterance of the *Survey*, one of the foremost organs of the new conscience, is it not true that the workers are fighting for their livings, while the employers are fighting only for their profits? It would appear, then, that there can be no question as to the side to which justice inclines. A living is more sacred than a profit.

It is virtually never true, however, that the workers are fighting for their "living." Contrary to Marx's exploded "iron law" they probably had that and more before the trouble began. But of course we would not wish to restrict them to a living, if they can produce more, and want all who can't produce that much to be provided with it — and something more at the expense of others.

It may be urged that the employer's profits also represent the livings of a number of human beings; but this passes nowadays for a reactionary view. "We stand for man as against the dollar." If you say that the "dollar" is metonymy for "the man possessed of a dollar," with rights to defend, and reasonable expectations to be realized, you convict yourself of reaction. "These gentry" (I quote from the May *Atlantic*) "suppose themselves to be discussing the rights of man, when all they are discussing is the rights of stockholders." The true view, the progressive view, is obviously that the possessors of the dollar, the recipients of profits and dividends, are excluded from the communion of humanity. Labor is mankind.

The present instance is of course not the only instance in human history of the substitution of class criteria of judgment for social criteria. Such manifestations of class conscience are doubtless justified in the large economy of human affairs; an individual must often claim all in order to gain anything, and the same may be true of a class. Besides, the ultimate arbitration of the claims of the classes is not a matter for the rational judgment. What is subject to rational analysis, however, are the methods of gaining its ends proposed by the new social conscience. Of these methods one of wide acceptance is that of fixing odium upon certain property interests, with a view to depriving them immediately of the respect still granted to property interests in general, and ultimately of the protection of the laws. It is with the rationality of what may be called the excommunication and outlawing of special property interests, that the present paper is concerned.

In passing, it is worth noting that the same ethical spirit that insists upon fixing the responsibility for social ills upon particular property interests — or property owners — insists with equal vehemence upon absolving the propertyless evil-doer from personal responsibility for his acts. The Los Angeles dynamiters were but victims: the crime in which they were implicated was institutional, not personal. Their punishment was rank injustice; inexpedient, moreover, as provocative of further crime, instead of a means of repression. On the other hand, when it appears that the congestion of the slum produces vice and disease, we are not urged by the spokesmen of this ethical creed, to blame the chain of institutional causes typified by scarcity of land, high prices of building materials, the incapacity of a raw immigrant population to pay for better habitations, or to appreciate the need for light and air. Rather, we are urged to fix responsibility upon the individual owner who receives rent from slum tenements. Perhaps we can not imprison him for his misdeeds, but we can make him an object of public reproach; expel him from social intercourse (if that, so often talked about, is ever done); fasten his iniquities upon him if ever he seeks a post of trust or honor; and ultimately we can deprive him of his property. Let him and his anti-social interests be forever excommunicate, outlawed.

II

In the country at large the property interests involved in the production and sale of alcoholic beverages are already excommunicated. The unreformed "best society" may still tolerate the presence of persons whose fortunes are derived from breweries or distilleries; but the great mass of the social-minded would deny them fire and water. In how many districts would a well organized political machine urge persons thus enriched as candidates for Congress, the bench or even the school board? In the prohibition territory excommunication of such property interests has been followed by outlawry. The saloon in Maine and Kansas exists by the same title as did Robin Hood: the inefficiency of the law. On the road to excommunication is private property in the wretched shacks that shelter the city's poor. Outlawry is not far distant. "These tenements must go." Will they go? Ask of the police, who pick over the wreckage upon the subsidence of a wave of reform. Many a rookery, officially abolished, will be found still tenanted, and yielding not one income, but two, one for the owner and another for the police. The property represented by enterprises paying low wages, working men for long hours or under unhealthful conditions, or employing children, is almost ripe for excommunication. Pillars of society and the church have already been seen tottering on account of revelations of working conditions in factories from which they receive dividends. Property "affected by a public use," that is, investments in the instrumentalities of public service, is becoming a compromising possession. We are already somewhat suspicious of the personal integrity and political honor of those who receive their incomes from railways or electric lighting plants; and the odor of gas stocks is unmistakable. Even the land, once the retreat of high birth and serene dignity, is beginning to exhale a miasma of corruption. "Enriched by unearned increment" — who wishes such an epitaph? A convention is to be held in a western city in this very year, to announce to the world that the delegates and their constituencies — all honest lovers of mankind — will refuse in future to recognize any private title to land or other natural resources. Holders of such property, by continuing to be such, will place themselves beyond the pale of human society, and will forfeit all claim to sympathy when the day dawns for the universal confiscation of land.

III

The existence of categories of property interests resting under a growing weight of social disapprobation, is giving rise to a series of problems in private ethics that seem almost to demand a rehabilitation of the art of casuistry. A very intelligent and conscientious lady of the writer's acquaintance became possessed, by inheritance, of a one-fourth interest in a Minneapolis building the ground floor of which is occupied by a saloon. Her first endeavor was to persuade her partners to secure a cancellation of the liquor dealer's lease. This they refused to do, on the ground that the building in question is, by location, eminently suited to its present use, but very ill suited to any other; and that, moreover, the lessee would immediately reopen his business on the opposite corner. To yield to their partner's desire would therefore result in a reduction of their own profits, but would advance the public welfare not one whit. Disheartened by her partners' obstinacy, my friend is seeking to dispose of her interest in the building. As she is willing to incur a heavy sacrifice in order to get rid of her complicity in what she considers an unholy business, the transfer will doubtless soon be made. Her soul will be lightened of the profits from property put to an anti-social use. But the property will still continue in such use, and profits from it will still accrue to someone with a soul to lose or to save.

In her fascinating book, *Twenty Years at Hull House*, Miss Jane Addams tells of a visit to a western state where she had invested a sum of money in farm mortgages. "I was horrified," she says, "by the wretched conditions among the farmers, which had resulted from a long period of drought, and one forlorn picture was fairly burned into my mind. . . . The farmer's wife [was] a picture of despair, as she stood in the door of the bare, crude house, and the two children behind her, whom she vainly tried to keep out of sight, continually thrust forward their faces, almost covered by masses of coarse, sunburned hair, and their little bare feet so black, so hard, the great cracks so filled with dust, that they looked like flattened hoofs. The children could not be compared to anything so joyous as satyrs, although they appeared but half-human. It seemed to me quite impossible to receive interest from mortgages upon farms which might at any season be reduced to such conditions, and with great inconvenience to my agent and doubtless with hardship to the farmers, as speedily as possible I withdrew all my investment." And thereby made the supply of money for such farmers that much less and consequently that much dearer. This is quite a fair example of much current philanthropy.

We may safely assume that, however much this action may have lightened Miss Addams's conscience, it did not lighten the burden of debt upon the farmer, or make the periodic interest payments less painful, and it certainly did put them to the trouble and contingent expenses of a new mortgage. The moral burden was shifted, to the ease of the philanthropist, and this seems to exhaust the sum of the good results of one well intentioned deed. Do they outweigh the bad ones?

So, doubtless, there are among our friends persons who, upon proof that factories in which they have been interested pay starvation wages, have withdrawn their investments. And others who, stumbling upon a state legislature among the productive assets of a railway corporation, have sold their bonds and invested the proceeds elsewhere. It is a modern way of obeying the injunction, "Sell all thou hast and follow me." And not a very painful way, since the irreproachable investments pay almost, if not quite, as well as those that are suspect.

It is not, however, impossible to conceive of a property owner driven from one position to another, in order to satisfy this new requirement of the social conscience, without ever finding peace. Miss Addams put the money withdrawn from those hideous farm mortgages into a flock of "innocent looking sheep." Alas, they were not so innocent as they seemed. "The sight of two hundred sheep with four rotting hoofs each was not reassuring to one whose conscience craved economic peace. A fortunate series of sales of mutton, wool and farm enabled the partners to end the enterprise without loss." Sales of mutton? Let us hope those eight hundred infected hoofs are well printed on the butcher's conscience.

And the net result of all these moral strivings? The evil investments still continue to be evil, and still yield profits. Doubtless they rest, in the end, upon less sensitive consciences. Marvellous moral gain!

IV

We are bound to the wheel, say the sociological fatalists. All our efforts are of no avail; the Wheel revolves as it was destined. Not so. Our strivings for purity in investments, puny as may be their results in the individual instance, may compose a sum that is imposing in its effectiveness. How their influence may be exerted will best appear from an analogy.

It is a settled conviction among Americans of Puritan antecedents, and among all other Americans, native born or alien, that have come under Puritan influence, that the dispensing of alcoholic beverages is a degrading function. This conviction has not, to be sure, notably impaired the performance of the function. But it has none the less produced a striking effect. It has set apart for the function in question those elements in the population that place the lowest valuation upon the esteem of the public, and that are, on the whole, least worthy of it. In consequence the American saloon is, by common consent, the very worst institution of its kind in the world. Such is the immediate result of good intentions working by the method of excommunication of a trade.

This degradation of the personnel and the institution proceeds at an accelerated rate as public opinion grows more bitter. In the end the evil becomes so serious, so intimately associated with all other evils, social and political, that you hear men over their very cups rise to proclaim, with husky voices, "The saloon must go!" At this point the community is ripe for prohibition: accordingly, it would seem that the initial stages in the process, unpleasant as were their consequences, were not ill-advised, after all. But prohibition does not come without a political struggle, in which the enemy, selected for brazenness and schooled in corruption, employs methods that leave lasting scars upon the body politic. And even when vanquished, the enemy retreats into the morasses of "unenforcible laws," to conduct a guerilla warfare that knows no rules. Let us grant that the ultimate gain is worth all it costs: are we sure that we have taken the best possible means to achieve our ends?

In the poorer quarters of most great American cities, there is much property that it is difficult for a man to hold without losing the respect of the enlightened. Old battered tenements, dingy and ill lighted tumbledown shacks, the despair of the city reformer. Let us say that the proximity of gas tanks or noisy railways or smoky factories consign such quarters to the habitation of the very poor. Quite possibly, then, the replacement of the existing buildings by better ones would represent a heavy financial loss. The increasing social disapprobation of property vested in such wretched forms leads to the gradual substitution of owners who hold the social approval in contempt, for those who manifest a certain degree of sensitiveness. The tenants certainly gain nothing from the change. What is more likely to happen, is a screwing up of rents, an increasing promptness of evictions. Public opinion will in the end be roused against the landlords; the more timid among them will sell their holdings to others not less ruthless, but bolder and more astute. Attempts at public regulation will be fought with infinitely greater resourcefulness than could possibly have been displayed by respectable owners. Perhaps the final outcome will be that more drastic regulations are adopted than would have been the case had the shifting in ownership not taken place. There would still remain the possibility of the evasion of the law, and it is not at all improbable that the progress in the technique of evasion would outstrip the progress in regulation, thus leaving the tenant with a balance of disadvantage from the process as a whole.

The most illuminating instance of a business interest subjected first to excommunication — literally — and

then to outlawry, is that of the usurer, or, in modern par-
lance, the loan shark. To the mediæval mind there was
something distinctly immoral in an income from property
devoted to the furnishing of personal loans. We need
not stop to defend the mediæval position or to attack it;
all that concerns us here is that an opportunity for profit —
that is, a potential property interest — was outlawed.
In consequence it became impossible for reputable citizens
to engage in the business. Usury therefore came to be
monopolized by aliens, exempt from the current ethical
formulation, who were "protected," for a consideration,
by the prince, just as dubious modern property interests
may be protected by the political boss.

Let us summarize the results of eight hundred years of
experience in this method of dealing with the usurer's
trade. The business shifted from the control of citizens
to that of aliens; from the hands of those who were aliens
merely in a narrow, national sense, to the hands of those
who are alien to our common humanity. Such lawless,
tricky, extortionate loan sharks as now infest our cities
were probably not to be found at all in mediæval or early
modern times. They are a product of a secular process of
selection. Their ability to evade the laws directed against
them is consummate. It is true that from time to time
we do succeed in catching one and fining him, or even
imprisoning him. For which risk the small borrower is
forced to pay, at a usurer's rate.

Social improvement through the excommunication of
property interests is inevitably a disorderly process.
Wherever it is in operation we are sure to find the successive stages indicated in the foregoing examples. First,
a gradual substitution of the conscienceless property
holder for the one responsive to public sentiment. Next,
under the threat of hostile popular action, the timid and
resourceless property owner gives way to the resourceful
and the bold. The third stage in the process is a vigorous
political movement towards drastic regulation or aboli-

tion, evoking a desperate attempt on the part of the interests threatened to protect themselves by political means — that is, by gross corruption; or, if the menaced interest is a vast one, dominating a defensible territory, by armed rebellion, as in our own Civil War. If the interest is finally overwhelmed politically, and placed completely under the ban of the law, it has been given ample time to develop an unscrupulousness of personnel and an art of corruption that long enable it to exist illegally, a lasting reproach to the constituted authorities.

V

Suppression of anti-social interests by the methods in vogue amounts to little more than their banishment to the underworld. And we can well imagine the joy with which the denizens of the underworld receive such new accessions to their numbers and power. For in the nature of the case, it is inevitable that all varieties of outcasts and outlaws should join forces. The religious schismatic makes common cause with the pariah; the political offender with the thief and robber. Such association of elements vastly increases the difficulty of repressing crime. The band of thieves and robbers in the cave of Adullam doubtless found their powers of preying vastly increased through the acquisition of such a leader as David. The problem of mediæval vagabondage was rendered wellnigh incapable of solution by the fact that any beggar's rags might conceal a holy but excommunicated friar.

Let us once more review our experience with the usurer. As an outcast he offers his support to other outcasts, and is in turn supported by them. The pawnbroker and the pickpocket are closely allied: without the pawnshop, pocketpicking would offer but a precarious living; without the picking of pockets, many pawnshops would find it impossible to meet expenses. The salary loan shark often works hand in glove with the professional gambler; ach procures victims for the other. The "hole-in-the-wall" or "blind tiger" provides a rendezvous for all the outcasts of society. "Boot-legging" is a common subsidiary occupation for the pander, the thief and the cracksman. Where it flourishes, it serves to bridge over many a period of slack trade. Franchises whose validity is subject to political attack, bring to the aid of the underworld some of the most powerful interests in the community. The police are almost helpless when confronted by a coalition of persons of wealth and respectability with professional politicians commanding a motley array of yeggs and thugs, pimps and card-sharpers.

Let us suppose that the developing social conscience places under the ban receipt of private income from land and other natural resources, and that a powerful movement aiming at the confiscation of such resources is under way. It is superfluous to point out that the vast interests threatened would offer a desperate resistance. The warfare against an incomparably lesser interest, the liquor trade, has taxed all the resources of the modern democratic state — on the whole the most absolute political organization known. In no instance has the state come out of the struggle completely victorious; the proscribed interest is yielding ground, if at all, only very slowly. What, then, would be the outcome of a struggle against the vastly greater landed interest? Perhaps the state would be victorious in the end. But for generations the landed interest would survive, if not by title of common law, at least by title of common corruption. And in the course of the conflict, we can not doubt that political disorder would flourish as never before, and that under its shelter private vice and crime would develop almost unchecked.

We should disabuse ourselves of the notion that the will of a mere majority is absolute in the state. The law is a reality only when the outlawed interests represents an insignificant minority. Arbitrarily to increase the outlawed interests is to undermine the very foundations of society.

VI

The trend of the foregoing discussion, it will be said, is reactionary in the extreme. There are, as all must admit, private interests that are prejudicial to the public interest. Are they to be left in possession of the privilege of trading upon the public disaster — entrenching themselves, rendering still more difficult the future task of the reformer? By no means. The writer opposes no criticism to the extinction of anti-social private interests; on the contrary, he would have the state proceed against them with far greater vigor than it has hitherto displayed. It is important, however, to be sure first that a private interest is anti-social. Then the question is merely one of method. It is the author's contention that the method of excommunication and outlawry is the very worst conceivable.

We are wont to hold up to scorn the British method of compensating liquor sellers for licenses revoked. It is an expensive method. But let us weigh its corresponding advantages. The licensee does not find himself in a position in which he must choose between personal destitution and the public interest. He dares not employ methods of resistance that would subject him to the risk of forfeiting the right to compensation. He may resist by fair means, but if he is intelligent, he will keep his skirts clear of foul. If his establishment is closed, he is not left, a ruined and desperate man, to project methods for carrying on his trade illicitly. ·On the contrary, the act of compensation has placed in his hands funds in which he might be mulcted if convicted of violation of the law. And if natural perversity should drive him to illegal practices, he would not find himself an object of sympathy on the part of that considerable minority that resent injustice even to those whom they regard as evil-doers.

There can be little doubt that by the adoption of the principle of adequate compensation, an American commonwealth could extinguish any property interest that majority opinion pronounces anti-social. We may have industries that menace the public health. Under existing conditions the interests involved exert themselves to the utmost to suppress information relative to the dangers of such industries. With the principle of compensation in operation, these very interests would be the foremost in exposing the evils in question. It is no hardship to sell your interest to the public. Does any one feel aggrieved when the public decides to appropriate his land to a public use? On .the contrary, every possessor of a site at all suited for a public building or playground does everything in his power to display its advantages in the most favorable light.

And with this we have admitted a disadvantage of the compensation principle — over-compensation. We do pay excessively for property rights extinguished in the public interest. But this is largely because the principle is employed with such relative infrequency that we have not as yet developed a technique of compensation. German cities have learned how to acquire property for public use without either plundering the private owner or excessively enriching him. The British application of the Small Holdings Acts has duly protected the interests of the large landholder, without making of him a vociferous champion of the Acts.

Progressive public morality renders one private interest after another indefensible. Let the public extinguish such interests, by all means. But let the public be moral at its own expense.

A revolting doctrine, it will be said. Because men have been permitted, through gross defect in the laws, to build up interests in dealing out poisons to the public, are they to be compensated, like the purveyors of wholesome products, when the public decrees that their destructive activities shall cease? Because a corrupt legislature once gave away valuable franchises, are we and our children, and our children's children, forever to pay tribute, in the shape of interest on compensation funds, to the heirs of the shameless grantees? Because the land of a country was parcelled out, in a lawless age, among the unworthy retainers of a predatory prince, must we forever pay rent on every loaf we eat — as we should do, in fact, even if we transformed great landed estates into privately held funds? Did we not abolish human slavery, without compensation, and is there any one to question the justice of the act?

We did indeed extinguish slavery without compensation to the slave owners. But if no one had ever conceived of such a policy we should have been a richer nation and a happier one. We paid for the slaves, in blood and treasure, many times the sum that would have made every slave owner eager to part with his slaves. Such enrichment of the slave owner would have been an act of social injustice, it may be said. The saying would be open to grave doubt, but the doctrine here advanced runs, not in terms of justice, but in terms of social expediency.

And expediency is commonly regarded as a cheap substitute for justice. It is wrongly so regarded. Social justice, as usually conceived, looks to the past for its validity. Its preoccupation is the correction of ancient wrongs. Social expediency looks to the future: its chief concern is the prevention of future wrongs. As a guide to political action, the superiority of the claims of social expediency is indisputable.

VII

In the foregoing argument it has been deliberately assumed that the interests to be extinguished are, for the most part, universally recognized as anti-social. Slavery, health-destroying adulteration, the maintenance of tenements that menace life and morals, these at least represent interests so abominable that all must agree upon the wisdom of extinguishing them. The only point in dispute must be one of method. It is the contention of the present writer that when even such interests have had time to become clothed with an appearance of regularity, the method of extinction should be through compensation. By its tolerance of such interests, the public has made itself an accomplice in the mischief to which they give rise, and accordingly has not even an equitable right to throw the whole responsibility upon the private persons concerned.

Interests thus universally recognized to be evil are necessarily few. In the vast majority of cases the establishment of interests we now seek to proscribe took place in an epoch in which no evil was imputed to them. At first a small minority, usually regarded as fanatics, attack the interests in question. This minority increases, and in the end transforms itself into a majority. But long after majority opinion has become adverse, there remains a vigorous minority opinion defending the menaced interests. A hundred years ago the distilling of spirituous liquors was almost universally regarded as an entirely legitimate industry. The enemies of the industry were few and of no political consequence. Today in many communities the industry is utterly condemned by majority opinion. There is, however, no community in which a minority honestly defending the industry is absolutely wanting. Admitting that the majority opinion is right, it remains none the less true that adherents of the minority opinion would regard themselves as most grievously wronged if the majority proceeded to a destruction of their interests.

Where moral issues alone are involved, we may perhaps accept the view that the well considered opinion of the majority is as near as may be to infallibility. But it is very rarely the case that the question of the legitimacy of a property interest can be reduced to a purely moral issue. Usually there are also at stake, technical and broad economic issues in which majority judgment is notoriously fallible. Thus we have at times had large minorities who believed that the bank as an institution is wholly evil, and ought to be abolished. This was the majority opinion in one period of the history of Texas, and in accordance with it, established banking interests were destroyed by law. It is only within the last fifteen years that the majority of the citizens of that commonwealth have admitted the error of the earlier view.

In the course of the last twenty-five years, notable progress has been made in the art of preserving perishable foods through refrigeration. There are differences of opinion as to the effect upon the public health of food so preserved; and further differences as to the effect of the cold storage system upon the cost of living. On neither the physiological nor the economic questions involved is majority opinion worthy of special consideration. None the less, legislative measures directed against the storage interests have been seriously considered in a large number of states, and were it not for the difficulties inherent in the regulation of interstate commerce, we should doubtless see the practice of cold storage prohibited in some jurisdictions. Those whose property would thus be destroyed would accept their losses with much bitterness, in view of the fact that the weight of expert opinion holds their industry to be in the public interest.

What still further exacerbates the feeling of injury on the part of those whose interests are proscribed, is the fact that the purity of motives of the persons most active in the campaign of proscription is not always clear. Not many years ago we had a thriving manufacture of artificial butter. The persons engaged in the industry claimed that their product was as wholesome as that produced according to the time-honored process, and that its cheapness promised an important advance in the adequate provisioning of the people. We destroyed the industry, very largely because of our strong bent toward conservatism in all matters pertaining to the table. But among the influences that were most active in taxing artificial butter out of existence, was the competing dairymen's interest.

It is asserted by those who would shift the whole burden of taxation onto land that they are animated by the most unselfish motives, whereas their opponents are defending their selfish interests alone. Yet a common Single Tax appeal to the large manufacturer and the small house-owner takes the form of a computation demonstrating that those classes would gain more through the reduction in the burden on improvements than they would lose through increase in burden on the land. Let it be granted that personal advantage is not incompatible with purity of motives. The association of ideas does not, however, inspire confidence, especially in the breasts of those whose interests are threatened.

Extinction of property interests without compensation necessarily makes our legislative bodies the battleground of conflicting interests. Honest motives are combined with crooked ones in the attack upon an interest; crooked and honest motives combine in its defense. Out of the disorder issues a legislative determination that may be in the public interest or may be prejudicial to it. And most likely the law is inadequately supported by machinery of enforcement: it is effective in controlling the scrupulous; to the unscrupulous it is mere paper. In many instances its net effect is only to increase the risks connected with the conduct of a business.

When England prohibited importation of manufactures from France, the import trade continued none the less, under the form of smuggling. The risk of seizure was merely added to the risk of fire and flood. Just as one could insure against the latter risks, so the practice arose of insuring against seizure. At one time, at any rate, in the French ports were to be found brokers who would insure the evasion of a cargo of goods for a premium of fifteen per cent. At the safe distance of a century and a half, the absurd prohibition and its incompetent administration are equally comic. At the time, however, there was nothing comic in the contempt for law and order thus engendered, in the feeling of outrage on the part of those ruined by seizures, and in the alliance of respectable merchants with the thieves and footpads enlisted for the smuggling trade.

VIII

It is a common observation of present day social reformers that an excessive regard is displayed by our governmental organs for security of property, while security of non-property rights is neglected. And this would indeed be a serious indictment of the existing order if there were in fact a natural antithesis between the security of property and security of the person. There is, however, no such antithesis. In the course of history the establishment of security of property has, as a rule, preceded the establishment of personal security, and has provided the conditions in which personal security becomes possible. Adequate policing is essential to any form of security. Property can pay for policing; the person can not. This is a crude and materialistic interpretation of the facts, but it is essentially sound.

How much personal security existed in England, five centuries and a half ago, when it was possible for Richard to carve his way through human flesh to the throne? The lowly, certainly, enjoyed no greater security than the high born. How much personal security exists in the late Macedonian provinces of the Turkish Empire, or in northern Mexico? It is safe to issue a challenge to all the world to produce an instance, contemporary or historical, of a country in which property is insecure and in which human life and human happiness are not still more insecure. On the other hand, it is difficult to produce an instance of a state in which security of property has long been established, in which there is not a progressive sensitiveness about the non-propertied rights of man. It is in the countries where the sacredness of private property is a fetich, that one finds recognition of a universal right to education, of a right to protection against violence and against epidemic disease, of a right to relief in destitution. These are perhaps meagre rights; but they represent an expanding category. The right to support in time of illness and in old age is making rapid progress. The development of such rights is not only not incompatible with security of property, but it is, in large measure, a corollary of property security. Personal rights shape themselves upon the analogy of property rights; they utilize the same channels of thought and habit. One of the most powerful arguments for "social insurance" is its very name. Insurance is recognized as an essential to the security of property; it is therefore easy to make out a case for the application of the principle to non-propertied claims.

Some may claim that the security of property has now fulfilled its mission; that we can safely allow the principle to decay in order to concentrate our attention upon the task of establishing non-propertied rights. But let us remember that we are not removed from barbarism by the length of a universe. The crust of orderly civilization is deep under our feet: but not six hundred years deep. The primitive fires still smoke on our Mexican borders and in the Balkans. And blow holes open from time to time through our own seemingly solid crust — in Colorado, in West Virginia, in the Copper Country. It is evidently premature to affirm that the security of property has fulfilled its mission.

IX

The question at issue, is not, however, the rights of property against the rights of man — or more honestly — the rights of labor. The claims of labor upon the social income may advance at the expense of the claims of property. In the institutional struggle between the propertied and the propertyless, the sympathies of the writer are with the latter party. It is his hope and belief that an ever increasing share of the social income will assume the form of rewards for personal effort.

But this is an altogether different matter from the crushing of one private property interest after another, in the name of the social welfare or the social morality. Such detailed attacks upon property interests are, in the end, to the injury of both social classes. Frequently they amount to little more than a large loss to one property interest, and a small gain to another. They increase the element of insecurity in all forms of property; for who shall say which form is immune from attack? Now it is the slum tenement, obvious corollary of our social inequalities; next it may be the marble mansion or gilded hotel, equally obvious corollaries of the same institutional situation. Now it is the storage of meat that is under attack; it may next be the storage of flour. The fact is, our mass of income yielding possessions is essentially an organic whole. The irreproachable incomes are not exactly what they would be if those subject to reproach did not exist. If some property incomes are dirty, all property incomes become turbid.

The cleansing of property incomes, therefore, is a first obligation of the institution of property as a whole. The compensation principle throws the cost of the cleansing upon the whole mass, since, in the last analysis, any considerable burden of taxation will distribute itself over the mass. The principle is therefore consonant with justice. What is not less important, the principle, systematically developed, would go far toward freeing the legislature from the graceless function of arbitrating between selfish interests, and the administration from the necessity of putting down powerful interests outlawed by legislative act. It would give us a State working smoothly, and therefore an efficient instrument for social ends. Most important of all, it would promote that security of economic interests which is essential to social progress.

A STUBBORN RELIC OF FEUDALISM

THERE is a persistent question regarding the distribution of property which is of peculiar interest in the season of automobile tours and summer hotels. Most thinking people acknowledge a good deal of perplexity over this question, while on most parallel ones they are generally cock-sure — on whichever is the side of their personal interests. But in this question the bias of personal interest is not very large, and therefore it may be considered with more chance of agreement than can the larger questions of the same class which parade under various disguises.

The little question is that of tipping. After we have squeezed out of it such antitoxic serum as we can, we will briefly indicate the application of it to larger questions.

Tipping is plainly a survival of the feudal relation, long before the humbler men had risen from the condition of status to that of contract, when fixed pay in the ordinary sense was unknown, and where the relation between servant and master was one of ostensible voluntary service and voluntary support, was for life, and in its best aspect was a relation of mutual dependence and kindness. Then the spasmodic payment was, as tips are now, essential to the upper man's dignity, and very especially to the dignity of his visitor. This feudal relation survives in England to-day to such an extent that poor men refrain from visiting their rich relations because of the tips. In the great country-houses the tips are expected to be in gold, at least so I was told some years ago. And in England and out of it, Don Cesar's bestowal of his last shilling on the man who had served him, still thrills the audience, at least the tipped portion of it.

Europe being on the whole less removed from feudal institutions than we are, tipping is not only more firmly established there, but more systematized. It is more nearly the rule that servants' places in hotels are paid for, and they are apt to be dependent entirely upon tips. The greater wealth of America, on the other hand, and the extravagance of the *nouveaux riches*, has led in some institutions to more extravagant tipping than is dreamed of in Europe, and consequently has scattered through the community a number of servants from Europe who, when here, receive with gratitude from a foreigner, a tip which they would scorn from an American.

In the midst of general relations of contract — of agreed pay for agreed service, tipping is an anomaly and a constant puzzle.

It would seem strange, if it were not true of the greater questions of the same kind, that in the chronic discussion of this one, so little attention, if any, has been paid to what may be the fundamental line of division between the two sides — namely, the distinction between ideal ethics and practical ethics.

An illustration or two will help explain that distinction:

First illustration: "Thou shalt not kill" which is ideal ethics in an ideal world of peace. Practical ethics in the real world are illustrated in Washington and Lee, who for having killed their thousands, are placed beside the saints!

Second illustration: Obey the laws and tell the truth. This is ideal ethics, which our very legislatures do much to prevent being practical. For instance; they ignore the fact that in the present state of morality, taxes on personal property can be collected from virtually nobody but widows and orphans who have no one to evade the taxes for them. So the legislatures continue the attempt to tax personal property, and a judge on the bench says that a man who lies about his personal taxes shall not on that account be held an unreliable witness in other matters.

Or to take an illustration less radical: it is not in legal testimony alone that ideal ethics require everybody to tell the truth, the whole truth, and nothing but the truth —

that the world should have as much truth as possible; and if the world were perfectly kind, perfectly honest and perfectly wise (which last involves the first two), that ideal could be realized. For instance, in our imperfect world a man telling people when he did not like them, would be constantly giving needless pain and making needless enemies, whereas in an ideal world — made up of perfect people, there would be nobody to dislike, or, pardon the Hibernicism, if there were, the whole truth could be told without causing pain or enmity. Or again, in a world where there are dishonest people, a man telling everything about his schemes, would have them run away with by others, though in an ideal world, where there were no dishonest people, he could speak freely. In fact, the necessity of reticence in this connection does not even depend on the existence of dishonesty: for in a world where people have to look out for themselves, instead of everybody looking out for everybody else, a man exposing his plans might hurry the execution of competing plans on the part of perfectly honest people.

Farther illustration may be sufficiently furnished by the topic in hand.

In the case of most poor folks other than servants, what to do about it has lately been pretty distinctly settled: the religion of pauperization is pretty generally set aside: almsgiving, the authorities on ethics now generally hold, should be restricted to deserving cases — to people incapacitated by constitution or circumstance from taking proper care of themselves.

Now is tipping almsgiving, and are servants among the deserving classes?

How many people have asked themselves these simple questions, and how many who are educated up to habitually refusing alms unless the last of the questions is affirmatively answered, just as habitually tip servants?

Is tipping almsgiving? Not in the same sense that alms are given without any show of anything in return: the servant does something for the tipper. Yes, but he is paid for it by his employer. True, but only sometimes: at other times he is only partly paid, depending for the rest on tips; and sometimes the tips are so valuable that the servant pays his alleged employer for the opportunity to get them. Yet I know one hotel in Germany, and probably there are others, there and elsewhere, where the menus and other stationery bear requests against tipping. But in that one hotel I know tipping to be as rife as in hotels generally: the customers are not educated up to the landlord's standard. And here we come to the fundamental remedy for all questionable practices — the education of the people beyond them. But this is simply the ideal condition in which ideal ethics could prevail. Meanwhile we must determine the practical ethics of the actual world.

The servant's position is different from that of most other wage-earners, in that he is in direct contact with the person who is to benefit from his work. The man who butchers your meat or grinds your flour, you probably never see; but the man who brushes your clothes or waits on your table, holds to you a personal relation, and he can do his work so as merely to meet a necessity, or so as to rise beyond mere necessity into comfort or luxury. Outside of home servants, the necessity is all that, in the present state of human nature, his regular stipend is apt to provide; the comfort or the luxury, the feeling of personal interest, the atmosphere of promptness and cheerfulness and ease, is apt to respond only to the tip. Only in the ideal world will it be spontaneous. In the real world it must be paid for.

And why should it not be — why is it not as legitimate to pay for having your wine well cooled or carefully tempered and decanted, as to pay for the wine itself? The objection apt to be first urged is that it degrades the servant. But does it? He is not an ideal man in an ideal world, already doing his best or paid to do his best. You are not degrading him from any such standard as that, into the lower one of requiring tips: you are simply taking him as he is. True, if he got no tips, he would not depend upon them; but without them he would not do all you want him to; before he will do that, he must be developed into a different man — he must become a creature of an ideal world. You may in the course of ages develop him into that, and as you do, he will work better and better, and tips may grow smaller and smaller, until he does his best spontaneously, and tips have dwindled to nothing. But to withdraw them now would simply make him sulky, and lead to his doing worse than now.

Another objection urged against tips is that they put the rich tipper at an advantage over the poor one. But the rich man is at an advantage in nearly everything else, why not here? The idea of depriving him of his advantages, is rank communism, which destroys the stimulus to energy and ingenuity that, in the present state of human nature, is needed to keep the world moving. In an ideal state of human nature, the man with ability to create wealth may find stimulus enough, as some do to a considerable extent now, in the delight of distributing wealth for the general good; but we are considering what is practicable in the present state of human nature.

Another aspect of the case, or at least a wider aspect, is the more sentimental one where the tip is prompted as reciprocation for spontaneous kindness.

But in the service of private families, as distinct from service to the general public or to visitors it is notorious that constant tipping is ruinous. Occasional holidays and treats and presents at Christmas and on special occasions are useful, as promoting the general feeling of reciprocation. But from visitors the tip is generally essential to ensuring the due meed of respect. Yet we can reasonably imagine a time when it may not be; and even now, for the casual service of holding a horse or brushing off the dust, a hearty "thank you" is perhaps on the whole better than a tip.

Considering the morality of the question all around —
the practical ethics as well as the ideal, the underlying
facts are that no man ought to be a servant in the servile
sense, and indeed no man ought to be poor; and in an ideal
world no man would be one or the other. Just how we are
to get a world without servants or servile people, is perhaps a little more plain than how we are to get Mr. Bel-
lamy's world without poor people, which, however,
amounts to nearly the same thing. At least we will get a
less servile world, as machinery and organization make
service less and less personal. Bread has long been to a
great extent made away from home; much of the washing
is also done away in great laundries, and organizations
have lately been started to call for men's outer clothes,
and keep them cleaned, repaired and pressed. There is a
noticeable rise, too, in the dignity of personal service:
witness the college students at the summer hotels, and the
self-respecting Jap in the private family. These influences
are making for the ideal world in relation to service, and
when we get it, no man will take tips, and nobody will
offer them.

But in our stage of evolution, the tip, like the larger
prizes, is part of the general stimulus to the best exertion
and the best feeling, and is therefore legitimate; but it, like
every other stimulus, should not be applied in excess, and
the tendency should be to abolish it. The rich man often
is led by good taste and good morals to restrain his expenditure in many directions, and there are few directions,
if any, in which good taste and good morals more commend the happy medium than in tips. Excess in them,
however, is not always prompted by good nature and
generosity and reciprocation of spontaneous kindness, but
often by desire for comfort, and even by ostentation. But
all such promptings require regulation for the same reason
that, it is now becoming generally recognized, the promptings of even charity itself require regulation.

The head of one of the leading Fifth Avenue restaurants

once said to the writer, substantially: "We don't like tips: they demoralize our men. But what can we do about it? We can't stop it, or even keep it within bounds. Our customers will give them, and people who have too much money or too little sense, give not only dollar bills or five dollar bills, but fifty dollar bills and even hundred dollar bills. We have tried to stave off customers who do such things: we believe that in the long run it would pay us to; but we can't."

When all the promptings of liberality or selfishness or ostentation are well regulated, we will be in the ideal world. Until then, in the actual world, it is the part of wisdom to regulate ideal ethics by practical ethics — and tip, but tip temperately.

And now to apply our principles to a wider field.

The ideal is that all men should have what they produce. The ideal is also that all men should have full shares of the good things of life. These two ideals inevitably combine into a third — that all men should produce full shares of the good things of life. But the plain fact is that they cannot — that no amount of opportunity or appliances will enable the average day laborer to produce what Mr. Edison or Mr. Hill or even the average deviser of work and guide of labor does. Then even ideal ethics cannot say in this actual world: Let both have the same. That would simply be Robin Hood ethics: rob the man who produces much, and give the plunder to the man who produces little. Hence comes the disguising of the schemes to do it, even so that they often deceive their own devisers. What then do practical ethics say? They can't say anything more than: Help the less capable to become capable, so that he may produce more. But that is at least as slow a process as raising the servant beyond the stage of tips. Meantime the socialists are unwilling to wait, and propose to rob the present owners of the means of production, and take the control of industry from the men who manage it now, and put it in the hands of the men who merely can influence votes. These men certainly are no less selfish and dishonest than the captains of industry, and are vastly less able to select the profitable fields of industry, and organize and economize industry; whatever product they might squeeze out would be vastly less than now, and it would stick to their own fingers no less than does what the politicians handle now. Dividing whatever might reach the people, without reference to those who produced it, could yield the average man no more than he gets now. That's very simple mathematics. One of the saddest sights of the day is the number of good people to whom these facts are not self-evident.

In no state of human nature that any persons now living, or the grandchild of any person now living, will witness, could such conditions be permanent. Their temporary realization might be accomplished; but if it were, the able men would not be satisfied with either the low grade of civilization inevitable unless they worked, or with being robbed of the large share of production that must result from their work. The more intelligent of the rank and file, too, would rebel against the conditions inevitably lowering the general prosperity, and they would soon realize the difference in industrial leadership between "political generals" and natural generals. Insurrection would follow, and then anarchy, after which things would start again on their present basis, but some generations behind.

But I for one do not expect these experiences, especially in America: for here probably enough men have already become property holders to make a sufficient balance of power for the preservation of property. If not, the first step toward ensuring civilization, is helping enough men to develop into property holders, and *continue* property holders, which general experience declares that they will not unless they develop their property themselves.

AN EXPERIMENT IN SYNDICALISM

DURING the last twenty years New Zealand has tried many social and economic experiments; these experiments have been made by her own Legislature, and her own people; and as a rule they have been remarkably successful: during the last few months she has had the experience of a new one conducted by strangers, and made at her expense. Fortunately there is reason to believe that this one will be found to have resulted in benefit to New Zealand and its people, while it may prove of service to older and larger countries. It is probable that the most widely known of New Zealand's experiments is that which aimed at doing justice to employers and employees alike by the substitution for the Industrial strike of a Court of Arbitration, fairly constituted, on which both Workers and Employers were equally represented. This law has been branded by the supporters of the usual Strike policy with the name of "Compulsory Arbitration," the object being to discredit it in the eyes of the workers, as an infringement of their liberty. The title is unfair and misleading. Unlike most laws, it never has been of universal application either to Workers or Employers, but only to those among them that chose to form themselves into industrial Unions, and to register those Unions as subject to the provisions of the Statute. The purpose of the Statute was an appeal to the common sense of the people, by offering them an alternative method of settling disputes and securing that fair-play for both parties which experience had shown could seldom be secured by the strike. The law, which was first introduced in 1894, had gradually appealed both to workers and employers, as worth trying, and before the close of the last century it had rendered the country prosperous, and had attracted the attention of thoughtful people in many other parts of the world to the "Country Without Strikes." Efforts were made in several countries to introduce the principle of the New Zealand Statute, but with very little success, as it was generally opposed both by workers and employers: — the workers feeling confident they could obtain greater concessions by the forceful methods of the strike, and the employers suspecting that any Court of Arbitration would be likely to give the workers more than, without arbitration, they could compel the employers to surrender.

In the mean time the statutory substitute for the strike continued to succeed in New Zealand. Nearly every class of town workers, and some in the country, had formed Unions, and registered them under the arbitration law. With a single trifling exception, that was speedily put an end to by the punishment of the Union with the alternative of heavy fine or imprisonment, the country was literally as well as nominally a country without a strike. And it was something more than that: its prosperity increased year by year, and its production of goods — agricultural, pastoral, and manufactured — increased at a pace unequalled elsewhere. Yet the prosperity was most apparent in its effect on the conditions of the workers: under the successive awards of the arbitration court, wages had steadily increased until they had reached a point as high as in similar trades in America, while the cost of living was very little more than half the rate in any town in the United States. To all intelligent observers these facts were evident, and could not be concealed from the workers in other countries, especially in Australia, as the nearest geographically to New Zealand and commercially the most closely connected.

The effect, however, on the workers of Australia was not what might have been expected. Attempts had been made by some of the State Legislatures to introduce arbitration laws more or less like the New Zealand statute, but with very partial success. From the first these laws were opposed by the leaders of the Labor Unions, who naturally saw a menace to their influence in the fact that they became subject to punishment if they attempted to use their accustomed powers over their fellow unionists. The example of New Zealand was lauded in the Australian Legislatures and newspapers, and even in the courts, till at last a feeling of strong antagonism was developed among the more advanced class of socialistic Labor men, and it was decided by their leaders to undertake a campaign in the neighboring Dominion against the system of settling industrial questions by courts, and in favor of substituting the system of strikes, with their attendant power and profit to the Labor leaders. The first steps taken were sending men from Australia or England on lecturing tours through New Zealand, to create dissatisfaction with the Arbitration Courts by representing them as leaning to the side of the employers, and ignoring the claims of the workers. When this had gone on for about a year, workers of various classes were induced to cross from Australia, and join the Unions in New Zealand, for the purpose of influencing their fellow unionists to disloyalty towards the system under which they were registered. These men were generally competent workers and clever agitators, and many of them soon obtained prominence and official position in the Unions. As was natural, a good many of these new-comers were miners — either for coal or gold — and many of them joined the miners' union at the great gold mine known as the Waihi, from which upwards of thirty million dollars worth of gold had been dug, and which was still yielding between three and four million dollars a year. There were nearly a thousand miners employed there, and all of them were members of a Union that was duly registered under the Arbitration statute.

There had been several questions in dispute between

the miners and the owners, and these had been referred
to the Arbitration Court some time before the arrival of
the new Australian miners. The result, while it favored
the Union in some respects, favored the Company in
others, and this fact was used by the new-comers to convince the older hands that the Court had been unfair, and
that they could secure much better terms for themselves
if they would cease work, and so inflict immense loss by
permitting the lower levels of the mine to become flooded.
After a few months the Union decided to take advantage
of the provision of the law which enabled any registered
Union to withdraw its registration at six months' notice.
When the time had expired, the Union repeated the demand which had been refused by the Court, and on the
refusal of the Company to agree, a strike was at once declared, and the whole of the miners ceased work. This
had the effect, within a very short time, of rendering all the
deeper levels of the mine unworkable. Close to the mine
was a prosperous little town occupied chiefly by the miners
and their families, most of the houses being the property
of the mining company, and the men continued to occupy
the houses while the strike was in progress. Other miners
were found who were ready to take their places, but the
men in possession refused to move out, and threatened
with violence any miners that should attempt to work the
mine. The men who had been prepared to work, finding
this to be the position, withdrew. As there was no actual
violence shown, there seemed to be a difficulty in the way
of any interference by the Government: so several months
passed, during which the mine lay idle while the miners
on strike continued to occupy the houses and pay the very
moderate rents demanded from employees of the company.
This they were able to do partly from their savings, partly
from the sympathetic contributions from Australia, and
partly by some of the miners having scattered over the
country and got work on the farms, and throwing their
earnings into the common fund.

After repeated appeals by the mine-owners to the Government, an arrangement was made that the Company should employ miners willing to become members of a new Union registered under the Arbitration statute, and that the Government should send a police force sufficient to protect these in working the mine, and also to enforce the judgment of the local court in dispossessing the occupants of the houses belonging to the Company. An attempt was made by the strikers to defy this police force and prevent the new Union from working the mine; but when most of the new unionists had been sworn in as special constables, and a number of the militant strikers had been arrested, the others saw that they could not continue the struggle, and within a week or two abandoned the district, giving place to the members of the arbitration Union in both the mine and town.

Thus the first strike organized by the "Federation of Labor" in New Zealand resulted in a failure, but the miners thus defeated and driven from the little town that had been their home, in many cases for a good many years, were naturally embittered by their failure, and became an element of mischief in other districts, and especially in the coal mines, to which they turned when they found it hard to obtain employment in any of the gold mines.

The Australian Federation of Labor and its branch in New Zealand fully appreciated the fact that their first attempt to establish a system of Unionism opposed to the one recognized by the law, having proved a failure, it was necessary either to give up the attempt altogether or to make it more deliberately and on a much wider scale. The method they adopted was one that did credit to their foresight and determination. The Australian Federation is, and has always been, highly socialistic in its policy, and latterly its leaders have adopted and preached syndicalism, as promising to give the workers the control of society. New Zealand, alone among self-governing countries, having struck at the very root of their policy by trying to substitute a statute and a Court for the will of the associated workers, was a very tempting country for syndicalism. An island country which, owing to climate and soil, was specially suited for the production of all kinds of agricultural wealth beyond the needs of its own people, must depend on free access to the ports of other countries. This, it seemed plain, could be prevented by well managed syndicalism. It would be only necessary to organize the seamen who worked the vessels that kept the smaller harbors of such a country in touch with the larger ports at which the ocean going ships loaded and unloaded; and to organize also the stevedores at the larger ports. The bitterness of feeling that had followed the destruction of the Waihi Union, and the loss to its members not only of a good many months of good wages but of the homes they and their families had occupied for years, was a valuable asset in such a campaign. At first, of course, some of the working classes blamed the agents of "The Federation of Labor" who were responsible for the disastrous strike, but it was not difficult to turn attention from the past failure of a single strike, to the certain success that must attend a great syndical strike that would involve all the industries of the country. Most, indeed nearly all, of the disappointed Waihi strikers were ready to join with enthusiasm in carrying out the plans of The Federation, and removed to the places where they could be most effective in preparing the way for what they looked upon as a great revenge. Thus they either joined the old Unions at the principal ports, especially Auckland and Wellington, or formed new Unions, no longer registered under the Arbitration statute, but openly affiliated to The Federation of Labor, which had been established in New Zealand, but was really a branch of the Australian Federation. The four principal ports of New Zealand, indeed the only ports much frequented by the large export and import vessels, are Auckland, Wellington, Lyttleton, and Dunedin, the two first named being in the north island,

and the other two in the south. Auckland is considerably
the largest city in The Dominion, containing at least
25,000 more inhabitants than Wellington, which is not
only the capital of the Dominion, but also the great distributing centre for the South island and the southern
part of the North island, at the southern extremity of
which it is situated. The remarkable situation of Auckland, on a very narrow isthmus about a hundred and
eighty miles from the northern point of the country, is no
doubt largely responsible for the growth of the city, which
is the chief centre of the young manufactures of the
Dominion, and the largest port of export for almost all the
country produces, except wool and mutton, which are
mainly raised in the South island. Thus it happens that
Auckland and Wellington are at present the chief shipping
ports of the Dominion, and it was to them that the Federation of Labor turned its chief attention when its leaders
had definitely decided to undertake the campaign of syndicalism against the system of arbitration which had
prevailed for sixteen years.

There had already been formed Unions of Waterside
Workers and Seamen at each of these ports; but they were
in all cases registered under the arbitration law, and of
course subject to its penalties against both officials and
members in cases of any breach of the statute. The
Federation's agents proceeded to collect the members of
these unions who were in any way dissatisfied with the
existing awards of the Arbitration Courts, and to form
them into new Unions outside the statute. They had little
difficulty in persuading the men that the new Unions would
be free to act in many directions that were barred to the
members of the old Unions. A good many of the men were
thus persuaded to resign their membership in the existing
Unions, and as they were very often the most active
members, they gradually persuaded others to leave with
them. There was nothing either in the law or custom of
the ports to prevent unionists and non-unionists working

together on the wharves or the coasting vessels; so within a comparatively short time the members of the new Fedcration Unions were more numerous than those that clung to the older ones. When this became the case, the officials of the new Unions approached the shipping companies with proposals for an agreement between them and the Federation Unions in some respects more favorable to the employers than the arbitration award under which the older Unions were working, and in this way gained a position which enabled them to undermine the old Unions, till they either died out for want of members or withdrew their registration, and at the end of their six months' notice merged their Unions in those of The Federation. The Federation's plans had been so carefully prepared that there was little or no suspicion on the part of the employers or of the public generally as to the true meaning of the movement. It was evident, of course, that it indicated a revolt against the arbitration law, but as the new unions appeared ready to give the employers rather better terms than the old ones, many reasons were found by employers for defending what began to be called the "Free Unions." In this way things had gone on at the shipping ports for about two years from the failure of the gold miners' strike at Waihi, before anything happened to open the eyes of the public to the real meaning of what The Federation of Labor had been doing. In that time the new Unions at each of the principal ports of the country had quietly obtained the entire control of the hands at waterside and local shipping, as well as of the Carters Unions. The time had arrived when the syndicalists believed themselves able to compel the public to submit to any demands they might see fit to make.

The occasion finally arose, as might have been expected, at Wellington, where the Federation of Labor had established its head-quarters. There was no definite dispute between the employers and workers, but for a few weeks there had been an uneasy feeling in relation to the Waterside Workers who, it was said, were growing more lazy and slovenly in handling cargo on the wharves and piers. A meeting had been called by The Federation to discuss some grievances of the coal miners at Westport, from which most of the coal landed in Wellington is brought. The meeting was called for the noon dinner hour, and a number of the waterside workers engaged in discharging cargo from a steamer about to sail, at once went to the meeting, and did not return to work in the afternoon. The shipping company at once engaged other men to finish their work, and when the men came back some hours later, they found their places filled up. The new men belonged to the same Union, but the men dispossessed demanded that the new ones should be dismissed at once. When the company refused the demand, the men appealed to the Council of the Federation, who at once called on the Waterside Workers and Seamens Unions at Wellington to cease work. Within a few days the position looked so serious that the Premier invited both parties to a conference, at which he presided in person, in the hope of bringing about an agreement to refer the matters in dispute to an arbitrator to be mutually agreed upon. The officials of The Federation, however, said there was nothing to submit to an arbitrator: they had made a demand, and unless it was complied with by the shipping company and the Union of merchants at Wellington who were in league with the Company in victimizing the men who took part in the meeting in aid of the Coal-miners, the strike must go on. The Merchants and Shipping Company's Unions pointed out that what had been done was in direct opposition to the terms of the formal agreement signed less than a year before, and they refused to have anything more to do with the Federation on any terms. The conference thus ended in an open declaration of war. The time had evidently come for the Federation of Labor to make good the assertions so often made by its lecturers and agitators, of its power to force the rest of the community to submission. It would be difficult to imagine a more favorable position for carrying such a policy into effect: New Zealand, it must be borne in mind, is a country without an army. For some years past, it is true, a system of military training for all her young men between eighteen and twenty-five has been enforced by law, but except for training purposes, there is no military force in the Dominion, either of regulars or militia; and it is now forty-five years since the last company of British soldiers left its shores. Law has been maintained, and order enforced, by a police force under the control of the Government of the Dominion, and while the force is undoubtedly a good and trustworthy one, its numbers have never been large in proportion to the population. This year the entire force throughout the country is very little more than 850, which includes officers as well as men. It can hardly be wondered at that the officials of The Federation of Labor were convinced that, if they could arrange a general strike of the workers, the police force would be powerless to deal with it. On the failure of the attempt of the Premier to bring about a settlement between the parties by arbitration, the Federation proclaimed a general strike of all Unions affiliated to themselves throughout the country, and of all other Unions that were in sympathy with them in their policy of giving united Labor the control of society. The order to cease work was at once obeyed, as a matter of course, by all the Federation Unions, which practically meant all the workers engaged on vessels registered in the Dominion and trading on the coast, all workers on wharves and piers, carters in the cities, and coal miners throughout the country. The appeal for sympathetic assistance from Unions unconnected with the Federation was largely successful in the chief centres, though it was, of course, a direct defiance of the arbitration law under which they were registered. It has since been discovered that in nearly every case it was brought about by the unprincipled scheming of the secretaries, assisted by a few of the officials, who called meetings, of which notice was given only to a selected minority, and at which the question of joining a sympathetic strike was settled by a large majority of those present, but in fact in many cases a small minority of the whole membership. The sympathetic strike of Arbitration Unions was mainly confined to the cities, and Auckland, as the largest city, was the most affected by it. In Auckland the members of practically every Union ceased work, somewhere about ten thousand persons going on strike simultaneously.

The result during the first days of the strike seemed likely to confirm the expectations of the Federation orators. Industry was practically dead. At every port vessels lay at anchor, having been withdrawn from the wharves before they were deserted by their crews, and the wharves were in the possession of the Waterside strikers. The streets of the cities were empty, and a large proportion of the stores were closed, partly owing to want of business, and partly from fear of violence in case they kept open. These first few days in both New Zealand and Australia were days of triumph for the Federation leaders but the triumph was a short-lived one. The Government of the Dominion did not interfere, indeed, but the public, through their municipal authorities, did. The people of New Zealand have throughout their history been accustomed to manage their own affairs, and within four days of the declaration of war by the syndical Federation, steps were taken to meet the emergency. At Auckland and Wellington it had been evident from the first that the small police force available could not safely attempt to cope with the main body of strikers, or do more than prevent acts of aggressive violence to the citizens and their property. The local authorities, however, had confidence in the general public, and at Auckland, and afterwards at Wellington, the Mayor of the city appealed to the public to come forward as volunteers to maintain law and order, by acting as Special Constables. In both cities the appeal was responded to readily, nearly two thousand young men coming forward at Auckland in twenty-four hours, and upwards of a thousand at Wellington. These were at once sworn in as special constables, and armed with serviceable batons, while all the fire-arms and ammunition for sale in the city was taken charge of and withdrawn from sale by the municipal authorities. In this way the maintenance of order was fairly provided for, and the temporary closing of all licensed hotels by order of the city magistrates removed the danger of riot as the result of intemperance.

There had been some rioting in Wellington, though with little serious injury, but there was nothing that could be called a riot in Auckland. The Federation Unions waited, under the impression that time was on their side, owing to the impossibility of doing anything or getting anything done without the help of the associated workers. This had been the basis of their scheme, but like all such schemes it failed to take into account the instinct of self-preservation on the part of the people outside the Unions. As long as the strike leaders could point to the fleet of vessels lying idle in the harbor, the mills silent, and the street railroads without a moving car, and almost deserted by carts, it was easy for them to persuade their followers that complete victory was only a matter of days, or at most of weeks; they had not remembered that there were others besides themselves and their fellow townsmen interested in the question of a paralyzed industry. The trade that has been making the people of New Zealand increasingly rich during the last twenty years has been mainly derived from the land. Small holdings and close settlement have been the rule, and the rate of production has been increasingly rapid. The exports — mainly the produce of the land — have grown in proportions quite unknown in any other country, and the farmers knew that the prosperity of the country, and most directly of all the workers on the land, depended on the freedom and facilities for shipment of their ports. It was the workers on the land, accordingly, that came to the rescue, and solved the industrial problem. An offer was made by the President of The Farmers' Coöperative Union to bring a sufficient number of the members into the cities to work the shipping and to prevent any interruption of the work by the men on strike. The offer was at once accepted by the municipal authorities at Auckland and Wellington, and within two days fully eighteen hundred mounted farmers rode into Auckland, and nearly a thousand into Wellington, all prepared to carry on the work and protect the workers. Their arrival practically settled the question. New Waterside Unions were formed at every port, and registered under the provisions of the Arbitration Statute; such of the country workers as were able to do so, enrolled themselves as members of the new Unions; the wharves and water fronts were taken possession of and guarded by the special constables enlisted in the cities, while the streets were patrolled by parties of the mounted volunteers. Within twenty-four hours of their arrival, some of the vessels in harbor had been brought to the wharves, and the work of unloading them was begun.

At first there were many threats of violent opposition on the part of the strikers, and crowds assembled in the principal streets and in the neighborhood of the wharves; but these were dispersed before they became dangerous, by the mounted constables, and a proclamation having been issued by the mayor calling attention to the fact that collections of people that obstructed traffic in the streets were contrary to law, the police and mounted constables cleared the streets, and forcibly arrested any persons who attempted opposition. Within two or three days, at each of the principal cities, new Unions of seamen and of carters had been formed and registered under the arbitration law, and those members of the old Federation Unions who were not enthusiastic, and began to see that the assurances of success were not likely to be realized, began to resign and apply for admission to the new Unions. After about two weeks the Council of The Federation of Labor, recognizing the failure of the sympathetic strike, invited the Unions that were not connected with them to declare the strike at an end, and tried by confining the strike to their own members, to maintain a solid front, which, with the help of the Australian Federation both in money for the strikers and in refusing to handle any goods either from or for New Zealand, they still hoped would carry them to at least a compromise, if not to the victory they had expected. The hopes of the Federation of Labor were not realized. Within a week or two a large proportion of the members of their own Unions, seeing their places filled, and their work being done, not by free labor, which they might hope to deal with, but by new Unions, whose members would be entitled, under the arbitration law, to preference and many other privileges, began to desert and to seek admission to the Arbitration Unions that had taken their place. For a time this was fiercely denied by the Federation officials, but as the days went on, and business of every kind was resumed in the cities, the groups of strikers at street corners and around the Federation head-quarters dwindled away; the hotels were reopened, the shops and stores were busy, the mills were at work, and even the coastal steamers were manned and running, and the federationists were forced to admit that they were hopelessly defeated. For a time they still hoped that the Australian Boycott might save them from absolute disaster, and the Labor Ministry of New South Wales tried to help the Federation by making an appeal to the New Zealand Government to arrange an arbitration to settle the dispute between The Wellington Waterside Workers and the merchants and shipping companies. The absolute refusal of the New Zealand Government to recognize The Federation of Labor, or to interfere with the new Unions under the Arbitration Act that had taken their place, finally settled the question, and completed the defeat of the strikers. The officials of the Federation declared the strike at an end, and the Australian Federation announced that the boycott was also at an end.

At first sight it may seem that, after all, the experiment in syndicalism was on a small scale, and that its lesson can hardly be of great value to a country like America. A little consideration may correct such a misapprehension. New Zealand was deliberately selected by the Syndicalists as a test case, for two reasons. In the first place it was the only country that had for years adopted a policy of justice according to law for both workers and employers, and from the syndicalist's point of view it was therefore the only country that seriously attacked their own policy by showing that it was unnecessary. In the second place New Zealand was the only country with a population of British origin that could be dealt with practically by itself. With the aid of an Australian boycott it seemed as if her people must be helpless in the hands of the Federation. The result proved to be not only the defeat of the principle of lawless syndicalism, but the destruction of the industrial association that represented it in the country. No compromise was accepted, and except it may be in name, no Union attached to the Federation of Labor remains at work. The question, of course, suggests itself: What was the reason? Minor reasons may be found, no doubt, to account for failure where success was so confidently expected; but there can be little doubt that the real cause is the policy pursued by the Legislature and people of New Zealand for the last twenty years. Syndicalism, like all plans for the over turn, or reform, as their advocates would perhaps prefer to call it, of existing institutions, depends for success on the existence of wrongs by which part of the people is impoverished, while another, and very small part, has more than enough. The workers of our own race, at any rate, have enough common-sense to understand, at least when they are not hysterically excited, that imaginary wrongs are not a sufficient reason for great sacrifices.

New Zealand's legislation has not created an ideal society, it is true; but for twenty years it has proceeded step by step in the direction of righting the wrongs of the past, and giving opportunity to that part of its people that needed it most, on the single condition that they would use it, and respect the rights of others. To such a people, increasing steadily, year by year, in all that makes for well-being, the wild denunciations, and if possible wilder promises, of paid agitators can have little attraction. It may be possible by careful generalship to stir a small section of such a people to the hysterical excitement of an industrial war, but the mass of the people would be certain to resent it, and the movement will be doomed to a speedy collapse.

Other countries have been less enlightened and less fortunate than New Zealand in their legislation, and perhaps still less fortunate in the administration of the laws passed for the betterment of the masses of their people. They have done little to convince the great majority that they are aware of the wrongs that have been done that majority in the supposed interest of the small class of the over rich. They have not provided opportunity for those who hitherto have had none, nor have they even provided a reasonable alternative for industrial warfare. Had they done these things in the past, or were they even to begin honestly to provide for them in the future, they might confidently expect that the reign of industrial warfare, which exasperates their people, and retards the prosperity of their nation, would be as easily and effectually suppressed as the experiment of the Syndicalists has just been in New Zealand.

LABOR: "TRUE DEMAND" AND IMMI-
GRANT SUPPLY

A RESTATEMENT OF THE ECONOMIC ASPECTS OF IMMI-
GRATION POLICY

RECENT historians and economists have been showing that it was anything but pure and unadul-
terated sense of brotherhood that prompted many of
our forefathers' fine speeches about opening the doors of
America to the down-trodden and oppressed of Europe.
Emerson, fifty years ago, in his essay on *Fate* noted the
current exploitation of the immigrant: "The German and
Irish millions, like the Negro, have a great deal of guano
in their destiny. They are ferried over the Atlantic, and
carted over America, to ditch and to drudge, to make corn
cheap, and then to lie down prematurely to make a spot of
green grass on the prairie." Indeed it would not be hard
to show that there was always a real or potential social
surplus back of our national hospitality to the alien.

The process began long before our great nineteenth century era of industrial expansion. Colonial policies with
regard to the immigrant varied according to latitude and
longitude. Most of the New England colonies viewed the
foreigner with distrust as a menace to Puritan theocracy.
New York, Pennsylvania, and some of the Southern colonies were much more hospitable, for economic reasons.
That this hospitality sometimes resembled that of the
spider to the fly is evident from observations of contemporary writers. That it included whites as well as negroes
in its ambiguous welcome is equally evident.

John Woolman writes in his *Journal* (1741-2): "In a
few months after I came here my master bought several

45

Scotchmen as servants, from on board a vessel, and brought them to Mount Holly to sell." Isaac Weld, traveling in the United States in the last decade of the eighteenth century, noted methods of securing aliens in the town of York, Pennsylvania: "The inhabitants of this town as well as those of Lancaster and the adjoining country consist principally of Dutch and German immigrants and their descendants. Great numbers of these people emigrate to America every year and the importation of them forms a very considerable branch of commerce. They are for the most part brought from the Hanse towns and Rotterdam. The vessels sail thither from America laden with different kinds of produce and the masters of them on arriving there entice as many of these people on board as they can persuade to leave their native country, without demanding any money for their passages. When the vessel arrives in America an advertisement is put into the paper mentioning the different kinds of people on board whether smiths, tailors, carpenters, laborers, or the like and the people that are in want of such men flock down to the vessel. These poor Germans are then sold to the highest bidder and the captain of the vessel or the ship holder puts the money into his pocket."

These may be, it is true, extreme cases of the economic motive for immigration. But they are quite in line with eighteenth century Mercantilist economic philosophy. Josiah Tucker, for example, in his *Essay on Trade*, 1753, urges the encouragement of immigration from France, and cites the value of Huguenot refugees. "Great was the outcry against them at their first coming. Poor England would be ruined! Foreigners encouraged! And our own people starving! This was the popular cry of the times. But the looms in Spittle-Fields, and the shops on Ludgate-Hill have at last sufficiently taught us another lesson . . . these *Hugonots* have . . . partly got, and partly saved, in the space of fifty years, a balance in our favour of, at least, fifty millions sterling. . . . And as England and

France are rivals to each other, and competitors in almost all branches of commerce, every single manufacturer so coming over, would be our gain, and a double loss to France."

The obverse side of the case appears in British hindrances to the free emigration of artisans during the eighteenth and early nineteenth centuries. Laws forbade any British subject who had been employed in the manufacture of wool, cotton, iron, brass, steel, or any other metal, of clocks, watches, etc., or who might come under the general denomination of artificer or manufacturer, to leave his own country for the purpose of residing in a foreign country out of the dominion of His Britannic Majesty. Recall the difficulty early American manufacturers encountered in introducing new English improvements in cotton manufacture; a virtual embargo was laid upon the migration of either men or machinery. Recall, too, an expression of American resentment in our Declaration of Independence at this English attitude: "He has endeavored to prevent the population of these states; for that purpose, obstructing the laws for naturalization of foreigners, refusing to pass others to encourage migration hither, and raising the conditions of new appropriations of lands."

On the whole, the economic motive seems to have been uppermost in the minds of both those who fostered and those who opposed foreign immigration into the United States, up to, say, 1870. Likewise in perhaps more than ninety-nine of every hundred cases the economic motive holds in the mind of the present day immigrant, or his protagonist. Escape from political tyranny or religious persecution, at least since the revolutionary period of 1848, has operated only as a secondary motive. The industrial impulse is all the more striking in the so-called "new immigration" from the Mediterranean and South-Eastern Europe. The temporary migrant laborer, the "bird of passage," roams about seeking his fortunes in much the same spirit that certain Middle Age Knights or Crusades camp followers sought theirs. This is in no way to his discredit. It is simply a fact that we are to reckon with when called upon to work out a satisfactory immigration policy. At least its recognition would eliminate a good deal of wordy sentimentality from discussions of the immigration problem.

Professor Fairchild discovered that three things attract the Greek immigrant. First and foremost, financial opportunities. Second, corollary to the first, citizenship papers which will enable him to return to Turkey, there to carry on business under the greater protection which such citizenship confers. There is a hint here to the effect that mere naturalization does not mean assimilation and permanent acceptance of the status and responsibilities of American citizenship. Third, enjoyment of certain more or less factitious "comforts of civilization."

But the Greeks are by no means untypical. The conclusion of the Immigration Commission as to the causes of the new immigration is that while "social conditions affect the situation in some countries, the present immigration from Europe to the United States is in the largest measure due to economic causes. It should be stated, however, that emigration from Europe is not now an absolute economic necessity, and as a rule those who emigrate to the United States are impelled by a desire for betterment rather than by the necessity of escaping intolerable conditions. This fact should largely modify the natural incentive to treat the immigration movement from the standpoint of sentiment, and permit its consideration primarily as an economic problem. In other words, the economic and social welfare of the United States should now ordinarily be the determining factor in the immigration policy of the Government."

This delimitation of the immigration problem to its economic aspects led the Immigration Commission to recommend a somewhat restrictionist policy. That they

were not without warrant in so delimiting it is evident
from the utterances of such ardent opponents of restric-
tion as Dr. Peter Roberts and Max J. Kohler. The latter,
writing in the *American Economic Review* (March, 1912)
said: "In fact, the immigrant laborer is indispensable to
our economic progress today, and we can rely upon no
one else to build our houses, railroads and subways, and
mine our ores for us." Dr. Roberts' plea is almost identical.

What a glaring misconception of the whole economic
and social problem is here involved will appear if we add a
clause or two to Mr. Kohler's sentence. He should have
said: "We can rely upon no one else to build our houses,
railroads and subways, and mine our ores for us *at $455 a
year; for workers of native birth but of foreign fathers would
cost us $566, and native born White Americans $666 a year.*"
(See Abstracts of Rep. of Immigr. Comm. vol. i., pp. 405–
8.) These are the facts. This is the social situation as it
should be stated if a candid discussion of the problem is
sought.

Now what are the economic arguments for restricting
somewhat the tide of immigration? Several studies of
standards of living among American workingmen within
the past ten years have shown that a large proportion of
American wage earners fall below a minimum efficiency
standard. Studies of American wages indicate that only a
little over ten per cent of American wage earners receive
enough to maintain an average family in full social efficiency. The average daily wage for the year ranges from
$1.50 to $2. One-half of all American wage earners get
less than $600 a year; three-quarters less than $750; only
one-tenth more than $1,000.

Take in connection with these wage figures the statistics
for unemployment. The proportion of idleness to work
ranges from one-third in mining industries to one-fifth in
other industries. In Massachusetts, 1908, manufacturers
were unemployed twelve per cent of the working time.

Professor Streightoff estimated three years ago that the average annual loss in this country through unemployment is 1,000,000 years of working time. Perhaps one-tenth of working time might be taken as a very conservative general average loss. But the worst feature of the whole problem is that, in certain industries at least, the tendency to seasonal unemployment is increasing. Ex-Commissioner Neill in his report on the Lawrence strike said: " . . . it is a fact that the tendency in many lines of industry, including textiles, is to become more and more seasonal and to build to meet maximum demands and competitive trade conditions more effectively. This necessarily brings it about that a large number of employés are required for the industry during its period of maximum activity who are accordingly of necessity left idle during the period of slackness." (Senate Document 870, 62d Cong., 2d sess., 1912.)

If we recall still further that the casual laborer, who suffers most from seasonal unemployment, is the chief stumbling block in the way to a solution of the problem of poverty; that he furnishes the human power in "sweated trades:" that immigrants form the majority of unskilled and sweated laborers; if we remember that there is not a shred of evidence (except the well-meant enthusiasm of the protagonists of the immigrant) to show that immigration has "forced-up" the American laborer and his standard of living, instead of displacing him downward; if we remember that probably 10,000,000 of our people are in poverty, and that though the immigrant may not seek charity in any larger proportions than the poor of native stock, yet he does contribute heavily to our burden of relief for dependents and defectives: we are justified in assuming that an analysis of the causes of poverty confirms the evidence from studies of wages and standards of living as to the depressing effect of the new immigration, in particular, upon working conditions for the American laborer.

Consider, too, the question of "social surplus." Several American economists, among them Professors Hollander, Patten and Devine, agree that we are creating annually in the United States a substantial social surplus. But it is evident from the figures of wages and standards of living quoted above that the American laborer is not participating as he might expect to participate in this economic advantage. Three factors conspire against him. First, we have yet no adequate machinery for determining exactly what the surplus is, or how to distribute it equitably. Mr. Babson with his "composite statistical charts" has made a beginning in the mathematical determination of prosperity; but it is only a beginning. Second, organized labor is not yet sufficiently organized nor sufficiently self-conscious to perceive and demand its opportunity for a larger share. The significant point here is that recent immigration has hampered and hindered the development of labor organizations, and thus indirectly held back the normal tendency of wages to rise. Third, inadequate education, particularly economic and social education. The adult illiterate constitutes a tremendous educational problem. Over 35 per cent of the "new immigration" of 1913 was illiterate, and this new immigration included over two-thirds of the total. Ignorance prevents the laborer from demanding the very education that would give him a better place in the economic system; it hinders the play of intelligent self-interest; and it actually prevents effective labor-organization, which is one of the surest means of labor-education. Jenks and Lauck, after experience with the Immigration Commission, concluded that "the fact that recent immigrants are usually of non-English speaking races, and their high degree of illiteracy, have made their absorption by the labor organizations very slow and expensive. In many cases, too, the conscious policy of the employers of mixing the races in different departments and divisions of labor, in order, by a diversity of tongues, to prevent concerted action on the part of employés, has made unionization of the immigrant almost impossible."

For these reasons, and others, we are driven to the conclusion that future policies of immigration must be based on sound principles of social welfare and social economy, and not upon the economic advantage of certain special industries. Whether we want the brawn of the immigrant must be determined by what it will contribute to the general social surplus, and not by what it adds to A's railroads or B's iron mines.

We are told that the three classes of our population demanding unrestricted immigration are large employers of unskilled labor, transportation companies, and revolutionary anarchists. Since this is by definition an economic and not a philosophical question, we may neglect the third class. To the other two classes should be directed certain brief tests of economic good faith. Take at its face value their claim that European brawn by the ship-load is indispensable to American industry. It is becoming an accepted maxim that industry should bear its own charges, should pay its own way. American industry has long fought the contract-labor exclusion feature in current immigration law. Suppose we frankly admit that it is much better for the immigrant to come over here to a definite job than to wander about for weeks after he arrives, a prey to immigrant banks, fake employment agents, and other sharks. Suppose, accordingly, we repeal the laws against contract-labor. Let the employer contract for as many foreign laborers as he likes or says he needs. But make the contractor liable for support and deportation costs if the laborers become public charges. Also require him to assume the cost of unemployment insurance. Exact a bond for the faithful performance of these terms, guaranteed in somewhat the same way that National Banks are safeguarded. Immigration authorities now commonly require a bond from the relatives of admitted aliens who seem likely to become public charges, but who are allowed to enter with the benefit of the doubt. Customs and revenue rules admit dutiable goods in bond. Hence the principle of the bond is perfectly familiar, and its application to contract-immigrants would be in no sense an untried or dangerous experiment. It would establish no new precedent: for precedents, and successful ones, are already established, accepted and approved. It would be understood that all admissions of aliens can be only provisional, with no time limit on deportation. It would be understood further — and the plan would work automatically if the contractor were made such a deeply interested party — that intending immigrants must be rigidly inspected, that they be required to produce consular certificates of clean police record, freedom from chronic disease, insanity, etc.

The result of such a scheme would probably cut away entirely contract-labor; for it would not longer pay. But this does not mean barring the gate to all foreign labor. As an aid to the employer and to our own native working-man, we must, sooner or later, and the sooner the better, establish a chain of labor bureaus throughout the Union. The system must be placed under Federal direction, largely because the Department of Labor would be charged, *ex officio*, with ascertaining the "true demand" for immigrant labor, and it could only accomplish this end effectively through such an employment clearing system. This true demand would, of course, be based not only upon mere numerical excess of calls for labor over demands for jobs, but would also take into account the nature of the work, working conditions, and above all the prevailing level of wages. According to this true demand the Department would adjust a sliding scale of admissions of immigrant laborers.

Much might be said in favor of an absolute embargo upon all immigration until such a body as the Industrial Relations Commission has time to make an authoritative economic survey of the whole country, or until the Unem-

ployment Research Commission recently called for by
Miss Kellor could make the three years' study contemplated by her as the only way out of the unemployment
morass. Twenty years ago men of the type of General
Walker frankly urged that the immigration gates be closed
for a flat period of ten years or so. But the sliding scale
plan contemplates no such radical step. Indeed it is
radical in no sense whatever. The proposed immigration
act now before Congress (The Burnett Bill, H. R. 6060)
paves the way for it, and provides a working principle,
which apparently is accepted on all sides. Section 3 includes this clause: "That skilled labor, if otherwise ad-
missible, may be imported if labor of like kind unemployed
can not be found in this country, and the question of the
necessity of importing such skilled labor in any particular
instance may be determined by the Secretary of Labor. . . ." A really workable test for immigration, superior by far to the literacy test or any other so far suggested, might easily be developed by simply enlarging the
scope of this clause, making it include unskilled as well as
skilled labor. No machinery other than that contemplated by the present act would be required.

The immigration problem can never be satisfactorily
handled until we fix upon some such means of determining
just what the economic need is. There is no danger of
hindering legitimate industrial expansion in times of sudden business prosperity: for the transportation companies
may be safely trusted to supply in three or four weeks
aliens enough to fill all the gaps in the industrial army.
Neither would injustice be done to the immigrant himself.
On the contrary, he would be assured of a job and re-
spectful consideration when he arrived. The "dago" or
the "bohunk" would acquire a new dignity and a more
enviable status than he now occupies. The selective
process thus involved would much improve the quality of
the immigrant admitted, and would incidentally render
assimilation of the foreigner all the easier.

The precise details of selection, and the machinery, are mere matters of detail. But the consular service, as long ago suggested by Catlin, Schuyler and others, seems to offer the proper base of operations. We have already recommended charging consuls with viséing certificates from police, medical, and poor-relief authorities. We should further require that declarations of intention to migrate be published (somewhat as marriage banns are published) at local administrative centers (arrondissement, Bezirk, etc.) and at United States consular offices; the consular declaration should be obligatory; perhaps the other might be optional, though in all probability foreign governments would coöperate in demanding it. These validated declarations of intention should be filed in the consular offices. When notice comes from the United States Department of Labor that so many laborers will be admitted from such and such district, the declarations are to be taken up in the order of their filing, and the proper number of persons certified for admission. The apportionment of admissions from each country might be calculated on a basis of its population, also upon the nature of the employment offered, and upon the desirability of the alien himself, his general assimilability, his willingness to become naturalized, to adopt the English language and the American standard of living among efficient workers, etc., — all as proved by past experience with his countrymen. This plan, in so far as it provides for a sliding scale of admissions, is in line with that proposed by Professor Gulick. He advocates making all nations eligible for admission and citizenship, but would admit them only in proportion as they can be readily assimilated. This would admit annually, say, five per cent of those already naturalized, with their American children. The principle here seems to be that we can assimilate from any land in, and only in, proportion to the number already assimilated from that land. But the difficulty of applying such a test lies in the complexity of the assimilative process. No measure yet exists for assimilation. Anthropologists are convinced that various strains in the populations, for example of France, or Great Britain, which have been dwelling together for centuries, are not by any means assimilated. Mere naturalization is not a sufficient test of assimilation; it is only the expression of a desire to be assimilated; and it may only be a device for the promotion of business success here or in foreign parts, as we have already indicated in the case of the Greeks. Hence in working out the basis of a sound immigration policy, it would seem more practicable to consider first the question of economic utilization rather than assimilation. This, of course, does not exclude from the Secretary of Labor's judgment the category of assimilability as one of the factors in determining the apportionment of admissions.

It will appear that the plan outlined above limits immigration policy to purely national and economic considerations. But it is, as matters now stand, a national question. And it must remain so for some time to come, even if we are reproached with a narrow Mercantilist economics. The admission of aliens is not yet a fundamental international *right*, or *duty;* it is only an example of *comity* within the family of nations. And the matter must rest in this state of limbo until we develop some institution or method of registering our sentiments of internationalism, and especially of determining *international surplus*. As it is idle to talk or dream of abolishing poverty until at least the concept of social or national surplus is pretty clearly fixed and its realization either actually at hand or fairly imminent, just so is it vain to expect an international adjustment of the immigration problem on economic grounds until the existence of an international surplus is demonstrated, and the methods of apportioning it worked out.

How soon we may expect these things it is not our province to predict. It is too early to pass final judgment on Professor Patten's dictum that inter-racial coöperation is impossible without integration, and that races must therefore stand in hostile relations or finally unite. But it is perfectly apparent that we have a long way to travel before the path to integration is cleared. Such assemblages as the First Universal Races Congress which met in London in 1911 can do much to prepare the way. But it must not be forgotten that the German representative at that Congress pleaded for the maintenance of strict racial and national boundaries, and summed up his plea in the rather ominous sentence: "The brotherhood of man is a good thing, but the struggle for life is a far better one." Meanwhile we need not anticipate serious international difficulties in the way of the sliding-scale plan; for foreign governments are watching the tide of immigration with mixed feelings. They welcome the two or three hundred million dollars sent home annually by alien residents in the United States. But they also resent the dislocations of industry, the fallow fields, the dodging of military service, and the disturbance of the level of prices which such wholesale emigrations inflict upon the mother country.

Since the protagonists of unrestricted immigration have taken largely an economic line of argument, it seemed desirable to accept their terms, and meet them on their own ground. But I should not wish to be misunderstood as limiting the immigration question to its economic phases. When we have said that the *latifondisti* of Southern Italy are in despair at the scarcity of laborers to work their lands at starvation wages, and that the railway builders and mine operators of America are equally anxious to have those selfsame South Italian laborers for their own exploitive enterprises, we have told a bare half of the tale. There remain all those cultural, educational, political, religious and domestic variations and adjustments which make up the general problem of assimilability of the alien and of the strength of our own national digestion. America had a giant's undiscriminating appetite in the great days of expansion from 1850 to 1890. But there are many signs, economic and other, that we can no longer play Gargantua and continue a healthy nation. An unwise engineer sometimes over-stokes his boilers, and courts disaster. Is it not equally possible that national welfare may suffer from an over-dose of human fuel in our industry?

"THE next great task of preventive medicine is the inauguration of universal periodic medical examinations as an indispensable means for the control of all diseases, whether arising from injurious personal habits, from congenital or constitutional weakness, or from social and vocational conditions." That this declaration by the Commissioner of Health of the city of New York is not the mere expression of an individual opinion, there is abundant evidence. And no one who has watched the growth of other movements towards such regulation of life as only a few years ago would have seemed wholly outside the domain of practical probability can doubt that the "Life Extension" movement, as thus outlined, will rapidly grow into prominence. Nor is there much room for doubt that, whether explicitly contemplated at present or not, compulsion as well as universality is tacitly implied in the movement.

I say that the movement is sure to grow into prominence, that it is a thing which must be seriously reckoned with; I do not say that it will march straight on to victory, or even that it is sure to prevail in the end. It is instructive, in this regard, to hark back to a recent experience in a more special, but yet an extremely important, domain. Several years ago a report on university efficiency was issued under the auspices — though, it should be added, without the official endorsement — of the Carnegie Foundation. The central feature of this report lay in its advocacy of the application to universities of those principles of system and of standardization which have been successfully applied on a large scale to the promotion of industrial efficiency, and are generally referred to by the catchword, "scientific management." In spite of the merits of the report in certain matters of detail, and of the high standing of the expert who wrote it in his own department of industrial engineering, the report evoked an almost universal chorus of contemptuous rejection not only in university circles, but also from those organs of public opinion which have any claim to be regarded as enlightened judges in questions of education and culture. The thing seemed to have been laughed out of court. And yet it turned out that a year or two afterwards a full-fledged scheme for carrying out some of the crudest and most objectionable features of this "efficiency" program was presented to the professors of Harvard University, apparently with the expectation that they would fall in with its requirements without hesitation or protest. For some days there seemed to be real danger that this would actually happen. It turned out to be a false alarm; the faculty of the foremost of American universities were guilty of no such supineness. The project was ignominiously shelved, with some sort of explanation that the springing of it on the professors was due to an error or misunderstanding. But that the attempt should have been made, and in a manner that argued so total a lack of any sense of its grossness and crudity, is a significant warning of the extent to which the notions underlying it have fastened upon the general mind.

The story of the eugenics movement in this country affords a striking illustration at once of the almost startling rapidity with which innovating ideas as to the regulation of life gain acceptance, and of the fact that this rapidity is by no means conclusive proof that their progress will be continuous. The one thing clear is that there is a large, active, and influential element in the population that is extremely hospitable to such ideas, and manifests a naïve, an almost childish, readiness to put them into immediate execution. Since, in the nature of things, this element is lively and active — since, too, what is novel and in motion is more interesting than what is old and at rest — at first there is almost sure to be produced a deceptive appearance that the new thing is sweeping everything before it. Just now there is evidently a lull in the onward march of legislative eugenics. This is sufficient proof of the conservatism of the people as a whole; we may be quite sure that anything beyond a very restricted application of eugenical notions will take a long time to get itself established in our laws or even in our customs. Nevertheless, it would be a great mistake to suppose that even the more extreme forms of eugenical doctrine are not forces to be reckoned with as affecting practical possibilities of a not distant future. Though no results may appear on the surface, the leaven is working. It is consonant with tendencies which in so many directions are becoming more and more dominant. So long as those tendencies continue in anything like their present strength, there can be little doubt that the idea of control in the direction of eugenics, like that of the regulation of human life in other fundamental respects, will continue to make headway, and may at any time become one of the central issues of the day.

To adduce prohibition as an illustration of this same character in the thought and the tendencies of our immediate time may seem like forcing the point. It is true, it may be said, that there has been within the past few years a rapid spread of prohibition in almost every part of the country; but the thing itself is sixty years old, has had its periods of advance and recession, and is now, in the fullness of time, reaping the fruits of two generations of agitation, investigation, and education. But to say this is to overlook the distinctive feature of the present situation regarding prohibition in the United States. A Constitutional amendment providing for the complete prohibition of the sale of liquor throughout the Union is pending in Congress. A year ago — probably six months ago — there was hardly a human being in the United States, other than those in the councils of the Anti-saloon League, who had so much as thought of national prohibition as a question of present-day practical politics. Suddenly it is announced that there is a distinct possibility of a prohibition amendment being passed by Congress in the near future; and one of the foremost representatives of the Anti-saloon League states, and with good show of reason, that if the amendment be passed by Congress, its ratification by the Legislatures of three fourths of the States can be only a matter of time. What the probabilities actually are, I do not undertake to say; neither am I concerned at this moment with the merits of the issue itself. What I *am* concerned with is the simple fact that in this situation, brought upon the country with dramatic suddenness, nobody seems to have been in the least startled, or so much as disturbed in his equanimity. There will of course be a great struggle over the question, sooner or later. But neither in Congress nor in the press has there as yet been any sign of such an assertion of the claims of personal liberty as, at any time previous to the past ten years, would have been sure to be made in such a situation. This collective silence, on an issue affecting so intimately the lives, the habits, the traditions of millions of people, is, in my judgment, by far the most impressive proof of the degree in which the public mind has grown accustomed to the inroads of regulation upon the domain of individuality.

A number of years ago, when the mathematical concept of space of more than three dimensions was attracting great popular interest, an ingenious writer undertook to make the idea intelligible to "the general" by picturing the state of mind in regard to three dimensions of a race of beings whose life and whose sensual experience was limited to space of two dimensions. He gave his little book the title "Flatland," and it gained wide attention. In his Commencement address at Columbia last year, President

Butler had the happy thought of applying the term in the characterization of certain aspects of the intellectual and political life of our time. He was speaking particularly of that absorption in the immediate problems of the day which makes almost impossible a true study and contemplation of the lasting concerns of mankind as embodied in history and literature. "Every ruling tendency," he said, "is to make life a Flatland, an affair of two dimensions, with no depth, no background, no permanent root." That this is a literal truth probably neither Dr. Butler nor anyone else would contend; but it hits off with great force and with substantial accuracy the prevailing character of thought in the circles most active and most influential in almost every department of human activity at the present time. And the tendency which President Butler describes as arising out of our absorption in current problems is still more manifest in the spirit of our actual dealings with those problems themselves. On every hand we find a surprising readiness to accept views which explicitly tend to take out of life that which gives it depth and significance and richness. Each one of the four movements we have mentioned affords an illustration of this: in following any one of them we travel straight toward Flatland. They differ very much, one from another; they have very different degrees and kinds of justification; it may be difficult in the case of some of them to strike a balance between the gain and the loss. The remarkable thing — the ominous thing, if we are to suppose that the present tone of thought will long persist — is that the loss involved in the flattening of life, as such, apparently almost wholly fails to get consideration. I say apparently, because there is, no doubt, a deep and strong undercurrent of opposition which, sooner or later, will manifest itself; in speaking of "ruling tendencies" we are apt to mean merely the tendencies that are most in evidence. But after all, it is to these that criticism of contemporary life and thought must, of necessity, be chiefly directed.

As I have already indicated, the attack on individuality and personal dignity in the universities was met in a spirit that is highly gratifying, and which is quite out of keeping with the tendency that I am discussing and deploring. Yet it is doubtful whether, outside the circle of the universities themselves, and of those individuals who are thoroughly imbued with the university spirit, there is any true realization of what it is that constituted the head and front of that offending. If some bureau of research were to present a formidable array of figures showing that the "output" of professorial work could be increased by so and so many per cent. through the adoption of some definitely formulated system of "scientific management," it is by no means certain that the scheme would not receive powerful support in the highest quarters of efficiency propaganda. We should be told just how many millions of dollars a year we are spending on university education, and just how many of these millions go needlessly to waste. Even the opponents of the "reform" would probably find themselves compelled to use as their most powerful argument this and that example of great practical results which have flowed from letting men of genius go their own way. It would be pointed out that many an investigation which, to the authorities of the time, appeared wholly unpromising, turned out to be of cardinal value. We should be warned that what we gain in a thousand cases through time-clock and card-catalogue methods, might be lost ten times over through the shackling of the initiative of a single man of unrecognized genius. And all this would be very much to the purpose; but it is not upon any such special pleading that the case ought to be made to rest. The loss that would be suffered transcends all these concrete and definable instances of it. It would be pervasive, fundamental, immeasurable. Grievous as might be the injury caused by the prevention of specific achievements of exceptional importance, this would be as nothing in comparison with the intellectual and spiritual loss entailed by the lowering of the human level, the devitalizing of the intellectual atmosphere, which must inevitably follow upon the application of factory methods to university life.

The case of the eugenics propaganda is far more complex. In its origin, and doubtless in some of its present manifestations, it may lay claim to being directed toward aims which are particularly concerned with the higher interests of life. The author of "Hereditary Genius" certainly could not be accused of indifference to the part played in the past, or to be played in the future, by exceptional minds and characters; nor is it necessary to charge any of the present promoters of the propaganda with explicit failure to appreciate the importance of such minds and characters. The criticism is often made, from this standpoint, that the hard-and-fast rules which the eugenists propose would, in point of fact, have put under the ban some of the most illustrious names in the annals of mankind — men whose genius was accompanied with some of the very traits which they hold should most positively be prevented from appearing. But, however weighty this objection to the methods of eugenics may be, it is to be looked upon rather as an item on the debit side of the reckoning than as marking an ingrained defect, a fault at the very heart of the matter. The eugenists may well challenge those who urge merely this kind of objection to show that the losses thus pointed out are great enough to offset the gains, in the very same direction, which they regard their program as promising. Whatever the truth of the matter may be, they can at least set up the contention that, as a mere affair of quantity, genius will do better under their system than without it.

What brings the eugenics movement into the Flatland category is not its attitude toward the question of genius, or perhaps even of singularity, but its attitude toward the life of mankind as a whole — if indeed it can be said to have any attitude toward the life of mankind as a whole. The profound elements of that life seem not to come at all within the range of its contemplation. Of course this does not apply to everything that comes from the eugenics camp, nor to every person that calls himself a eugenist. But on the other hand it is by no means only of the crude projects of half-educated reformers, or the outgivings of the prophets of our popular magazines, that it *is* true. The agitation has derived much of its impetus, directly or indirectly, from the teachings of men of high scientific eminence who have attacked the question without any apparent realization of its deeper bearings on the whole character of human life. This influence often comes in the shape of exhortations, or suggestions, addressed to the public at a time when attention is centered upon some conspicuous crime or some particular phase of evil in the community; sweeping and radical regulation of the right of parenthood being urged as necessary for the prevention of all such distressing phenomena. Thus, after the attempted assassination of Mayor Gaynor, there was much talk of a " national campaign for mental hygiene," which should have the effect of "preventing Czolgoszes and Schranks." Its program was thus indicated by one of the foremost professors of medicine in the United States:

Provision must be made for the birth of children whose brains shall, so far as possible, be innately of good quality; this means the denial of the privilege of parenthood to those likely to transmit bad nervous systems to their offsprings.

What the carrying out of such a programme would mean to mankind at large, how profoundly it would modify those ideas about life, those standards of human dignity and human rights, which are so fundamental and so pervasive that they are taken for granted without express thought in every act and every feeling of all normal men and women — this does not seem ever to trouble the mind of the devotee of universal regulation. He sees the possibility of effecting a certain definite and measurable improvement; that the means by which this is accomplished must fatally impair those elemental conceptions of human life whose value transcends all measurement, he has not the insight or the imagination to recognize. The distinctions of social class, of wealth, of public honor, leave untouched the equality of men in the fundamentals of human dignity. They do not go to the vitals of self-respect; they do not interfere with a man's sense of what is due to him, and what is due from him, in the primary relations of life. If nature has been unkind to him in his physical or mental endowments, he does not therefore feel in the least disqualified, as regards his family, his friends, his neighbors, the stranger with whom he chances to come into contact, from receiving the same kind of consideration, in the essentials of human intercourse, that is accorded to those who are more fortunate; nor does he feel in any respect absolved from the duty of playing the full part of a man. Under the régime of medical classification — and the "mental hygiene" programme can mean nothing less than that — all this would disappear. Some men would be men, others would be something less. It is true that, so far as regards the imbecile, the insane, and the criminal, such a state of things obtains as it is; but this stands wholly apart from the general life of the race, and has no influence whatever on the habitual feelings and experiences of human beings. The normal life of mankind is shot through and through with the idea that a man's a man; all that is highest in feeling and conduct is closely bound up with it. Lessen its sway over our feelings and thoughts and instincts, and how much benefit in the shape of "preventing Czolgoszes and Schranks" would be required to compensate for the loss in nobleness, in depth, which human life would suffer?

The prohibition movement belongs, in the main, to a wholly different order of things. The fight against the evils of drink, as it has been carried on for a century or more, has been animated by a moral fervor which classes it rather with the fight against slavery, or with the great revivals of religion, than with those movements which owe their origin to a calculating and cold-blooded perfectionism. Its leaders have been fired with the ardor of a war directed against a devastating monster, to whose ravages was to be ascribed a large part of the misery and wickedness that afflict mankind. It is true that the economic and physiological aspects of the drink question were not ignored; the total-abstinence men were glad enough to have this second string to their bow. But the real fight was not against alcohol as one of many things concerning which the habits of men are more or less unwise; it was a fight against the Demon Rum, the ally of all the powers of .darkness· The plea of the moderate drinker was rejected with scorn, not because there was any objection to moderate drinking in itself, but because total abstinence was the only true preventive of drunkenness, and drunkenness must be stamped out if mankind was to be saved. The moderate drinker was censured not because he was wasting his money, or failing to "conserve his efficiency," but because for the sake of a trivial self-indulgence he was giving countenance to a practice which was consigning millions of his fellow men to wretchedness in this world and to everlasting damnation in the next.

Now the remarkable thing about the present extraordinary manifestation of growth and strength in the prohibition movement is that it is not in the least due to a strengthening of this sentiment. On the contrary, it is safe to say that feeling about drunkenness, about the drink evil in the sense in which it was understood a generation ago, is far less intense than it was then. The prohibition movement in its present stage is not the old prohibition movement advancing to triumph through the onward march of its proselyting zeal; of true prohibitionist zealots the number is probably less, in proportion to the

population, than it was forty years ago. Its great accession of strength has come from the growth of that order
of ideas which is common to all the "efficiency" movements of the time. And that growth helps it in two ways.
On the one hand, to the little army of crusaders against
the Demon Rum there has come the accession of a
host of men who are not thinking about demons at all,
but who calmly hold that the world would be better off
without drinking, and that this is an all-sufficient reason
for prohibiting it. And on the other hand, millions of
persons who, in former days would have cried out against
this way of improving the world — against the impairment of personal liberty and the sacrifice of social enjoyment and social variety — have no longer the courage of
their convictions. The temper of the time is unfavorable
to the assertion of the value of things so incapable of
numerical measurement. Against the heavy battalions
led by the statisticians, and the experimental psychologists, and the efficiency experts, what chance is there for
successful resistance? On the opposing side can be rallied only such mere irregulars as are willing to fight for
airy nothings — for the zest and colorfulness of life, for
sociability and good fellowship, for preserving to each man
access to those resources of relaxation and refreshment
which, without injury to others, he finds conducive to his
own happiness.

It is hardly necessary to say that, in taking up these
various movements, no attempt has been made at anything like comprehensive discussion of their merits.
Whatever may be the balance between good and ill in any
of them, they all have in common one tendency that
bodes danger to the highest and most permanent interests of mankind; and it is with this alone that I am
concerned. What that tendency is has, I trust, been made
sufficiently clear; but it will perhaps be brought out more
distinctly by a consideration of the "Life Extension"

propaganda more detailed and specific than that given to the other three.

Conspicuous in the literature of this propaganda is the appeal to standard modern practice in regard to machinery. "Those to whom the care of delicate mechanical apparatus is entrusted," says the New York Commissioner of Health, "do not wait until a breakdown occurs, but inspect and examine the apparatus minutely, at regular intervals, and thus detect the first signs of damage." "This principle of periodic inspection," says the prospectus of the Life Extension Institute, "has for many years been applied to almost every kind of machinery, except the most marvelous and complex of all, — the human body." To find fault with the drawing of this comparison, with the utilization of this analogy, would be foolish. That many persons would be greatly benefited by submitting to these inspections is certain; it is not impossible that they are desirable for most persons. And the analogy of the inspection of machinery serves excellently the purpose of suggesting such desirability. What is objectionable about its use by the Life Extension propagandists is their evident complacent satisfaction with the analogy as complete and conclusive. Yet nothing is more certain than that, even from the strictly medical standpoint, it ignores an essential distinction between the case of the man and the case of the machine. The machine is affected only by the measures that may be taken in consequence of the knowledge arising from the inspection; the man is affected by that knowledge itself. Whether the possible physical harm that may come to a man from having his mind disturbed by solicitude about his health is important or unimportant in comparison with the good that is likely to be done him by the following of the precautions or remedies prescribed, is a question of fact to which the answer varies in every individual case. It may be that in the great majority of cases the harm is insignificant in comparison with the good. However that may

be, the question is there, and it is of itself fatal to the con-
clusiveness of the *argumentum ex machina*. That this is
not a captious criticism, that it is based on substantial
facts of life, ordinary experience sufficiently attests; but
it may not be amiss to point to a conspicuous contemporary phenomenon which throws an interesting light on
the matter. The Christian Scientists regard the *ignoring*
of disease as the primary requisite for health and longevity.
That the Christian Science doctrine is a sheer absurdity,
no one can hold more emphatically than the present
writer; but it cannot be denied that in thousands of cases
its acceptance has been of physical benefit through its
subjective effect upon the believer. Personally, I would
not purchase any benefit to my physical life at such sacrifice of my intellectual integrity; I mention the point only
by way of accentuating the undisputed fact that the presence or absence of concern about health may have a
potent influence on one's bodily welfare.

Although it is a still further digression from the main
purpose of this paper, I must permit myself a few words on
another point relating to the strictly medical claims of the
plan of "universal periodic medical examination." It
is natural that its advocates say nothing about the danger
of errors in diagnosis; everybody knows that this danger
exists, but sensible men do not allow it to deter them from
consulting a physician; in this, as in other affairs of life,
they do not cry for the moon, but do the best they can.
But it seems to be wholly overlooked by the advocates of
the propaganda of "universal periodic examination" that
the extent of this danger under present conditions affords
no indication at all of what it would be under the system
they contemplate. Its cardinal virtue, they constantly
proclaim, would be the detection of the very slightest indication of impairment: "The task before us is to discover the first sign of departure from the normal physiological path, and promptly and effectually to apply the
brake." The consequence must necessarily be that for

one case of false alarm that occurs today there will be a
score, or a hundred, under the new régime. For, in the
first place, the individuals seeking advice will not be, as
they now are in the main, selected cases in which there is
some antecedent presumption that there is something
wrong; and secondly, the examiner, bent upon the one
great object of overlooking nothing, however slight, will
give warnings which, whether technically justifiable or
not, will in great numbers of cases have a wholly unjusti-
fiable significance to the mind of the subject. Who shall
say how many persons will thus be made to carry through
life a burden of solicitude about their health from which,
if left to their own devices, they would have been wholly
free?

But it is not my design to find fault with this scheme as
a matter of medical benefit; if I have ventured to point
out some drawbacks, it is only by way of showing that,
even from the strictly medical standpoint the cult of
uniformity, of standardization, of mechanical perfection, is
not free from fault. But the great objection against that
attitude of mind which is typified in the appeal to the
analogy of machinery is far more vital. Our only interest
in a machine is that we shall get out of it as much, and
as exact, work as possible. Our interest in our bodies is
not so limited. We may deliberately choose to forego
the maximum of mechanical perfection for the sake of
living our lives in a way more satisfactory to us than
a constant care for that perfection would permit. Even
the most ardent of health enthusiasts — unless he be an
insane fanatic — draws the line somewhere. What he
forgets is that other people prefer to draw the line somewhere else. They choose to run a certain amount of risk
rather than have their health on their minds. To compel — whether by legal means or by social pressure —
every man to take precautions concerning his own body
which he deliberately prefers not to take; to make impossible, in this most intimate and personal of all human

concerns, the various ways of acting which the infinite
varieties of temperament and desire may dictate — this
would be such an invasion of personal liberty, such a
suppression of individuality, as would strike us all as ap-
palling, had we not grown so habituated to the mechanical, the statistical, measurement of human values — to
the Flatland view of life.

What gives to these movements that I have been discussing the character which I have been ascribing to them
is not so much the specific things which they severally
aim to accomplish, but the spirit in which they are carried
on, and perhaps still more the spirit, or want of spirit,
with which they are met. It is not that a balance is
falsely struck between the benefit of the concrete, circum-
scribed, measurable improvement aimed at and the injury done to some deeper, more pervading, and quite
immeasurable element or principle of life; it is that the
balance is not struck at all. The subtler, the less tangible,
element is simply ignored. It was not always so. It was
not so in the last generation, or the generation before that.
The phenomenon is one that is closely bound up with the
ruling tendency of thought and action in all directions; it
is not an accident of this or that particular agitation.
Perhaps in no direction is it more convincingly manifested than in the prevailing tone of opinion, or at least
of publicly expressed opinion, in regard to the objects and
ideals of universities. That in the present state of the
world's economic and social development on the one hand,
and of the various sciences on the other, "service" — that
is, service directly conducive to the general good —
should be regarded as one of the great objects of universities, is altogether right; that it should be spoken of as
their *only* object, which is the ruling fashion, is most
deplorable. The object of a university, said Mill, is to
keep philosophy alive; yet it would go hard with the
present generation to point to any one more truly and

profoundly devoted to the service, the uplifting, of the masses of mankind than was John Stuart Mill. Were he living he would recognize, as thoroughly as the best efficiency man of them all, that the universities of today have opportunities and duties which were undreamed of half a century ago. But he would know, too, that in those activities which are directed to the promotion of practical efficiency, the university is but one of many agencies, and that if it were not doing the work some other means would be found for supplying the demand. Its paramount value he would find now, as he did then, in the service it renders not to the ordinary needs of the community but to the higher intellectual interests and strivings of mankind. That so few of us have the courage clearly to assert a position even distantly approaching this — such a position as was mere matter of course among university men in the last generation — is perhaps the most significant of all the indications of our drift toward Flatland.

THE DISFRANCHISEMENT OF PROPERTY

I

IT is Hawthorne, I think, who tells us that when he was a boy he used once in a while to go down to the wharves in Salem, and lay his hand on the rail of some great East India merchantman, redolent of spices, and thus bring himself in actual touch with the mysterious orient. But there is nothing strange in this: almost anything that we can feel or see may start the flight of fancy, and open to us prophetic visions. This is even true of such dry symbols as figures, for our journalists would never publish statistics as they do, unless they knew that their readers liked to see them. Travellers from other parts of the world have often laughed at our fondness for revelling in the marvellous accounts of our material dimensions, but they should remember that people who do not have a taste for poetry may yet have a taste for romance, and that big figures do appeal to the imagination.

It is true that there may be something portentous in bigness. "Tom" Reed, as he was affectionately called, said many wise things in a jesting way. At a certain crisis in our history he exclaimed: "I don't want Cuba and Hawaii; I've got more country now than I can love." A foreigner might suppose that our politicians had similarly become terror-stricken at the extent of our wealth and the rate at which it was growing. They may well give the impression that there has been created in the "money power," a Frankenstein monster, the control of whose murderous propensities has put them at their wit's end.

Figures are notorious liars; they may arouse emotion if looked at in any light, but they must be looked at in many lights if we would get an emotional effect that is truly worth while. Some very large figures relating to Savings Banks have lately been published. The deposits in these banks amount to over four and two-thirds billions of dollars, and the number of separate accounts is about ten and two-thirds millions. Savings deposits in all banks are about $7,000,000,000, the number of accounts being 17,600,000. Probably the interest paid on the savings banks deposits is 160 millions of dollars a year. I confess that these figures give me much pleasure. I like to think that so many men have taken pains to guard their wives and children against miserable want; that so many women have to some extent made sure of their independence. It would not be surprising to find that twelve millions of families, possibly half the people of the country, were in this way protected against extreme penury. Viewed in this light, the growth of wealth does not seem so terrible. One might paraphrase Burke and say that such wealth as this loses half its evil through losing all its grossness. Indeed one might go further and say that if there were twice as much of this wealth, and every person in the country had an interest in it, it would lose all of its evil.

To young people, this is all dry enough. They like to think of spending money, not of saving it. But it is not at all dry to their elders. It is what St. Beuve said of literary enjoyment, a "pure délice du goût et du cœur dans la maturité." It is a "Pleasure of the Imagination" that can be appreciated only by those like the old Scottish lawyer, who justified his penurious prudence by saying that he had shaken hands with poverty up to the elbow when he was young, and had no intention to renew the acquaintance. We have not, at least in the Northern part of our country, had the terrible experiences of the people of Europe, who are even now hiding their money in a vague apprehension of danger, inherited from centuries of rapine; but there are few of those who have given hostages to fortune who have not had many hours, and even years, of distressing anxiety concerning the future of their families. The greater the provision made against this heart-corroding care by a people, the happier should that people be.

It seems so unselfish a luxury to revel in these comfortable statistics, that one is tempted to broaden his vision, and take in the four or five billions of assets heaped up by the six or seven millions of people who have insured their lives, and the one hundred and fifty or two hundred millions of dollars paid out yearly to lighten the distress attending the death of husbands and fathers of families, — to say nothing of a much greater sum repaid policy-holders. In many cases, happily, death causes no actual want; but against these cases we may offset the stupendous number of policies insuring against industrial accidents, possibly twenty-five millions of them, representing one quarter of the people of the country — for we may be sure that there are few payments made under these policies that do not actually alleviate suffering. We have here a colossal aggregate of altruism on the part of the policy-holders, an intangible national asset grander than all the material wealth which it represents; for the sordid element in all these savings is necessarily small. There is a point in the old story of the gambler on the Mississippi steamboat who listened attentively to the persuasive arguments of a life-insurance agent; he "allowed" that he was willing to bet on almost any kind of game, but declined to take a hand in one where he had to die to win. It is painful to think of the infinity of petty economies, of all the grievous deprivations, the positive hardships, undergone in so many millions of families, day by day, and year by year, to secure these policies of insurance; but, as Plato said, "the good is difficult." There is no heroism where there is no self-sacrifice. Whoever is disquieted by the growth of "materialism" may be relieved by reflecting that when so many millions of people are denying themselves present enjoyments in order that others may be spared pain in the future, there is such a leaven of high motive among us as may leaven the whole lump.

It would be easy to keep on in this exalted strain, but perhaps it is a little too much in the style of a life-insurance advertisement. We may correct any such impression, by changing our point of view. When we consider the difficulties and the hindrances in the way of laying up these savings, while the moral effect of the self-sacrifice hitherto involved is enhanced, the question comes up whether this altruistic exertion can be maintained in the future. How many of the ten millions of depositors in the savings banks have considered that their rulers at Washington give away every year in military pensions a sum equal to all, and more than all, the income earned by the four billions of dollars in the banks? When after many years, it seemed that this burden might at last begin to be lightened, it was suddenly increased by the last Congress perhaps thirty millions a year. Why should so many people scrimp, year in and year out, when the equivalent of all the toil and all the self-denial is thus swept away?

Senator Aldrich has told the country that its affairs could be carried on for three hundred millions of dollars a year less than it now pays. He is a very competent witness, and no one has contradicted him. If the attempt had been made, he could perhaps have shown — he could certainly show now — that three hundred millions was an understatement. But this sum is nearly equal to the income earned by the investments of all the savings banks and all the life-insurance companies of the country. If our rulers had borrowed ten billions of dollars at three per cent. and had wasted it all, the country would be financially about where it is now. They have not borrowed this ten billions of dollars, but if Mr. Aldrich is right, they are spending the interest on it. They have in effect mortgaged the wealth of the people to the extent of all their deposits in the savings banks, and all their investments in life-insurance companies, and are wasting the income of these funds faster than it is earned. If anyone thinks this is stating the case too strongly, he may add the waste of our state and municipal rulers to that of those at Washington, and Mr. Aldrich's figure will seem moderate enough.

People who are comfortably off will reply to all this that we are getting on pretty well, and seem to be on the whole doing better from year to year. There is a well known passage in Macaulay's History which may be thought to give support to optimism of this kind. "No ordinary misfortune," he said, "no ordinary misgovern-ment, will do so much to make a nation wretched as the constant progress of physical knowledge, and the constant effort of every man to better his condition will do to make a nation prosperous."

No one will deny that the history of England justifies this statement; but let us remember the reason that Macaulay gave for this insuperable prosperity. "Every man has felt entire confidence that the State would pro-tect him in the possession of what had been earned by his diligence and hoarded by his self-denial."

It is impossible to maintain that every man now feels this entire confidence. The income "earned by his dili-gence" is henceforth to be taxed at a progressive rate, and the demagogues are already complaining that the rate is not high enough. The inheritance of his family, "hoarded by his self-denial," protected by the State until within a few years, now pays taxes which amount to the interest on a billion of dollars. We are assured by a railroad officer that three measures of legislation have increased the expenses of his corporation alone by a sum equal to the interest on $32,000,000, with no appreciable benefit to the public. The number of such laws is incal-culable, and the cost of complying with them has become an almost intolerable burden. The income of the railroads declines, while their taxes increase, in some cases two or three fold. Lawyers and office holders thrive and are cheerful; investors suffer and tremble.

The people of New York seem just now to be in a way to find out how the enormous taxes which their rulers have levied on them are expended; but New York has no monopoly of corrupt rulers, and the cost of investigating extravagance is itself extravagant. And yet people wonder at the increased cost of living! Unfortunately the oppressions of government do worse than discourage business enterprise; they tend to demoralize society. There are too many men who hesitate to marry because they do not have confidence in the future, too many married people who do not dare to have more than one or two children, if they dare to have any, to make it possible to maintain that there is now no dread of more than ordinary misgovernment.

It is difficult to ascertain the total wealth of the country. The census bureau is notoriously dilatory. Its latest estimate was for 1904, when this aggregate was computed to be $107,000,000,000, or about $1,300 *per caput*. Assuming this ratio, the wealth of our people should now be over $120,000,000,000; but the figures are largely conjectural. It happens, however, that we possess some figures that are altogether trustworthy. In the year 1909 the Federal Government imposed a tax of one per cent. on the net income of every corporation, joint stock company, or association, including insurance companies, organized for profit, whenever this net income is over $5,000. There are some other exemptions, but they are not sufficient to demand consideration, and may be disregarded. Now we may be absolutely certain of one thing, and that is that the net income of those concerns will not be overestimated. Their net income may be more than what they report for the purposes of taxation, but it surely cannot be less. For the past year it seems probable that this tax will produce nearly thirty-five millions of dollars net income, after deducting all expenses, losses, depreciation, interest on debts and on deposits paid by banks, and dividends from other companies subject to the tax.

It may be more, but it cannot be less. Here our certainty ends. Guesses will vary, but in view of what we know in a general way of the conditions of business during the past year, we may perhaps venture to assume that the net income of these concerns is six per cent. of their real wealth. If this assumption is correct, their total wealth is 60 billions of dollars, or one half of the total wealth of the nation.

This estimate may be confirmed to some extent by other statistics. Calling the physical value of the railroads fourteen billions, their net earnings at five per cent. would be 700 millions, which corresponds well enough with the figures of the government, although some railroad men would make their net earnings much less. We do not know the net income of the untaxed corporations. Their returns would show its amount, but the government does not supply the information. As there must be now nearly 250,000 such corporations, if their average income is only $2,000 a year, the total could be $500,000,000. If it is $4,000, their income would be almost a billion dollars. On a 5 per cent. basis, the wealth of these corporations would be nearly 20 billion dollars. It seems, on the whole, that the wealth held by corporations is probably more than half our total wealth rather than less.

The bearing of these figures on our subject is now apparent. All of this property is disfranchised. It is, economically, to a very great extent disfranchised; politically, it is altogether disfranchised. What I mean by this is that the owners of this wealth, as owners, have very little to say, and nothing to do, about its care and management. Prob-

ably more than half of our people are directly or indirectly
interested in it as owners. They have been attracted by
a desire to share, however humbly, in big and famous
enterprises, by the freedom from liability of the portion
of their estates outside the particular investments, and
by the freedom at death or withdrawal of associates from
appraisals and accountings and probable closing of the
business, as is the inevitable practice in mere partnerships.
Two centuries ago people who saved money could hardly
find ways to invest it. The practice of incorporation has
enormously increased our wealth by putting a stop to
hoarding without interest, stimulating saving, and broad-
cning industry. The number of individual owners of the
bonds and stocks of corporations is incalculable, and their
holdings added to those of savings banks, insurance companies, trust companies and other fiduciary institutions,
churches, hospitals, and colleges, make up a total of almost fabulous extent. It is true that large sums are loaned
to persons, and on mortgages of real estate; but for most
people such investments are not desirable or convenient,
and they are altogether inadequate to absorb the vast
sums that are available. In fact probably most investments of this character are now made by corporations who
gather the savings of little depositors and premium payers;
and it would cost much more to make them in any other
way.

Corporations, therefore, are necessary, but they necessarily separate the ownership of wealth from its management. To invest is generally to entrust your money to
another, and those who invest in corporations, unless
they control them, are economically disfranchised, because the stockholders in all large corporations almost
never influence the management of their property, and
as a rule do not know anything about it. They don't
because they can't. A few years ago a very large number
of people were much worried by the exposure of some

scandalous doings by the managers of certain great life-insurance companies. They would have been very glad to combine and choose better managers if they could; but they couldn't. Laws were passed for the purpose of enabling the policy-holders to select their trustees, but the only result has been a ridiculous and rather expensive fiasco. As in politics, the rank and file select the managers selected for them by a few men who understand the situation. When many thousands of people own stock in a concern, they live all over this continent and in foreign parts, and it is a physical impossibility to bring them together. They do not know one another, and very few of them know much about the affairs of the concern, and if they know anything of the candidates that may be suggested, it is generally only by hearsay.

How many of the eighty-eight thousand stockholders in the Pennsylvania Railroad, for instance, have ever attended a meeting? For that matter, how many of them have ever studied the report of the railroad? Not one in ten could spare the time to read it, perhaps not one in a hundred could master it. The report may be read in a few hours; it would take as many months, if not years to verify it. Very nearly half these stockholders are women; the average holding is 120 shares, (par $50), and one-sixth of the stockholders own less than 10 shares each. Ten thousand of them are abroad. Much stock is held by trustees, whose beneficiaries are probably very numerous, and totally incompetent to understand railroad management. There are also more than twenty thousand holders of stock in subsidiary corporations controlled by the Pennsylvania Railroad. No one can tell the number of bondholders; perhaps there are as many as there are employees, making an aggregate of almost half a million.

Sometimes trustees abuse their office; but on the whole they have done pretty well, and whether they have or not, there is no other way in which large capitals can be managed. All civilization rests on confidence. Such a vast fabric could not be built on confidence unless confidence was deserved. As a matter of fact, a man invests his money just as he invests in a surgeon. He does not think of directing the surgeon how to operate. If the operation does not succeed, he tries another surgeon next time — if there is a next time.

Of course all this applies chiefly to the large corporations. There are many thousands of small ones, having few stockholders, who reside where the business is established. These stockholders know more or less of the details of the business; they can judge to some extent how it is carried on, they are often acquainted with the managers, or are the managers themselves, and if not, they are able sometimes to combine and change the management. And I will anticipate a little and say here that the property of such a corporation located in a small town is often to some extent not politically disfranchised, because the people of the town understand that they are directly interested in the prosperity of the business. But it seems almost impossible for the stockholders to change the management of a large corporation. It has been done a few times. Mr. Harriman notoriously did it by using the money of one concern to buy the stock of another, and that is almost the only way in which it has been done. No doubt there has been an immense deal of combination which has resulted in change of management, but this has not been because the stockholders combined to oust their trustees, but because they thought they saw a good chance to sell their stock to those who would pay high for the control, or to participate in these combinations. There have been a good many cases where an enterprising speculator has managed to get hold of a majority of the stock and change the control, and powerful bankers can sometimes get proxies enough to put a stop to bad management; but spontaneous movements of this kind on the part of the mass of the stockholders are extremely rare.

Beyond dispute then, the great mass of wealth held by corporations is almost wholly under the control of their managers, and not the mass cf the owners. Mr. Hill has recently testified that he never knew a stockholder to attend a meeting except to make trouble; by which he perhaps meant that when a single stockholder appeared, it was to get paid for not making trouble.

It need hardly be said that no such thing as legitimate representation of corporate wealth is known in our politics, and the representation of individual wealth is very limited. The theory of government by manhood suffrage, so far as there is any theory, is now entirely personal. In early times the freemen of the town, or little commune, met and legislated according to their needs. To be a freeman one had to own property; to "have a stake in the country." Nowadays nearly all the men who have no property can vote, and some that have property cannot. In England, they are doing away with "plural voters." Heretofore it was thought just, when a man owned land in more than one place, that he should have his say in the government of all; but this is now forbidden. The right was never recognized in this country, partly because formerly men seldom owned property in two places, but as transportation improved the conditions changed. The "commuters" are legion. Their business and their capital are under one jurisdiction and their dwellings and families under another; but they can vote in only one. Many thousands of men own houses in both city and country. They could help in the government of both, but are disfranchised in one or the other. Under our complicated systems of registration, they are often disfranchised at both.

Of course when population increases, the town meeting becomes a physical impossibility. There is no more direct legislation; it has to be delegated. The power is transferred to the city councils, and to the state and national legislatures. In other words, the interests of the owners of wealth are put in charge of trustees. According to Hamilton, the theory of our government is that the people will "naturally" choose the wisest of their number to represent them. There is not much basis for this assumption. Rousseau scouted it. According to him, the *volonté générale* could be ascertained only in the town meeting, and he seriously maintained that the ideal government for the Roman empire was by the gangs of rioters that the politicians marshalled in the Forum at Rome under the name of *comitia*. All that the theory of our government requires, is that our rulers shall be such men as are designated by the majority of the voters. That they should be wise and good men may accord with the theory of aristocracy; it is no part of the theory of democracy, and is certainly a very small part of the practice.

When I say that half of the property of this country is disfranchised, I mean that the nature of this property is such that it is peculiarly subject to the power of rulers, and that the owners of it have hardly any legitimate-way of defending it against the arbitrary exercise of this power. The corporation is created by the legislature; men cannot combine their capitals and avoid unlimited liability for the debts of the combination, unless the law specifically authorizes the proceeding. Of course, if the legislature has power to make such grants, it must have power to alter them. In short, property held by a corporation is held at the will of the legislature, and in a way and to an extent that property held by an individual is not. It is not very easy for the legislature to plunder or blackmail individuals, even when they are disfranchised, because it has to be done by general laws, and direct methods arouse direct opposition. But, as we have seen, stockholders as a class cannot defend their rights, and as things are now, their trustees cannot have much to say concerning the laws that affect their property. Managers of large corporations are now commonly denounced as unfit to be legislators, and are practically excluded from the halls of legislation. In some states they are even specifically disfranchised, so far as holding office is concerned, and, under the new despotism, ironically dubbed the new freedom, every man whose wealth and ability make his aid important to many enterprises, is to be forbidden to participate in more than one. Yet property is almost entirely subject to the disposition of the legislature! not entirely, for the courts afford some protection; but even this is now threatened: we may "progress" so far as to make it unconstitutional for a judge to declare any law unconstitutional.

It goes without saying that half the property of the country will not submit to spoliation without a struggle. If it cannot have representation legitimately, it will try to get it illegitimately or extra legitimately. The managers of corporations have in the past found many ways to influence legislation. Despite the prejudices against them, some of them have had themselves chosen as legislators; even as judges. Some have brought about the election of legislators who would act in their favor, and have even bribed legislators. Until recently it was not even unlawful for these managers to use the money of their stockholders in political contributions; some managers acted on the "Good Lord! Good Devil!" principle. Probably most of the politicians paid no railroad fares. Many of them got passes for their families and their friends; and it was certainly to be expected that they should listen to the requests of those who granted these favors. The situation became grotesque when a great ruler, seeking a nomination to office with the proclaimed purpose of enforcing the laws against rebates and passes, required the railroad managers to furnish him free transportation on his righteous mission.

There were obvious objections to these practices, and

public opinion finally compelled our rulers to pass laws prohibiting them. Theoretically the managers of corporations are now effectually disfranchised. They dare not offer themselves as candidates for office. They scarcely dare to favor, even secretly, the choice of rulers who will listen to them. Fortunately, however, they hardly longer dare to offer bribes. Anyone on friendly terms with them is politically a suspicious character. Any lawyer who has been employed by them becomes unavailable as a candidate for office. Our legislators, as was to be expected, at once showed the effect of release from restraint. It has been uncharitably said that in revenge for the loss of their passes and other favors, they attacked the railroads; but there has been considerable voting of more mileage, and our congressmen at least voted themselves ample indemnity in larger salaries, and they opened fire on corporations in general and railroads in particular, with a broadside of statutes. Against this fire the property of millions of small holders in the corporations has been almost defenceless. Some of these statutes are so drawn that the plain business man does not know whether he is a criminal or not; if he could afford to consult the best of lawyers it would not help him much. The only safe course to pursue is to agree with the adversary quickly; to plead guilty to whatever charge is made, and beg for mercy. That one is innocent is immaterial. The expense of litigation is nothing to the rulers of the United States; but it may be ruinous to their subjects. The cost of the commissions and investigations and prosecutions of the last few years has been enormous. Only lawyers can contemplate it without consternation.

True, the managers of large corporations can make their protests heard. They can publish their pleas in the newspapers, and issue pamphlets, and they can appear before committees and commissions, and submit arguments. The managers of small corporations cannot afford such measures. You might as well refer a servant-girl who couldn't collect her wages, to the Hague Tribunal, as to send a plain business man to Washington to plead his cause.

The animus of these statutes is hostility to great corporations. But it is impossible to legislate against great corporations without hitting the small ones. Take the case of the recent corporation income tax; the 244,000 corporations exempt from the tax had to make out their inventories and keep their books and report their proceedings precisely as if they were liable to the tax. A fine of from $1,000 to $10,000 and a 50 per cent. increased assessment were the penalties for failure. But the cost of complying with all the requirements of the law, for a corporation having an income of two or three thousand dollars, cannot be figured at much less than the tax. Many corporations have no net income. The managers of these concerns are not expert book-keepers, and their returns must be in many cases so inaccurate as to expose them to prosecution if the game were worth the candle. If we assume that the average cost of making out the return is only ten dollars, we have a bill of $2,400,000, which the stockholders, or the employees, or the customers, must pay for the privilege of demonstrating that the small corporations are not liable to pay anything at all.

The corporation income tax law was really an act of popular dislike of corporations exercising great monopolies. Grouping all the little corporations with them was an absurdity and a cruelty.

Corporations have no feelings. They are not wounded by the hostility of legislatures. The managers of corporations of large capital have feelings, and some of them are wounded in their pride by this hostility. But they need not suffer in their pockets. They are abundantly able to protect their own property; they know how to make money on the short side of the market as well as the long side. But the managers of the concerns of small capital are seldom able to do this. Oppressive laws cause suffering to them, to the mere holders of stock in all corporations, to the creditors of all, to the employees, and to the customers. Many of these laws profess to be meant to favor small people as against big people — to restrain the rich corporations so that the poor ones may have more liberty. There is no evidence to show that this result is attained, or that the country would be better off if it were attained. But there is plenty of evidence to show that half the people of the country are suffering from these legislative attacks on their property. The men who manage the great corporations, whatever their faults, are men of enterprise and courage. They are the true progressives; the prosperity that they diffuse among the whole people is ordinarily more than can be destroyed by our progressive politicians. They are now beginning to feel that their rulers are discriminating against them as a class, and are uneasy and disheartened, and reluctant to embark in new enterprises; and the progress of the country is halted by their apprehension. It is not the rich who suffer most: it is "the unemployed," and the millions of dumb, helpless, struggling thrifty men and women whose hard earned savings constitute a large part of the capital of the corporations; and who are already alarmed at the shrinking value of these savings. It is, perhaps most of all, the mass of ignorant unthrifty poor, whose chief wealth is the wages paid them by the corporations which they are taught to look on as their oppressors.

RAILWAY JUNCTIONS

IN his illuminating essay on *The Lantern-Bearers*, Stevenson complains of the vacuity of that view of life which he finds expressed in the pages of most realistic writers. "This harping on life's dulness and man's meanness is a loud profession of incompetence; it is one of two things: the cry of the blind eye, *I cannot see*, or the complaint of the dumb tongue, *I cannot utter*." And then, with a fine flourish, he declares: — "If I had no better hope than to continue to revolve among the dreary and petty businesses, and to be moved by the paltry hopes and fears with which they surround and animate their heroes, I declare I would die now. But there has never an hour of mine gone quite so dully yet; if it were spent waiting at a railway junction, I would have some scattering thoughts, I could count some grains of memory, compared to which the whole of one of these romances seems but dross."

"If it were spent waiting at a railway junction" . . . Here, with his instinct for the perfect phrase, Stevenson has pointed a finger at the one experience which is commonly accepted as the acme of imaginable dulness. This man, who could be happy at a railway junction, could not have found a prouder way of boasting to posterity that he had never "faltered more or less in his great task of happiness."

It is because railway junctions are the most unpopular places in the world that they have been singled out for praise in THE UNPOPULAR REVIEW. Poor places, lonely and forlorn, cursed by so many, celebrated by so few, — surely they have waited over-long for an apologist. . . . But first of all, in order to be fair, we must consider the customary view of these points of punctuation in the text of travel.

Far up in Vermont, at a point vaguely to the east of Burlington, there is a place called Essex Junction. It consists of a dismal shed of a station, a bewildering wilderness of tracks, and an adjacent cemetery, thickly populated (according to a local legend) with the bodies of people who have died of old age while waiting for their trains. This elegiac locality was visited, many years ago, by the Honorable E. J. Phelps, once ambassador of the United States to the court of St. James's. He was allotted several hours for the contemplation of the cemetery; and his consequent meditations moved him to the composition of a poem, in four stanzas, which is a little classic of its kind. Space is lacking for a quotation of more than the initial stanza; but the taste of a poem, as of a pie, may conveniently be judged from a quadrant of the whole. —

> With saddened face and battered hat
>   And eye that told of blank despair,
> On wooden bench the traveller sat,
>   Cursing the fate that brought him there.
> "Nine hours," he cried, "we've lingered here
>   With thoughts intent on distant homes,
> Waiting for that delusive train
>   That, always coming, never comes:
>   Till weary, worn,
>   Distressed, forlorn,
> And paralyzed in every function!
>   I hope in hell
>   His soul may dwell
> Who first invented Essex Junction!"

It was apparently the purpose of the writer to convey the impression that his period of waiting had been passed without pleasure; but yet we may easily confute him with another quotation from *The Lantern-Bearers*. "One pleasure at least," says Stevenson, "he tasted to the full — his work is there to prove it — the keen pleasure of successful literary composition." Was this honorable author ever moved to such eloquence by an audience with Queen

Victoria? Never; so far as we know. Was not Essex Junction, therefore, a more inspiring spot than Buckingham Palace? Undeniably. Then, why complain of Essex Junction?

For, indeed, the pleasure that we take from places is nothing more nor less than the pleasure we put into them. A person predisposed to boredom can be bored in the very nave of Amiens; and a person predisposed to happiness can be happy even in Camden, New Jersey. I know: for I have watched American tourists in Amiens; and once, when I had gone to Camden, to visit Walt Whitman in his granite tomb, I was wakened to a strange exhilaration, and wandered all about that little dust-heap of a city amazing the inhabitants with a happiness that required them to smile. "All architecture," said Whitman, "is what you do to it when you look upon it; . . . all music is what awakes from you when you are reminded by the instruments": and I must have had this passage singing in my blood when I enjoyed that monstrous court-house dome which stands up like a mushroom in the midst of Camden.

I have never been to Essex Junction; but I should like to go there — just to see (in Whitman's words) what I could do to it. Imagine it upon a windy night of winter, when a hundred discommoded passengers are turned out, grumbling, underneath the stars, — coughing invalids, and kicking infants, and indignant citizens, scrambling haphazard among tottering trunks, and picking their way from train to train. Imagine their faces, their voices, their gesticulations: here, indeed, you will see more than a theatre-full of characters. Or, if human beings do not interest you, imagine the mysterious gleam of yellow windows veiled behind a drift of intermingled smoke and steam. Listen, also, to the clang of bells, the throb and puff of the engines, and the shrill shriek of their whistles. Or peer into the station-shed, made stuffy by the breath of many loiterers; and contrast their death in life with the life in death of those others who loiter through eternity beneath the gravestones of the cemetery. I can imagine being happy with all this (and even writing a paragraph about it afterwards): but, above all, I should like to gather those hundred discommoded passengers upon the station-platform, and to rehearse and lead them in a solemn chant of the refrain of Phelps's poem. Imagine a hundred voices singing lustily in unison,

"I hope in hell
His soul may dwell
Who first invented Essex Junction,"

under the vast cathedral vaulting of the night, until the adjacent dead should seem to stand up in their graves and join the anthem of anathema. . . . Who is there so bold to tell me that enjoyment is impossible in such a place as this?

There is very little difference between places, after all: the true difference is between the people who regard them. I should rather read a description of Hoboken by Rudyard Kipling than a description of Florence by some New England schoolmarm. To the poet, all places are poetical; to the adventurous, all places are teeming with adventure: and to experience a lack of joy in any place is merely a sign of sluggish blood in the beholder.

So, at least, it seems to me; for not otherwise can I explain the fact that, like my beloved R. L. S., I have always enjoyed waiting at railway junctions. I love not merely the marching phrases, but also the commas and the semi-colons of a journey, — those mystic moments when "we look before and after" and need not "pine for what is not." I have never done much waiting in America, which is in the main a country of express trains, that hurl their lighted windows through the night like what Mr. Kipling calls "a damned hotel;" but there is scarcely a country of Europe except Russia whose railway junctions are unknown to me. In many of these little nameless places I have experienced memorable hours: and because the less enthusiastic Baedeker has neglected to star and double-star them, I have always wanted to praise them, in print somewhat larger than his own. Space is lacking in the present article for a complete guide to all the railway junctions of Europe; but I should like to commemorate a few, in gratitude for what befell me there.

There is a junction in Bavaria whose name I have forgotten; but it is very near Rothenburg, the most picturesquely medieval of all German cities. It consists merely of a station and two intersecting tracks. When you enter the station, you observe what seems to be a lunch-counter; but if you step up to it and innocently order food, a buxom girl informs you that no food is ever served there — and then everybody laughs. This pleasant cachinnation attracts your attention to the assembled company. It consists of many peasants, in their native costumes (which any painter would be willing to journey many miles to see), who are enjoying the delicious experience of travel. They are great travelers, these peasants. Once a month they take the train to Rothenburg, and once a month they journey home again, to talk of the experience for thirty days. All of them have heard of Nuremberg [which is actually less than a hundred miles away], — that vast and wonderful metropolis, so far, so very far, beyond the ultimate horizon of their lives. They would like to see it some day — as I should like to see the Taj Mahal — but meanwhile they content themselves with the great adventure of going to Rothenburg, — a city that is really much more interesting, if they could only know. In the very midst of these congregated travelers, I casually set down a suit-case which was plastered over with many labels from many lands; and this suit-case affected them as I might be affected by a messenger from Mars. They spelled out many unfamiliar languages, and a murmur of amazement swept through

the entire company when one of them discovered that
that suit-case had been to Morocco. Morocco, they
assured me, was a place where black men rode on camels;
and I had no heart to tell them that it was a country where
white men rode on mules. Then another of these travelers
— an old man, with a face like one of Albrecht Dürer's
drawings — discovered a label that read "Venezia." "Is
that," he said, "Venedig?" with a little gasp. "Yes;
Venedig," I responded, "where the streets are water."
Slowly he removed his hat. "Ach, Venedig!" he sighed;
and then he stooped down, and, with the uttermost
solemnity, he kissed the label. . . . And then I understood
the vast impulsion of that *wanderlust* which has pushed so
many, many Germans southward, to overrun that golden
city that is wedded to the sea. I have forgotten the name
of that junction, as I said before; but I have never been
so happy in Munich as in this lonely station where there
is no food.

Speaking of food reminds me of Bobadilla, in southern
Spain. Bobadilla sounds as if it ought to be the name of
a medieval town, with ghosts of gaunt imaginative knights
riding forth to tilt with windmills; but there is no town
at all at Bobadilla, — merely two railway restaurants set
on either side of several intersecting tracks. For some
mysterious reason, passengers from the four quarters of
the compass — that is to say, from Cordoba, Granada,
Algeciras, or Sevilla — are required to alight here, and
eat, and change their trains. I remember Bobadilla as
the place where you spend your counterfeit money. Many
of the current coins of southern Spain are made of silver;
and the rest are made of lead. For leaden five-peseta
pieces there is a local name, "Sevillan dollars," which
ascribes their coinage to the crafty artisans of the capital
of Andalucia. These pieces, which are plentiful, are just
as good as silver dollars — when you can persuade anyone
to take them. The currency of any coinage, except gold,
depends entirely upon the faith of those who pass and take

it and has no reference to its intrinsic value; and, in southern Spain, the leaden dollars serve as counters for just as many commercial transactions as the dollars made of silver. The only difference is that they are commonly accepted only after protest. In every Spanish shop, a slab of marble is built into the counter, and on this slab all proffered coins are slapped before they are accepted by the merchant. The traveler soon learns to fling his change upon the pavement; and many merry arguments ensue regarding the *timbre* of their ring. I remember how once, in the wondrous town of Ronda, when a beggar had imposed himself upon me as a guide and led me into a church where High Mass was being chanted, I gave him a peseta to get rid of him, and at once he flung it upon the pavement of the church, and chased it, listening, across the nave. Thereafter, he protested loudly that the piece was lead, and disrupted the intoning of the priests. "Very well," said I, "it is, in any case, a gift; if you don't want it, I will take it back": and he accepted it with bows and smiles, and allowed the weary priests to continue their intonings. But Bobadilla is the one place in southern Spain where money is never jingled upon marble. There is no time between trains to quibble over minor matters; and a "Sevillan dollar" accepted from one passenger is blithely handed to another who is traveling in the opposite direction. I discovered this fact on the occasion of my first visit to this interesting junction; and on subsequent occasions I have eaten my fill at one or another of the railway restaurants and settled the account with all the leaden money garnered up from weeks of traveling. There is surely no dishonesty in observing the custom of a country; and Bobadilla may be treasured by all travelers as a clearing-house for counterfeit coins.

Again, in northern France, it was merely by some accident of changing trains that I discovered the lovely little town of Dol. I found myself in Saint Malo, for obvious reasons; and I desired to go to Mont Saint-Michel, for reasons still more obvious — Mother Poulard's omelettes, and architecture, and the incoming of the tide. Between them — the map told me — was situated Dol. I made inquiries of the porter in the Saint Malo hotel. He responded in English, — the English of *Ici on parle anglais.* "Dol," said he, "is a dull place." He pronounced "Dol" and "dull" in precisely the same manner, and smiled at his sickly pun. I did not like that smile; and I alighted at the town that he despised. It was a little picture-book of a place, with many toy-like medieval houses clustered side by side around a market-place where peasants twisted the tails of cows. I strolled to the cathedral — and found myself mysteriously in England. It was a manly Norman edifice, sane and reticent and strong, set in a veritable English green, with little houses round about, reminding one of Salisbury. I entered the Cathedral; and found the nave to be composed in what is called in England the "decorated" style, and the choir to give hints of "perpendicular." And then I remembered, with a start, that the ancestors of all that is most beautiful in England had migrated from Normandy, and that here I was visiting them in their antecedent home. "Saxon and Norman and Dane are we;" and all that was Norman in me reached forth with groping hands to grasp the palms of those old builders who reared this little sacrosanct cathedral in the far-off times when one dominion extended to either side of the English Channel.

It was by a similar accident — desiring to transfer myself from Bourges to Auxerre — that I discovered the wonderful junction-town of Nevers, which, despite the guide-books, is more interesting than either of the others. It possesses a Gothic cathedral with an apse at either end, that looks as if two churches had collided and telescoped each other. There is also a Romanesque church at Nevers which is just as simple and as manly as either of the famous abbeys in Caen; and a chateau with rounded towers, which once belonged to Mazarin. But the most amusing feature of this town is that, though Bourges packs itself to bed at ten o'clock, Nevers sits blithely up till twelve, listening to music in cafés, and watching moving-pictures; and this amiable incongruity in a medieval town makes you bless that complication of the time-table which has forced you, against forethought, to stay there over night.

It is difficult for me to remember a railway junction in which there was nothing to do; but perhaps Pyrgos, in Greece, comes nearest to this description. At this point, you change cars on your way from Patras to Olympia. The town is made of mud: that is to say, the single-storied houses are built of unbaked clay. There is nothing to see in Pyrgos. But I amused myself by addressing the inhabitants, in the English language, with an eloquent oration that soon gathered them under my control; and thereafter I set a hundred of them at the pleasant task of trying to push the train for Olympia on its way to take me to the Hermes of Praxiteles. I knew no word of their language, nor did they of mine; but they understood that that train should be started, if human force were sufficient to help the cars upon their way: and finally, when the engine puffed and snorted with a tardily awakened sense of duty, the train was cheered by the entire population as I waved my hand from the rear platform and quoted one of Daniel Webster's perorations.

Is it — I have often wondered — so difficult as people think, to be happy in an hour "spent waiting at a railway junction"? . . . The kingdom of happiness is within us; or else there is no truth in our assumption that the will of man is free: and I am inclined to pity a man who, being happy in Amalfi — the loveliest of all the places I have ever seen — cannot also manage to be happy in Pyrgos — or in Essex Junction — and to communicate his happiness to his responsive fellow-travelers.

The true enjoyment of traveling is to enjoy traveling; not to relish merely the places you are going to, but to relish also the adventure of the going. The most difficult train-journey I remember is the twenty-hour trip from Lisbon to Sevilla, with a change of cars in the ghastly early morning at the border-town of Badajoz and another change at noon at the sun-baked, parched, and God-forsaken town of Merida; and yet I relish as red letters on my personal map of Spain a pleasant quarrel over the price of sandwiches at Badajoz and the way a muleteer of Merida flung a colored cloak over his shoulder and posed for an unconscious moment like a painting by Zuloaga.

And this philosophy has a deeper application to life at large: for all life may be figured as a journey, and few there are who are natively equipped for the enjoyment of all the waste and waiting places on the way. The minds of most people are so fixed upon the storied capitals that are featured in those works of fiction known as guide-books that they are impeded from enjoying the minor stations on their journey. "Hurry me to Sevilla," cries the traveler — and misses the sight of my muleteer of Merida. In America, our society is crammed with people who fail to enjoy life on five thousand a year because their minds are fixed upon that distant time when they hope to enjoy life on twenty thousand a year. And if ever they attain that twenty thousand they will not enjoy it either; but will merely peer forward to a hypothetical enjoyment at fifty thousand a year. And this is the essence of their tragedy: — they have not learned to wait with happiness.

Is there any reason for this inordinate ambition to "get on"? Louis Stevenson was happier, as a small boy with a bull's-eye lantern at his belt, than any king upon his throne. The secret of enjoyment is to learn to look about us, to value what our destiny has given us, to transform it into magic by some contributory gift of poetry or humor, to consider with contentment the lilies of the field. The zest of life is in the living of it; and "to travel hopefully is a better thing than to arrive."

How often, in the roaring and tumultuary tide of life,

we meet a man who sighs, "If only I could have a single day in which there was nothing that I had to do, nothing even that I had to think of, how happy I should be!" and yet this self-same man, if set down at a railway junction, will at once bestir himself to seek something to think of, something to do, and will spurn the gift of leisure. The incessant hurry of our current life has tragically lured us to forget the art of loitering. We are no longer able — like Wordsworth, on his "old gray stone" — to sit upon a trunk at some railway junction of our lives and listen reverently to the "mighty sum of things forever speaking."

One of the loveliest women I have ever known — the late Alison Cunningham — told me a little anecdote of the author of *The Lantern-Bearers* which, so far as I know, has never yet been published. When little Louis was about five years old, he did something naughty, and Cummy stood him up in a corner and told him he would have to stay there for ten minutes. Then she left the room. At the end of the allotted period, she returned and said, "Time's up, Master Lou: you may come out now." But the little boy stood motionless in his penitential corner. "That's enough: time's up," repeated Cummy. And then the child mystically raised his hand, and with a strange light in his eyes, "Hush . . .," he said, "I'm telling myself a story. . . ."

And, in the *Christian Morals* of Sir Thomas Browne, we may read the following passage: — "He who must needs have company, must needs have sometimes bad company. Be able to be alone. Lose not the advantage of solitude, and the society of thyself; nor be only content, but delight to be alone and single with Omnipresency. He who is thus prepared, the day is not uneasy nor the night black unto him. Darkness may bound his eyes, not his imagination. In his bed he may lie, like Pompey and his sons, in all quarters of the earth; may speculate the universe, and enjoy the whole world in the hermitage of himself."

Wordsworth sitting quiescent and receptive in a lake-side landscape, little Louis standing in a corner, Sir Thomas Browne enjoying the whole world in the hermit-age of himself: — what a rebuke is offered by these images to those who fret and fume away the leisure that is granted them at all the waiting places of their lives! . . . These disgruntled travelers *nel mezzo del cammin di nostra vita* miss their privilege and duty of enjoying life merely be-cause they miss the point that life is, in itself, enjoyable. They are so busy reading guide-books to the vague beyond that they shut their minds to all that may be going on about them, or within them, at way-stations. They close their eyes and ears to the immediate. They veto all per-ception of the here and now. But life itself is always here and now; and, truly to enjoy it, we must learn to look forever with unfaltering eyes into the bright face of im-mediacy.

And there is another point about railway junctions that reveals an important application to the larger journey of our life. A friend of mine, who is a great lover of painting, had occasion once (and only once) to change trains at Basle, in the course of a journey from Lucerne to Heidel-berg. He had to wait two hours at this railway junction; and this time he pleasantly expended in eating many dishes at a restaurant, and amusing the lax porters by teaching them a method of economizing energy in shifting trunks. It should be noted that this friend of mine was not trying to "kill time;" for, like all genuine humani-tarians, he of course regards that tragic process as the least excusable of murders. He was entirely happy for two hours in that railway station. But — having packed his guide-book in a trunk — it was not until he reached Darmstadt, some days later, that he discovered that several of the very greatest works of Holbein are now resi-dent in Basle. The two hours that he had spent playing and eating might have been devoted to an examination of many masterpieces of that art which, more than any other, he had crossed the seas to seek. He has never yet been able to return to Basle; but for a sight of those lost portraits of the most honest and straightforward of all German painters, he would gladly sell his memories of both Lucerne and Heidelberg.

Here we have a record of a great disappointment that was occasioned merely by the common habit of despising railway junctions, and presuming them to be inevitably dull. But this same unfortunate presumption, applied to life at large, leads many people to overlook the nearness of some great adventure. Interrogate a thousand men, and you will find that none of them has first set eyes upon his greatest friend in the Mosque of Cordoba or in Trafalgar Square. Every adventure of lasting consequence has confronted all of them, without exception, in some hidden nook or cranny of the world, — some place unknown to fame. Anybody is as likely to meet the woman who is destined to become his wife, at Essex Junction on a wintry night, as in the Parthenon by moonlight in the month of May. The most romantic places in the world are often those that promised, in advance, to be the least romantic.

Since this is so, how can anybody ever dare to shut his eyes to that incalculable imminency of adventure which environs him even when he is merely changing trains on some island-platform of the New York Subway? In our daily living we are never safe from destiny; and who can ever know in what vacuous and sedentary period of his experience he may suddenly be called upon to entertain an angel unawares? It is best to be prepared for anything, at any hour of our lives, — even at those moments that must, perforce, be "spent waiting at a railway junction."

TO assert today that the rich are for the most part entirely harmless is to dare much, for the contrary opinion is greatly in favor. Such wholesale condemnation of the rich assumes a more general and a more specific form. They are said to be harmful to the body politic simply because they have more money than the average: their property has been wrongly taken from persons who have a better right to it, or is withheld from people who need it more. But aside from being constructively a moral detriment from the mere possession of wealth, the rich man may do specific harm through indulging his vices, maintaining an inordinate display, charging too much for his own services, crushing his weaker competitor, corrupting the legislature and the judiciary, finally by asserting flagrantly his right to what he erroneously deems to be his own. Such are the general and specific charges of modern anti-capitalism against wealth. Like many deep rooted convictions, these rest less on analysis of particular instances than upon axioms received without criticism. The word spoliation does yeoman service in covering with one broad blanket of prejudice the most diverse cases of wealth. But spoliation is assumed, not proved. My own conviction that most wealth is quite blameless, whether under the general or specific accusation, is based on no comprehensive axiom, but simply on the knowledge of a number of particular fortunes and of their owners. Such a road towards truth is highly unromantic. The student of particular phenomena is unable to pose as the champion of the race. But the method has the modest advantage of resting not on a priori definitions, but on

inductions from actual experience; hence of being relatively scientific.

Before sketching the line of such an investigation, let
me say that in logic and common sense there is no presumption against the wealthy person. Ever since civilization began and until yesterday it has been assumed that
wealth was simply ability legitimately funded and transmitted. Even modern humanitarians, while dallying
with the equation wealth=spoliation, have been unwilling
wholly to relinquish the historic view of the case. I have
always admired the courage with which Mr. Howells
faced the situation in one of those charming essays for
the Easy Chair of *Harper's*. Driving one night in a comfortable cab he was suddenly confronted by the long
drawn out misery of the midnight bread line. For a moment the vision of these hungry fellow men overcame him.
He felt guilty on his cushions, and possibly entertained
some St. Martin-like project of dividing his swallowtail
with the nearest unfortunate. Then common sense in
the form of his companion came to his rescue. She remarked "Perhaps we are right and they are wrong." Why
not? At any rate Mr. Howells was not permitted to condemn in a moment of compassion the career of thrift, industry and genius, that had led him from a printer's case to
a premier position in American letters, or, more concretely,
he received a domestic dispensation to cab it home in
good conscience, though many were waiting in chilly discomfort for their gift of yesterday's bread. The why so
and why not of this incident are my real subject. For
Mr. Howells is merely a particularly conspicuous instance
of the kind of prosperity I have in mind. We are all too
much dazzled by the rare great fortunes. The newly rich
have spectacular ways with them. By dint of frequently
passing us in notorious circumstances, they give the impression of a throng. They are much in the papers, their
steam yachts loom large on the waters, they divorce
quickly and often, they buy the most egregious, old mas-

ters. By such more or less innocent ostentations, a handful
stretches into a procession, much as a dozen sprightly
supernumeraries will keep up an endless defile of Macduff's
army on the tragic stage. Let us admit that some of the
great wealth is more or less foolishly and harmfully spent;
my subject is not bank accounts, but people; and very
wealthy people constitute an almost negligible minority
of the race. Their influence too is much less potent than
is supposed. A slightly vulgarizing tendency proceeds from
them, but in waves of decreasing intensity. Their vogue
is chiefly a *succès de scandale*. Sensible people will gape
at the spectacle without admiration, and even the reader
of the society column in the sensational newspapers keeps
more critical detachment than he is usually credited with.
In any case neither the boisterous nor the shrinking multi-
millionaire has any representative standing. He is not
what a poor person means by a rich person. Ask your
laundress who is rich in your neighborhood, and she will
name all who live gently and do not have to worry about
next month's bills. True pragmatist, she sees that to be
exempt from any threat of poverty is to all intents and
purposes to be rich. Her classification ignores certain
niceties, but corresponds roughly to the fact, and has the
merit of corresponding to government decree. Rich
people, since the income tax, are officially those who pay
the tax but not the surtax. Families with an income not
less than four thousand dollars nor more than twenty
thousand comprise the harmless, middling rich. Let us
once for all admit that in the surtaxed classes there are
many cases of quite harmless wealth, while in the lower
level of the rich, harmful wealth will sometimes be found.
Such exceptions do not invalidate the general rule that
all but a negligible fraction of the rich are included in
the first class of income taxpayers — on from four to
twenty thousand, that most of the property here held
is blamelessly held in good hands — wealth that in
no fair estimate can be regarded as harmful. In terms

of British currency, our category of the middling rich
would include the poorer individuals of the upper classes,
the richer persons of the lower middle class, and the upper
middle class as a whole. This comparison is made not to
apply an alien class system which holds very inadequately
here in America, but simply to avow the difficulty of my
task of apology. The bourgeoisie is equally suspect among
radicals, reactionaries, and artists. My middling rich are
nothing other than what an European essayist would quite
brazenly call the *haute bourgeoisie*. It is quite a comprehensive class, made up chiefly of professional men, mod-
erately successful merchants, manufacturers, and bankers
with their more highly paid employees, but including also
many artists, and teachers of all sorts. Incidentally it is
an employing and borrowing class in various degrees,
hence especially subject to the exactions of the labor union
at one end, and of the great capitalist and the Trust at the
other.

The general harmlessness of the wealth of this class
rests upon the fact that it is in small part inherited, but
mostly earned by individual effort, while such effort has
usually been honestly and efficiently rendered and paid
for at a moderate rate. In fact the amount of capacity
that can be hired for the slightest rewards is simply amazing. It is the distinction of this class as compared both
with the wage earning and the capitalist class — both of
which agree in overvaluing their services and extorting
payment on their own terms — that it respects its work
more than it regards rewards. Consider the amount of
general education and special training that go to make a
capable school superintendent, or college professor; a good
country doctor or clergyman — and it will be felt that no
money is more honestly earned. This is equally true of
many lawyers and magistrates, who are wise counsellors
for an entire country side. It is no less true of hosts of
small manufacturers who make a superior product with
conscience. For the wealth, small enough it usually is,

that is thus gained in positions of especial skill and confidence, absolutely no apology need be made. I sometimes wish that the Socialists for whom any degree of wealth means spoliation, would go a day's round with a country doctor, would take the pains to learn of the cases he treats for half his fee, for a nominal sum, or for nothing; would candidly reckon his normal fee against the long years of college, medical school and hospital, and against the service itself; would then deduct the actual expenses of the day, as represented by apparatus, motor, or horse service — I can only say that if such an investigator could in any way conceive that physician as a spoliator, because he earned twice as much as a master brick-layer or five times as much as a ditch digger — if, I say, before the actual fact, our Socialist investigator in any way grudges that day's earnings, his mental and emotional confusion is beyond ordinary remedy. And such a physician's earnings are merely typical of those of an entire class of devoted professional men.

We do well to remind ourselves that the great body of wealth in the country has been built up slowly and honestly by the most laborious means, and accumulated and transmitted by self-sacrificing thrift. A rich person in nine cases out of ten is merely a capable, careful, saving person, often, too, a person who conducts a difficult calling with a fine sense of personal honor and a high standard of social obligation. We are too much dazzled by the occasional apparition of the lawyer who has got rich by steering guilty clients past the legal reefs, of the surgeon who plays equally on the fears and the purses of his patients, of the sensational clergyman who has made full coinage of his charlatanism. All these types exist, and all are highly exceptional. Most rich persons are self-respecting, have given ample value received for their wealth, and have less reason to apologize for it than most poor folks have to apologize for their poverty.

Furthermore: for the maintenance of certain humdrum

but necessary human virtues, we are dependent upon these middling rich. It has been frequently remarked that a lord and a working man are likely to agree, as against a bourgeois, in generosity, spontaneous fellowship, and all that goes to make sporting spirit. The right measure of these qualities makes for charm and genuine fraternity; the excess of these qualities produces an enormous amount of human waste among the wage earners and the aristocrats impartially. The great body of self-controlled, that is of reasonably socialized people, must be sought between these two extremes. In short the building up of ideals of discipline and of habits of efficiency and of good manners and of human respect is very largely the task of the middle classes. Whereas the breaking down of such ideals is, in the present posture of society, the avowed or unavowed intention of a considerable portion of laboring men and aristocrats. The scornful retort of the Socialist is at hand: "Of course the middle classes are shrewd enough to practice the virtues that pay." Into this familiar moral bog that there are as many kinds of morality as there are economic conditions of mankind, I do not consent to plunge. I need only say that the so-called middle class virtues would pay a workman or a lord quite as well as they do a bourgeois. Moreover, while workmen and lords are prone to scorn the calculating virtues of the middle classes, there is no indication that the *bourgeoisie* has selfishly tried to keep its virtues to itself. On the contrary there is positive rejoicing in the middle classes over a workman who deigns to keep a contract, and an aristocrat who perceives the duty of paying a debt. In fine we of the middle classes need no more be ashamed of our highly unpicturesque virtues than we are of our inconspicuous wealth.

So far from being in danger of suppression, we middling rich people are likely to last longer than the capitalists who exploit us in practice, and the workmen who exploit us on principle. Theoretically, and perhaps practically, the very rich are in danger of expropriation. Theoretically the course of invention may limit or almost abolish all but the higher grades of labor. The need of the more skilful sort of service in the professions, in manufacture, in agency of all sorts, is sure to persist. The socialists expect to get such service for much less than it at present brings, that is to make us poor and yet keep us working. Such a scheme must break down, not through the refusal of the middling rich to keep at work; — for I think there is loyalty enough to the work itself to keep most necessary activities going after a fashion, even under the most untoward conditions; — but because to make us poor is to destroy the conditions under which we can efficiently render a somewhat exceptional service. Our wealth is not an extraneous thing that can be readily added or taken away. It is our possibility of self-education and of professional improvement, it is the medium in which we can work, it is our hope of children. To take away our wealth is to maim us. There is nothing humiliating in such an avowal. It is merely an assertion of the integrity of one's life and work. As a matter of fact no class is so well fitted to face the threat of a proletarian revolution as we harmless rich. It is the class that produces generals, explorers, inventors, statesmen. A social revolution with its stern attendant regimentation would bear most heavily on the relatively undisciplined class of working people. The disciplined class of the middling rich is better prepared to meet such an eventuality. Accordingly it is no mere selfishness or complacency that leads the middling rich to oppose the pretensions of proletarianism on one side and of capitalism on the other. It is rather the assertion of sound middle class morality against two opposite yet somewhat allied forms of social immorality — the strength that exaggerates its claims, and the weakness that claims all the privileges of strength.

We are useful too as conserving certain valuable ideas. When I mention the idea of the right of private property, I expect to be laughed at by a large class of enthusiasts. Yet all of civilization has been built up on the distinction between *meum* and *tuum*. Without this idea there is not the slightest inducement to persistent individual effort nor possibility of progress for the individual or for the race. The fruitful diversities, the germinative inequalities between men all depend on this right. And today the right to one's own is doubly under attack from the violence of laboring men, and the guile of those in positions of financial trust. The strikers who offer as an argument the burning of a mine or wrecking of a mill, and the directors who manipulate corporation accounts to pay unearned dividends, are both undermining the right of property. Against such counsels of force and fraud, the representatives of the common sense and funded wisdom of mankind are the middling rich. It is an unromantic service — doubtless breaking other people's windows or scaling their bank accounts is much more thrilling — it is a public service obviously tinged with self-interest, but none the less a public service of high and timely importance. The business of keeping the sanity of the world intact as against the wilder expressions of social discontent, and the uglier expressions of personal envy and greed, may seem to lack zest and originality today. History may well take a different view of the matter. It would not be surprising to find a posthumous aureole of idealism conferred upon those who amid the trumpeting of money market messiahs, and the braying of self-appointed remodellers of the race, simply stood quietly on their own inherited rights and principles.

Such are some not wholly minor uses for the middling rich. Should they be abolished, many of the pleasanter facts and appearances of the world would disappear with them. The other day I whisked in one of their motor cars through miles of green Philadelphia suburbs dappled with pink magnolia trees and white fruit blossoms — everywhere charming houses, velvety lawns, tidy gardens. The establishing of a little paradise like that is of course a selfish enterprise — a mere meeting of the push and foresight of real estate operators with the thrift and sentiment of householders, yet it is an advantage inevitably shared, a benefit to the entire community, an example in reasonable working, living, and playing.

On the side of play we should especially miss these harmless rich. The sleek horses on a thousand bridle paths and meadows are theirs, the smaller winged craft that still protest against the pollution of the sea by the reek of coal and the stench of gasoline; of their furnishing are the graceful and widely shared spectacles not only of the minor yacht racing but of the field sports generally. They constitute our militia. The survival in the world of such gentler accomplishments as fencing, canoeing, and exploration rests with the middling rich. They write our books and plays, compose our music, paint our pictures, carve our statues. The pleasanter unconscious pageantry of our life is conducted by their sons and daughters. To be nice, to indulge in nice occupations, to express happiness — this is not even today a reproach to any one. Indeed if any approach to the dreamed socialized state ever be made, it will come less through regimentation than through imitation of those persons of middle condition who have managed to be reasonably faithful in their duties, and moderate in their pleasures. To keep a clean mind in a clean body is the prerogative of no class, but the lapses from this standard are unquestionably more frequent among the poor and the very rich.

It is instructive in this regard to compare with the newspapers that serve the middling rich, those that address the poor, and those that are owned in the interest of well understood capitalistic interests. The extremes of yellow journalism and of avowedly capitalistic journalism, meet in a preference for salacious or merely shocking news, and in a predilection for blatant, sophistical, or merely nugatory and time-serving editorial expressions. Between the two really allied types of newspapers are a few which exercise a decent censorship over questionable news, and habitually indulge in the luxury of sincere editorial opinion. There are some exceptions to the rule. In our own day we have seen a proletarian paper become a magnificent editorial organ, while somewhat illogically maintaining a random and sensational policy in its news columns. But generally the distinction is unmistakable. Imagine the plight of New York journalism if four papers, which I need not mention, ceased publication. It would mean a distinct and immediate cheapening of the mentality of the city. Then observe on any train who are reading these papers. It is plain enough what class among us makes decent journalism possible.

Much is to be said for the abolition of poverty, and something for the reduction of inordinate wealth. Poverty is being much reduced, and will be farther, the process being limited simply by the degree to which the poor will educate and discipline themselves. We shall never wholly do away with bad luck, bad inheritance, wild blood, laziness, and incapacity: so some poverty we shall always have, but much less than now, and less dire. The fact that the large class of middling rich has been evolved from a world where all began poor, is a promise of a future society where poverty shall be the exception. But such increase of the wealth of the world, and of the number of the virtually rich, will never be attained by the puerile method of expropriating the present holders of wealth. That would produce more poor people beyond doubt — but its effect in enriching the present poor would be inappreciable. You cannot change a man's character and capacity simply by giving him the wealth of another. In wholesale expropriations and bequests the experiment has been many times tried, and always with the same results. The wealth that could not be assimilated and administered has always left the receiver or grasper in all essentials poorer than he was before. Wealth is an attribute of personality. It is not interchangeable like the parts of a standardized machine. The futility of dispossessing the middling rich would be as marked as its immorality.

This essentially personal character of wealth must affeet the views of those who would attack what are called the inordinate fortunes. I hold no brief for or against the multi-millionaire. In many cases I believe his wealth is as personal, assimilated and legitimate as is the average moderate fortune. In many cases too, I know that such gigantic wealth is in fact the product of unfair craft and favoritism, is to that extent unassimilated and illegitimate. Yet admitting the worst of great fortunes, I think a prudent and fair minded man would hesitate before a general programme of expropriation. He would consider that in many cases the common weal needs such services as very wealthy people render, he would reflect on the practical benefits to the world, of the benevolent enterprises for education, research, invention, hygiene, medicine, which are founded and supported by great wealth. In our time The Rockefeller Institute will have stamped out that slow plague of the south, the hook worm. To the obvious retort that the government ought to do this sort of thing, the reply is equally obvious, that historically governments have not done this sort of thing until enlightened private enterprise has shown the way. Our prudent observer of mankind in general, and of the very rich in particular, would again reflect that, granting much of the socialist indictment of capital as illgained, common sense requires a statute of limitations. At a certain point restitution makes more trouble than the possession of illegitimate wealth. Debts, interest, and grudges cannot be indefinitely accumulated and extended. It is the entire disregard of this simple and generally admitted principle that has marred the socialist propaganda from the first. From the point of view of fomenting hatred between classes, to make every workingman regard himself as the residuary legatee of all the grievances of all workingmen, at all times, may be clever tactics, it is not a good way of making the workingman see clearly what his actual grievance and expectancy of redress are in his own day and time.

With increasingly heavy income and inheritance taxes, the very rich will have to reckon. Yet the multi-millionaire's evident utility as the milch cow of the state, will cause statesmen, even of the anti-capitalistic stamp, to waver at the point where the cow threatens to dry up from over-milking. If the case, then, for utterly despoiling the harmful rich, is by no means clear, the prospect for the harmless rich may be regarded as fairly favorable. For the moment, caught between the headiness of working folk, the din of doctrinaires, and the wiles of corporate activity, the lot of the middling rich is not the most happy imaginable. But they seem better able to weather these flurries than the windy, cloud-compelling divinities of the hour. From the survival of the middling rich, the future common weal will be none the worse, and it may even be better.

LECTURING AT CHAUTAUQUA

TO render any real impression of the Chautauqua Summer Assembly, I must approach this many-mooded subject from a personal point of view. Others, more thoroughly informed in the arcana of the Institution, have written the history of its development from small beginnings to its present impressive magnitude, have analyzed the theory of its intentions, and have expounded its extraordinary influence over what may be called the middle-class culture of our present-day America. It would be beyond the scope of my equipment to add another solemn treatise to the extensive list already issued by the tireless Chautauqua Press. My own experience of Chautauqua was not that of a theoretical investigator, but that of a surprised and wondering participant. It was the experience of an alien thrust suddenly into the midst of a new but not unsympathetic world; and, if the reader will make allowance for the personal equation, some sense of the human significance of this summer seat of earnest recreation may be suggested by a mere record of my individual reactions.

I had heard of Chautauqua only vaguely, until, one sunny summer morning, I suddenly received a telegram inviting me to lecture at the Institution. I was a little disconcerted at the moment, because I was enjoying an amphibious existence in a bathing-suit, and was inclined to shudder at the thought of putting on a collar in July; but, after an hour or two, I managed to imagine that telegram as a Summons from the Great Unknown, and it was in a proper spirit of adventure that I flung together a few books, and climbed into the only available upper berth on a discomfortable train that rushed me westward.

In some sickly hour of the early morning, I was cast out at Westfield, on Lake Erie, — a town that looked like the back-yard of civilization, with weeds growing in it. Thence a trolley car, climbing over heightening hills that became progressively more beautiful, hauled me ultimately to the entrance of what the cynical conductor called "The Holy City." A fence of insurmountable palings stretched away on either hand; and, at the little station, there were turn-stiles, through which pilgrims passed within. Most people pay money to obtain admittance; but I was met by a very affable young man from Dartmouth, whose business it was to welcome invited visitors, and by him I was steered officially through unopposing gates. I liked this young man for his cheerful clothes and smiling countenance; but I was rather appalled by the agglomeration of ram-shackle cottages through which we passed on our way to the hotel.

I say "the hotel," for the Chautauqua Settlement contains but one such institution. It carries the classic name of Athenæum; but the first view of it occasioned in my sensitive constitution a sinking of the heart. The edifice dates from the early-gingerbread period of architecture. It culminates in a horrifying cupola, and is colored a discountenancing brown. The first glimpse of it reminded me of the poems of A. H. Clough, whose chief merit was to die and to offer thereby an occasion for a grave and twilit elegy by Matthew Arnold. Clough's life-work was a continual asking of the question, "Life being unbearable, why should I not die?" — while echo, that commonplace and sapient commentator, mildly answered, "Why?": and this was precisely the impression that I gathered from my initial vista of the Athenæum between trees.

On entering the hotel I was greeted over the desk (with what might be defined as a left-handed smile) by one of the leading students of the university with which I am associated as a teacher. He called out, "Front!" in the manner of an amateur who is amiably aping the professional, and assigned me to a scarcely comfortable room.

My first voluntary act in the Chautauqua Community was to take a swim. But the water was tepid, and brown, and tasteless, and unbuoyant; and I felt, rather oddly, as if I were swimming in a gigantic cup of tea. From this initial experience I proceeded, somewhat precipitately, to induce an analogy; and it seemed to me, at the time, as if I had forsaken the roar and tumble of the hoarse, tumultuous world, for the inland disassociated peace of an unaware and loitering backwater.

With hair still wet and still dishevelled, I was met by the Secretary of Instruction, — a man (as I discovered later) of wise and humorous perceptions. By him I was informed that, in an hour or so, I was to lecture, in the Hall of Philosophy, on (if I remember rightly) Edgar Allan Poe. I combed my hair, and tried to care for Poe, and made my way to the Hall of Philosophy. This turned out to be a Greek temple divested of its walls. An oaken roof, with pediments, was supported by Doric columns; and under the enlarged umbrella thus devised, about a thousand people were congregated to greet the new and unknown lecturer.

I honestly believe that that was the worst lecture I have ever imposed upon a suffering audience. I had lain awake all night, in an upper berth, on the hottest day of the year; I had found my swim in inland water unrefreshing; and, at the moment, I really cared no more for Edgar Allan Poe than I usually care for the sculptures of Bernini, the paintings of Bouguereau, or the base-ball playing of the St. Louis "Browns." This feeling was, of course, unfair to Poe, who is (with all his emptiness of content) an admirable artist; but I was tired at the time. It pained me exceedingly to listen, for an hour, to my own dull and unilluminated lecture. And yet (and here is the pathetic point that touched me deeply) I perceived gradually that the audience was listening not only attentively but eagerly. Those people really wanted to hear whatever the lecturer should say: and I wandered back to the depressing hotel with bowed head, actuated by a new resolve to tell them something worthy on the morrow.

That afternoon and evening I strolled about the summer settlement of Chautauqua; and (in view of my subsequent shift of attitude) I do not mind confessing that this first aspect of the community depressed me to a perilous melancholy. I beheld a landscape that reminded me of Wordsworth's Windermere, except that the lake was broader and the hills less high, deflowered and defamed by the huddled houses of the Chautauqua settlers. The lake was lovely; and, with this supreme adjective, I forbear from further effort at description. Upon the southern shore, a natural grove of noble and venerable trees had been invaded by a crowded horror of discomfortable tenements, thrown up by carpenters with a taste for machine-made architectural details, and colored a sickly green, an acid yellow, or an angry brown. The Chautauqua Settlement, which is surrounded by a fence of palings, covers only two or three square miles of territory; and, in the months of July and August, between fifteen and twenty thousand people are crowded into this constricted area. Hence a horror of unsightly dormitories, spawning unpredictable inhabitants upon the ambling, muddy lanes.

There have been, in the history of this Assembly, a few salutary fires, — as a result of which new buildings have been erected which are comparatively easy on the eyes. The Hall of Philosophy is really beautiful, and is nobly seated among memorable trees at the summit of a little hill. The Aula Christi tried to be beautiful, and failed; but at least the good intention is apparent. The Amphitheatre (which seats six or seven thousand auditors) is admirably adapted to its uses; and some of the more recent business buildings, like the Post Office, are inoffensive to the unexacting observer. A wooded peninsula, which is pleasantly laid out as a park, projects into the lake; and, at the point of this, has lately been erected a *campanile* which is admirable in both color and proportion. Indeed, when a fanfaronnade of sunset is blown wide behind it, you suffer a sudden tinge of homesickness for Venice or Ravenna. It is good enough for that. But beside it is a helter-skelter wooden edifice which reminds you of Surf Avenue at Coney Island. Indeed, the Settlement as a whole exhibits still an overwhelmment of the unæsthetic, and appals the eye of the new-comer from a more considerative world.

On the way back from the lovely *campanile* to the hotel, I stumbled over a scattering of artificial hillocks surrounding two mud-puddles connected by a gutter. This monstrosity turned out to be a relief-map of Palestine. Little children, with uncultivated voices, shouted at each other as they lightly leaped from Jerusalem to Jericho; and waste-paper soaked itself to dingy brown in the insanitary Sea of Galilee. — Then I encountered a wooden edifice with castellated towers and machicolated battlements, which called itself (with a large label) the Men's Club; and from this I fled, with almost a sense of relief, to the hotel itself, now sprawling low and dark beneath its Boston-brown-bread cupola.

Thus my first impression of Chautauqua was one of melancholy and resentment. But, in the subsequent few days, this emotion was altered to one of impressible satiric mirth; and, subsequently still, it was changed again to an emotion of wondering and humble admiration. I had been assured at the outset, by one who had already tried it, that, if I stayed long enough, I should end up by liking Chautauqua; and this is precisely what happened to me before a week was out.

But meanwhile I laughed very hard for three days. The thing that made me laugh most was the unexpected experience of enduring the discomfiture of fame. Chautauqua is a constricted community; and any one who lectures there becomes, by that very fact, a famous person in this little backwater of the world, until he is supplanted (for fame is as fickle as a ballet-dancer) by the next new-comer to the platform. The Chautauqua Press publishes a daily paper, a weekly review, a monthly magazine and a quarterly; and these publications report your lectures, tell the story of your life, comment upon your views of this and that, advertise your books, and print your picture. Everybody knows you by sight, and stops you in the street to ask you questions. Thus, on your way to the Post Office, you are intercepted by some kindly soul who says: "I am Miss Terwilliger, from Montgomery, Alabama; and do you think that Bernard Shaw is really an immoral writer?" or, "I am Mrs. Winterbottom, of Muncie, Indiana; and where do you think I had better send my boy to school? He is rather a backward boy for his age — he was ten last April — but I really think that if, etc."

Then, when you return to the hotel, you observe that everybody is rocking vigorously on the veranda, and reading one of your books. This pleases you a little; for, though an actor may look his audience in the eyes, an author is seldom privileged to see his readers face to face. Indeed, he often wonders if anybody ever reads his writings, because he knows that his best friends never do. But very soon this tender sentiment is disrupted. There comes a sudden resurrection of the rocking-chair brigade, a rush of readers with uplifted fountain-pens, and a general request for the author's autograph upon the flyleaf of his volume. All of this is rather flattering; but afterward these gracious and well-meaning people begin to comment on your lectures, and tell you that you have made them see a great light. And then you find yourself embarrassed.

It is rather embarrassing to be embarrassed.

One enthusiastic lady, having told me her name and her address, assaulted me with the following commentary: — "I heard you lecture on Stevenson the other day; and ever since then I have been thinking how very much

like Stevenson you are. And today I heard you lecture on
Walt Whitman: and all afternoon I have been thinking
how very much like Whitman you are. And that is rather
puzzling — isn't it? — because Stevenson and Whitman
weren't at all like each other, — were they?"

I smiled, and told the lady the simple truth; but I do not
think she understood me. "Ah, madam," I said, "wait
until you hear me lecture about Hawthorne. . . ."

For (and now I am freely giving the whole game away)
the secret of the art of lecturing is merely this: — on your
way to the rostrum you contrive to fling yourself into complete sympathy with the man you are to talk about, so
that, when you come to speak, you will give utterance to
his message, in terms that are suggestive of *his* style.
You must guard yourself from ever attempting to talk
about anybody whom you have not (at some time or
other) loved; and, at the moment, you should, for sheer
affection, abandon your own personality in favor of his,
so that you may become, as nearly as possible, the person
whom it is your business to represent. Naturally, if
you have any ear at all, your sentences will tend to fall into
the rhythm of his style; and if you have any temperament
(whatever that may be) your imagined mood will diffuse
an ineluctable aroma of the author's personality.

This at least, is my own theory of lecturing; and, in the
instance of my talk on Hawthorne, I seem to have carried
it out successfully in practice. I must have attained a
tone of sombre gray, and seemed for the moment a medi-
tative Puritan under a shadowy and steepled hat; for, at
the close of the lecture, a silvery-haired and sweet-faced
woman asked me if I wouldn't be so kind as to lead the
devotional service in the Baptist House that evening.
I found myself abashed. But a previous engagement
saved me; and I was able to retire, not without honor,
though with some discomfiture.

This previous engagement was a steamboat ride upon
the lake. When you want to give a sure-enough party at

Chautauqua, you charter a steamboat and escape from the enclosure, having seduced a sufficient number of other people to come along and sing. On this particular evening, the party consisted of the Chautauqua School of Expression, — a bevy of about thirty young women who were having their speaking voices cultivated by an admired friend of mine who is one of the best readers in America; and they sang with real spirit, so soon as we had churned our way beyond remembrance of (I mean no disrespect) the Baptist House. But this boat-ride had a curious effect on the four or five male members of the party. We touched at a barbarous and outrageous settlement, named (if I remember rightly) Bemus Point; and hardly had the boat been docked before there ensued a hundred-yard dash for a pair of swinging doors behind which dazzled lights splashed gaudily on soapy mirrors. I did not really desire a drink at the time; but I took two, and the other men did likewise. I understood at once (for I must always philosophize a little) why excessive drinking is induced in prohibition states. Tell me that I may not laugh, and I wish at once to laugh my head off, — though I am at heart a holy person who loves Keats. This incongruous emotion must have been felt, under this or that influence of external inhibition, by everyone who is alive enough to like swimming, and Dante, and Weber and Fields, and Filipino Lippi, and the view of the valley underneath the sacred stones of Delphi.

Within the enclosure of Chautauqua one does not drink at all; and I infer that this regulation is well-advised. I base this inference upon my gradual discovery that all the regulations of this well-conducted Institution have been fashioned sanely to contribute to the greatest good of the greatest number. That is my final, critical opinion. But how we did dash for the swinging doors at Bemus Point! — we four or five simple-natured human beings who were not, in any considerable sense, drinking men at all.

Then the congregated School of Expression tripped ashore with nimble ankles; and there ensued a general dance at a pavilion where a tired boy maltreated a more tired piano, and one paid a dime before, or after, dancing. One does not dance at Chautauqua, even on moon-silvery summer evenings: — and again the regulation is right, because the serious-minded members of the community must have time to read the books of those who lecture there.

And this brings me to a consideration of the Chautauqua Sunday. On this day the gates are closed, and neither ingress nor egress is permitted. Once more I must admit that the regulation has been sensibly devised. If admittance were allowed on Sunday, the grounds would be overrun by picnickers from Buffalo, who would cast the shells of hard-boiled eggs into the inviting Sea of Galilee; and unless the officers are willing to let anybody in, they can devise no practicable way of letting anybody out. Besides, the people who are in already like to rest and meditate. But alas! (and at this point I think that I begin to disapprove) the row-boats and canoes are tied up at the dock, the tennis-courts are emptied, and the simple exercise of swimming is forbidden. This desuetude of natural and smiling recreation on a day intended for surcease of labor struck me (for I am in part an ancient Greek, in part a mediæval Florentine) as strangely ir-religious. All day the organ rumbles in the Amphi-theatre (and of this I approved, beause I love the way in which an organ shakes you into sanctity), and many meetings are held in various sectarian houses, the mood of which is doubtless reverent — though all the while the rippling water beckons to the high and dry canoes, and a gathering of many-tinted clouds is summoned in the windy west to tingle with Olympian laughter and Universal song. How much more wisely (if I may talk in Greek terms for the moment) the gods take Sunday, than their followers on this forgetful earth!

But we must change the mood if I am to speak again of what amused me in the pagan days of my initiation at Chautauqua. Life, for instance, at the ginger-bread hotel amused me oddly. To one who lives in a metropolis throughout the working months, the map of eating at Chautauqua seems incongruous. Dinner is served in the middle of the day, at an hour when one is hardly encouraged to the thought of luncheon; and at six P. M. a sort of breakfast is set forth, which is denominated *Supper*. This Supper consists of fruit, followed by buckwheat cakes, followed by meat or eggs; and to eat one's way through it induces a curious sense of standing on one's head. After two days I discovered a remedy for this undesired dizziness. I turned the *menu* upside down, and ordered a meal in the reverse order. The Supper itself was a success; but the waitress (who, in the winter, teaches school in Texas) disapproved of what she deemed my frivolous proceeding. Her eyes took on an inward look beneath the pedagogical eye-glasses; and there was a distinct furrowing of her forehead. Thereafter I did not dare to overturn the *menu*, but ate my way heroically backward. After all, our prandial prejudices are merely the result of custom. There is no real reason why stewed prunes should not be eaten at three A. M.

But this philosophical reflection reminds me that there is no such hour at Chautauqua. At ten P. M. a carol of sweet chimes is rung from the Italian *campanile;* and at that hour all good Chautauquans go to bed. If you are by profession (let us say) a writer, and are accustomed to be alive at midnight, you will find the witching hours sad. Vainly you will seek companionship, and will be reduced at last to reading the base-ball reports in the newspapers of Cleveland, Ohio.

At the Athenæum you are passed about, from meal to meal, like a one-card draw at poker. The hotel is haunted by Old Chautauquans, who vie with each other to receive you with traditional cordiality. The head-waitress steers

you for luncheon (I mean Dinner) to one table, for Supper
to another, and so on around the room from day to day.
The process reminds you a little of the procedure at a
progressive euchre party. At each meal you meet a new
company of Old Chautauquans, and are expected to converse: but many (indeed most) of these people are humanly
refreshing, and the experience is not so wearing as it
sounds.

But you must not imagine from all that I have said that
the life of the lecturer at Chautauqua is merely frivolous.
Not at all. You get up very early, and proceed to Hig-
gins Hall, a pleasant little edifice (named after the late
Governor of New York State) set agreeably amid trees
upon a rising knoll of verdure; and there you converse
for a time about the Drama, and for another time about
the Novel. In each of these two courses there were,
perhaps, seventy or eighty students, — male and female,
elderly and young. I found them much more eager than
the classes I had been accustomed to in college, and at
least as well prepared. They came from anywhere, and
from any previous condition of servitude to the general
cause of learning; but I found them apt, and interested,
and alive.

Now and then it appeared that their sense of humor was
a little less fantastic than my own; but I liked them very
much, because they were so earnest and simple and human
and (what is Whitman's adjective?) adhesive.

And now I come to the point that converted me finally
to Chautauqua. I found myself, after a few days, liking
the people very much. In the afternoons I talked in the
Doric Temple about this man or that, — selected from
my company of well-beloved friends among "the famous
nations of the dead"; and the people came in hundreds
and listened reverently — not, I am very glad to know,
because of any trick I have of setting words together, but
because of Stevenson and Whitman and the others, and
what they meant by living steadfast lives amid the hurly-

burly of this roaring world, and steering heroically by
their stars. Some elderly matrons among the listeners
brought their knitting with them and toiled with busy
hands throughout the lecture; but they listened none the
less attentively, and reduced me to a mood of humble
wonderment.

For I have often wondered (and this is, perhaps, the
most intimate of my confessions) how anybody can endure
a lecture, — even a good lecture, for I am not thinking
merely of my own. It is a passive exercise of which I am
myself incapable. I, for one, have always found it very
irksome — as Carlyle has phrased the experience — "to
sit as a passive bucket and be pumped into." I always
want to talk back, or rise and remark "But, on the other
hand . . ." ; and, before long, I find myself spiritually
itching. This is, possibly, a reason why I prefer canoeing
to listening to sermons. Yet these admirable Chautauquans submit themselves to this experience hour after
hour, because they earnestly desire to discover some glim-
mering of "the best that has been known and thought in
the world."

These fifteen or twenty thousand people have assembled for the pursuit of culture — a pursuit which the
Hellenic-minded Matthew Arnold designated as the
noblest in this life. But from this fact (and here the
antithetic formula asserts itself) we must deduce an
inference that they feel themselves to be uncultured. In
this inference I found a taste of the pathetic. I discovered
that many of the colonists at Chautauqua were men and
women well along in life who had had no opportunities
for early education. Their children, rising through the
generations, had returned from the state universities of
Texas or Ohio or Mississippi, talking of Browning, and
the binominal theorem, and the survival of the fittest, and
the grandeur and decadence of the Romans, and the
entassus of Ionic columns, and the doctrine of *laissez
faire;* and now their elders had set out to endeavor to

catch up with them. This discovery touched me with both reverence and pathos. An attempt at what may be termed, in the technical jargon of base-ball, a "delayed steal" of culture, seemed to me little likely to succeed. Culture, like wisdom, cannot be acquired: it cannot be passed, like a dollar bill, from one who has it to one who has it not. It must be absorbed, early in life, through birth or breeding, or be gathered undeliberately through experience. A child of five with a French governess will ask for his mug of milk with an easier Gallic grace than a man of eighty who has puzzled out the pronunciation from a text-book. There is, apparently, no remedy for this. Love the *Faerie Queene* at twelve, or you will never really love it at seventy: or so, at least, it seems to me. And yet the desire to learn, in gray-haired men and women who in their youth were battling hard for a mere continuance of life itself, and founding homesteads in a book-less wilderness, moved me to a quick exhilaration.

Most of the people at Chautauqua come either from the south or from the middle west. They pronounce the English language either without any *r* at all, or with such excessive emphasis upon the *r* as to make up for the deficiency of their fellow-seekers. In other words, these people are really American, as opposed to cosmopolitan; and to live among them is — for a world-wandering adventurer — to learn a lesson in Americanism. Mr. Roosevelt once stated that Chautauqua is the most American institution in America; and this statement — like many others of his inspired platitudes — begins to seem meaningful upon reflection.

At one time or another I have drifted to many different corners of the world; but my residence at Chautauqua was my only experience of a democracy. In this community there are no special privileges. If the President of the Institution had wished to hear me lecture (he never did, in fact — though we used to play tennis together, at which game he proved himself easily the better man) he would have been required to come early and take his chance at getting a front seat; and once, when I ventured to attend a lecture by one of my colleagues, I found myself seated beside that very waitress in the Athenæum who had disapproved of my method of ordering a meal. All the exercises are open equally to anybody — first come, first served — and the boy who blacks your boots may turn out to be a Sophomore at Oberlin. Teachers in Texas high-schools sweep the floors or shave you, and the raucous newsboy is earning his way toward the University of Illinois. All this is a little bewildering at first; but in a day or two you grow to like it.

This free-for-all spirit that permeates Chautauqua reminds me to speak of the economic conduct of the Institution. The only charge — except in the case of certain special courses — is for admission to the grounds. The visitor pays fifty cents for a franchise of one day, and more for periods of greater length, until the ultimate charge of seven dollars and fifty cents for a season ticket is attained. On leaving the grounds, he has to show his ticket; and if it has expired he is taxed according to the term of his delinquent lingering. Once free of the grounds, he may avail himself of any of the privileges of the Assembly. Lectures, on an infinite variety of subjects, are delivered hour after hour; and a bulletin of these successive lectures is posted publicly and printed in the daily paper. Every evening an entertainment of some sort is given in the Amphitheatre, and this is eagerly attended by swarming thousands. The Institution owns all the land within the bounding palisades. Private cottages may be erected by individual builders on lots leased for ninety-nine years; but the Institution owns and operates the only hotel, and exercises an absolute empery over the issuance of franchises to necessary tradesmen. The revenue of the corporation is therefore rich; but all of it is expended in importing the best lecturers that may be obtained, and in furthering the general good of the general assembly. The entire system suggests the theoretic observation that an absolute democracy can be instituted and maintained only by an absolute monarchy. If all the people are to be free and equal, the government must have absolute control of all the revenue. Here is, perhaps, a principle for our presidential candidates to think about.

But I do not wish to terminate this summer conversation on a serious note, and I must revert, in closing, to some of the recreations at Chautauqua. The first of these is tea. Every afternoon, from four to five o'clock, the visitor lightly flits from tea to tea, — making his excuses to one hostess in order to dash onward to another. This is rather hard upon the health, because it requires the deglutition of innumerable potions. I have always maintained that tea is an admirable entity if it be considered merely as a time of day, but that it is insidious if it be considered as a beverage. At Chautauqua, tea is not only an hour but a drink, and (though I am a sympathetic soul) I can only say that those who like it like it. For my part, I preferred the concoction sold at rustic soda-fountains, which is known locally as a "Chautauqua highball," — a ribald term devised by college men who make up the by-no-means-despicable ball-team. This beverage is compounded out of unfermented grape-juice and foaming fizz-water; and, if it be taken absent-mindedly, seems to taste like something.

But the standard recreation at Chautauqua is the habit of impromptu eating in the open air. Every one invites you to go upon a picnic. You take a steamer to some point upon the lake, or take a trolley to a wild and deep ravine known by the somewhat unpoetic name of the Hog's Back; and then everybody sits around and eats sandwiches and hard-boiled eggs, and considers the occasion a debauch. This formality resembles a great good fun, especially as there are girls who laugh and play, and threaten to disconcert you on the morrow when you solemnly arise to lecture on the Religion of Emerson.

But picnic-baskets out of doors are rather hard on the digestion.

Perhaps I should record also, as a curious experience, that I was required to appear as one of the guests of honor at a large reception. This meant that I had to stand in line, with certain other marionettes, and shake hands with an apparently endless procession of people who were themselves as bored as were the guests of honor. I determined then and there that I should never run for President, not even in response to an irresistible appeal from the populace. I had never suspected before that there could be so many hands without the touch of nature in them. I shook hands mechanically, chatting all the while with a humorous and human woman who stood next to me in the line of the attacked — until suddenly I felt the sensitive and tender grasp of a sure-enough hand, reminding me of friends and one or two women it has been a holiness to know. My attention was attracted by the thrill. I turned swiftly and I looked upon a little bent old woman who was blind. She had a voice, too, for she spoke to me, and, well, I was very glad that I went to that reception.

And many other matters I remember fondly, a certain lonely hill at sunset, whence you looked over wide water to distant, dream-enchanted shores; the urbanity and humor of the wise directors of the Institution; the manner of many young students who discerned an unadmitted sanctity beneath the smiling conversations of those summer hours; my own last lecture, on "The Importance of Enjoying Life"; the people who walked with me to the station and whom I was sorry to leave; and the oddly-minded student behind the desk of the hotel; and an old man from Kentucky who cared about Walt Whitman after I had talked about his ministrations in the army hospitals; and the trees, and the reverberating organ, and, beneath a benison of midnight peace, the hushed moon-silvery surface of the lake. It is, indeed, a memorable experience to have lectured at Chautauqua.

ANY one who has traveled much about the country of recent years must have been impressed by the growing uneasiness of mind among thoughtful men. Whether in the smoking car, or the hotel corridor, or the college hall, everywhere, if you meet them off their guard and stripped of the optimism which we wear as a public convention, you will hear them saying in a kind of sad amazement, "What is to be the end of it all?" They are alarmed at the unsettlement of property and the difficulties that harass the man of moderate means in making provision for the future; they are uneasy over the breaking up of the old laws of decorum, if not of decency, and over the unrestrained pursuit of excitement at any cost; they feel vaguely that in the decay of religion the bases of society have been somehow weakened. Now, much of this sort of talk is as old as history, and has no special significance. We are prone to forget that civilization has always been a *tour de force*, so to speak, a little hard-won area of order and self-subordination amidst a vast wilderness of anarchy and barbarism that are with difficulty held in check and are continually threatening to overrun their bounds. But that is equally no reason for over-confidence. Civilization is like a ship traversing an untamed sea. It is a more complex machine in our day, with command of greater forces, and might seem correspondingly safer than in the era of sails. But fresh catastrophes have shown that the ancient perils of navigation still confront the largest vessel, when the crew loses its discipline or the officers neglect their duty; and the analogy is not without its warning.

Only a year after the sinking of the *Titanic* I was crossing the ocean, and it befell by chance that on the anniversary of that disaster we passed not very far from the spot where the proud ship lay buried beneath the waves. The evening was calm, and on the lee deck a dance had been hastily organized to take advantage of the benign weather. Almost alone I stood for hours at the railing on the windward side, looking out over the rippling water where the moon had laid upon it a broad street of gold. Nothing could have been more peaceful; it was as if Nature were smiling upon earth in sympathy with the strains of music and the sound of laughter that reached me at intervals from the revelling on the other deck. Yet I could not put out of my heart an apprehension of some luring treachery in this scene of beauty — and certainly the world can offer nothing more wonderfully beautiful than the moon shining from the far East over a smooth expanse of water. Was it not in such a calm as this that the unsuspecting vessel, with its gay freight of human lives, had shuddered, and gone down, forever? I seemed to behold a symbol; and there came into my mind the words we used to repeat at school, but are, I do not know just why, a little ashamed of to-day:

> Thou, too, sail on, O Ship of State!
> Sail on, O Union, strong and great!
> Humanity with all its fears,
> With all its hopes of future years,
> Is hanging breathless on thy fate! . . .

Something like this, perhaps, is the feeling of many men — men by no means given to morbid gusts of panic — amid a society that laughs overmuch in its amusement and exults in the very lust of change. Nor is their anxiety quite the same as that which has always disturbed the reflecting spectator. At other times the apprehension has been lest the combined forces of order might not be strong enough to withstand the ever-threatening inroads of those

who, envy, barbarously, and desire recklessly; whereas today the doubt is whether the natural champions of order
themselves shall be found loyal to their trust, for they
seem no longer to remember clearly the word of command
that should unite them in leadership. Until they can
rediscover some common ground of strength and purpose
in the first principles of education and law and property
and religion, we are in danger of falling a prey to the
disorganizing and vulgarizing domination of ambitions
which should be the servants and not the masters of
society.

Certainly, in the sphere of education there is a growing
belief that some radical reform is needed; and this dissatisfaction is in itself wholesome. Boys come into college
with no reading and with minds unused to the very practice of study; and they leave college, too often, in the same
state of nature. There are even those, inside and outside
of academic halls, who protest that our higher institutions
of learning simply fail to educate at all. That is slander;
but in sober earnest, you will find few experienced college
professors, apart from those engaged in teaching purely
utilitarian or practical subjects, who are not convinced
that the general relaxation is greater now than it was
twenty years ago. It is of considerable significance that
the two student essays which took the prizes offered by
the Harvard *Advocate* in 1913 were both on this theme.
The first of them posed the question, "How can the
leadership of the intellectual rather than the athletic
student be fostered?" and was virtually a sermon on
a text of President Lowell's: "No one in close touch
with American education has failed to notice the lack
among the mass of undergraduates of keen interest
in their studies and the small regard for scholarly
attainment." Now the *Advocate* prizeman has his specific remedy,
and President Lowell has his, and other men propose other
systems and restrictions; but the evil is too deep-seated

to be reached by any superficial scheme of honors or to be charmed away by insinuating appeals. The other day Mr. William F. McCombs, chairman of the National Committee which engineered a college president into the White House, gave this advice to our academic youth: "The college man must forget — or never let it creep into his head — that he's a highbrow. If it does creep in, he's out of politics." To which one might reply in Mr. McCombs's own dialect, that unless a man can make himself a force in politics (or at least in the larger life of the State) precisely by virtue of being a "highbrow," he had better spend his four golden years otherwise than in college. There it is: the destiny of education is intimately bound up with the question of social leadership, and unless the college, as it used to be in the days when the religious hierarchy it created was a real power, can be made once more a breeding place for a natural aristocracy, it will inevitably degenerate into a school for mechanical apprentices or into a pleasure resort for the *jeunesse dorée* (sc. the "gold coasters"). We must get back to a common understanding of the office of education in the construction of society, and must discriminate among the subjects that may enter into the curriculum, by their relative value towards this end.

A manifest condition is that education should embrace the means of discipline, for without discipline the mind will remain inefficient, just as surely as the muscles of the body, without exercise, will be left flaccid. That should seem to be a self-evident truth. Now it may be possible to derive a certain amount of discipline out of any study, but it is a fact, nevertheless, which cannot be gainsaid, that some studies lend themselves to this use more readily and effectively than others. You may, for instance, if by extraordinary luck you get the perfect teacher, make English literature disciplinary by the hard manipulation of ideas; but in practice it almost inevitably happens that a course in English literature either degenerates into the dull

memorizing of dates and names or, rising into the O Alti-
tudo, evaporates in romantic gush over beautiful passages.
This does not mean, of course, that no benefit may be obtained from such a study, but it does preclude English
literature generally from being made the backbone, so to
speak, of a sound curriculum. The same may be said of
French and German. The difficulties of these tongues in
themselves, and the effort required of us to enter into their
spirit, imply some degree of intellectual gymnastics, but
scarcely enough for our purpose. Of the sciences it be-
hooves one to speak circumspectly, and undoubtedly
mathematics and physics, at least, demand such close attention and such firm reasoning as to render them an essential part of any disciplinary education. But there are
good grounds for being sceptical of the effect of the non-
mathematical sciences on the immature mind. Any one
who has spent a considerable portion of his undergraduate
time in a chemical laboratory, for example, as the present
writer has done, and has the means of comparing the results of such elementary and pottering experimentation
with the mental grip required in the humanistic courses,
must feel that the real training obtained therein was almost
negligible. If I may draw further from my own observation I must say frankly that, after dealing for a number of
years with manuscripts prepared for publication by college
professors of the various faculties, I have been forced to
the conclusion that science, in itself, is likely to leave the
mind in a state of relative imbecility. It is not that the
writing of men who got their early drill too exclusively, or
even predominantly, in the sciences lacks the graces of
rhetoric — that would be comparatively a small matter —
but such men in the majority of cases, even when treating
subjects within their own field, show a singular inability
to think clearly and consecutively, so soon as they are
freed from the restraint of merely describing the process of
an experiment. On the contrary, the manuscript of a
classical scholar, despite the present dry-rot of philology,

almost invariably gives signs of a habit of orderly and well-governed cerebration.

Here, whatever else may be lacking, is discipline. The sheer difficulty of Latin and Greek, the highly organized structure of these languages, the need of scrupulous search to find the nearest equivalents for words that differ widely in their scope of meaning from their derivatives in any modern vocabulary, the effort of lifting one's self out of the familiar rut of ideas into so foreign a world, all these things act as a tonic exercise to the brain. And it is a demonstrable fact that students of the classics do actually surpass their unclassical rivals in any field where a fair test can be made. At Princeton, for instance, Professor West has shown this superiority by tables of achievements and grades, which he published in the *Educational Review* for March, 1913; and a number of letters from various parts of the country, printed in the *Nation*, tell the same story in striking fashion. Thus, a letter from Wesleyan (September 7, 1911) gives statistics to prove that the classical students in that university outstrip the others in obtaining all sorts of honors, commonly even honors in the sciences. Another letter (May 8, 1913) shows that in the first semester in English at the University of Nebraska the percentage of delinquents among those who entered with four years of Latin was below 7; among those who had three years of Latin and one or two of a modern language the percentage rose to 15; two years of Latin and two years of a modern language, 30 per cent.; one year or less of Latin and from two to four years of a modern language, 35 per cent. And in the *Nation* of April 23, 1914, Prof. Arthur Gordon Webster, the eminent physicist of Clark University, after speaking of the late B. O. Peirce's early drill and life-long interest in Greek and Latin, adds these significant words: "Many of us still believe that such a training makes the best possible foundation for a scientist." There is reason to think that this opinion is daily gaining ground among those who are

zealous that the prestige of science should be maintained
by men of the best calibre.

The disagreement in this matter would no doubt be less,
were it not for an ambiguity in the meaning of the word
"efficient" itself. There is a kind of efficiency in manag-
ing men, and there also is an intellectual efficiency, properly speaking, which is quite a different faculty. The
former is more likely to be found in the successful engineer
or business man than in the scholar of secluded habits, and
because often such men of affairs received no discipline at
college in the classics, the argument runs that utilitarian
studies are as disciplinary as the humanistic. But efficiency of this kind is not an academic product at all, and
is commonly developed, and should be developed, in the
school of the world. It comes from dealing with men in
matters of large physical moment, and may exist with a
mind utterly undisciplined in the stricter sense of the
word. We have had more than one illustrious example in
recent years of men capable of dominating their fellows,
let us say in financial transactions, who yet in the grasp
of first principles and in the analysis of consequences
have shown themselves to be as inefficient as children in the first semester in English at the University.
Probably, however, few men who have had experience
in education will deny the value of discipline to the classics,
even though they hold that other studies, less costly from
the utilitarian point of view, are equally educative in this
respect. But it is further of prime importance, even if
such an equality, or approach to equality, were granted,
that we should select one group of studies, and unite in
making it the core of the curriculum for the great mass of
undergraduates. It is true in education as in other matters that strength comes from union, and weakness from
division, and if educated men are to work together for a
common end, they must have a common range of ideas,
with a certain solidarity in their way of looking at things.
As matters actually are, the educated man feels terribly

his isolation under the scattering of intellectual pursuits, yet too often lacks the courage to deny the strange popular fallacy that there is virtue in sheer variety, and that somehow well-being is to be struck out from the clashing of miscellaneous interests rather than from concentration. In one of his annual reports some years ago, President Eliot, of Harvard, observed, from the figures of registration that the majority of students still at that time believed the best form of education for them was in the old humanistic courses; and *therefore*, he argued, the other courses should be fostered. There was never perhaps a more extraordinary syllogism since the *largo* of Shakespeare's gravedigger. I quote from memory, and may slightly misrepresent the actual statement of the influential "educationalist" but the spirit of his words, as indeed of his practice, is surely as I give it. And the working of this spirit is one of the main causes of the curious fact that scarcely any other class of men in social intercourse feel themselves, in their deeper concerns, more severed one from another than those very college professors who ought to be united in the battle for educational leadership. This estrangement is sometimes carried to an extreme almost ludicrous. I remember once, in a small but advanced college, the consternation that was awakened when an instructor in philosophy went to a colleague — both of them now associates in a large university — for information in a question of biology. "What business has he with such matters!" said the irate biologist; "let him stick to his last, and teach philosophy — if he can!" That was a polite jest, you will say. Perhaps; but not entirely. Philosophy is indeed taught in one lecture hall, and biology in another; but of conscious effort to make of education a harmonious driving force there is next to nothing. And, as the teachers, so are the taught, as I have argued at length in my article on Natural Aristocracy. Such criticism does not imply that advanced work in any of the branches of human knowledge should be cut-tailed; but it does demand that, as a background to the professional pursuits, there should be a common intellectual training through which all students should pass, acquiring thus a single body of ideas and images in which they could always meet as brother initiates.

We shall, then, make a long step forward when we determine that in the college, as distinguished from the university, it is better to have the great mass of men, whatever may be the waste in a few unmalleable minds, go through the discipline of a single group of studies — with, of course, a considerable freedom of choice in the outlying field. And it will probably appear in experience that the only practicable group to select is the classics, with the accompaniment of philosophy and the mathematical sciences. Latin and Greek are, at least, as disciplinary as any other subjects; and if it can be further shown that they possess a specific power of correction for the more disintegrating tendencies of the age, it ought to be clear that their value as instruments of education outweighs the service of certain other studies which may seem to be more immediately utilitarian.

For it will be pretty generally agreed that efficiency of the individual scholar and unity of the scholarly class are, properly, only the means to obtain the real end of education, which is social efficiency. The only way, in fact, to make the discipline demanded by a severe curriculum and the sacrifice of particular tastes required for unity seem worth the cost, is to persuade men that the resulting form of education both meets a present and serious need of society and promises to serve those individuals who desire to obtain society's fairer honors. As for the specific need of society at the present day, it is not my purpose to open this matter now, for the good reason that the editor of THE UNPOPULAR REVIEW has already permitted me to argue it at length in my article on *Natural Aristocracy*. Mr. McCombs, speaking for the "practical" man, declares that there is no place in politics for the intellectual aristocrat.

A good many of us believe that unless the very reverse of this is true, unless the educated man can somehow, by virtue of his education, make of himself a governor of the people in the larger sense, and even to some extent in the narrow political sense, unless the college can produce a hierarchy of character and intelligence which shall in due measure perform the office of the discredited oligarchy of birth, we had better make haste to divert our enormous collegiate endowments into more useful channels.

And here I am glad to find confirmation of my belief in the stalwart old *Boke Named the Governour*, published by Sir Thomas Elyot in 1531, the first treatise on education in the English tongue, and still, after all these years, one of the wisest. It is no waste of time to take account of the theory held by the humanists when study at Oxford and Cambridge was shaping itself for its long service in giving to the oligarchic government of Great Britain whatever elements it possessed of true aristocracy. Elyot's book is equally a treatise on the education of a gentleman, and on the ordinance of government; for, as he says elsewhere, he wrote "to instruct men in such virtues as shall be expedient for them which shall have authority in a weal public." I quote from various parts of his work with some abridgment, retaining the quaint spelling of the original, and I beg the reader not to skip, however long the citation may appear:

Beholde also the ordre that god hath put generally in al his creatures, begynning at the moste inferiour or base, and assendynge upwarde; so that in euery thyng is ordre, and without ordre may be nothing stable or permanent; and it may nat be called ordre, excepte it do contayne in it degrees, high and base, accordynge to the merite or estimation of the thyng that is ordred. And therfore hit appereth that god gyueth nat to euery man like gyftes of grace, or of nature, but to some more, some lesse, as it liketh his diuine maiestie. For as moche as understandyng is the most excellent gyfte that man can receiue in his creation, it is therfore congruent, and accordynge that as one excelleth an other in that influence, as therby beinge next to the similitude of his maker, so shulde the astate of his persone be auanced in degree or place where understandynge may profite. Suche oughte to be set in a more highe place than the residue where they may se and also be sene, that by the beames of they'r excellent witte, shewed throughe the glasse of auctorite, other of inferiour understandynge may be directed to the way of vertue and commodious liuynge. Thus I conclude that nobilitie is nat after the vulgare opinion of men, but is only the prayse, and surname of vertue, whiche the lenger it continueth in a name or lignage, the more is nobilitie extolled and meruailed at.

If thou be a gouernour, or haste ouer other soueraygntie, knowe thy selfe. Knowe that the name of a soueraigne or ruler without actuall gouernaunce is but a shadowe, that gouernaunce standeth nat by wordes onely, but principally by acte and example; that by example of gouernours men do rise or falle in vertue or vice. Ye shall knowe all way your selfe, if for affection or motion ye do speke or do nothing unworthy the immortalitie and moste precious nature of your soule. In semblable maner, the inferiour persone or subiecte aught to consider, that, all be it he in the substaunce of soule and body be equall with his superior, yet for als moche as the powars and qualities of the soule and body, with the disposition of reason, be nat in euery man equall, therfore god ordayned a diuersitie or pre-eminence in degrees to be amonge men for the necessary derection and preseruation of them in conformitie of lyuinge.

Where all thynge is commune, there lacketh ordre; and where ordre lacketh, there all thynge is odiouse and uncomly.

Such is the goal which the grave Sir Thomas pointed out to the noble youth of his land at the beginning of England's greatness, and such, within the bounds of human frailty, has been the ideal even until now which the two universities have held before them. Naturally the method of training prescribed in the sixteenth century for the attainment of this goal is antiquated in some of its details, but it is no exaggeration, nevertheless, to speak of the *Boke Named the Governour* as the very Magna Charta of our education. The scheme of the humanist might be described in a word as a disciplining of the higher faculty of the imagination to the end that the student may behold, as it were in one sublime vision, the whole scale of being in its range from the lowest to the highest under the divine decree of order and subordination, without losing sight of the immutable veracity at the heart of all variation, which "is only the praise and surname of virtue." This was no new vision, nor has it ever been quite forgotten. It was the whole meaning of religion to Hooker, from whom it passed into all that is best and least ephemeral in the Anglican Church. It was the basis, more modestly expressed, of Blackstone's conception of the British Constitution and of liberty under law. It was the kernel of Burke's theory of statecraft. It is the inspiration of the sublimer science, which accepts the hypothesis of evolution as taught by Darwin and Spencer, yet bows in reverence before the unnamed and incommensurable force lodged as a mystical purpose within the unfolding universe. It was the wisdom of that child of Stratford who, building better than he knew, gave to our literature its deepest and most persistent note. If anywhere Shakespeare seems to speak from his heart and to utter his own philosophy, it is in the person of Ulysses in that strange satire of life as "still wars and lechery" which forms the theme of *Troilus and Cressida*. Twice in the course of the play Ulysses moralizes on the causes of human evil. Once it is in an outburst against the devastations of disorder:

Take but degree away, untune that string,
And, hark, what discord follows! each thing meets
In mere oppugnancy: the bounded waters
Should lift their bosoms higher than the shores,
And make a sop of all this solid globe:
Strength should be lord of imbecility,
And the rude son should strike his father dead:
Force should be right; or rather, right and wrong,

Between whose endless jar justice resides,
Should lose their names, and so should justice too.
Then every thing includes itself in power,
Power into will, will into appetite.

And, in the same spirit, the second tirade of Ulysses is
charged with mockery at the vanity of the present and at
man's usurpation of time as the destroyer instead of the
preserver of continuity:

For time is like a fashionable host
That slightly shakes his parting guest by the hand,
And with his arms outstretch'd, as he would fly,
Grasps in the comer: welcome ever smiles,
And farewell goes out sighing. O, let not virtue seek
Remuneration for the thing it was;
For beauty, wit,
High birth, vigor of bone, desert in service,
Love, friendship, charity, are subjects all
To envious and calumniating time.

To have made this vision of the higher imagination a
true part of our self-knowledge, in such fashion that the
soul is purged of envy for what is distinguished, and we
feel ourselves fellows with the preserving, rather than the
destroying, forces of time, is to be raised into the nobility
of the intellect. To hold this knowledge in a mind trained
to fine efficiency and confirmed by faithful comradeship,
is to take one's place with the rightful governors of the
people. Nor is there any narrow or invidious exclusiveness in such an aristocracy, which differs in its free hospitality from an oligarchy of artificial prescription. The
more its membership is enlarged, the greater is its power,
and the more secure are the privileges of each individual:
Yet, if not exclusive, an academic aristocracy must by its
very nature be exceedingly jealous of any levelling process
which would shape education to the needs of the intellectual proletariat, and so diminish its own ranks. It can-

not admit that, if education is once levelled downwards, the whole body of men will of themselves gradually raise the level to the higher range; for its creed declares that elevation must come from leadership rather than from self-motion of the mass. It will therefore be opposed to any scheme of studies which relaxes discipline or destroys intellectual solidarity. It will look with suspicion on any system which turns out half-educated men with the same diplomas as the fully educated, thinking that such methods of slurring over differences are likely to do more harm by discouraging the ambition to attain what is distinguished than good by spreading wide a thin veneer of culture. In particular it will distrust the present huge overgrowth of courses in government and sociology, which send men into the world skilled in the machinery of statecraft and with minds sharpened to the immediate demands of special groups, but with no genuine training of the imagination and no understanding of the longer problems of humanity, with no hold on the past, "amidst so vast a fluctuation of passions and opinions, to concentre their thoughts, to ballast their conduct, to preserve them from being blown about by every wind of fashionable doctrine." It will set itself against any regular subjection of the "fierce spirit of liberty," which is the breath of distinction and the very charter of aristocracy, to the sullen spirit of equality, which proceeds from envy in the baser sort of democracy. It will regard the character of education and the disposition of the curriculum as a question of supreme importance; for its motto is always, *abeunt studia in mores.*

Now this aristocratic principle has, so to speak, its everlasting embodiment in Greek literature, from whence it was taken over into Latin and transmitted, with much mingling of foreign and even contradictory ideas, to the modern world. From Homer to the last runnings of the Hellenic spirit you will find it taught by every kind of precept and enforced by every kind of example; nor was

Shakespeare writing at hazard, but under the instinctive guidance of genius, when he put his aristocratic creed into the mouth of the hero who to the end remained for the Greeks the personification of their peculiar wisdom. In no other poetry of the world is the law of distinction, as springing from a man's perception of his place in the great hierarchy of privilege and obligation, from the lowest human being up to the Olympian gods, so copiously and magnificently set forth as in Pindar's *Odes of Victory*. And Aeschylus was the first dramatist to see with clear vision the primacy of the intellect in the law of orderly development, seemingly at variance with the divine immutable will of Fate, yet finally in mysterious accord with it. When the philosophers of the later period came to the creation of systematic ethics, they had only the task of formulating what was already latent in the poets and historians of their land; and it was the recollection of the fulness of such instruction in the *Nicomachean Ethics* and the Platonic Dialogues, with their echo in the *Officia* of Cicero, as if in them were stored up all the treasures of antiquity, that raised our Sir Thomas into wondering admiration:

Lorde god, what incomparable swetnesse of wordes and mater shall he finde in the saide warkes of Plato and Cicero; wherin is ioyned grauitie with dilectation, excellent wysedome with diuine eloquence, absolute vertue with pleasure incredible, and euery place is so infarced [crowded] with profitable counsaile, ioyned with honestie, that those thre bokes be almoste sufficient to make a perfecte and excellent gouernour.

There is no need to dwell on this aspect of the classics. He who cares to follow their full working in this direction, as did our English humanist, may find it exhibited in Plato's political and ethical scheme of self-development, or in Aristotle's ideal of the Golden Mean which combines magnanimity with moderation, and elevation with self-knowledge. If a single word were used to describe the character and state of life upheld by Plato and Aristotle, as spokesmen of their people, it would be *eleutheria, liberty:* the freedom to cultivate the higher part of a man's nature — his intellectual prerogative, his desire of truth, his refinements of taste — and to hold the baser part of himself in subjection; the freedom, also, for its own perfection, and indeed for its very existence, to impose an outer conformity to, or at least respect for, the laws of this inner government on others who are of themselves ungoverned. Such liberty is the ground of true distinction; it implies the opposite of an equalitarianism which reserves its honors and rewards for those who attain a bastard kind of distinction by the cunning of leadership, without departing from common standards — the demagogues who rise by flattery. But it is, on the other hand, by no means dependent on the artificial distinctions of privilege, and is peculiarly adapted to an age whose appointed task must be to create a natural aristocracy as a *via media* between an equalitarian democracy and a prescriptive oligarchy or plutocracy. It is a notable fact that, as the real hostility to the classics in the present day arises from an instinctive suspicion of them as standing in the way of a downward-levelling mediocrity, so, at other times, they have fallen under displeasure for their veto on a contrary excess. Thus, in his savage attack on the Commonwealth, to which he gave the significant title *Behemoth,* Hobbes lists the reading of classical history among the chief causes of the rebellion. "There were," he says, "an exceeding great number of men of the better sort, that had been so educated as that in their youth, having read the books written by famous men of the ancient Grecian and Roman commonwealths concerning their polity and great actions, in which books the popular government was extolled by that glorious name of liberty, and monarchy disgraced by the name of tyranny, they became thereby in love with their forms of government; and out of these men were chosen the greatest part of the House of Commons; or if they were not the greatest part, yet by advantage of their eloquence were always able to sway the rest." To this charge Hobbes returns again and again, even declaring that "the universities have been to this nation as the Wooden Horse was to the Trojans." And the uncompromising monarchist of the *Leviathan*, himself a classicist of no mean attainments, as may be known by his translation of Thucydides, was not deceived in his accusation. The tyrannicides of Athens and Rome, the Aristogeitons and Brutuses and others, were the heroes by whose example the leaders of the French Revolution (rightly, so far as they did not fall into the opposite, equalitarian extreme) were continually justifying their acts:

> There Brutus starts and stares by midnight taper,
> Who all the day enacts — a woollen-draper.

And again, in the years of the Risorgimento, more than one of the champions of Italian liberty went to death with those great names on their lips.

So runs the law of order and right subordination. But if the classics offer the best service to education by inculcating an aristocracy of intellectual distinction, they are equally effective in enforcing the similar lesson of time. It is a true saying of our ancient humanist that "the longer it continueth in a name or lineage, the more is nobility extolled and marvelled at." It is true because in this way our imagination is working with the great conservative law of growth. Whatever may be in theory our democratic distaste for the insignia of birth, we cannot get away from the fact that there is a certain honor of inheritance, and that we instinctively pay homage to one who represents a noble name. There is nothing really illogical in this: for, as an English statesman has put it, "the past is one of the elements of our power." He is the wise democrat who, with no opposition to such a decree of Nature, endeavors to control its operation by expecting noble service where the memory of nobility abides. When last year Oxford bestowed its highest honor on an American, distinguished not only for his own public acts but for the great tradition embodied in his name, the Orator of the University did not omit this legitimate appeal to the imagination, singularly appropriate in its academic Latin:

. . . Statim succurrit animo antiqua illa Romae condicio, cum non tam propter singulos cives quam propter singulas gentes nomen Romanum floreret. Cum enim civis alicujus et avum et proavum principes civitatis esse creatos, cum patrem legationis munus apud aulam Britannicam summa cum laude esse exsecutum cognovimus; cum denique ipsum per totum bellum stipendia equo meritum, summa pericula "Pulcra pro Libertate" ausum, . . . Romanae alicujus gentis — Brutorum vel Deciorum — annales evolvere videmur, qui testimonium adhibent "fortes creari fortibus," et majorum exemplis et imaginibus nepotes ad virtutem accendi.

Is there any man so dull of soul as not to be stirred by that enumeration of civic services zealously inherited; or is there any one so envious of the past as not to believe that such memories should be honored in the present as an incentive to noble emulation?

Well, we cannot all of us count Presidents and Ambassadors among our ancestors, but we can, if we will, in the genealogy of the inner life enroll ourselves among the adopted sons of a family in comparison with which the Bruti and Decii of old and the Adamses of to-day are veritable *new men*. We can see what defence against the meaner depredations of the world may be drawn from the pride of birth, when, as it sometimes happens, the obligation of a great past is kept as a contract with the present; shall we forget to measure the enlargement and elevation of mind which ought to come to a man who has made himself the heir of the ancient Lords of Wisdom? "To one small people," as Sir Henry Maine has said, in words often quoted, "it was given to create the principle of

Progress. That people was the Greek. Except the blind forces of Nature, nothing moves in this world which is not Greek in its origin." That is a hard saying, but scarcely exaggerated. Examine the records of our art and our science, our philosophy and the enduring element of our faith, our statecraft and our notion of liberty, and you will find that they all go back for their inspiration to that one small people, and strike their roots into the soil of Greece. What we have added, it is well to know; but he is the aristocrat of the mind who can display a diploma from the schools of the Academy and the Lyceum, and from the Theatre of Dionysus. What tradition of ancestral achievement in the Senate or on the field of battle shall broaden a man's outlook and elevate his will equally with the consciousness that his way of thinking and feeling has come down to him by so long and honorable a descent, or shall so confirm him in his better judgment against the ephemeral and vulgarizing solicitations of the hour? Other men are creatures of the visible moment; he is a citizen of the past and of the future. And such a charter of citizenship it is the first duty of the college to provide.

I have limited myself in these pages to a discussion of what may be called the public side of education, considering the classics in their power to mould character and foster sound leadership in a society much given to drifting. Of the inexhaustible joy and consolation they afford to the individual, only he can have full knowledge who has made the writers of Greece and Rome his friends and counsellors through many vicissitudes of life. It is related of Sainte-Beuve, who, according to Renan, read everything and remembered everything, that one could observe a peculiar serenity on his face whenever he came down from his study after reading a book of Homer. The cost of learning the language of Homer is not small; but so are all fair things difficult, as the Greek proverb runs, and the reward in this case is precious beyond estimation.

Nor need we forget another proverb from Greece, with its spirit of "accommodation" — that the half is sometimes greater than the whole. Even a moderate acquaintance with the language, helped out by good translations (especially in such form as the Loeb Classics are now offering, with the original and the English on opposite pages), will go a surprising length towards keeping a man, amid the exactions of a professional or otherwise busy life, in possession of the heritage to which our age has grown so perilously indifferent.

A GOOD many good judges find the world more out of joint, and moving with a more threatening rattling, than at any previous time since the French Revolution, and think that this is largely because the machine has lost too much of that regulation it used to get from the religions. Much of the regulation came from an interest in things wider than those directly revealed by sense.

Possibly a revival of such an interest may be promised by the recent indications of a range of our forces, both physical and psychic, far wider than previous experience has indicated. This leads us to invite attention to some unusual psychic phenomena evinced by persons of exceptional sensibilities not yet as well understood, or even as carefully investigated, as perhaps they deserve to be. The physical phenomena are outside of our present purpose.

There are hundreds of well authenticated reports of super-usual visions. The vast majority of them, however, were experienced when the percipients were in bed, but believed themselves awake. But almost everybody has often believed himself awake in bed, when he was only dreaming. Hence the probability is overwhelming that most of these super-usual experiences were had in dreams.

But it is certain that not all were, at least in dreams as ordinarily understood; but there seems to be a waking dream state. Foster's visions virtually all came while he was awake, and they were generally at once described by him as if he were describing a landscape or a play. At times he very closely identified himself with some personality of his visions, and acted out the personality, just as Mrs. Piper has habitually done. The following is an approximate instance, quoted by Bartlett (*The Salem Seer*, p. 51*f.*):

Says a writer in the New York *World*, Dec. 27, 1885:

. . . While we were talking one night, Foster and I, there came a knock at the door. Bartlett arose and opened it, disclosing as he did so two young men plainly dressed, of marked provincial aspect. . . . I saw at once that they were clients, and arose to go. Foster restrained me.

"Sit down," he said. "I'll try and get rid of them, for I'm not in the humor to be disturbed. . . ."

Foster hinted that he had no particular inclination to gratify them then and there, but they protested that they had come some distance, and, with a characteristically good-natured smile, he gave in. . . .

Then follows an account of a fairly good séance — taps on the marble table, reading pellets, describing persons, etc., until I thought Foster was tired of the interview and was feigning sleep to end it. All of a sudden he sprang to his feet with such an expression of horror and consternation as an actor playing Macbeth would have given a good deal to imitate. His eyes glared, his breast heaved, his hands clenched. . . .

"Why did you come here?" cried Foster, in a wail that seemed to come from the bottom of his soul. "Why do you come here to torment me with such a sight? Oh, God! It's horrible! It's horrible! . . . It is your father I see! . . . He died fearfully! He died fearfully! He was in Texas — on a horse — with cattle. He was alone. It is the prairies! Alone! The horse fell! He was under it! His thigh was broken — horribly broken! The horse ran away and left him! He lay there stunned! Then he came to his senses! Oh! his thigh was dreadful! Such agony! My God! Such agony!"

Foster fairly screamed at this. The younger of the men . . . broke into violent sobs. His companion wept, too, and the pair of them clasped hands. Bartlett looked on concerned. As for me, I was astounded.

"He was four days dying — four days dying — of starvation and thirst," Foster went on, as if deciphering some terrible hieroglyphs written on the air. "His thigh swelled to the size of his body. Clouds of flies settled on him — flies and vermin — and he chewed his own arm and drank his own blood. He died mad. And my God! he crawled three miles in those four days! Man! Man! that's how your father died!"

So saying, with a great sob, Foster dropped into his chair,

his cheeks purple, and tears running down them in rivers. The younger man . . . burst into a wild cry of grief and sank upon the neck of his friend. He, too, was sobbing as if his own heart would break. Bartlett stood over Foster wiping his forehead with a handkerchief. . . .

"It's true," said the younger man's friend; "his father was a stock-raiser in Texas, and after he had been missing from his drove for over a week, they found him dead and swollen with his leg broken. They tracked him a good distance from where he must have fallen. But nobody ever heard till now how he died." . . .

Now it is hardly to be supposed that the young visitor could ever have had this scene in his mind as vividly as Foster had. In that case where and how did Foster get the vividness and emotion? How do we get them in dreams? He dreamed while he was awake.

As Bartlett quotes this, and as it declares him to have been present, he of course attests it by quoting it. So in each of Bartlett's quoted cases, the original witness is the reporter in the newspaper, and Bartlett, who was present (he was Foster's traveling companion and business agent) thus confirms it. We know Mr. Bartlett personally, and have thorough confidence in his sanity and sincerity. We have also been at the pains to learn that he commands the confidence and respect of his fellow townsmen in Tolland, Connecticut, where he is passing a green old age. Moreover, he does not interpret these phenomena by "spiritism."

We also had a sitting with Foster, in which he undoubtedly showed abundant telepathy, and satisfied us that he was fundamentally honest, though not always discriminating between his involuntary impressions, and his natural impulses to help out their coherence and interest.

Those who explain these things by denying their existence, were at least excusable thirty, or even twenty, years ago, but since the carefully sifted and authenticated and recorded evidence of recent years, especially that gathered by the Society for Psychical Research, the makers of such explanations simply put themselves in the category of those who, in Schopenhauer's day, denied the telopsis which is now quite generally recognized. He said their attitude should not be called skeptical, but merely ignorant. This brings to mind an excellent very practical friend who read the first number of this REVIEW, and praised it, but said: "Don't fool any more with Psychical Research and Simplified Spelling." We refrained from saying that we had not known that he had ever studied either, and we would not say it here if we were not confident that his aversion from the subject will prevent his reading this.

To return to the manifestations: here are some other cases where Foster identified himself with a personality of his vision. (Bartlett, *op. cit.*, 93.)

From Sacramento *Record*, December 8, 1873:
Foster at one time seized A.'s hand, explaining, "God bless you, my dear boy, my son. I am thankful I at last may speak to you. I want you to know I am your father, who loved you in life and loves you still. I am near to you; a thin veil alone separates us. Good-by. I am your father, Abijah A——"
"Good heavens!" exclaimed A—, "that was my father's name, his tone, his manner, his action."
"And," said Foster, "it was a good influence; he was a man of large veneration."

The above indicates what we will provisionally call Possession. But it is not possession to the extent of complete expulsion of the original consciousness, as in the trances of Home, Moses, and Mrs. Piper.

And which is the following? (Bartlett, *op. cit.*, 103):

[Letter to editor, written Nov. 30, 1874]
New York *Daily Graphic:* . . . He told me he saw the spirit of an old woman close to me, describing most perfectly my grandmother, and repeating: "Resodeda, Resodeda is here; she kisses her grandson." Arising from his chair, Foster embraced and kissed me in the same peculiar way as my grandmother did when alive.

But here the Possession seems complete (Bartlett, *op. cit.*, 140). From the Melbourne *Daily Age:*

Mr. Foster . . . in answer to the question, What he died of? suddenly interrupted, "Stay, this spirit will enter and possess me," and instantaneously his whole body was seized with quivering convulsions, the eyes were introverted, the face swelled, and the mouth and hands were spasmodically agitated. Another change, and there sat before me the counterpart of the figure of my departed friend, stricken down with complete paralysis, just as he was on his death-bed. The transformation was so life-like, if I may use the expression, that I fancied I could detect the very features and physiognomical changes that passed across the visage of my dying friend. The kind of paralysis was exactly represented, with the palsied hand extended to me to shake, as in the case of the original. Mr. Foster recovered himself when I touched it, and he said in reply to one of my companions that he had completely lost his own identity during the fit, and felt like waves of water flowing all over his body, from the crown downwards.

Now for some tentative explanation of these rather unusual proceedings. It is generally known that a hypnotized person will imagine things and do things willed by the hypnotizer, that the sensibility of persons to hypnotism varies, and that persons frequently hypnotized become increasingly susceptible to the influence.

Now what is ordinarily called thought transference has all these symptoms, and the combined indications seem to be that persons who readily experience thought-transference are specially susceptible to hypnotic influence, and get the transferred thought from almost anybody, just as the recognized hypnotic subject gets it from his hypnotizer; and that persons of excessive sensibility, like Foster, Home, Mrs. Holland, Mrs. Piper and mediums generally — the genuine ones, — simply get their impressions hypnotically from their sitters.

But this explanation (?) by no means covers the whole situation. In the first place, it does not cover the vividness and the emotional content often displayed by the sensitive. The sitter is very seldom conscious of anything approaching it. It comes nearer to, in fact almost seems identical with, the frequent vividness and intensity of dreams. But where do dreams come from, whether in sleep, or in a waking "dream state" like that of Foster and many other sensitives? They don't come from any assignable "sitter." This present scribe dreams architecture and bric-a-brac finer than any he ever saw, or than any ever made. Yet he is no architect, or artist of any kind. Where does it all come from?

Dreams, moreover, are filled with memories of forgotten things. Where do they come from? Dreams, too, are by no means devoid of truths not previously known to the dreamer, or, it would sometimes seem, to anybody else. Where do they come from?

Du Prel and his school say they come from a "subliminal self," and Myers picks up the term and spreads it through Anglo-Saxondom. But those queer dreams frequently include persons who oppose the self — argue with it, and even down it, sometimes very much for its information, regeneration and increased stability. That does not seem like a house divided against itself; such an one, we have on very high authority, is apt to fall. James, cornered by his studies in Psychical Research, was inclined to posit a "cosmic reservoir" of all thoughts and feelings that ever existed, and of potentialities of all the thoughts and feelings that are ever going to exist; and under various designations, this cosmic reservoir or, — it seems a better metaphor — the cosmic soul filling it, and dribbling into our little souls, — is a guess of virtually all the philosophers from James back to Plato, and farther still — into the mists.

Moreover this guess is powerfully backed up by another guess: men's speculations have been reaching back for the beginning of mind, until they recognize that a consistent doctrine of evolution finds no beginning, and demands mind as a constituent of the star-dust, and, when it really comes down to the scratch, is unable to imagine matter unassociated with mind. This is admirably expressed by James (Psychology I, 140):

> If evolution is to work smoothly, consciousness in some shape must have been present at the very origin of things. Accordingly we find that the more clear-sighted evolutionary philosophers are beginning to posit it there. Each atom of the nebula, they suppose, must have had an aboriginal atom of consciousness linked with it; and, just as the material atoms have formed bodies and brains by massing themselves together, so the mental atoms, by an analogous process of aggregation, have fused into those larger consciousnesses which we know in ourselves and suppose to exist in our fellow-animals.

That mind is not limited to this connection with matter, we see proved *a posteriori* every day by the appearance from *some* source, it may be only from the memories of survivors, of minds whose accompanying matter is long since dissipated.

Moreover, in life, the matter is changing constantly and entirely — " renewed once in seven years." Yet not only does the "plan," the "idea," of the material man remain the same, but his mind grows for forty, sixty, sometimes eighty years, while the body begins to go down hill at twenty-eight.

Moreover, we never see the sum of matter in the universe increasing, and we do see the sum of mind increasing every time two old thoughts coalesce into a new one, or even every time matter assumes a new form before a perceiving intelligence, not to speak of every time Mr. Bryan or Mr. Roosevelt opens his mouth. We cite these last as the extreme examples of increase — in quantity. We see another sort of increase every time Lord Bryce takes up his pen — the mental treasures of the world are added to — the contents of the cosmic reservoir worthily increased — the cosmic soul greater and more significant than before.

Parts of it farther and farther removed in time and space

seem to be manifesting themselves through the sensitives every day: so the evidence is increasing that none of it has ever been extinguished. The evidence that any part has been, is merely the evidence that it has stopped flowing through each man when he dies. But there are pretty strong indications that it has welled up occasionally through another man, and yet with the original individuality apparently even stronger than it was in the first man — strong enough to make an alien body — Foster's, in the instances quoted, look and act like the original twin body.

Yet while the cosmic soul idea seems very illuminating, and even stimulating, as far as it goes, it soon lands us in the swamp of paradox surrounding all our knowledge. How reconcile it with our individuality — the individuality as dear as life itself — virtually identical with life itself? Well, we can't reconcile them, at least just yet. But we can pull our feet up from the swamp, and make a step that may be towards a reconciliation. Each of our brains is a network of channels through which the cosmic soul flows; and there are no two brains alike — hence our individuality.

But those brains perish. Must individuality be conceded at the cost of our mental continuity? Perhaps not. Grant even the original mind-atom to be a constituent, or inseparable companion, of an original matter-atom (wouldn't it be more up to date to say vibration in each case?), mind, as we have already tried to demonstrate, is not limited, as matter seems to be, to those primitive atoms.

The vague but almost unescapable notion of the cosmic soul also opens up some hint of an explanation of hypnotism, including, of course, thought transference. These vague hints or gleams on the borderland of our knowledge are of course something like what must be such hints of what we know as color, as go through the pigment spots

on the surface of one of the lower creatures. Such as our
limits are, we can express them only in metaphors. But
for that matter all of our language beyond a few material
conceptions, is metaphor from them. Well, on the hypothesis (or facing the fact, if you prefer) of the cosmic
soul, telepathy, hypnotism and all that sort of thing at once
affiliates itself with all our easy conceptions of interflow —
in fluids, gases, sounds, colors, magnetism, electricity,
etc. It's all a vague groping, but there seems something
there which, as we evolve farther, we may get clearer
impressions of.

Well, to return to our sheep. Foster didn't get the clearness and intensity of his visions from the comparatively in-
distinct and placid impressions in his sitters' minds. There
must be something more than hypnotism from the sitter.

Now here is a tougher case which opens a new element
of the problem. It is from *The Autobiography of a Journalist*, by W. J. Stillman, Boston, 1901, Vol. I, pp. 192–4:
Not many of our older readers will require any introduction of Stillman. For the younger ones, we may say that
he was a very eminent art-critic; spent most of the latter
half of his life abroad, being part of the time our consul at
Crete; wrote a history of the Cretan Rebellion, and other
books; and was a regular correspondent of *The Nation*,
and of *The London Times*. We never knew his veracity
questioned.

Here is the story:

A "spiritual medium," Miss A. was "under the control" of Stillman's dead cousin "Harvey." The "possession" seems to have been throughout free from trance.
Stillman says:

I asked Harvey if he had seen old Turner, the landscape
painter, since his death, which had taken place not very long
before. The reply was "Yes," and I then asked what he was
doing, the reply being a pantomime of painting. I then asked
if Harvey could bring Turner there, to which the reply was,
"I do not know; I will go and see," upon which Miss A. said,

"This influence [Harvey's. Editor] is going away — it is gone";
and after a short pause added, "There is another influence coming, in that direction," pointing over her left shoulder. "I don't
like it," and she shuddered slightly, but presently sat up in her
chair with a most extraordinary personation of the old painter
in manner, in the look out from under the brow, and the pose of
the head. It was as if the ghost of Turner, as I had seen him
at Griffiths's, sat in the chair, and it made my flesh creep to the
very tips of my fingers, as if a spirit sat before me. Miss A.
exclaimed, "This influence has taken complete possession of me,
as none of the others did. I am obliged to do what it wants me
to." I asked if Turner would write his name for me, to which
she replied by a sharp, decided negative sign. I then asked if
he would give me some advice about my painting, remembering
Turner's kindly invitation and manner when I saw him. This
proposition was met by the same decided negative, accompanied by the fixed and sardonic stare which the girl had put on
at the coming of the new influence. This disconcerted me, and
I then explained to my brother what had been going on, as, the
questions being mental, he had no clue to the pantomime. I
said that as an influence which purported to be Turner was
present, and refused to answer any questions, I supposed there
was nothing more to be done.

But Miss A. still sat unmoved and helpless, so we waited.
Presently she remarked that the influence wanted her to do
something she knew not what, only that she had to get up and
go across the room, which she did with the feeble step of an
old man. She crossed the room and took down from the wall
a colored French lithograph, and, coming to me, laid it on the
table before me, and by gesture called my attention to it. She
then went through the pantomime of stretching a sheet of
paper on a drawing-board, then that of sharpening a lead pencil,
following it up by tracing the outlines of the subject in the
lithograph. Then followed in similar pantomime the choosing
of a water-color pencil, noting carefully the necessary fineness of
the point, and then the washing-in of a drawing, broadly.
Miss A. seemed much amused by all this, but as she knew nothing of drawing she understood nothing of it. Then with the
pencil and her pocket handkerchief she began taking out the
lights, "rubbing-out," as the technical term is. This seemed to
me so contrary to what I conceived to be the execution of
Turner that I interrupted with the question, "Do you mean to
say that Turner rubbed out his lights?" to which she gave the

affirmative sign. I asked further if in a drawing which I then had in my mind, the well-known " Llanthony Abbey," the central passage of sunlight and shadow through rain was done in that way, and she again gave the affirmative reply, emphatically. I was so firmly convinced to the contrary that I was now persuaded that there was a simulation of personality, such as was generally the case with the public mediums, and I said to my brother, who had not heard any of my questions [He says above that they were mental. Ed.] that this was another humbug, and then repeated what had passed, saying that Turner could not have worked in that way.

Six weeks later I sailed for England, and, on arriving in London, I went at once to see Ruskin, and told him the whole story. He declared the contrariness manifested by the medium to be entirely characteristic of Turner, and had the drawing in question down for examination. We scrutinized it closely, and both recognized beyond dispute that the drawing had been executed in the way that Miss A. indicated. Ruskin advised me to send an account of the affair to the *Cornhill*, which I did; but it was rejected, as might have been expected in the state of public opinion at that time, and I can easily imagine Thackeray putting it into the basket in a rage.

I offer no interpretation of the facts which I have here recorded, but I have no hesitation in saying that they completed and fixed my conviction of the existence of invisible and independent intelligences to which the phenomena were due.

To me they seem perhaps the nearest I have come to a communication of something not known to any earthly intelligence, and yet it *may* have been so known.

When manifestations of this general nature first attracted systematic study, they were attributed, as already stated, to telepathy from the sitter. Stillman knew Turner, and as Stillman had an artist's vividness of impression, the sensitive could have got from him a pretty good idea of Turner, and have acted it out. But how about the innumerable cases not unlike the Foster cases quoted, where sensitives get impressions much more vivid than the sitter appears capable of holding, and act them out with dramatic verisimilitude of which the sitter is absolutely incapable; and how about the innumerable cases where the sensitive gets impressions and memories which the sitter never had?

These have been accounted for as being picked up from absent persons, by a kind of wireless telegraphy, for which we have ventured, with the assistance of a couple of Grecian friends, to suggest the name teloteropathy.

Well! In this Turner case, *somebody* somewhere, *may* have known what neither the sensitive nor Stillman knew of Turner's method of work, and the sensitive's wireless *may* have picked up all those detailed impressions and dramatic impressions of them from that unknown *somebody*. But is that any easier to swallow than that old Turner himself was the somebody — that his share of the cosmic soul, or a sufficient portion of his share, flowed into or hypnotized the sensitive, and made her act as she did?

And now let us go on to some of the developments of these phenomena manifested by Mrs. Piper. Unlike the manifestations already given, hers are not from waking dreams, but from dreams in trance. Moreover, so far the sensitives have manifested impressions of but one personality at a time, but Mrs. Piper has manifested one by speech and, at the same time, another by writing, the expressions of the two apparent personalities progressing independently, with full coherence and consistency. Moreover, in many of her trances she seemed as if surrounded by a crowd of persons endeavoring, with different degrees of success, to express themselves through her, or she endeavoring to express them. All this of course, is counter to the impression prevailing during the early years of her career, that her soul had left her body, and the body was "possessed" by a postcarnate soul expressing itself through her. The present aspect of the facts is more as if she had impressions such as we all have in dreams, of any number of personalities around her. Some of her typical manifestations may give still further indications of interflowing of mental impressions.

The George "Pelham" famous in the annals of Psychical Research was a friend of the present writer, and his alleged postcarnate self appeared through Mrs. Piper to the following effect.   There could not have been anything cooked up about it; it was my first and only sitting with Mrs. Piper, who knew nothing about me or my friends. In fact, the old theories of some form of fraud, now, in the light of the vast accumulation of later knowledge, seem ridiculous.   However the phenomena have to be explained, that explanatiou is out of date.

G. P. speaks. — "A" [assumed initial. Ed.] "is in a critical state. He's not himself now. He's terribly depressed." Sitter — "Can you tell anything [more] about A?" G. P. — "Friend of yours in body." S. — "Of Hodgson?" [Who was present. This question and the following were mild "tests": I knew the man well. Ed.] G. P. — "Yes." S. — "Did I ever know him?" G. P. — "Yes, you knew him very well. You're connected with him." S. — "Through whom?" G. P. — "Do you know any B——?" [assumed initial. Ed.] S. — "Are A. and I connected through B?" G. P. — "Write to B. and he'll tell you all about it."

It turned out later that A. actually was low in his mind, and that B., whom nobody present knew, *was* trying to get him occupation.   I knew nothing whatever about any such circumstances, nor did Hodgson.   To suppose that Mrs. Piper did, would be absurd.   *But* they were known to other minds "in the body," and hence the medium's utterance of them is open to the interpretation of teloteropathy.   Similar instances are not rare, but the interpretation of teloteropathy seems to be rapidly losing probability.

In this instance, I *was* "connected with" B., but only so far as he had become a professor at Yale long after my graduation: I did not know him personally.   But my intimate connection with A. was not only direct, but through several persons intimate with us both, including G. P. when living.   Mere telepathy, certainly mere telepathy from my mind, would have "spotted" some one of these connections much more readily than the alleged one with B., which was hardly a connection at all.

The *simplest* solution for the whole business, though perhaps not the most "scientific," or even probable, is that the spirit of G. P. was troubled about A. and habitually thinking of me at the University Club as a Yale man, on my turning up at the séance, was reminded of the solution of A.'s troubles proposed through B., and wanted me to help.

And now to this rather commonplace manifestation comes an interesting sequel illustrating the reach of mind spoken of at the outset. Out of a perfectly clear sky came to me in New York on April 8, 1894, the message from G. P., to look out for A., who was low in his mind, and that B. was trying to get a place for him. On May 29th, Hodgson writes me as follows, showing that the same thing had come up *through the heteromatic writing of A.'s wife at Granada in Spain*, and meant nothing to her or to A.

———— You may be interested in the inclosed. Keep private. [This injunction is of course outlawed by time, but I still conceal the names of the parties. Ed.] and please return. I am writing from my den, and haven't copy of your sitting at hand. But I remember that something was said at your sitting *re* B. and A.

(Copy of Enclosure.)

"Granada, May 6, 1894.

"Dear H. [odgson]:

"Those suggestions from Geo. that I write to B. prove interesting in the light of what I first learned here: that he had been lamenting my silence and had been urging me to a place as ———— [at] Yale where he is. I had no notion of this move on his part till four days ago when I received a letter telling me. Of course nothing came of it, but anything less known than that cannot be imagined. The message came once earlier thro' [his wife. Ed.] to whom George wrote it [heteromatically. Ed.]. George [in life. Ed.] never heard of B. nor saw him, nor did we ever speak of B. to Geo. or Phinuit. . . . Of course I don't want mention made of the effort of B. to get me the Yale place. What

Geo. said was to write to B.; he is a good friend of yours [*i. e.*, of A.   Ed.]

"All send kind messages.   Yrs. ever.

"A——."

Being intensely busy, and not as much interested in the matter as later experiences have made me, I did not at the moment catch the full purport of Hodgson's letter, or write him till June 5th, and did not keep any copy that I can find of my letter.   He wrote me on the 8th:

"Thanks for yours of June 5th, with return of A.'s letter.   I knew nothing whatever of the circumstances connected with B., neither, so far as I can tell by cross-questioning, did Mrs. Piper."

And I, the present scribe, certainly did not.   A. did not.   B. alone did, with whatever persons he may have approached on the matter, and Mrs. Piper had presumably never seen one of the group.   So where did Mrs. Piper and Mrs. A. get it?   The only answers that seem possible are that she and Mrs. A. either got it teloteropathically from one of those absent, or that the postcarnate George Pelham himself wrote her about it, and also told me of it through Mrs. Piper's organism in New York, and four days later was working it into a cross-correspondence through Mrs. A. in Spain.   At first blush the latter seems easier; and I am not sure but that it does on reflection.

Hodgson's letter continues:

"I never knew of any B. connected with Yale.   When B. was first mentioned at the sitting, I had a vague notion that some B. or other had gone to England or France as United States consul.   I also knew the name of —— —— B. [a celebrated author.   Ed.], and met her after she became Mrs. C. two or three years ago.

"On questioning Mrs. Piper, which I did by referring to books first, I found that she remembered the name of —— —— B. when I mentioned it, and connected it in some way with [a certain book.   Ed.], which was widely circulated some years ago. This was the only B. that she seemed to know anything about. . . .

"Yours sincerely,

"R. Hodgson."

Now does not all this give a strong impression of an interflow among minds all over — in New York (the place of the sitting), Granada (Mrs. A.'s place of sojourn), Boston (A.'s home), New Haven (B.'s home), and the universe in general (G. P.'s apparent home) — of an interflow free from the limitations of time and space, and independent of all means of communication known to us?

This impression tends to grow deeper with farther study. We have had a cross-correspondence between two incarnate intelligences and one apparently postcarnate. Mr. Piddington has unearthed a cross-correspondence between one apparently postcarnate intelligence and seven "living" ones.

Perhaps the significance of cross-correspondences justifies a little more specific treatment, and even the repetition of a paragraph from the first number of this REVIEW. The topic has lately attracted more attention from the S. P. R. than any other.

If Mrs. Verrall in London and Mrs. Holland in India both, at about the same time, write heteromatically about a subject that they both understand, that is probably coincidence; but if both write about it when but one of them understands it, that is probably teloteropathy; and if both write about it when neither understands it, and each of their respective writings is apparently nonsense, but both make sense when put together, the only obvious hypothesis is that both were inspired by a third mind.

There are many instances of strict cross-correspondence of this type. The one we have given was perhaps more impressive than a stricter one would be apt to be.

Accounts of sittings generally suggest apparent intercommunication independent of time and space between postcarnate intelligences: often the controls say that they will go and find other controls, and, generally, after a short interval, the new control manifests. It is impossible to read many of the accounts, whether one regards them as fictitious or not, without getting an impression — like that given by a good story-teller, if you please, of a life outside this one, among a host of personalities who communicate freely with each other and, through difficulties, with us. The nature of the communication we have already tried to express by "interflow." But all metaphors are weak beside the impression of the Cosmic Soul that has been brought to most of those who have persistently studied the phenomena, as to nearly all those who have speculated *a priori* on the nature of mind.

Judged by the foregoing specimens, the literature of what we are provisionally considering as hypnotic telepathy would not be regarded as very cheerful. As a whole, however, the pictures it presents from an alleged postcarnate life, are cheerful, and some of them very attractive.

Below are some from an alleged George Eliot. They are from notes of Piper sittings kindly placed at our disposal by Professor Newbold.

To my taste the matter savors *very* little of the reputed author. And yet assuming for the moment that our great authors survive in a fuller life, presumably they would have to communicate under very embarrassing conditions: for not only would they have to cramp themselves to produce work comprehensible here, but the System of Things would have to limit them, lest their competition should upset the whole system of our literary development, or rather would have involved a different one from the beginning.

My first reading of the alleged George Eliot matter inclined me to scout it entirely. It is certainly not in all particulars what that great soul would have sent from a better world if she had been permitted to communicate anything more profound than we have been left to find out for ourselves, or even if she had had the commonplace chance to revise her manuscript. But on reflection I realized that, although the matter came through Mrs. Piper, it could not have come *from* her, wherever it came from; and that if George Eliot were communicating tidings naturally within our comprehension, and merely descriptive of superficial experience as distinct from reflection, and were communicating, through a poor telephone, words to be recorded by an indifferent scribe, this material would not seem absolutely incongruous with its alleged source, and to a reader knowing that the stuff claimed to be hers, might possibly suggest the weakest possible dilution or reflection of her. Yet in ways which I have no space for, it abounds in the sort of anthropomorphism that might be expected from the average medium or average sitter, but not from George Eliot.

And now, since writing the last paragraph and going through the material half a dozen times more, I have about concluded, or perhaps worked myself up to the conclusion, that if a judicious blue pencil were to take from it what could be attributed to imperfect means of communication, and what could be considered as having slopped over from the medium, there would be a pretty substantial and not unbeautiful residuum which might, without straining anything, be taken for a description by George Eliot, of the heaven she would find if, as begins to seem possible, she and the rest of us, have or are to have heavens to suit our respective tastes. But what would have to be taken out is often ludicrously incongruous with George Eliot, and taking it out would certainly be open to serious question.

Yet whatever may be the qualities, merits, or demerits of this. "George Eliot" matter, what character it has is its own, and different materially from any I have seen recorded from any other control. What is vastly more important, despite the lapses in knowledge, taste, and

style, which negative its being the unmodified production
of George Eliot, it nevertheless presents, *me judice*, the
most reasonable, suggestive, and attractive pictures of a
life beyond bodily death that I know of: it is not a reflection of previous mythologies, it is congruous with the
tastes of what we now consider rational beings, and might
well fill their desires; and it *tallies with our experiences —*
in dreams. Yet it is not a great feat of imagination; but
in recent times no great genius has attacked the subject,
and George Eliot would not have been expected to devote
her imagination to it, which raises a slight presumption
that what is told is really told by her from experience.

If I had to venture a guess as to how it came into existence, I should guess that somebody within range, hardly
Mrs. Piper herself, had been reading George Eliot, or
about George Eliot, and the musk-melon pollen had affected the cucumbers. Professor Newbold, for instance,
was entirely able involuntarily to create and telepath the
stories, and better shaped ones. Some real George Eliot
influence may have flowed in too, but on that my judgment
is in suspense.

"George Eliot" comes in abruptly to Hodgson, on
February 26, 1897. After a few preliminaries, in response
to a remark of Hodgson's on her dislike of and disbelief
in spiritism, she says:

" . . . You may have noted the anxiety of such as I to return and enlighten your fellow men. It is more especially confined to unbelievers before their departure to this life."

This remark and the persistent efforts of the alleged
G. P. who, living, was a thorough skeptic, would seem
strongly "evidential."

March 5, 1897.   *Hodgson sitting.*
[G. E. writes:] "Do you remember me well? . . . I had a
sad life in many ways, yet in others I was happy, yet I have
never known what real happiness was until I came here. . . .
I was an unbeliever, in fact almost an agnostic when I left my

body, but when I awoke and found myself alive in another form superior in quality, that is, my body less gross and heavy, with no pangs of remorse, no struggling to hold on to the material body, I found it had all been a dream. . . ." R. H.: "That was your first experience?" G. E.: " . . . The moment I had been removed from my body I found at once I had been thoroughly mistaken in my conjectures. I looked back upon my whole life in one instant. Every thought, word, or action which I had ever experienced passed through my mind like a wonderful panorama as it were before my vision. You cannot begin to imagine anything so real and extraordinary as this first awakening. . . . I awoke in a realm of golden light. I heard the voices of friends who had gone before calling to me to follow them. At the moment the thrill of joy was so intense I was like one standing spellbound before a beautiful panorama. The music which filled my soul was like a tremendous symphony. I had never heard nor dreamed of anything half so beautiful. . . .

"Another thing which seemed to me beautiful was the tranquillity of everyone. You will perhaps remember that I had left a state where no one ever knew what tranquillity meant."

March 13, 1807: "I was speaking about the songs of our birds. Then the birds seemed to pass beyond my vision, and I longed for music of other kinds. . . . When, to my surprise, my desires were filled. . . . Just before me sat the most beautiful bevy of young girls that eyes ever rested upon. Some playing stringed instruments, others that sounded and looked like silver bugles, but they were all in harmony, and I must truly confess that I never heard such strains of music before. No mortal mind can possibly realize anything like it. It was not only in this one thing that my desires were filled, but in all things accordingly. I had not one desire, but that it was filled without any apparent act of myself.

"I longed to see gardens and trees, flowers, etc. I no sooner had the desire than they appeared. . . . Such beautiful flowers no human eye ever gazed upon. It was simply indescribable, yet everything was real. . . . I walked and moved along as easily as a fly would pass through a ray of sunlight in your world. I had no weight, nothing cumbersome, nothing. . . . I passed along through this garden, meeting millions of friends. As they were all friendly to me, each and every one seemed to be my friend. . . . I then thought of different friends I had once known, and my desire was to meet some one of them, when like every other thought or desire that I had expressed, the friend of whom I thought instantly appeared."

How much all this is like dreams!

March 27, 1897. (A good deal of confusion, out of which appears) "He will insist upon calling me Miss, but let him if he wishes. I am very much Mrs. Never mind so long as it suits him. . . .

"I have a desire for reading, when instantly my whole surrounding is literally filled with books of all kinds and by many different authors. . . . When I touched a book and desired to meet its author, if he or she were in our world, he or she would instantly appear. [Is this purely incidental reiterated claim for female authors, by one of them, 'evidential,' or was Mrs. Piper ingenious enough to invent it? Ed.] . . . .

The change of the instrument below is a specially dream-like touch.

March 30, 1897. "I wished to see and realize that some of the mortal world's great musicians really existed, and asked to be visited by some one or more of them. When this was expressed, instantly several appeared before me, and Rubinstein stood before me playing upon an instrument like a harp at first. Then the instrument was changed and a piano appeared and he played upon it with the most delightful ease and grace of manner. While he was playing the whole atmosphere was filled with his strains of music."

She wanted to see Rembrandt, and he came, with a quantity of pictures. She wanted a symphony, and an orchestra "of some thirty musicians" at once appeared and gave her several, which she enjoyed to the full.

Now George Eliot was a remarkably good musician. If she wanted an orchestra, she would have wanted at least sixty, and probably more than a hundred. Perhaps they do these things with more limited resources in Heaven? Such an incongruity as this, and the inane dilution of the writing (which of course does not appear at its worst in the selected passages) make a genuine George Eliot control hard to predicate, and yet this control, like virtually every other one, is an individuality, and is less unlike

George Eliot than is any other control I know. Will difficulties of communication or any other *tertium quid*, make up the difference? I first read the record with repulsion, and now find in it some elements of attraction.

Do you care for a little more? She wanted to see "angels," and gives a very pretty picture of an experience with a bevy of children. Telepathy from the sitter will hardly account for the following, especially the strange turn at the end, which is signally dreamlike.

"I being fond, very fond of writers of ancient history, etc., felt a strong desire to see Dante, Aristotle and several others. Shakespeare if such a spirit existed. [An odd bunch of 'writers of ancient history'! Ed.] As I stood thinking of him a spirit instantly appeared who speaking said 'I am Bacon.' . . . As Bacon neared me he began to speak and quoted to me the following words 'You have questioned my reality. Question it no more. I am Shakespeare.'"

June 4, 1897. ". . . Speak to me for a moment and if you have anything to say in the nature of poetry or prose would you kindly recite a line or two to me. It will give me strength to remain longer than I could otherwise do. [R. H. recites a poem of Dowden's beginning,

'I said I will find God and forth I went

To seek him in the clearness of the sky,' etc. Excitement.] G. E.: 'I will go and see G. and return presently (R. H.: Who says that?) I do. (R. H.: I do not understand what you mean by G.) I do. My husband. Do you not know I had a husband? (R. H.: Do you mean by G. Mr. George Henry Lewes?) [Hand is writing Lewes while I am saying George Henry] Lewes. Yes I do. Oh I am so happy. And when I did not mistake altogether my deeds I am more *happy than tongue can utter*.

As bearing on her feeling for Lewes not many months after his death, the foregoing does not correspond with some widely credited but unpublished allegations.

Now does not all this read as if Mrs. Piper were dreaming of George Eliot, just as any of us might dream? Its quality seems as if it might be a transcript of one of my own dreams, with the important exceptions that the dreamer wrote it all out, and that it is made up from a series of dreams, coming up at intervals for about six months, and apparently only when Hodgson was present, though there are records of George Eliot appearing to other sitters at other seances.

We have, then, groped our way to a vague notion of a dream-life on the part of certain sensitives, which seems to participate in another life, in some ways similar, that is led by intelligences who have passed beyond the body.

We are not saying that this interpretation of the phenomena is the correct one: on the contrary we are constantly haunted by a suspicion that any day it may be exploded by some new discovery. But we do say, with considerable confidence, that of all the interpretations yet offered — even including the pervasive one that "the little boy lied," it surpasses all the others in the portion of the facts that it fits, and in the weight attached to it by the most capable students — even by James, who, however, did not accept it as established, though he gave many indications that he felt himself likely to. Myers definitely accepted it, not from the impressions of the sensitives, but from having them capped by a veridical impression of his own. Through the church service one Sunday morning, he felt an inner voice assuring him: "Your friend is still with you." Later he found that Gurney, with whom he had a manifestation-pact, had died the night before. We are not aware that Myers ever published this, but he told it to the present writer and presumably to others. The convictions of Hodgson and Sir Oliver Lodge were interpretations of the phenomena of the sensitives, though Hodgson, it is now known, was probably mainly influenced by communications from the alleged postcarnate soul of all possible ones most dear to him.

But to return to the sensitives. They seem to be somnambulists who talk out and write out what they see and hear in their dreams. What they see, and consequently what they say, is a good deal of a jumble. They see and hear persons they never saw before. Sometimes they identify themselves more or less with these personalities. Mrs. Piper nearly always does. Those others say many things, and very often correct things, unknown to sensitives, to anybody present, or to anybody else that can be found. Rather unusual among ordinary dreamers, but by no means unprecedented. But from here on the experiences of the sensitives are more and more unusual.

Some of the people Mrs. Piper (I speak of her as the representative of a class) never saw before, and of whom she never saw portraits, she identifies from photographs. Very few people have done that: perhaps very few have had the chance. There have been many times when I am sure I could, if photographs had been presented.

Her personalities and those of many sensitives are nearly always "dead" friends, not of the sensitives, but of the sitters, and abound in indications of genuineness in scope and accuracy of memory, in distinctness of in-dividual recollections and characteristics, and in all the dramatic indications that go to demonstrate personalities. She sees and hears these personalities again and again, and *keeps them distinct* in feature and character.

Now what do we mean by personalities? Is one, after all, anything more or less than an individualized aggregate of cosmic vibrations, physical and psychical, with the power of producing on us certain impressions. You and I know our friends as such aggregates, and nothing more.

And what do we mean by discarnate personalities? In most minds, the first answer will probably bear a pretty close resemblance to Fra Angelico's angels, and very nice angels they are! But to some of the more prosy minds that have thought on the subject in the light of the best and fullest information, or misinformation, probably the answer will be more like this: A personality, incarnate or postcarnate, in the last analysis, is a manifestation of the Cosmic Soul. From that the raw material is supplied

with the star dust, and later, through our senses, from
the earliest reactions of our protozoic ancestors, up to
our dreams; and the material is worked up into each personality through reactions with the environment. Thus
it becomes an aggregate of capacities to impress another
personality with certain sensations, ideas, emotions. As
already said, the incarnate personality impresses us thru
certain vibrations. But after that portion of the vibrations constituting "the body" disappears, there still
abides somewhere the capacity of impressing us, at least
in the dream life. Perhaps it abides only in the memory
of survivors, and gets into our dreams telepathically,
though that is losing probability every day; and, with our
anthropomorphic habits, we want to know "where" this
capacity to impress us abides. The thinkers generally
say: In the Cosmic reservoir, which I would rather express as the psychic ocean, boundless, fathomless, throb-
bing eternally. It seems to be made up of the original
mind-potential plus all thoughts and feelings that have
ever been. And into this ocean seem to be constantly
passing those currents that we know as individualities, that can each influence, and even intermingle with,
other individualities, here as well as there: for here really
is there. While each does this, it still retains its own individuality. This is, of course, a vague string of guesses
venturing outward from the borderland of our knowledge.
It may be a little clearer, the more we bear in mind that
the apparent influencings and interminglings seem to be
telepathic.

Now apparently among the accomplishments of a
personality, does not *necessarily* inhere that of depressing
a scale x pounds: for when that capacity is entirely absent, from the apparent personalities who visit us in the
dream state, they can impress us in every other way, even
to all the reciprocities of sex. But for some reasons not
yet understood, with ordinary dreamers these impressions
are not as congruous, persistent, recurrent, or regulable in

the dream life as in the waking life. But with Mrs. Piper, Hodgson after his death, and especially G. P. and others, were about as persistent and consistent associates as anybody living, barring the fact that they could not show themselves over an hour or two at a time, which was the limit of the medium's psychokinetic power, on which their manifestations depended. But that these personalities are not in time to be evolved so that they will be more permanent and consistent with dreamers generally, would be a contradiction to at least some of the implications of evolution.

Accepting provisionally the identity of a postcarnate life with the life indicated in dreams, are there any further indications of its nature? There are some, which may lend some slight confirmation to the theory of identity.

It seems to show itself not only in the visions of the sensitives, but in the dream life of all of us. If Mrs. Piper's dream state (I name her only as a type) is really one of communication with souls who have passed into a new life, dream states generally may not extravagantly be supposed to be foretastes of that life. And so far as concerns their desirability, why should they not be? Our ordinary dreams are, like the dreams of the sensitives, superior to time, space, matter and force — to all the trammels of our waking environment and powers. In dreams we experience unlimited histories, and pass over unlimited spaces, in an instant; see, hear, feel, touch, taste, smell, enjoy unlimited things; walk, swim, fly, change things, with unlimited ease; do things with unlimited power; make what we will — music, poetry, objects of art, situations, dramas, with unlimited faculty, and enjoy unlimited society. Unless we have eaten too much, or otherwise got ourselves out of order in the waking life, in the dream life we seldom if ever know what it is to be too late for anything, or too far from anything; we freely fall from chimneys or precipices, and I suppose it will soon be aeroplanes, with no worse consequences than comfortably waking up into the everyday world; we sometimes solve the problems which baffle us here; we see more beautiful things than we see here; and, far above all, we resume the ties that are broken here.

The indications seem to be that if we ever get the hang of that life, we can have pretty much what we like, and eliminate what we don't like — continue what we enjoy, and stop what we suffer — find no bars to congeniality, or compulsion to boredom. To good dreamers it is unnecessary to offer proof of any of these assertions, and to prove them to others is impossible.

The dream life contains so much more beauty, so much fuller emotion, and such wider reaches than the waking life, that one is tempted to regard it as the real life, to which the waking life is somehow a necessary preliminary. So orthodox believers regard the life after death as the real life: yet most of their hopes regarding that life — even the strongest hope of rejoining lost loved ones — are realized here during the brief throbs of the dream life.

There seems to be no happiness from association in our ordinary life which is not obtainable, by some people at least, from association in the dream life. And as this appears to exist between incarnate A and postcarnate B, there is at least a suggestion that it may exist between postcarnate A and postcarnate B, and to a degree vastly more clear and abiding than during the present discrepancy between the incarnate and postcarnate conditions? This of course assumes, that B's appearance in A's dream life, just as he appeared on earth (though, as I know to be the case, sometimes wiser, healthier, jollier, and more lovable generally), is something more than a mild attack of dyspepsia on the part of A.

Dreams do not seem to abound in work, and are often said not to abound in morality, but I know that they sometimes do — in morality higher than any attainable in our waking life. Certainly the scant vague indications from the dream suggestions of a future life do not necessarily preclude abundant work and morality, any more than work and sundry self-denials are precluded on a holiday because one does not happen to perform them. Moreover, the hoped-for future conditions may not contain the necessities for either labor or self-restraint that present conditions do: they may not be the same dangers there as here in the *dolce far niente*, or in Platonic friendships.

Men are not consistent in their attitude regarding dreams. They admit the dream state to be ideal — constantly use such expressions as "A dream of loveliness," "Happier than I could even dream," "Surpasses my fondest dreams," and yet on the other hand they call its experience "but the baseless vision of a dream." What do they mean by "baseless"? Certainly it is not lack of vividness or emotional intensity. It is probably the lack of duration in the happy experiences, and of the possibility of remembering them, and, still more, of enjoying similar ones at will. Yet the sensitives do both in recurrent instalments of the dream life, and like the rest of us, through the intervening waking periods, after the first hour or so, generally know nothing of the dreams. It is not vividness of the dream life itself that is lacking, but vividness in our memories of it. James defines our waking personality as the stream of consciousness: the dream life gives no such stream. To-night does not continue last night as to-day continues yesterday. The dream life is not like a stream, but more like a series, though hardly integral enough to be a series, of disconnected pools, many of them perhaps more enchanting than any parts of the waking stream, but not, like that stream, an organic whole with motion toward definite results, and power to attain them. But suppose the dream life continues after the body's death, and under direction toward definite ends, at least so far as the waking life is, and still free from the tram-

mels of the waking life — suppose us to have at least as
much power to secure its joys and avoid its terrors as we
have regarding those of the waking life; and with all the
old intimacies which it spasmodically restores, restored
permanently, and with the discipline of separation to make
them nearer perfect. What more can we manage to want?

The suggestion has come to more than one student,
that when we enter into life — as spermatazoa, or star
dust if you please — we enter into the eternal life, but
that the physical conditions essential to our development
into appreciating it, are a sort of veil between it and our
consciousness. In our waking life we know it only through
the veil; but when in sleep or trance, the material environment is removed from consciousness, the veil becomes
that much thinner, and we get better glimpses of the
transcendent reality.

Does it not seem then as if, in dreams, we enter upon
our closer relation with the hyper-phenomenal mind? All
sorts of things seem to be in it, from the veriest trifles
and absurdities up to the highest things our minds can
receive, and presumably an infinity of things higher still.
They appear to flow into us in all sorts of ways, presumably depending upon the condition of the nerve apparatus
through which they flow. If that is out of gear from any
disorder or injury, what it receives is not only trifling,
but often grotesque and painful; while if it is in good estate, it often receives things far surpassing in beauty and
wisdom those of our waking phenomenal world.

Apparently every dreamer is a medium for this flow,
but dreamers vary immensely in their capacity to receive
it — from Hodge, who dreams only when he has eaten
too much, or Professor Gradgrind who never dreams at
all, up to Mrs. Thompson and Mrs. Piper.

As oft remarked, dreams generally are nonsense, but
some dreams, or parts of some dreams, are perhaps the
most significant things we know. Each vision, waking or
sleeping, must have a cause, and as an expression of that

cause, must be veridical. On the one hand, the cause of a trivial dream is generally too trivial to be ascertained: it may be too much lobster, or impaired circulation or respiration; while on the other hand (and here the paradox seems to be explained), the cause of an important dream must, *ex vi termini*, be some important event. But important events are rare, and therefore significant dreams are rare; while trivial events are frequent, and therefore trivial dreams are frequent.

The important and rare event *may* be such a conjunction of circumstances and temperaments as makes it possible for a postcarnate intelligence, assuming the existence of such, to communicate with an incarnate one. That such apparent communications are rare tends to indicate their genuineness.

Now to develop a little farther the time-honored hypothesis of a cosmic soul as explaining dreams, and supported by them.

Admit, provisionally at least, that the medium is merely an extraordinary dreamer. Does a man do his own dreaming, or is it done for him? Does a man do his own digesting, circulating, assimilating, or is it done for him? If he does not do these things himself, who does? About the physical functions through the sympathetic nerve, we answer unhesitatingly: the cosmic force. How, then, about the psychic functions? Are they done by the cosmic psyche?

Like respiration, they are partly under our control, but that does not affect the problem. Who runs them when we do not run them, even when we try to stop them that we may get to sleep? Even when, after they have yielded to our entreaties to stop, and we are asleep, they begin going again — without our will. The only probability I can make out is that our thinking is run by a power not ourselves, as much as our other partly involuntary functions.

To hold that a man does his own dreaming — that it is done by a secondary layer of his own consciousness — is to hold that we are made up of layers of consciousness, of which the poorest layer is that of what we call our waking life, and the better layers are at our service only in our dreams — that when a man is asleep or mad he can solve problems, compose music, create pictures, to which, when awake and in his sober senses, and in a condition to profit by his work, and give profit from it, he is inadequate.

Nay more, the theory claims that a man's working consciousness — his self — the only self known to him or the world, will hold and shape his life by a set of convictions which, in sleep, he will *himself* prove wrong, and thereby revolutionize his philosophy and his entire life. Wouldn't it be more reasonable to attribute all such results — the solutions of the problems, the music, the pictures, the corrections of the errors — to a power outside himself?

I cannot believe that there's anything in my individual consciousness which my experience or that of my ancestors has not placed there — in raw material at least; or that in working up that raw material *I* can exert any genius in my sometimes chaotic dreams that I cannot exert in my systematized waking hours. All the people I meet and talk with in my dreams *may* have been met and talked with by me or my forebears, though I don't believe it; but the works of art I see have not been known to me or my ancestors or any other mortal; nor have I any sign of the genius to combine whatever elements of them I may have seen, into any such designs. And when in dreams *other* persons tell me things contrary to my firmest convictions, in which things I later discover germs of most important workable truth, the persons who tell me that, and who are different from me as far as fairly decent persons can differ from each other, are certainly not, as the good Du Prel would have us believe, myself. All these things are not figments of *my* mind—if they are figments of a mind, it's a mind bigger than mine. The biggest claim I can make, or assent to anybody else making, is that my mind is telepathically receptive of the product of that greater mind.

Here are some farther evidences of the greater mind, given by Lombroso (*After Death, What?*, 320f.):

"It is well known that in his dreams Goethe solved many weighty scientific problems and put into words many most beautiful verses. So also La Fontaine (*The Fable of Pleasures*) and Coleridge and Voltaire. Bernard Palissy had in a dream the inspiration for one of his most beautiful ceramic pieces. . . .

Holde composed while in a dream *La Phantasie*, which reflects in its harmony its origin; and Nodier created *Lydia*, and at the same time a whole theory on the future of dreaming. Condillac in dream finished a lecture interrupted the evening before. Kruger, Corda, and Maignan solved in dreams mathematical problems and theorems. Robert Louis Stevenson, in his *Chapters on Dreams*, confesses that portions of his most original novels were composed in the dreaming state. Tartini had while dreaming one of his most portentous musical inspirations. He saw a spectral form approaching him. It is Beelzebub in person. He holds a magic violin in his hands, and the sonata begins. It is a divine adagio, melancholy-sweet, a lament, a dizzy succession of rapid and intense notes. Tartini rouses himself, leaps out of bed, seizes his violin, and reproduces all that he had heard played in his sleep. He names it the *Sonata del Diavolo*, . . .

Giovanni Dupré got in a dream the conception of his very beautiful *Pietà*. One sultry summer day Dupré was lying on a divan thinking hard on what kind of pose he should choose for the Christ. He fell asleep, and in dream he saw the entire group at last complete, with Christ in the very pose he had been aspiring to conceive, but which his mind had not succeeded in completely realizing.

It is a quite frequent experience that a person perplexed by a problem at night finds it solved on waking in the morning. Efforts to remember, which are unsuccessful before going to sleep, on waking are often found accomplished.

A dream is a work of genius, and in many respects, perhaps most, especially in vividness of imagination, the best
example we have. It is the most spontaneous, constructed
with the least effort from fewest materials, the least
restrained, and often immeasurably surpassing all works
of waking genius in the same department. A genius gets
a trifling hint, and being inspired by the gods (anthropomorphic for: flowed in upon by the cosmic soul?) builds
out of the hint a poem or a drama or a symphony. You
and I build dreams surpassing the poem or the drama or
the symphony, but our friends Dryasdust and Myopia
inquire into our experiences, and sometimes find a little
hint on which a dream was built, and then all dreams are
demonstrated things unworthy of serious consideration.
Is it not a more rational view that the fact that the soul
can in the dream state elaborate so much from so little,
indicates it to be then already in a life which has no
limits?

Havelock Ellis, in his *World of Dreams*, says (p. 229):

Our eyes close, our muscles grow slack, the reins fall from
our hands. But it sometimes happens that the horse knows the
road home even better than we know it ourselves.

He puts "the horse" outside of the dreamer plainly
enough here. He further says (p. 280).

If we take into account the complete psychic life of dreaming, subconscious as well as conscious, it is waking, not sleeping,
life which may be said to be limited. . . . Sleep, Vaschide
has said, is not, as Homer thought, the brother of Death, but of
Life, and, it may be added, the elder brother. . . .

He quotes from Bergson (*Revue Philosophique*, December, 1908, p. 574):

This dream state is the substratum of our normal state.
Nothing is added in waking life; on the contrary, waking life
is obtained by the limitation, concentration, and tension of that
diffuse psychological life which is the life of dreaming. . . .
To be awake is to will; cease to will, detach yourself from life,
become disinterested: in so doing you pass from the waking

ego to the dreaming ego, which is less *tense*, but more *extended* than the other.

Ellis continues (p. 281):

I have cultivated, so far as I care to, my garden of dreams, and it scarcely seems to me that it is a large garden. Yet every path of it, I sometimes think, might lead at last to the heart of the universe.

But with the exception of a few spasmodic inspirations, the records of dreams, ordinary or from the sensitives, contain nothing new — nothing to relieve man from the blessed necessity of eating his bread, intellectual as well as material, in the sweat of his brow; and, perhaps more important still, little to make the interests or responsibilities of this life weaker because of any realized inferiority to those of a possible later life.

It would apparently be inconsistent in Nature, or God, if you prefer, to start our evolution under earthly conditions, educating us in knowledge and character through labor and suffering, but at the same time throwing open to our perceptions, from another life, a wider range of knowledge and character attainable without labor or suffering.

I have no time or space or inclination to argue with those who deny a plan in Nature. He who does, probably lives away from Nature. It appears to have been a part of that plan that for a long time past most of us should "believe in" immortality, and that, at least until very lately, none of us should know anything about it. Confidence in immortality has been a dangerous thing. So far we haven't all made a very good use of it. Many of the people who have had most of it and busied themselves most with it, so to speak, have largely transferred their interests to the other life, and neglected and abused this one. "Otherworldliness" is a well-named vice, and positive evidence of immortality might be more dangerous than mere confidence in it.

All this, I think, supports the notion that whatever, if anything, is in store for us beyond this life, it would be a self-destructive scheme of things (or Scheme of Things, if you prefer) that would throw the future life into farther competition with our interests here, at least before we are farther evolved here. Looking at history by and large, we children have not generally been trusted with edge tools until we had grown to some sort of capacity to handle them. If the Mesopotamians or Egyptians or Greeks or Romans had had gunpowder, it looks as if they would have blown most of themselves and each other out of existence, and the rest back into primitive savagery, and stayed there until the use of gunpowder became one of the lost arts. But the new knowledge of evolution has given the modern world a new intellectual interest; and the new altruism, a new moral one. The reasons for doing one's best in this life, and doing it actively, are so much stronger and clearer than they were when so many good people could fall into asceticism and other-worldliness, that perhaps we are now fit to be trusted with proofs of an after life. It is very suggestive that these apparent proofs came contemporaneously with the new knowledge tending to make them safe; and equally suggestive that it is when we have begun to suffer from certain breakdowns in religion, that we have been provided with new material for bracing it up.

At the opposite extreme, it also is suggestive that these new indications that our present life is a petty thing beside a future one, have come just when modern science has so increased our control over material nature that we are in peculiar danger of having our interest in higher things buried beneath material interests, and enervated by over-indulgence in material delights.

If it be true that, roughly speaking, we are not entrusted with dangerous things before we are evolved to the point where we can keep their danger within bounds, the fact that we have not until very lately, if yet, been entrusted with any verification of the dream of the survival of bodily death, would seem to confer upon the spiritistic interpretation of the recent apparent verifications, a pragmatic sanction — an accidental embryo pun over which the historic student is welcome to a smile, and which, since the preceding clause was written, I have seen used in all seriousness by Professor Giddings. Conclusive or not, that "sanction" is certainly an addition to the arguments that existed before, including the general argument from evolution. And, so far as the phenomena go to establish the spiritistic hypothesis, surely they are not to be lightly regarded because as yet they do not establish it more conclusively.

When during the last century science bowled down the old supports of the belief in immortality, there grew up a tendency to regard that belief as an evidence of ignorance, narrowness, and incapacity to face the music. May not disregard of the possible new supports be rapidly becoming an evidence of the same characteristics?

When the majority of those who have really studied the phenomena of the sensitives, starting with absolute skepticism, have come to a new form of the old belief; and when, of the remaining minority, the weight of respectable opinion goes so far as suspense of judgment, how does the argument look? Isn't it at least one of those cases of new phenomena where it is well to be on guard against old mental habits, not to say prejudices?

Is it not now vastly more *reasonable* to believe in a future life than it was a century ago, or half a century, or quarter of a century? Is it not already more reasonable to believe in it than not to believe in it? Is it not already appreciably harder *not* to believe in it than it was a generation ago?

So far as I can see, the dream life, from mine up to Mrs. Piper's, vague as it is, is an argument for immortality *based on evidence.*

The sensitives are not among the world's leading thinkers or moralists — are not more aristocratic founders for a new faith than were a certain carpenter's son and certain fishermen; and only by implication do the sensitives suggest any moral truths, but they do offer more facts to the modern demand for facts.

Spiritism has a bad name, and it has been in company where it richly deserved one; but it has been coming into court lately with some very important-looking testimony from very distinguished witnesses; and some rather comprehensive minds consider its issues supreme — the principal issues now upon the horizon, between the gross, luxurious, unthinking, unaspiring, uncreating life of today, and everything that has, in happier ages, given us the heritage of the soul — the issues between increasing comforts and withering ideals — between water-power and Niagara.

The doubt of immortality is not over the innate reasonableness of it: the universe is immeasurably more reasonable with it than without it; but over its practicability after the body is gone. We, in our immeasurable wisdom, don't see how it can work — we don't see how a universe that we don't begin to know, which already has given us genius and beauty and love, and which seems to like to give us all it can —- birds, flowers, sunsets, stars, Vermont, the Himalayas, and the Grand Canyon; which, most of all, has given us the insatiable soul, can manage to give us immortality. Well! Perhaps we ought not to be grasping — ought to call all we know and have, enough, and be thankful — thankful above all, perhaps, that as far as we can see, the hope of immortality cannot be disappointed — that the worst answer to it must be oblivion. But on whatever grounds we despair of more (if we are weak enough to despair), surely the least reasonable ground is that we cannot see more: the mole might as well swear that there is no Orion.

" HOW to be efficient though incompetent" is the title suggested by a distinguished psychologist for the vocational appeals of the moment. Among these raucous calls none is more annoying to the ear of experience than the one which summons the college girl away from the bounty of the sciences and the humanities to the grudging concreteness of a domestic science, a household economy, from which stars and sonnets must perforce be excluded. We have, indeed, no quarrel with the conspicuous place now given to the word "home" in all discussions of women's vocations. Suffragists and anti-suffragists, feminists and anti-feminists have united to clear a noble term from the mists of sentimentality and to reinstate it in the vocabulary of sincere and candid speakers. More frankly than a quarter of a century ago, educated women may now glory in the work allotted to their sex. The most radical feminist writer of the day has given perfect expression to the home's demand. Husband and children, she says, have been able to count on a woman "as they could count on the fire on the hearth, the cool shade under the tree, the water in the well, the bread in the sacrament." We may go farther and say that our high emprise does not depend upon husband and children. Married or unmarried, fruitful or barren, with a vocation or without, we must make of the world a home for the race. So far from quarrelling with the hypothesis of the domestic scientists, we turn it into a confession of faith. It is their conclusions that will not bear the test of experience. Because women students can anticipate no more important career than home-making, it is argued that within their four undergraduate years training should be given in the practical details of house-keeping. Any woman who has been both a student and a housekeeper knows that this argument is fallacious.

Before examining it, however, we must clear away possible misunderstandings. Our discussion concerns colleges and not elementary schools. Those who are loudest in denouncing the aristocratic theory of a college education must admit that colleges contain, even today, incredible as it sometimes seems, a selected group of young women. It is also true that the High Schools contain selected groups. Below them are the people's schools. The girls who do not go beyond these are to be the wives of working men, in many cases can learn nothing from their mothers, and before marriage may themselves be caught in the treadmill of daily labor. It is probable that to these children of impoverished future we should give the chance to learn in school facts which may make directly for national health and well-being. But the girls in the most democratic state university in this country are selected by their own ambition, if by nothing else, for a higher level of life. Their power and their opportunities to learn do not end on Commencement Day. The higher we go in the scale of education, until we reach the graduate professional schools, the less are we able and the less need we be concerned to anticipate the specific activities of the future.

Furthermore, we are discussing colleges of "liberal" studies, not technical schools. Into the former have strayed many students who belong in the latter. The tragic thing about their errantry is that presidents and faculties, instead of setting them in the right path, try to make the college over to suit them. The rightful heirs to the knowledge of the ages are despoiled. The most downtrodden students are those who cherish a passion for the intellectual life. Among these are as many women as men. If domestic science were confined to separate schools, as all applied sciences ought to be, we should have nothing but praise for a subject admirably conceived, and often admirably taught. In these schools it may be studied by such High School graduates as prefer to deal with practical rather than with pure science, and, in a larger way, by such college graduates as wish to supplement theory with practice for professional purposes. But in liberal colleges domestic science is but dross handed out to seekers after gold. Against its intrusion into the curriculum no protest can be too stern.

Faith in this study seems to rest upon the belief that the actual experiences of life can be anticipated. This is a fallacy. There is no dress rehearsal for the rôle of "wife and mother." It is a question of experience piled on experience, life piled on life. The only way to perform the tasks, understand the duties, accept the joys and sorrows of any given stage of existence is to have performed the tasks, learned the duties, fought out the joys and sorrows of earlier stages. In so far as "housekeeping" means the application of principles of nutrition and sanitation, these principles can be acquired at the proper time by an active, well-trained mind. The preparation needed is not to have learned facts three or five or ten years in advance, when theories and appliances may have been very different, but to have taken up one subject after another, finding how to master principles and details. This new subject is not recondite nor are we unconquerably stupid. To learn as we go — *discere ambulando* — need not turn the home into an experiment station.

But "every woman knows" that housekeeping, when it is a labor of love and not a paid profession, goes far deeper than ordering meals or keeping refrigerators clean, or making an invalid's bed with hospital precision. We are more than cooks. We furnish power for the day's work of men, and for the growth of children's souls. We are more than parlor maids. We are artists, informing material objects with a living spirit. We are more even than trained nurses. We are companions along the roads of pain, comrades, it may be, at the gates of death. Back

of our willingness to do our full work must lie something
profounder than lectures on bacteria, or interior decora-
tion, or an invalid's diet or a baby's bath. Specific knowledge can be obtained in a hurry by a trained student.
What cannot be obtained by any sudden action of the
mind is *the habit* of projecting a task against the background of human experience as that experience has been
revealed in history and literature, and of throwing into
details the enthusiasm born of this larger vision. She is
fortunate who comes to the task of making a home with
this habit already formed. Her student life may have
cast no shadow of the future. When she was reading
Æschylus or Berkeley, or writing reports on the Italian
despots, or counting the segments of a beetle's antennæ,
she may not have foreseen the hours when the manner of
life and the manner of death of human beings would depend upon her. She was merely sanely absorbed in the
tasks of her present. But in later life she comes to see
that in performing them, she learned to disentangle the momentary from the permanent, to prefer courage to cowardice, to pay the price of hard work for values received. Age
may bring what youth withholds, a sense of humor, a mel-
low sympathy. But only youth can begin that habitual
discipline of mind and will which is the root, if not of all
success, at least of that which blooms in the comfort of
other people. Carry the logic of the vocation-mongers to
its extreme. Grant that every girl in college ought some-
day to marry, and that we must train her, while we have
her, for this profession. Then let the college insist on
honest work, clear thinking and bright imagination in
those great fields in which successive generations reap
their intellectual harvest. Captain Rostron of the Car-
pathia once spoke to a body of college students who were
on fire with enthusiasm for the rescuer of the Titanic's
survivors. He ended with some such words as these: "Go
back to your classes and work hard. I scarcely knew that
night what orders were coming out when I opened my

mouth to speak, but I can tell you that I had been preparing to give those orders ever since I was a boy in
school." Many a home may be saved from shipwreck in
the future because today girls are doing their duty in their
Greek class rooms and Physics laboratories.

But this fallacy of domesticity probes deeper than we
have yet indicated. It is, in the last analysis, superficial
to ticket ourselves off as house-keepers or even as women.
What are these unplumbed wastes between housekeepers
and teachers, mothers and scholars, civil engineers and
professors of Greek, senators and journalists, bankers and
poets, men and women? A philosopher has pointed out
that what we share is vastly greater than what separates
us. We walk upon and must know the same earth. We
live under the same sun and stars. In our bodies we are
subject to the same laws of physics, biology and chemistry.
We speak the same language, and must shape it to our
use. We are products of the same past, and must understand it in order to understand the present. We are vexed
by the same questions about Good and Evil, Will and
Destiny. We all bury our dead. We shall all die ourselves. Back of our vocations lies human life. Back of
the streams in which we dabble is that immortal sea which
brought us hither. To sport upon its shore and hear the
roll of its mighty waters is the divine privilege of youth.

If any difference is to be made in the education of boys
and girls, it must be with the purpose of giving to future
women more that is "unvocational," "unapplied," "un-
practical." As it happens, such studies as these are the
ones which the mother of a family, as well as a teacher
or writer, is most sure to apply practically in her vocation.
The last word on this aspect of the subject was said by a
woman in a small Maine town. Her father had been a
day laborer, her husband was a mechanic. She had five
children, and, of course, did all the house-work. She also
belonged to a club which studied French history. To a
foolish expression of surprise that with all her little chil-

dren she could find time to write a paper on Louis XVI she retorted angrily: "With all my children! It is for my children that I do it. I do not mean that they shall have to go out of their home, as I have had to, for everything interesting." But the larger truth is that the value of a woman as a mother depends precisely upon her value as a human being. And it is for that reason that in her youth we must lead one who is truly thirsty only to fountains pouring from the heaven's brink. It might seem cruel if it did not merely illustrate the law of risk involved in any creative process, that the more generously women fulfil the "function of their sex" the more they are in danger of losing their souls to furnish a mess of pottage. The risk of life for life at a child's birth is more dramatic but no truer than the risk of soul for body as the child grows. In the midst of petty household cares the nervous system may become a master instead of a servant, a breeder of distempers rather than a feeder of the imagination. The unhappiness of homes, the failure of marriage, are due as often to the poverty-stricken minds, the narrowed vision of women as to the vice of men.

> Their sense is with their senses all mix'd in,
> Destroyed by subtleties these women are.

George Meredith's prayer for us, "more brain, O Lord, more brain!" we shall still need when "votes for women" has become an outworn slogan.

No one claims that character is produced only by college training or any other form of education. There are illiterate women whose wills are so steady, whose hearts are so generous, and whose spirits seem to be so continuously refreshed that we look up to them with reverence. They have their own fountains. It would be a mistake to suppose that because they are "open at the outlet" they are "closed at the reservoir." But there is a class of women who are impelled toward knowledge (as still others are impelled toward music or art) and whose success in anything they do will depend upon their state of mind. We ought to assume that the girls who go to college belong to this class, however far from the springs of Helicon they mean to march in the future. It is a terrible thing that we should think of taking one hour of their time while they are in college for any course that does not enrich the intellect and add to the treasury of thoughts and ideas upon which the woman with a mind will always be drawing. Spirit is greater than intellect, and may survive it in the course of a long life. But in the active years, for this kind of woman, the mental life becomes one with the spiritual. A lusty serviceableness will issue from their union. If mental interests seem sterile, the cure, as far as the college is concerned with it, is to deepen, not to lessen the love of learning. The renewal of sincerity, humility and enthusiasm in the age-old search for truth is more necessary than the introduction of new courses, which must be applied to be of value, and which at this time in a girl's experience, and under these conditions, can give only partial and superficial data.

Our lives are subject to a thousand changes. In the home as well as out of it, we shall meet, face to face, fruition and disappointment, rapture and pain, hope and despair. In these tests of the soul's health what good will *domestic* science do us? Not by sanitation is sanity brought forth. Women do not gather courage from calories, nor faith from refrigerators. But every added milestone along the road from youth to age shows us the truth of Cicero's claim, made after he had borne public care and known private grief, for the faithful, homely companionship of intellectual studies: "For other things belong neither to all times and ages nor all places; but these pursuits feed our growing years, bring charm to ripened age, adorn prosperity, offer a refuge and solace to adversity, delight us at home, do not handicap us abroad, abide with us through the watches of the night, go with us on our travels, make holiday with us in the country."

Upon women, in crucial hours, may depend the peace of the old, the fortune of the middle-aged, the hopefulness of the young. In such an hour we do not wish to be dismissed as were the women of Socrates's family, who had had no part in the bright life of the Athens of which he was taking leave. Shall we become the bread in the sacrament of life, ourselves unfed? the fire on the hearth, ourselves unkindled?

THE LAND OF THE SLEEPLESS
WATCHDOG

IF from almost any given point in the United States you start out towards the Southwest, you will reach in time the Land of the Sleepless Watchdog. On each of the scattered farms, defending it against all intruders, you will find a band of eager and vociferous dogs — dogs who magnify their calling because they have no other, and who, by the same token lose all sense of proportion in life. It is "theirs not to reason why," but to put up warnings and threats, and to be ready for the fight that never comes.

If you enter a domain without previous understanding with them, you are powerless for mischief, for you are in the center of a publicity beside which any other publicity is that of a hermit's cell. The whole farm knows where you are, and all are suspicious of your predatory intentions. You can have none under these conditions. Meanwhile the whole pack voices its opinion of you and your unworthiness.

This is supposing that you are actually there. If you are not, it amounts to the same thing. Every dog knows that you meant to be there, or at any rate, that to be there was the scheme of someone equally bad. The slightest rustle of the wind, the call of a bird, the ejaculation responsive to a flea — any of these, anything to set the pack going.

And one pack starts the next. And the cries of the two start the third and the fourth, and each of these reacts on the first. The cry passes along the line, "We have him at last, the mad invader." There being no other enemy, they cry out against each other. And of late

197

years, since the barbed wire choked the cattle ranges, and
gave pause to the coyote, there has been no enemy. But
the dogs are there, though their function has passed away.
It is but a tradition — a remembrance. Only to the dogs
themselves does any reality exist.

Yet, such is the nature of dogs and men, the watchdog was never more numerous nor more alert than today.
He was never in better voice, and having nothing whatever to do, he does it to the highest artistic perfection.
At least one justification remains. Civilization has not
done away with the moon. In the stillness of night, its
great white face peeps over the hills at intervals no dog
has yet determined. Under this weird light, strange
shadowy forms trip across the fields. The watchdogs of
each farm have given warning, and the whole countryside
is eager with vociferation.

Men say the Sleepless Watchdog's bark is worse than
his bite. This may be, but it is certain that his feed is
worse than both bark and bite together. In the language
of economics, the Sleepless Watchdog is an unremunerative investment. He has "eaten his master out of house
and home," and by the same token, he imagines that he
himself is now the master.

By this time, the gentle but astute reader has observed
that this is no common "Dog Story," but a parable of
the times we live in; and that the real name of the Land of
the Sleepless (but unremunerative) Watchdog is indeed
Europe.

And because of the noisy and costly futility of the whole
system in his own and other countries, Professor Ottfried
Nippold of Frankfort-on-the-Main, has made a special
study of the Watchdogs of Germany.

The good people of the Fatherland some forty years
ago were drawn into a great struggle with their neighbors
beyond the Rhine. To divert his subjects' attention from
their ills at home, the Emperor of France wagered his

Rhine provinces against those of Prussia, in the game of War. The Emperor lost, and the King of Prussia took the stakes: for in those days it was a divine right of Kings to deal in flesh and blood.

The play is finished, the board is cleared, Alsace and Lorraine were added to Germany, and the mistake is irretrievable. A fact accomplished cannot be blotted out. But hopeless as it all is, there are watchdogs who, on moonlight nights, call across the Vosges for revenge — for honor, for War, War, War. And the German watchdogs cry War, War, War. The word sounds the same in all languages. The watchdogs bark, but the battle will never begin.

It is Professor Nippold's purpose, in his little book *Der Deutsche Chauvinismus*, to show that the clamor is not all on one side. The watchdogs of the Paris Boulevards are noisy enough, but those of Berlin are just the same. And as these are not all of Germany, so the others are not all of France. A great, thrifty, honest, earnest, cultured nation does not find its voice in the noises of the street. On the other hand, Germany, industrious, learned, profound and brave, is busy with her own affairs. She would harm no one, but mind her own business. But she is entangled in mediæval fashions. She has her own band of watchdogs, as noisy, as futile, as unthinkingly clamorous as ever were those of France. The "Sleepless Watchdog" in France is known as a Chauvinist, in England as a Jingo, in Prussia as a Pangermanist. They all bay at the same moon, are excited over the same fancies; they hear nothing, see nothing but one another. All alike live in an unreal world, in its essentials a world of their own creation. With all of them the bark is worse than the bite, and their "Keep" is more disastrous than both together.

And as each nation should look after its own, Dr. Nippold lists — blacklists if you choose — the Chauvinists of Germany.

At first glance, they make an imposing showing. A long series of newspapers, dozens of pamphlets, categories of bold and impressive warnings against the schemes of England and France, a set of appeals in the name of patriotism, of religion, of force, of violence. A long-drawn call to hate, to hate whatever is not of our own race or class; and above all the banding together of the "noblest" profession as against the encroachments of mere civilians, of men whose hands are soiled with other stains than blood.

We have, first and foremost, General Keim, Keim the invincible, Keim the insatiable, Keim of the Army-League, Keim the arch hater of England and of Russia and of France, Keim the jewel of the fighting Junker aristocracy of Prussia — the band of warriors who despise all common soldiers — "white slave" conscripts, and with them all civilians, who at the best are only potential common soldiers. "War, war, on both frontiers," is Keim's obsessing vision. War being inevitable and salutary, it cannot come too soon. The duty of hate, he urges on all the youth of Germany, maidens as well as men. It is said that Keim is the only man of the day who can maintain before an audience of Christians such a proposition as this: "We must learn to hate, and to hate with method. A man counts little who cannot hate to a purpose. Bismarck was hate."

From Gaston Choisy's clever character sketch of General Keim, we learn that as a soldier or tactician, he was a man of no note. He has no ability as a thinker or as a speaker, but this he has: "the courage of his vulgarity." At the age of 68, suffering from Bright's Disease, he travelled all Germany, his great head always in ebullition, gathering everywhere for the war-fire all the news, all the stories and all the lies susceptible of aiding the Cause." "Without Bismarck's authority, he had his manner — a mixture of baseness, of atrocious joviality, a studied cynicism and a lack of conscience." "How generous are circumstances! The spirit of Von Moltke the silent, with the speech of an *enfant terrible*, an endless flow of language, an endless course of words."

To the Chauvinists of France, Keim is indeed Germany. As to his own country, Von Ferlach sagely remarks: "Keims and Keimlings unfortunately are all about us. But they are a vanishing minority." The great culture peoples do not hate one another. ("Die grossen Kultur-völker hassen einander nicht.")

Next on the black list, comes General Frederick von Bernhardi, with his *Germany and the Next War*, the need to obliterate France, while giving the needed chastisement to England. A retired officer of cavalry, said to be disgruntled through failure of promotion, a tall, spare, serious, prosy figure, a writer without inspiration, a speaker without force. Germany has never taken him seriously; for he lacks even the clown-charm of his rival Keim, but the mediæval absurdities and serious extravagances in his defense of war are well tempered to stir the eager watchdogs in the rival lands. In spite of his pleas, "historical, biological and philosophical," for war, he is a man of peace, for which, in the words of General Eichhorn, "one's own sword is the best and strongest pledge."

Doubtless other retired officers hold views of the same sort, as do doubtless many who could not be retired too soon for the welfare of Germany. Into the nature of their patriotism, the Zabern incident has thrown a great light. "Other lands may possess an army," a Prussian officer is quoted as saying, "the army possesses Germany."

The vanities and follies of Prussian militarism are concentrated in the movement called Pangermanism. Behind this, there seem to be two moving forces, the Prussian Junker aristocracy, and the financial interests which center about the house of Krupp. The purposes of Pangermanism seem to be, on the one hand, to prevent parliamentary government in Germany; and on the other, to take part in whatever goes on in the world outside.

Just now, the control of Constantinople is the richest prize
in sight, and that fateful city is fast replacing Alsace in
the passive role of "the nightmare of Europe." The
journalists called Conservative find that "Germany needs
a vigorous diplomacy as a supplement to her power on
land and sea, if she is to exercise the influence she deserves." And a vigorous foreign policy is but another
name for the use of the War System as a means of pushing
business. From the daily press of Germany may be culled
many choice examples of idle Jingo talk, but analysis of
the papers containing it shows their affiliation with the
"extreme right," a small minority in German politics,
potent only through the indiscretions of the Crown Prince,
and through the fact that the Constitution of Germany
gives its people no control over administrative affairs.
The journals of this sort — the *Tägliche Rundschau*, the
Berliner Post, the *Deutsche Tageszeitung*, and the *Berliner Neueste Nachrichten* are the property of Junker
reactionists, or else, like the *Lokal Anzeiger*, the *Rheinisch-
Westphalische Zeitung*, the organs merely of the War trade
House of Krupp. Out from the ruck of hack writers, there
stands a single imposing figure, Maximilian Harden, the
"poet of German politics," who "casts forth heroic ges-
tures and thinks of politics in terms of æsthetics, the
prophet of a great, strong and saber-rattling nation,"
whose force shall be felt everywhere under the sun.

Bloodthirsty pamphlets in numbers, are listed by Nippold. But the anonymous writers ("Divinator" "Rhe-
nanus," "Lookout," "Deutscher," "Politiker," "Activer
General" and "Deutscher Officier" count for less than
nothing in personal influence. They do little more than
bay at the moon.

Impressive as Nippold's list seems at first, and dangerous to the peace of the world, after all one's final thought
is this: How few they are, and how scant their influence,
as compared with the wise, sane, commonsense of sixty
millions of German people. The two great papers that

stand for peace and sanity, the *Berliner Tageblatt* and the *Frankfurter Zeitung*, with the *Münchener Neueste Nachrichten*, are read daily by more Germans than all the reactionary sheets combined. The Socialist organ *Vorwaerts*, avowedly opposed to monarchy as well as to militarism, carries farther than all the organs of Pan-germanism of whatever kind.

We may justly conclude that the war spirit is not the spirit of Germany, a nation perforce military because the people cannot help themselves. So far as it goes, it is the spirit of a narrow clique of "sleepless watchdogs" whose influence is waning, and would be non-existent were it not for the military organization which holds Germany by the throat, but which has pushed the German people just as far as it dares.

A second lesson is that while forms of government, and social traditions, may differ, the relation of public opinion towards war is practically the same in all the countries of Western Europe. It is in its way the test of European civilization. Each nation has its "sleepless watchdogs," and those of one nation fire the others, when the proper war scares are set in motion by the great unscrupulous group of those who profit by them. The war promoters, the apostles of hate, form a brotherhood among themselves, and their success in frightening one nation reacts to make it easier to scare another.

This the reader may remember, as a final lesson. There is no civilized nation which longs for war. There is nowhere a reckless populace clamoring for blood. The schools have done away with all that. The spread of commerce has brought a new Earth with new sympathies and new relations, in which international war has no place.

If you are sure that your own nation has no design to use violence on any other, you may be equally sure that no other has evil designs on you. The German fleet is not built as a menace to England; whether it be large or small should concern England very little. Just as little does the size of the British fleet bear any concern to Germany. The German fleet is built against the German people. The growth of the British army and navy has in part the same motive. Armies and navies hold back the waves of populism and democracy. They seem a bulwark against Socialism. But in the great manufacturing and commercial nations, they will not be used for war, because they cannot be. The sacrifice appalls: the wreck of society would be beyond computation.

But still the sleepless watchdogs bark. It is all that they can do, and we should get used to them. In our own country, whatever country it may be, we have our own share of them, and some of them bear distinguished names. No other nation has any more, and no nation takes them really seriously, any more than we do. And one and all, their bark is worse than their bite, and the cost of feeding them is doubtless worse than either.

Special to our Readers

THOSE of you who have not received your REVIEWS on time will probably now find a double interest in the article in the last number, on *Our Government Subvention to Literature*. In conveying periodicals so cheaply, not only is Uncle Sam engaged in a bad job, but he is doing it cheaply, and consequently badly, and he has more of it than he can well handle. *He is at length carrying them as freight,* and most of you know what that means. We are receiving complaints of delay on all sides, and an appreciable part of the unwelcome subvention Uncle Sam is giving us, goes in sending duplicates of lost copies. We don't acknowledge any obligation, legal or moral, to do this; but we love our subscribers — more or less disinterestedly — and try to do them all the kinds of good we can. Partly to enable us to do that, as long as the subvention is given, we follow the example of the excellent Pooh Bah, and put our pride (and the subvention) into our pockets. Even if we did not love our subscribers so, we should have to do the pocketing all the same, because our competitors do. Competitors are always a very shameless sort of people.

We wish, however, that Uncle Sam would keep his subvention in his own pocket, and so lead to a higher plane all competitors in the magazine business, including some of those who don't want to rise to a higher plane. The best of such a proceeding on his part would be that he would also, through the complicated influences described in the article referred to encourage up to a higher plane those who write for popular magazines. Those who write for THE UNPOPULAR REVIEW are, of course, on the highest possible plane already. This remark is made solely for the benefit of readers taking up the REVIEW for the first time. To others it is superfluous, and if there is anything we try to avoid, it is, as we have so many times to tell volunteer contributors, superfluities. Even popularity we do not try to avoid, but — !

The foregoing paragraph was written with little thought of what was coming to be added to it. You and we have something to be proud of. Our REVIEW has been doing its part in saving all Europe from the waste of hundreds of millions of money, and the literatures of all Europe from a degradation like that through which our own is passing. Read the following letter:

Dear Mr. [Editor]:

I have already sent a line through ————— thanking you for the copy of THE UNPOPULAR REVIEW, which you were good enough to send me, but I should like to repeat my thanks to you again direct, and at the same time, tell you how the REVIEW has been of service to European publishers.

The article in the last number entitled *Our Government Subvention to Literature* naturally interested me very much from a personal point of view, but the statistics you give showing the effect of second class matter rate on book sales was very valuable to me as the representative of the English Publishers on the Executive Committee of the International Publishers Congress.

At the Congress held at Budapest last June, a resolution was adopted instructing the Congress to press for a reduced rate of postage on periodicals, and an international stamp. The steps to be taken in order to carry out this resolution were discussed at the meeting of the Committee last week held at Leipzig, when I produced the copy of your article, and gave the Committee a summary of the statistics. The result was the unanimous decision to take no further steps in the matter.

I tremble to think of what might have happened if I had not had your article before me, for the point of view which you have put forward was one that had not occurred to anyone else connected with the Congress, and if the resolution had not been cut out at this last meeting of the Executive Committee, it would have gone before the Postal Conference which is to be held in Madrid this autumn, backed by practically every European country.

I feel we all owe you a debt of gratitude for bringing out the facts so clearly, and believe that you will like to know what has taken place.

While we are not slow to take all the credit that our supporters and ourselves are entitled to in this matter, we should be very slow tacitly to accept the lion's share of it, which is due to Colonel C. W. Burrows of Cleveland, who supplied all of the facts and nearly all of the expression of the article in question, and who has for years, lately as President of the One Cent Letter Postage League, been devoting himself with unsparing energy and self-sacrifice to stopping the waste of money and capacity that the mistaken outbreak of paternalism we are discussing has brought upon the country.

Demos is a good fellow — when he behaves himself, and that generally means when he is not abused or flattered; but how supremely ridiculous, not to say destructive, he is when he gets to masquerading in the robes of the scholar or the judge; and how criminal is the demagogue who seeks personal aggrandisement by dangling those robes before him.

Our modesty has been so anesthetized by the preceding letter, that it permits us to show you, in strict confidence of course, a paragraph from another. A new subscriber, apparently going it blind on the recommendation of a friend, writes:

"I am told it is the best gentleman's magazine in the United States."

Now, somehow, "gentleman" is a word that we are very chary of using. We couldn't put that remark on an advertising page, but perhaps there is no inconsistency in putting it here, and confessing that we like it — and that we even suspect that we have always had a subconscious idea that

it was just what we were after — that it includes, or ought
to include, about everything that we are trying to accomplish.   In any interpretation, it is certainly an encouragement to keep pegging away.

Most of our readers probably remember a letter on
pp. 432–3 of the *Casserole* of the April–June number, from
an individual who thought we were trying to humbug
the wage-receiving world into a false and dangerous contentment with existing conditions.   This inference was
probably drawn from our insistent promulgation of the
belief that a man's fortune depends more upon himself
than upon his conditions.

As a contrast to that remarkable letter, it is a great
pleasure to call attention to the following still more remarkable one.   It is from a printer—not one in our employ.

I wish to congratulate you on the excellence of the REVIEW,
both from a literary and mechanical standpoint.   As a "worker,"
"a member of the Union," it might be inferred that I endorse
the views of the critics given on page 432 of the second number.
Not so.   It is such views as his that harm the unthinking —
those who think capital is the emblem of wickedness.

I believe that individual merit and worth are the only things
worth while.   The workman who puts his best efforts into his
labor, and takes a personal pride in making his productions as
nearly perfect as possible, will be recognized, and his individual
worth to his employer will raise him above the "common level."
All this rot about a "ruling oligarchy" "grinding down the
poorer class" is dangerous.   The man who has no ambition
above ditch digging, and who endeavors to throw out as little
dirt in a day as he possibly can, will always be one of "the submerged."   It lies with each one — outside of unavoidable
physical or mental infirmities — whether he shall rise or sink.

Again I must congratulate you on the stand you are taking
in THE UNPOPULAR REVIEW.   I "take" and read twenty to
twenty-five magazines and for over forty years have been trying to educate myself to a right way of thinking, and the result
is I believe as above briefly outlined.

Especially good is *The Greeks on Religion and Morals*, also.
The Soul of Capitalism, *Trust-Busting as a National Pastime*,
and *Our Government Subvention to Literature*.

Possibly some of you are disappointed at not finding this number as full as the daily papers of wisdom on War and the Mexican situation. In one sense we are disappointed ourselves: for we had made arrangements for at least one article of that general nature from one of our best qualified contributors; but when it came time to write it (speaking by the calendar), he showed the excellence of his qualifications by saying that, considering the situation and the function of this REVIEW, it was *not* time — that the situation had not yet become mature enough or broad enough for any general conclusions — for any treatment beyond that already well given by the newspapers and other organs of frequent publication, and that they were giving all the details called for. We will wait, then, and try to philosophize when the time comes.

We find, however, that with little deliberate intention on our part, this number has turned out "seasonable" in another sense, and hope you will find it so. Witness the articles on *Chautauqua,* and *Railway Junctions,* and *Tips* (entitled *A Stubborn Relic of Feudalism*) and several others.

Philosophy in Fly Time

IN the old days, before the destruction of the white pines removed the chief source of American inventiveness — the universal habit of whittling — every boy had a jackknife, and also had boxes, sometimes of wood, sometimes of writing paper, in which he kept flies. Now he has neither flies nor jackknife.

Then, when he wanted a fly, nine times out of ten he could catch one with a sweep of the hand. That was before the fly was charged with an amount of bad deeds, if they really were as bad as represented, which would have destroyed the human race long before the plagues of Egypt; or if not before the fly plague, would have caused that plague to leave no Egyptians alive to enjoy the later ones. With these new opinions of the fly, began a crusade against him; and now the boys can't have any more fun with him — that is, only good boys can — the kind that catch him with illusive traps, for a cent a hundred. The other kind of boys may occasionally be sports enough to hunt him with the swatter; but it's pretty poor hunting: for the game is so shy that generally before you get within reach of him, he is off: so swatting him is difficult, while catching him by hand, as we boys used to, is virtually impossible.

Now for some questions profound enough to befit our pages. (I) Have only a select group of very alert and quick flies survived? or (II) Have the flies told each other that that big clumsy brute with only two legs to walk on, and two aborted ones which do all sorts of foolish things — the brute with only one lens to an eye (though he sometimes puts a glass one over it) and a pitifully aborted proboscis — the brute that has no wings, and can't get ahead more than about once his own length in a second — that this clumsy brute had at last got so jealous of the six legs, hundred-lensed eyes, proboscis, wings and speed of the fly, that he had started a new crusade against him, and must be specially avoided?

Then, after it is ascertained whether the timidity of the flies is because this story has been passed around among them, or only because men have already killed off all but the specially quick and timid ones; we hope our investigators may find an answer to the farther question: (III) How, if a tenth of what some folks say against flies is true, the human race has so long survived?

To avoid misapprehension, it should be added that despite the availability, in our boyhood, of flies as playmates, we don't like 'em, especially when they light on our hands to help us write articles for this REVIEW.

Setting Bounds to Laughter

THAT there is even a measure of personal liberty on the earth, is one of our most pointed proofs that the universe is governed by design. For liberty is loved neither by the many nor by the few; its defense has always been unpopular in the extreme, and can be manfully undertaken only in an age of moral heroism. The present is no heroic age, and hence our personal rights fall one by one, without defense, and apparently without regret. The losses thus incurred must be left to future historians to weigh and to lament. There is, however, one of our natural rights, now cruelly beset by its enemies, that is too precious to surrender to the threnodies of the future historians. This is the right to laugh.

It is scarcely a quarter of a century since the first appearance of organized efforts to curb the spirit of laughter. All good men and women were hectored into believing that one should weep, not laugh, over the absurdities of men in their cups. Next, we were warned that it is unseemly and unChristian to laugh at a fellow-man's discomfiture — an awkward social situation, a sermon or a political oration wrecked by stage fright, or a poem spoilt by a printer's stupidity. Under shelter of the dogma that to laugh at the ridiculous is unlawful. there have recently grown into vigor multitudinous anti-laughter alliances, racial, national and professional. Not many years ago a censorship of Irish jokes was established, and this was soon followed by an index expurgatorious of Teutonic jokes. Our colored fellow citizens promptly advanced the claim that jokes at the expense of their race are "in bad taste"; and country life enthusiasts solemnly affirmed that the rural and suburban jokes are nothing short of national disasters. A recent press report informs us that the suffragette joke has been excluded from the vaudeville circuits throughout the country. And the movement grows apace. Domestic servants, stenographers, politicians, college professors, and clergymen are organizing to establish the right of being ridiculous without exciting laughter.

But what does it all matter? What is laughter but an old-fashioned aid to digestion, more or less discredited by current medical authority? It is time we learned that laughter has a social significance: it is the first stage in the process of understanding one's fellow man. Professor Bergson to the contrary notwithstanding, you can not laugh with your intellect alone. An essential element of your laughter is sympathy. You can not laugh at an idiot, nor at a superman. You can not laugh at a Hindoo or a Korean; you can hardly force a smile to your lips over the conduct of a Bulgar, a Serb, or a Slovak. You are beginning to find something comic in the Italian, because you are beginning to know him. And all the world laughs at the Irishman, because all the world knows him and loves him.

When Benjamin Franklin walked down the streets of Philadelphia, carrying a book under his arm, and munching a crust of bread, just one person observed him, a rosy maiden, who laughed merrily at him. As our old school readers narrated, with naïve surprise, this maiden was destined to become Franklin's faithful wife. And yet psychology should have led us to expect such a result. The stupidest small boy making faces or turning somersaults before the eyes of his pig-tailed inamorata, evidences his appreciation of the sentimental value of the ridiculous. When did we first grant some small corner in our hearts to the Chinese? It was when we were introduced to Bret Harte's gambler:

> For ways that are dark and tricks that are vain,
> The heathen Chinee is peculiar.

The natural history of the racial or professional joke is easily written. At the outset it is crude and cruel, wholly at the expense of the group represented. In time the world wearies of an unequal contest, and we have a new order of jokes, in which the intended victim acquits himself well. This, too, gives way to a higher order, in which race, nationality or profession is employed merely as

a cloak for common humanity. The successive stages
mark the progress in assimilation, induced, in large measure, by laughter. There is no other social force so potent
in creating mutual understanding and practical fraternity
of spirit; in establishing the essential unity of mankind
underneath its phenomenal diversity. Setting bounds to
laughter: why, this is to indenture the angel of charity to
the father of lies and the lord of hate.

A Post Graduate School for Academic Donors

AT a recent meeting of an University Montessori
Club the case of donors to colleges and universities was
reported on by a special committee. The majority report drew a pretty heavy indictment. It was shown that
the givers to colleges and universities seldom considered
the real needs of their beneficiaries. Donors liked to give
expensive buildings without endowment for upkeep,
liked to give vast athletic fields, rejoiced in stadiums,
affected memorial statuary and stained glass windows,
dabbled in landscape gardening, but seldom were known
either to give anything unconditionally or, specifically, to
destine a gift for such uninspiring needs as more books or
professors' pay. The result of giving without first considering the needs of the benefited college or university,
was that every gift made the beneficiary more lopsided.
Certain universities were almost capsized by their incidental architecture. Others were subsidizing graduate
students to whom the conditions of successful research were
denied. Still others were calling great specialists to the
teaching force without providing the apparatus for the pursuit of these specialties. Others preferred to offer financial
aid to students who were poor — in every sense. Donors
apparently without exception had single-track minds.
They saw plainly enough what they wanted to give, but
never took the pains to see the donation in its relation to
the institution as a whole. The majority report, which was

drawn by our famous Latinist, Professor Claudius Senex, concluded with the despairing note *Timeo Danaos et dona ferentes*. The minority report was delivered orally by young Simpson Smith of the department of banking and finance. He "allowed" that everything alleged by the majority report was true, but saw no use in dwelling on such truths, since donors always had done and always would do just as they darned pleased.

The Club took a more hopeful view of the case, and it was voted that our Club should resolve itself into the trustees and faculty of a Post Graduate School for Academic Donors. Our committee recommended that we qualify our advanced students by conferring the lower degree of Heedless Donor (H. D.) every year upon all givers who can be shown to have given at random. No method of instruction seemed more appropriate than the seminar plan of practical exercises based on concrete instances. The first laboratory experiment was performed in the presence of a Seminar of seven H. D.'s. in a specially called meeting of married professors attired only in bath gowns borrowed from the crews and base ball teams. Into this assembly the class of H. D.'s was suddenly introduced. They naturally inquired into the meaning of the spectacle, and were informed that in no case did the mere salary of these professors enable them to wear clothes at all. "But you do usually wear clothes?" inquired a student of a favorite professor. "How do you get them?" "By University extension lecturing at ten dollars a lecture" was the quiet answer. Another professor explained that he got his clothes by tutoring dull students, another by book reviewing. One somewhat shamefacedly said the clothes came from his wife's money. One declined to answer, and, as a matter of fact, his clothes are habitually first worn by a more fortunate elder brother.

On the whole the results of our first seminary exercise were satisfactory. One student immediately drew a considerable check for the salary fund, another, who had been planning to give a hockey rink, said he would think things over. Still a third deposited forty pairs of slightly worn trousers with the university treasurer, "for whom it might concern." Only one accepted the demonstration contentedly. He admitted that low pay and extra work were hard on the Professors, but he also felt that these outside activities advertised the university and were good business. Of course you wore out some professors in the process, but you could always get others.

Our second seminary exercise was of a less spectacular sort. The post graduate donors were each provided with a bibliography. This in every instance contained the titles of books that a particular professor or graduate student in the university would need to consult for his studies of the ensuing week. It was briefly explained by Professor Senex that original research could not ·be successfully accomplished without reference to all the original sources and to the writings of other scholars. The bibliographies ran from ten titles or so to nearly a hundred, according to the nature of the particular research involved. The exercise consisted in going to the university library and matching these titles of desiderata with the books actually in the catalogue. After varying intervals, the post graduate donors returned with their report. Nobody had found more than half the books sought for: many had found less.

The effect of this demonstration was interesting. The donor who had tended towards the hockey rink, instead transferred his $100,000 to the book purchase fund. He said he guessed the old place needed real books more than it needed artificial ice. Others followed his example according to their ability.

The student who was satisfied with our bath robe faculty meeting, came back from the library equally pleased. He had not compared his bibliography with the catalogue, but a brief general inspection had convinced him that there were already more books in the library than anybody

could read.   His intention held firm to give his Alma
Mater a tower higher than any university tower on record
and containing a chime of bells that periodically played
the college song.   The tower was naturally to bear his
name, which was also his dear mother's.

A Suggestion Regarding Vacations

WHY wouldn't it be well for the country colleges to
shorten their summer vacations, and lengthen their winter
ones?   Then urban students would not, for so long a period
in summer, be put to their trumps to find out what to do
with themselves; and, what is more important, in winter
both faculty and students would have increased opportunity for metropolitan experience.   In the summer vacations, the cities are empty of music, drama, and most else
of what makes them distinctively worth while.   Intellectually, the country needs the city at least as much as,
morally, the city needs the country.

Advertisement

WE are disposed to do a little gratuitous advertising
for good causes.   Below is the first essay.   It is perfectly
genuine.   Please send us some more.

Help Wanted.   From a young gentleman of education,
leisure and energy, who desires to devote a part of his time,
in connection with scholars and philanthropists, to a reform
of world-wide importance.   Such a person may possibly
learn of a congenial opportunity by addressing.

X. T. C.
Care of THE UNPOPULAR REVIEW.

A few hundred persons of the kind whose help is sougth
by this advertisement would have the salvation of he
republic in their hands.   But somehow those who have
the leisure generally lack the desire; and those who have
the desire generally lack the leisure.

Simplified Spelling

AFTER receiving, in answer to the invitation in our first number, a few bitter objections to simplified spelling, we have felt like apologizing each time we approached the subject. Perhaps the best apology we can make is that apparently the majority of our readers are interested in it. Therefore we hope that the others will tolerate as equably as they can, the devotion of a little space to it in the interest of the majority. Perhaps the objectors may ultimately be able to settle the difficulty as we and our house have settled another unconquerable nuisance — the dandelions on our lawns —: we have concluded to like them.

Our recent correspondence regarding Simplified Spelling has developed a few points which we submit to those who abominate it, those who favor it, and those who, like the eminent school-superintendent we have already quoted, and like ourselves for that matter, do both:

To a leading Professor of Greek:

I am more hopeful than you that the repetition of a consonant beginning the second syllable of a dissyllable, to close the preceding syllable, as in "differ", "fiddle", "gobble", etc., *wil* "be generally accepted", especially in view of the fact that it is *alreddy* "generally accepted", and needs only to be extended to a minority of words.

"Annutther" is not "a fair illustration". On the contrary, it is an exception that I probably was very injudicious to call any attention to; and the trouble with you scholars, I find all the way thru, is that you permit those little exceptions to influence you too much. If a good simplification is ever effected, it will be by cutting Gordian knots, and you all of you seem absolutely incapable of anything of the kind. I don't expect anyhow to make much out of a man who will spell "peepl" "peopl". Imagine all this said with a grin, not a frown!!

You wil never get back to "the old sounds" of the vowels, in God's world.

As to the long sounds, I am going in for all I am worth on the double vowels. I alreddy agree with the English Society on

"faather", "feel" and "scuul", and am going to do all I can
for *niit*, and for spredding the *oo* in *floor* and *door* into *snore*,
more, hole, poke, etc. "Awl", "cow" and "go" are spelt wel, and
their spelling shoud be spred. These seem to be the lines of
least resistance. I find that they work first-rate in my own
riting.

You make enuf serious objections to diacritical marks, but
my serious objection to them is that they ar obstacles to lerners,
especially forreners.

From his answer:

All right; I catch the grin, and cheerfully grin back. The
business of a scholar (Emerson's "man thinking", Plato's
φιλόσοφος) is to take as long views as he can; in this case, to
look far beyond the possibilities of my life-time. The more
you people with the shorter views, as I venture to think them,
agitate for and practise each little partial solution, the more
you help on the threshing out which must go on for many years
before we can arrive at any general solution. So, more power to
your elbow!

Meantime my own spelling will continue to be — like the
conventional spelling of the printers of today — a hodge-podge
of inconsistencies, quite indefensible on rational grounds, and
varying with circumstances. Of course the rational way to
spell *people* is *piipl*, or *pīpl*.

Which we think is an attempt to bolster up a lost cause.

From another reader:

Your closing sentence in the first number of THE UNPOPULAR
REVIEW states with a most distressing combination of vowels
and outlandish collocation of consonants that you would like
to hear from your readers on the subject. . . . Z is not a pretty
letter, and to see it so frequently usurping the place so long
held by s is far from gratifying to the eye. . . .

Suppose you establish to your own satisfaction a method for
assigning sound values; how will you reach the differences in
vowel sounds that prevail in the United States? The New
Englander's mouthing of *a* differs from that of the Northern
New Yorker, and both differ greatly from that of the South-
erner — indeed, in the different Southern States there is variation. . . . At first I was interested in simplified spelling, but
the eccentricities developed by its advocates alienated me long
since, so I beg of you, drop it.

From our answer:

I delayed thanking you for your letter of the 29th until there should be time for you to see the April–June number.

I hope you are feeling better now.

If you are not, I do not think I can do much to console you, because when a man has been irritated into that position where the alleged beauty of a letter counts in so serious a question, he is probably beyond mortal help.

I have no desire "to reach the differences in vowel sounds that prevail in the United States". There is not much difference among cultivated people. Probably a fair standard would be the conversation at the Century Club, where there are visitors from Maine to California, and hardly any noticeable difference in pronunciation.

There seems to be no disagreement among authorities that a simplified spelling would save a great deal of time among children. . . .

Of course I have not been able to answer most of the letters I have received on the subject. I single yours out because you have had a fall from grace, and I feel guilty of having had something to do with it, by presenting stronger meat than was necessary, in our January number. I have fought on the Executive Committee of the Spelling Board against publishing anything of the English S. S. S.'s proposed improvements, for fear of arousing such prejudice as yours; and yet in our first number, I was insensibly led into, myself, publishing things that looked just as outlandish.

As I said at the outset, I hope you feel better since seeing the April–June number, and should be glad to know how you do feel.

From his reply:

Thank you very much for the courtesy of your letter of 9th April. I was surprised to receive it, as I did not suppose that your multifarious duties would permit you to notice my rather feeble protest. I was somewhat amused that you should think my irritation so extreme as to call for an effort to console me. I am sure I appreciate your attempt to do so. But really, I was not so hard hit as you thought, because I do not expect in my day (I am no longer a young man) to see the champions of "simplified spelling" (some of it seems to me the reverse of "simplified") gain such headway as to materially mar my pleasure in the printed page, for I do not believe you will allow the atrocities of the last few pages of your first number to creep

into the delightful essays which render THE UNPOPULAR REVIEW
such pleasant and profitable reading. . . .

I do not think any great respect is due the opinion of those
who think that a simplified spelling would save a great deal of
time among children, for it also seems to have its rules which
will present as much difficulty to memorize as do the peculiarities of our present system. . . .

Why *thru?* U does not always have the sound of double *o* —
very rarely in fact. Why not *throo* — if the aim is to make the
written sign correspond to the sound. Thru suggests *huh.*

From our answer:

Regarding "thru", you justly say that *u* does not always
have the sound of *oo.* The only sound of *oo* worthy of respect,
with which I have an acquaintance, is in "door" and "floor".
The idea of using it to represent a *u* sound is perhaps the culminating absurdity of our spelling.

Your statement that simplified spelling "seems to have its
rules which will present as much difficulty to memorize as do the
peculiarities of our present system" overlooks the advantage
that writing with a phonetic alphabet, like those of Europe, has
over writing with purely conventional characters, as in China.
Now English writing is probably the least phonetic in Europe.
Simplifying it in any of the well-known proposed methods would
be making it more phonetic, and consequently easier. At present
it is a mass of contradictions, and the rules that can be extracted
from it are overburdened with exceptions. Simplification will
decrease both the exceptions and the rules themselves. There
are now several ways of representing each of many sounds, and
therefore several "rules" to be learned for each of such sounds.
Simplification will tend to reduce those rules to one for each
sound, and so far as it succeeds, will *not* "present as much
difficulty to memorize as do the peculiarities of our present
system."

All the degrees of reformed spelling now in use are
professedly but transitional. They may gradually advance into a respectable degree of consistency, but we
expect that to be reached quicker by a coherent survival
among the warring elements proposed by the S. S. S., the
S. S. B. and the better individual reformers. Probably
there is already more agreement than disagreement among
these elements.

While the others are fighting it out, the various transition styles will do something to prepare parents to accept a more nearly perfect style for their children, and perhaps take an interest in seeing the various counsels of perfection fight each other.

A few words have already found their way into advertisements — *tho, thru, thoro* (a damnable way of spelling *thurro*), and the shortened terminal *gram (me)s, og(ue)s* and *et(te)s*; and these and a few more have found their way into correspondence on commonplace subjects; and the interest in the topic, especially among educators, is spreading. But most of the inconsistencies will probably bother and delay children and forreners until they are given something with some approach to consistency.

After we fight to something like agreement on a system, how are we to get it going?

It does not seem extravagant to expect that as soon as the weight of scholarly opinion endorses a vocabulary from our present alphabet consistent enough to afford a base for a reasonable spelling book, spelling books and readers will be prepared for the schools, and adopted by advanced teachers. Many are clamoring for such now. When the youngsters have mastered these, which they will do in a small fraction of the time wasted on their present books, they will of their own accord pick up without troubling their teachers a knowledge of the present forms. This they have always done when their teaching has been by the various phonetic methods with special letters, and have done both in much less time than they have needed for learning in the ordinary way. But they will prefer the reasonable forms, and this demand the publishers will probably not be slow to supply.

Cloth covers for Volume I (Nos. 1 and 2) of THE UN-POPULAR REVIEW are now ready and will be sent postpaid to any address on receipt of 50 cents. They are of brown cloth, stamped in gold, very like the paper covers of the numbers, minus the tables of contents, etc., and lettered on the back as cloth covers usually are.

The Index of Volume I accompanies this number, or will be mailed separately to any applicant.

Address THE UNPOPULAR REVIEW
35 WEST 32d STREET, NEW YORK CITY

The Unpopular Review

No. 4   OCTOBER—DECEMBER, 1914   Vol. II

SOME FREE-SPEECH DELUSIONS

A SINGULAR phenomenon of our time is the invention of a new species of martyrdom. Resistance to wrong, real or imaginary, revolt against oppression, the endeavor to overthrow an established order, has in all ages been attended with hardship and suffering. When repression or punishment has been cruel or vindictive, and the victims have cried out against it, in the more humane ages, they have had in their protest the sympathy and support of right-minded men, however opposed to the aims of the agitation or revolt in question. Those who have suffered for their convictions, whether at the hands of a court or through the bloody judgment of the sword, have won the name of hero or martyr. The time has been when those who were known to hold opinions which were regarded as dangerous to the State, or were obnoxious to the ruling power, fell under the ban of the Government as criminals. In the last two or three centuries, among the more liberal and advanced nations, outright persecution of this kind has been unknown; but between this merely negative freedom of opinion and that positive freedom which we understand by the terms "free speech" and "free press" there is a long distance, the traversing of which has been slow and irregular. It is possible to maintain that even now, and even in such countries as the United States or England, this freedom is not absolute; there are extremely few things, either in government or in common life, that *are* absolute. But the remarkable thing about the outcry for freedom of speech, of which we have lately been hearing so much, is that

this clamor has nothing whatever to do with the question
of the absolute completeness of that freedom. What the
agitators complain of is not that there are some things
which they are not permitted to say or to print; it is not
that their publications are censored or the circulation of
them obstructed; it is not that the doctrines in which they
are interested cannot be put before any assemblage, large
or small, which chooses to gather together in an orderly
way to hear them. Their grievance is that at certain times
or places, where the speaking they wish to do would be
either an invasion of ordinary private rights of others, or,
in the opinion of the authorities, an incitement to disorder,
the authorities intervene to prevent these results. The
restrictions to which they object are not limitations as to
the nature of the doctrine preached, nor yet limitations
that in any way confine the general spreading of the doctrine. What they are not allowed to do is — in principle,
at least; of course, there have been blundering applications
of it — simply what nobody else is allowed to do. In a
word, what they demand is not that they shall have the
same freedom as the ordinary citizen *in spite* of being
enemies of the established order, but that they shall have
special privileges and immunities *because* of being enemies
of the established order.

In keeping with the peculiar character of their grievance
is the character of that factitious martyrdom which they
seek to build upon it. The I. W. W. orator who wishes to
speak at the foot of the Franklin statue in Park Row considers himself — in a mild way, to be sure — a martyr if,
on account of the obstruction of traffic by the crowd that
gathers round him, he is required by the police to hold
his meeting a couple of hundred yards further north; his
martyrdom consisting in the fact that there is very little
fun or excitement to be had out of addressing a crowd
which does *not* obstruct traffic. In the crowd itself — say
the excited and more or less turbulent crowd in Union
Square soon after the Colorado trouble — a man may re-

fuse to move on at the command of the policeman, and may get a crack on his head from the policeman's club; this man certainly has a much more substantial claim to the title of martyr, and yet his claim is at least nine parts humbug to one part reality. It may be a pretty serious thing to the poor fellow himself, or it may not; as a social or political event it is simply nothing. It would only be something if it were part of a systematic persecution — an incident of a regular policy of oppression. Unfortunately there have been places, — say Lawrence or Paterson — where unwise or wrong-headed local administrations have been guilty of offences of this kind; but in such agitations as that of the I. W. W. and their "Free Speech" allies in New York the grievance has been wholly factitious. There has, indeed, occurred a tragic climax to these goings-on; the killing of three of the New York anarchists by the explosion of a bomb which they were handling, and which there is almost no doubt that they were engaged in preparing for some work of destruction or slaughter. But while this is in one sense a less factitious martyrdom than the others, for it was certainly serious enough, yet in the most vital element of martyrdom it was obviously lacking altogether. Nobody invited, still less compelled, these gentlemen to blow themselves up; and when they did it, they were not engaged in defending themselves against aggression, nor, presumably, did they feel that they were in the slightest danger of themselves incurring the fate they were preparing for others. But all this does not in the least impede their elevation to the honors of martyrdom; and incidentally it may be remarked that although those who thus publicly honor their dead comrades in the cause of revolutionary anarchy say their say without interference, and go about the city of New York without molestation, there are not wanting persons who are ready at any moment to tear their hair over the suppression of free speech in this community.

But it is in the hunger strike that the new martyrdom

is seen full-fledged, and in its true character. Here we
have the fiction of persecution raised to the second power.
The use of it by the free-speech anarchists is of course only
one instance of its exploitation, but it is the one that specially concerns us here. Whether from its small beginnings
it will develop into a serious nuisance, or perhaps even
take on the dimensions of a grave problem, remains to be
seen. But men of sense should be prepared for the possible
spread of a great deal of foolish and muddled thinking on
the subject, and should from the outset see the thing exactly as it is. In a land of free discussion, and where the
right to vote is exercised without distinction of class, a
certain number of persons are actively engaged in the
agitation of radical or revolutionary changes affecting the
whole social order. No impediment is put in the way of
this propaganda in the shape either of censorship, of hin-
drance to publicity, or of personal proscription. They are
free to make as many converts as they can, either by oral
persuasion or by the printed word; and when they have
won over a sufficient number, the government is theirs.
Of one instrument, it is true, they are deprived the use;
and it happens that that instrument is the one most to
their liking. They are not allowed to create turbulence or
disorder, or to persecute individuals who have incurred
their hostility. In this, they are treated no otherwise than
advocates of the most innocent or orthodox of causes
would be under like circumstances. If there should arise
a Puritan agitation against the theatre, its leaders would
be allowed to denounce the stage to their heart's content
as a device of the Devil for the corruption and damnation
of mankind; but they would not be permitted to harangue
excited crowds that were ready to mob the actors and
actresses or to burn down the theatres. They would have
to content themselves with bringing over to their way of
thinking as many persons as could be won by orderly
methods. It is of this kind of restraint that the anarchists,
and other pretended champions of so-called free speech,

complain; it is against this imaginary grievance that the fraudulent martyrdom of the hunger strike is a protest.

And it is the fraudulence of the hunger strike, the affront that is offered to human reason, first in the thing itself, and still more in the silly cry of "torture" that is raised about it, that every sane man must most deeply resent. Here is a handful of cheap revolutionists making themselves more or less of a menace, but certainly very much of a nuisance, to the constituted authorities. This they do, in general, without a particle of molestation from the government or of inconvenience to themselves. Once in a while, when, in these proceedings, they pass, or are thought to pass, beyond a certain line, marked out by considerations of public safety or comfort, they are arrested and subjected to the mild punishment of imprisonment for a short term, such as is meted out to thousands of petty offenders. Then they proceed to set themselves up as judges in their own case; they demand that the law shall surrender to their will. And when this preposterous demand is met by the application to them of the most humane methods which professional skill can devise for securing the accomplishment of their sentence, they rend the air with shrieks of "torture." If the sentence itself was unjust, let them make all possible to-do about it by all means; nobody would begrudge them that. But they know only too well how little could be made of any real grievance they could lay claim to; and they count on a combination of soft-heartedness and soft-headedness in a considerable part of the public to make a self-inflicted stage-play torture pass current as the equivalent of the thumb-screw and the rack. Precisely what the penal authorities had best do if this foolishness should prove persistent in our country, it may not be easy to say. The one thing certain is that it cannot be trifled with. It is an impudent challenge, not only of the law, but of reason and humanity; and, unless we have quite lost our grip on the realities of life and government, whatever measures it may be found necessary to take in order to meet the challenge effectively will receive the emphatic approval of the American people.

To what extent the fantastic notions of the nature of the right of free speech that we have been discussing are shared by men of intelligence and culture, it is difficult to say. They are to be found distinctly among a certain small and fairly well-defined class of socialist or semi-socialist clergymen and other humanitarians. In a wider circle, these notions, if not distinctly embraced, are at all events given a considerable amount of sympathetic toleration. In either case, it is not too harsh a judgment to say that the attitude is due to want of thought or to shallowness of mind. The true doctrine of free speech is a broad principle of civic conduct, having its foundations in reason and experience, and its justification in the highest public expediency; these people appear to think of it as a simple and absolute dogma, whose sanction transcends all considerations of expediency, and any violation of which is a sin against the divine order. Such a view can be entertained only by a shallow thinker or a one-ideaed fanatic; and it is the former class, unquestionably, to which nearly all of the "free speech" extremists are to be assigned. The contrast between their crude and childish notions and that conception of the doctrine of free speech which is alone worthy of respect or of serious consideration cannot be better shown than by quoting the words of one of the greatest champions of individual liberty the world has ever known. It will hardly be claimed by even the most effervescent of our sentimental apostles of free speech that his own convictions on the subject are more profound, or his courage more uncompromising, than that of John Stuart Mill. In his noble tractate "On Liberty," Mill goes as far as anyone can go — farther no doubt in some respects than many of these same emotional humanitarians would go — in demanding complete freedom of public expression, so far as the substance of the opinions or doctrines in question is concerned. He does not draw the line at immorality; he does not draw the line at the advocacy of tyrannicide. But the ardor of his devotion to this principle is that of a rational thinker, not that of the blind slave of a fetish. That freedom of speech is made for man, not man for freedom of speech, is to him so obvious as to require no insisting on. A single brief passage — introduced at the beginning of his discussion of the question whether "the same reasons" which prescribe freedom of opinion and of speech "do not require that men should be free to act upon their opinions" — will suffice to show this:

No one pretends that actions should be as free as opinions. On the contrary, even opinions lose their immunity when the circumstances in which they are expressed are such as to constitute their expression a positive instigation to some mischievous act. An opinion that corn-dealers are starvers of the poor, or that private property is robbery, ought to be unmolested when simply circulated through the press, but may justly incur punishment when delivered orally to an excited mob assembled before the house of a corn-dealer, or when handed about among the same mob in the form of a placard.

When we note the remark, a little further on, that "the liberty of the individual must be thus far limited: he must not make himself a nuisance to other people;" and when we observe that after maintaining the right of an advocate of the doctrine of tyrannicide freely to express his opinions, Mill adds that the instigation to it in a specific case may be a proper subject of punishment, provided "an overt act has followed, and at least a probable connection can be established between the act and the instigation," — we see plainly enough the difference between the working of a profound and rational conviction like Mill's, and that of the shallow-pated emotionalism which rallies to the support of a Berkman or a Bouck White.

The confusion of thought which is at the bottom of these vagaries has been strikingly illustrated in connection with two matters upon which it may be profitable to dwell at some length. In both instances, the trouble is in part due to misinformation, or misconception of the facts; but in both instances the misinformation, or misconception, is inextricably bound up with the confusion of thought.

Closely allied to the false notion we have been discussing of what constitutes suppression of free speech by the authorities is the false notion, even more prevalent, of what constitutes suppression of the news by the newspapers. That there are some items of news that do not get the degree of publicity to which they are entitled may be quite true; and as regards the treatment by some newspapers of some whole classes of items, the accusation may be entirely justified. But that there exists anything like wholesale suppression of news, among the newspapers of the country generally, and especially by the Associated Press, is a charge absolutely without foundation. Regarded as a matter of large and fundamental public interest — not as a mere matter of ordinary criticism, dealing with imperfections of execution rather than with wrongfulness of intent — the question simply lapses for want of body to the accusation. The things charged as suppressions are so trivial in amount, in comparison with the vast mass of matter of precisely the same, or graver, nature carried in the papers, that the idea of the so-called suppression being anything more than defect in execution — even though sometimes due to the dishonesty of individuals and not always to accident or want of adequate equipment — should be peremptorily dismissed by any man who is accessible to ordinary argument on the subject.

But in the minds of its chief exponents, the idea that there exists a wholesale and systematic suppression of news in the interest of conservatism does not rest upon the omission, or the misrepresentation, of specific items in the record of what are generally regarded as the day's happenings. Their conviction that the newspapers are guilty of a great and systematic crime against the truth cannot be overcome by any such comparison as I have indicated; simply because the scale of values which they habitually use is fundamentally different from the scale which is current in the community at large. To their minds, the one absorbing concern of mankind is to end the iniquities of the existing economic order; and accordingly, the ordinary news of the day is utterly trivial in comparison with anything that bears upon the social revolution which they are sure is impending. Now it would be perfectly possible to fill many columns of a newspaper every day with matter of this kind — indeed there would be no difficulty in making up an entire newspaper of nothing else. The world is very big — even the United States, even New York city, is very big; and a diligent search for tales of evil, of hardship, of injustice, of rapacity, of poverty, would be amply rewarded any day in the year. Moreover, there are strikes, little and big, in the thousands of industrial and mining centres; there is every now and then the formation of a Socialist club or the starting of a little Socialist newspaper; and then there are speeches, and meetings, and what not. From the point of view of the man who is convinced that the present order of society is on its last legs, and that the supreme duty of the journalist is to expose its rottenness, these are the things with which our papers ought to be filled, instead of the idle chatter about politics and business. This opinion they are, of course, fully entitled to entertain; but their charge that the newspapers suppress the news is essentially based on the notion that the owners or editors of the papers are themselves of that opinion, but have not the honesty or the courage to act upon it. And this is too absurd to call for denial.

The other illustration that I have in mind arises out of the history of the Chicago Anarchists of 1886. There has gradually spread throughout the country a notion that the execution of the four anarchist agitators who were hanged for instigation of the slaughter of the policemen in Haymarket Square was little better than a judicial murder. This opinion is expressed in only a little more extreme form than that which is widely current, by Charles Edward Russell (late Socialist candidate for Governor of New York) when he says:

The eight men were convicted, nominally by the jury, in reality by a misinformed public opinion resolutely bent upon having a hanging. Anything more like the spirit of a lynching I have never known under the forms of law.

That a man of Mr. Russell's type should talk in this way is natural enough; but it is truly regrettable that an impression approximating this should be widely entertained among persons of intelligence and soberness, and having no sympathy at all with the Socialist, not to speak of the Anarchist, movement. The explanation of this phenomenon is to be found in part in the absence of knowledge of the actual facts; but it is to be found in at least equal measure in the failure to grasp the essential character, and the natural and rational limits, of the right of free speech.

At a time of great public excitement, arising in connection with a strike, a bomb was thrown into the midst of a platoon of policemen, wounding sixty-six of them, seven of whom died of their wounds. The men who were tried and convicted of this murder had, every one of them, been engaged in anarchist agitation; they had, every one of them, been members of a revolutionary society; the two most conspicuous were active promoters of a propaganda of violence as editors of revolutionary sheets and as public speakers. But it was not on these general grounds that the men were convicted. What was proved at the trial, to the satisfaction of the twelve jurymen and of the judge, was that these men were guilty of direct incitement to the precise kind of act that was actually committed — the killing of policemen as the defenders of the rights of property and the maintainers of law and order. Now the trouble with the tender-minded people who so easily accept the view that the executed Anarchists were martyrs of free speech and victims of something like lynch law is that they never ask themselves the question whether, in point of fact, these men were really instigators of the crime in the sense required by the law to make them murderers, or were not. The trial lasted nearly six weeks; it was perfectly orderly; and this question — the question of whether these men were legally guilty of murder — was put before the jury in the sharpest possible way by the judge. It was that question which they decided; it was upon that question that Judge Gary, who presided over the trial, declared, in a remarkable and convincing article written seven years later and published in the *Century Magazine*, that the verdict was absolutely sound, and involved no stretching of the law. Finally, it should be remembered above all — and yet it is constantly forgotten — that the Supreme Court of Illinois, a year after the trial, sustained the proceedings in a unanimous judgment; its opinion, covering 150 pages of the Illinois reports, being an exhaustive review not only of the law, but also of the facts of the case. To speak of a trial so conducted, and stamped with such approval, as being a proceeding in the nature of a lynching, is not only preposterous, but impudent.

In the foregoing discussion, and in the illustrations that have been adduced, what I have chiefly endeavored to bring out is the unreasonableness, and the practical absurdity, of the unthinking view which passes current with many for the noble and rational doctrine of freedom of speech and of the press. It may be well to add, in conclusion, a few words on a broader aspect of the matter. Just as religion may be made repulsive and odious by narrowness and bigotry; just as scientific or philosophic thought may be perverted by a spirit of intolerant dogmatism; so a high and inspiring doctrine of human conduct and polity may degenerate into an object of merited contempt when divorced from those considerations upon which its justification rests, and erected into a mere formula, to be followed with superstitious servility. That the absurdities which have been put forward in the name of the doctrine of free speech will actually have the effect of thus degrading and discrediting that doctrine, is not likely; but it is not likely only because common sense and sound feeling may be counted on to keep the folly from spreading. Yet it is the duty of men of light and leading to make clear their own position on the subject whenever it comes conspicuously to the front. They can in no better way serve the permanent interests of the cause of true freedom of speech than by showing, beyond the possibility of mistake, their contempt for the cheap counterfeit of it. In all the clamor that has been set up by the Bouck Whites and the Berkmans and the Upton Sinclairs, has any one pointed to a single doctrine that has been suppressed, a single teacher that has been silenced, a single truth, or alleged truth, that the authorities have endeavored to stifle? Time was when the champions of free speech have had to fight in order that men who had a message to deliver should have a chance to deliver it; what these make-believe apostles and martyrs have to fight for now is a chance to be suppressed. Nobody asks what it was that Bouck White or Becky Edelson wanted to say; what they ask is how he came to be dragged out of a church, or how she came to be arrested for being disorderly. And nobody asks the former question for two reasons — first, that the newspapers freely print what these people have to say; and secondly, that what they have to say is utterly familiar and commonplace. Suppression is not, with them, an obstacle to the spread of their teachings; on the contrary, it is their chief stock-in-trade, their sole claim to the attention of the public. What has elevated the doctrine of freedom of opinion and of speech to the lofty place which it holds in the estimation of mankind is the conviction, slowly acquired through ages of physical and spiritual struggle, that by that freedom can best be served the cause of truth, and hence the advancement of humanity. But with this neither the vulgar stage business of the New York Anarchists of to-day, nor the crazy appeals to the pistol and the bomb of the Chicago Anarchists of 1886, has anything whatever to do. To identify either with the great historic doctrine of free speech is to debase the intellectual and moral coinage of the race.

IS SOCIALISM COMING?

And when the pedants bade us mark
What cold mechanic happenings
Must come; our souls said in the dark,
"Belike; but there are likelier things."
                        G. K. CHESTERTON.

EVERY historian today owes much to Karl Marx for his development of the "Economic Interpretation of History." Whatever that theory may fail to explain, it certainly succeeds in explaining the nature and growth of the Socialist movement. When the great attempt at real political and economic democracy made by the French people in their great Revolution had failed and left behind it as a legacy the memory of the Terror and the wars of Napoleon, every nation in Europe felt the reaction. Russia, Austria, Spain and non-industrial Europe generally reacted towards simple absolutism, noble against peasant. But in the countries within the boundary marked out by the industrial revolution, the wealth created by the new machines placed the balance of economic power in the hands of the commercial classes, and so forced the old landed aristocracy to admit them to political power as well. In the meanwhile the first shock of large scale production had widened the gap between the industrial workers and the employing class. Independent artisans were ruined or forced into factories, and in the wake of the new industry there trailed a network of industrial oligarchies which spread until they covered the civilized world. The already enfranchised classes refused to use their power to moderate the harshness of the competitive struggle, honestly believing that any interference with

236

"economic law" could work nothing but ruin and hardship in the end.

In view of the facts as they existed in the days of the *Communist Manifesto* it was practically inevitable that an economist in sympathy with the economically powerless and politically disfranchised masses should interpret history as did the Marxians. In an age of coal, iron and steam (that potent trinity), of large scale production, of capitalistic agriculture, of economic tyranny, of sharpening class divergence and increasing poverty, it seemed that there was no way to realize democracy but to wait until industry had been concentrated into the hands of a few rich men, till the middle class and the free peasantry had been reduced to the proletarian ranks, and till the ever increasing misery of the workers taught them to combine and seize the means of production and distribution by a single revolutionary stroke. Private property could have appeared only as a tool for robbing the workers of the "surplus value" of their labor, religion as an ingenious means of sidetracking revolutionary activities, and patriotism as an excuse for standing armies and protective tariffs. This was a tenable explanation of the world — in 1848!

But the world has moved since the day of the *Manifesto*. Now manhood suffrage is the rule and not the exception. The worst forms of factory serfdom have been ended by legislative and economic changes. The various reform parties of Europe and America and even the Conservatives compete with each other for the workingman's vote by programs of social amelioration which steadily grow more ambitious every year. Socialism itself has altered in a changing world. The "Revisionist" or common-sense wing of the party has abandoned both the "surplus value" metaphysics, and the prophecy, so happily falsified, of "increasing misery" and "cumulative panics," and has moderated the class war dogma far enough to permit working hand in hand with the once hated bourgeoisie for immediate reforms. Other Socialists still repeat the old catchwords, but modify them by a process of "interpretation" analogous to that which makes Liberal Christians content to repeat the historic creeds. Of course some revolutionists have looked upon this readjustment with misgivings, and, as a result, we have sporadic and badly led revolts against party discipline, such as Syndicalism in France, Larkinism in England and the I. W. W. in America.

The main citadel of Socialist theory still remains intact, however, in the eyes of its defenders; and so the loss of unessential outposts harms the party very little. If it is true that industry conducted in large units is *always* in the end more efficient than if undertaken by many small units, sooner or later all the means of production and distribution will be concentrated either in the hands of a closely-knit class of industrial magnates or else in the hands of society as a whole. The only choice then open will be between control by the few, and control by the many: there will no longer be a choice between individualism and collectivism. This must be, because individualism always involves some measure of free competition, and under a system of competition the less efficient competitor is forced into the background by the more efficient. The one hope of saving both democracy and private property, then, lies in the chance that centralization beyond a certain point is not an economic gain.

The factors that undoubtedly do make for greater concentration are numerous and important, but they are so well known that a brief mention of a few of the more important will be sufficient here. The first cause of monopoly is the fact that nature is also a monopolist. Many valuable mineral deposits are found in quantity in a small area, and hardly at all outside of it. Coal, iron, timber, water-power and a ready access to market are not to be had everywhere. There are also economies in the greater size of a plant, especially where, as in the telegraph service or the railroad lines, there is an enormous initial expense in any case, and profits increase directly with the amount of business which can be done on the basis of a given amount of fixed capital. Standardization of commodities, especially of commodities used in production — such as machine parts, is an advantage to the consumer, and hence to the largest producer. In the large factory, moreover, the subdivision and specialization of labor can be carried farther — more processes can be handled under one roof, and more patents can be united into one machine. But the chief advantage of the great factory is that it can afford great quantities of *power* in place of using hand labor. The reason why "handicraft revivals" have had such limited success is that the most skilled of artisans, working by hand, cannot produce in quantity as can the engineer with his machine. So long as this difference exists, individual industry can only be a decorative border to the main fabric of industrial life. The *type* of power now generally used gives an added advantage to concentration. "For steam can only be generated in a fixed spot, and the motive power furnished thereby can only be distributed over a small area." [1]

These advantages are due to the *size* of a unit of production. But large industry is usually also rich industry (or it could not be very large), and there are other advantages due to the *wealth* of the owners. The wealthy concern can buy goods cheaply in quantity, and, if its demand is great enough, even exercise some control over the production of needed raw materials. It can afford the best machinery, the best labor, the best management. This advantage notoriously applies, even to such organizations as churches and universities, since the ablest pastors and professors are attracted by the largest institutions. A great saving can also be made by such factors as combining clerical forces, managers, salesmen and other employees of several firms into one, thus reducing salary costs, and preventing du-

[1] See H. de B. Gibbins, *Industry in England*, p. 382.

plication of effort. Other advantages of the rich firm are diminished advertising costs, the abolition of premiums, the reduced need of borrowed capital and of extending credit to consumers, power over prices, middlemen, carriers and competitors, the ability to adjust supply to probable demand, and, as centralization approaches monopoly, the power to reduce wages without fear of losing employees to other firms. What then is left but to admit the contention of the Socialist that Socialism has no alternative except the undesirable one of a new feudalism differing from the old only in resting upon an industrial rather than an agricultural basis?

The first objection I would make to the positing of this dilemma is to the assumption that the farmer can be safely ignored. Socialists admit that concentration is proceeding more slowly in agriculture than in any other branch of production, but they say that as industry develops, the movement toward the city which is so strong today will become stronger than ever, until the manufacturing population will outnumber the agricultural many times. But there is a balance in these things. We must have food, and every person who leaves the country for the city subtracts one from the number of food producers, and adds a customer for other farmers to supply. Hence the growth of a large population divorced from the land means a continually augmenting profit for the agriculturist, and a growing inducement to go "back to the land." Agriculture must then remain a cardinal factor in our economic life. To be sure, in the past the great estate has often triumphed over the small farm, and the Socialists maintain that it will again. If the causes which produced the "latifundia" of Rome, the feudal land ownership of the middle ages, the sheep farms of sixteenth century England, the capitalist farming of the early nineteenth century and the cotton plantations and "bonanza" wheat farms of America, were operative today, this contention would be right. But just the contrary is the case. The vast estates of eastern Prussia,[1] heavily mortgaged and hard pressed for labor, are being rapidly alienated by the landlords themselves, who are encouraging the government they dominate to establish a system of peasant proprietorships in their place. In France the small holder is triumphant economically, and he controls by his vote the political destinies of the Republic. In Australia and New Zealand, the squatters' sheep farms have receded before the advance of selectors' holdings, which in turn are being parcelled out under "Closer Settlement Acts." In Ireland most of the landlords have already been bought out under the Wyndham act, and even in England, where the custom of primogeniture has tended to keep estates together, the Conservative or landlords' party has promised to establish small holdings by a policy of government purchase from the present owners.

If the Socialist theory as regards agriculture holds good anywhere, it must be in America. But on turning to the census of 1910 what do we find? Over 62 per cent. of our farms are worked by their owners, and these include about 65 per cent. of the improved land, and more than that of total area! In 1850 the average number of acres to a farm was over 202; today it is 138.1. More significant yet, while the number of owned and rented farms increased, the number of farms worked by managers shows an absolute *decrease* in the decade since 1900. This was the type of farm that was going to supplant all others, according to the Marxian prophecy. In the words of the census:[2] "That the number of farms increased more rapidly than the acreage of land in farms, is accounted for partly by the fact that in some sections of the country considerable numbers of small truck, poultry and fruit farms have been established, but still more by the fact that in the West large numbers of farms of moderate size have been

[1] See W. H. Dawson, The Evolution of Modern Germany, chapter XIII. On the general subject of agricultural decentralization see Prof. V. G. Simkhovitch, *Marxism versus Socialism.*
[2] Thirteenth Census, *Agriculture,* chapter I.

established where great cattle ranches were formerly found. Then, too, in the Southern states, the subdivision of many plantations into smaller tracts of land operated by tenants — a process begun soon after the Civil War — has continued, each of such tracts counting as a farm under the census definition."

It is further to be noted that the forces which have tended to bring about the triumph of the state and the plantation, are of less and less significance as we turn to the future, whereas the counter forces which make for agricultural decentralization increase with the progress of population, invention and popular education. Slave labor was alike the cause of the Roman manor and the Mississippi plantation, but the world will probably never see slavery extended again, for it is at once too inhumane for modern sentiment, and too wasteful for present-day scientific methods. On its economic side, the American Civil War was a fight to the death between the small farm run by free labor, and the slave plantation. So, virtually, is the present conflict in Mexico. Certainly in the first case, and probably in the second, victory belongs to the farm. Feudalism was partly a result of the disorders caused by barbarian raids, which forced men to put themselves and their holdings under the protection of some great lord, and partly of the exhaustion of the precious metals, which made it necessary for a king to pay his retainers in landed estates instead of money. Neither factor has been operative for centuries, or probably ever will be again. Nor is it probable that it will ever again pay to turn good arable land into pasture, as happened in Tudor England: the increasing density of population forbids it. Capitalistic farming in the eighteenth and nineteenth centuries rested upon the costliness of agricultural machinery, and the ignorance of the average farmer. Today the advance of industry puts cheap machinery within the pocket-range of the individual farmer, and scientific training is placed within reach of all by agricultural schools and colleges, state and national experiment stations, and the free distribution of information. Knowledge is no longer a monopoly: the farmer is becoming an engineer of intensive agriculture. What factors *are* now effective? The chief is the growth of population, the consequent increased value of land, and therefore the need for conservation rather than exploitation of its richness. Small diversified stock, fruit, poultry and dairy farms, where every acre can be watched over and put to its best use, yield a greater profit than where the land is covered with staple crops. The agricultural laborer or "hired man" is another factor in the situation. Few persons like to work for wages, some do not like agricultural life, almost no one enjoys the combination. Hence the laborer in the country will either buy a small holding of his own, if he can, or else go to the city. Whole provinces in Germany east of the Elbe have been depopulated just for that reason. No doubt the wholesaler has certain advantages in marketing his goods, but such voluntary systems of coöperative credit and sales as are so popular in western Germany and Denmark, reduce this to a minimum.

Is agriculture a solitary exception to a general law of the indefinite concentration of industry? In many cases, such as the telephone, telegraph, cable (possibly *not* wireless telegraphy), railroads, steamship lines, certain kinds of mining, certain wholesale physical and chemical processes, and the making of standardized goods, no doubt concentration has advantages which do not tend to diminish. Such industries will be either socialistically owned, or quasi-socialistically controlled by the government. But this leaves a wide range of trade and manufacture where other centralizing factors operate, which are not permanent but temporary. If the largest plant, even today, is the most efficient, why do separate establishments increase in number so rapidly? In 1909 [1] the num-

[1] Thirteenth Census, *Manufacturing*. Handicrafts and establishments producing less than $500 worth of goods per year are not considered.

ber of establishments in the continental United States were no less than 268,491, representing an increase of 24.2 per cent. over the number in 1904. But the most remarkable fact is that the number of persons engaged in manufacture increased in the same period by only 23.6 per cent. and the number of wage workers, as distinguished from owners and salaried persons, only by 21.0 per cent. Of course the Socialist will reply that many different plants are really controlled by single corporations, openly or secretly, according to the degree of enforcement of "anti-trust" laws. This is perfectly true, but it belongs to another aspect of the problem. What the census figures indicate is that the maximum efficiency point of a *plant* has not only a definite limit, but may even decrease with the progress of industry. The truth is that Socialism is a phenomenon of the age of coal burning, the nineteenth century. Steam power is being more and more replaced by electrical power, which, generated in one place, can be used over an immense area. It is true that most electricity is still derived, at some loss of efficiency but an immense gain in availability, from the burning of coal or other fuel. But the coal beds are far from inexhaustible, and sooner or later we must supplement our supply by the "white coal" of the waterfalls. The Age of Electricity will usher in a second great industrial revolution. By putting power in quantity at the disposal of the independent artisan, it will for the first time in history enable him to compete with the great factory. Our tiny remnant of handicraftsmen may thus become a great army of artisan-engineers, combining the skill and personal attention of the old-fashioned master craftsman, with the technical training and machinery of modern engineering. And if the supply of energy within the atom is ever tapped to a sufficient degree, power will be as cheap as water, and the greatest advantage of the large producer be wiped out forever.

These changes will make small production a possibility;

there must be other causes to make it the general rule of industry. As wealth increases and the standard of living rises, quality in commodities will come to be considered as well as quantity. If the small productive unit cannot compete on even terms with the large in wholesale production, it may more than do so in retail production for an exacting market. "Finishing" industries, "assembling" industries and the like will absorb an ever increasing proportion of the industrial population. The future will have use for the expert, and only the expert; the mere laborer will be eliminated by the advance of education and the specialization of machinery. There will yet come a time when it will pay the manufacturer better to keep "cheap labor" in opulent idleness than to let its unskillful fingers touch the machines. Mere routine duties in commerce can be left in large measure to calculating and recording machinery. The great concerns will then run with a small office force and a staff of engineers, and release a host of supernumerary clerks and laborers for individual industry. The only "proletariat" will be one of cogs and wires and dynamos.

There still remains the problem of distribution. Will the great stores, banks and exchanges continue to control the economic life of the nation? Will competition in buying and selling crush the small producer, no matter how efficient his production? It must be admitted that this is a possibility. The last moral I should wish anyone to draw from this article is that "everything is bound to work out all right" because of certain beneficent economic laws. Certainly it will need all our statesmanship to realize the possibilities I have sketched. All I contend is that they *are* possibilities, that we are not hopelessly driven to the alternative of aristocratic or democratic collectivism, that the stars in their courses do not, as is so often contended, fight against the small producer. But I see no cause for despair in the matter of exchange and control. The small shop still continues to exist beside the big store; the individual concern may fail, but the type endures. Perhaps all middlemen, big and small, will in the end disappear as the connection between producer and consumer becomes more direct. Even the poorest classes of the future will, I think, buy more goods to order than ready made. As to the power of the big establishment over carriers and middlemen, these can be controlled in part by law, as in the extirpation of the railway rebate. The advantages of credit and capital on the side of the large concerns, can be offset by coöperative credit and sales agencies, as readily in manufacturing as in agriculture. By ensuring a high level of competition unfair advantages can be eliminated, and the fight be purely one of industrial efficiency, which is not always on the side of the biggest battalions.

It is of the first importance to realize that each perceptible social change involves many other perceptible changes, that, in Spencer's happy analogy, the social constitution is a web, no strand of which can be moved without moving others. The changes we have tried to forecast cannot come effectively before the subsidence of the wave of fierce competition which was partly smoothed down by the trusts. In many businesses, competition in drumming and advertising is still at the point where it costs more to sell goods than to make them and hosts of men accomplish only the neutralizing of each other's efforts. The rationalizing of competition and the growth of a coöperative spirit would release men for other pursuits; and the growth of intelligence in learning what is to be had and discriminating what is best, must diminish the billions spent on advertising. These additions to productive labor and capital must diminish the ills which have made Socialism seem desirable as well as inevitable.

Suppose we do our best to realize these possibilities to the full. Suppose a Socialist then revisits the earth two or three hundred years from now. He may see in full operation what he has always declared impossible, a democratic individualism. Instead of an impoverished and disappearing farming class, he will find a populous countryside divided into small homesteads, and run at a handsome profit by specialists in intensive agriculture. Instead of a factory or mining proletariat, hungry and rebellious, he will find great wholesale establishments owned and run by a handful of engineers, turning out pulp, cloth, metal and standard parts for machinery, turning the products over to millions of independent artisan establishments supplied with cheap and plentiful power, to be worked into countless articles of art and utility. He will look to the processes of exchange to find great financial magnates and railway barons on the one hand, and a horde of miserable clerks and small shopkeepers in difficulties on the other. Instead, he will discover a network of voluntary credit and sales associations, information bureaus, individually owned freight automobiles (and possibly airships); with perhaps a few regulated railway lines and pneumatic delivery tubes, run by a prosperous association of experts. He will look for the old-time "servant class," and find that the scientifically trained housewife, with a power plant in the cellar, can run her own house, thank you, and consider it the most honorable of professions. Seeing everything so effectively managed for the happiness of the people, he will look to see in the government the universal owner and employer of his dreams, but he will find instead a clearing house of help and information, which puts its knowledge of efficient management, of technical processes, of economic and sociological conditions, at everyone's disposal, and comes to the rescue in the rare case of poverty, failure or crime. Will he rejoice that the world is happy, or be sorry that it is not happy his way? If I know the Socialist, he will claim that he was right all along, and that this state of society is really Socialism. Let him claim the word; I call it democratic individualism, because it means the greatest possible *distribution* of economic power and function consistent with efficient production.

THE REPUBLIC OF MEGAPHON

Persons of the Dialogue: *Socrates.*
Chærephon.
Megaphon.

Scene: At first a street in the Metropolis,[1] and afterward the
house of Megaphon.[2]

Time: Year 4 of Olympiad 25 after American Independence.

The narrator and leading person of the dialogue is Socrates.

I. I had gone into the city on the Fourth day of the
month to witness how they would observe the Festival,
and was returning at my leisure, when Chærephon,
catching sight of me at a distance, ordered his son
to run forward and bid me wait for him. And the boy,
taking hold of me by the cloak behind, said: "My father
bids you wait for him."

"By all means," said I.

And not long afterward Chærephon came.

"Socrates," he said, "you seem to be returning from
the city."

"You guess not badly," I replied.

We continued on our way, and soon came near the
crossing of two streets. Here, a boy was standing at the
curb, calling loudly to all who passed.

"What are the words he cries?" I said to Chærephon.

"The *Republic*," he answered. "It is the new paper,
that will come forth daily, and is to help the demos; for
you know that until now it has come but thrice a week,
and has been for the few. Have you not heard of it?"

"Yes," I said, "and I have thought about it much.

---

[1] Apparently there was a Greek colony in the city. — The notes are by the
Editor.

[2] The O in Megaphon is long, representing the Greek omega. Quite possibly
the author's use of the word is satirical.

Henceforth we shall have the news every day, and in a different way."

We had now come to the boy, and were passing him.

"Here, boy," I said, "give me your paper."

He gave it to me, still crying as before.

"And how much must I pay you for it?" I asked.

"An obol," [1] he replied.

"Very well," said I, and gave him the obol.

"Is it not cheap?" said Chærephon. "And do you not think the demos has great reason to rejoice? For now many more will be able to read of what takes place."

"It is indeed cheap," I said, "and now the demos may indeed read all it will. But I do not think it may rejoice."

"Do I hear aright?" he asked. "Can it be you do not like the change?"

"You do hear aright," I answered. "I do not like it."

"But 'twill educate the demos," he said.

"It will," I said, "and that is why I do not like it. My thought is that 'twill educate them wrongly, and we shall have trouble from it. But let us discuss the matter, if that will please you." [2]

II. "Most gladly," he said. "But look, yonder is Megaphon's house, and I told him I would stop. Will you go with me, and there discuss in the hearing of us both?"

"Yes," I said, "most willingly."

We drew near, and Chærephon beat gently upon the door with his sandal,[3] and we waited until someone should come from within.

The son of Chærephon, first asking his sire's permission, now joined other boys who were vying one with another in a game of making noises.

---

[1] About three cents.

[2] The language of this first section bears a striking resemblance to the beautiful translation, by Alexander Kerr, of a work called "The Republic of Plato."

[3] The ancient Greek manner of knocking for admission seems to have survived.

Now the playing of the game was on this wise. Chærephon's son would take from the store in his pocket a
crimson paper, tightly rolled, containing an explosive.
This he set off by means of a thread which projected from
the end of the roll, and contained the same explosive, but
not so much. The thread was called the fuse, and the
roll a "cracker." When lighted with a match, the fuse
would quickly carry fire to the cracker, which, straightway
bursting, made a loud report. But first Chærephon's son
would send it flying through the air, lest it harm his fingers. Yet there were lads of hardihood who boldly held
the cracker as it burst, and remained unharmed; and these
were the winners of the game.

This at that time was for young and old the manner of
celebrating the nation's freedom. For the people had once
been in thrall to the tyrant.

III. While we yet stood looking on at this sport, the
daughter of Megaphon opened to us.

"My sire is within," she said; and pointed to the door
of the megaron.

The door was open, and we entered. At first we saw
no one, but after some moments became aware of Megaphon's legs, which alone could be seen of all his body. For
the rest of his body was hidden by a printed sheet. This
sheet, we saw, was the *Republic;* for the letters were large.

"Hail, O Megaphon!" I cried in a loud voice.

Megaphon lowered the sheet until his face appeared,
and then leaped up.

"A thousand pardons, Socrates and Chærephon!" he
cried. "I was deep in the paper, and did not notice.
Pray seat yourselves."

We seated ourselves in front of him, and not far off.

Megaphon laid aside the paper, as it seemed, unwillingly.

"What were you reading, O Megaphon?" Chærephon
inquired, to start our discussion. For he knew well, without the asking.

"The *Republic*," Megaphon replied. "Ah, I see you have one, Socrates. Is it not fine, and should we not rejoice? The demos will surely make great progress now, and our nation will become much greater than ever, for we shall have news every day, and nearly all will be rich enough to read, and nearly all will thus become intelligent."

Chærephon gazed at me.

"But Socrates does not approve," he said.

"No," I said, "by Zeus, no!"[1]

Megaphon was greatly astonished.

"I do not understand," he said. "Will not knowledge be spread among our people as never before, and will not our demos become well informed and thinking citizens, no longer a prey to their own ignorance or to the deceits of their enemies? For we shall now have the news at trifling cost, I think. Is it not so, O Socrates?"

"At trifling cost, most certainly," I answered. "To speak truly, the cost is even too little. But shall we discuss the matter?"

"By all means," he said.

"And will you listen to me with patience," I said, "and answer what I ask, and not grow angry?"

"We will do as you say," he said. "Will we not, Chærephon?"

Chærephon agreed.

IV. "Well, then," I began, "I suppose we may assume that the *Republic*, and others — for without doubt there will in time be many like it — will be taken daily into the homes of the demos, as well as of the few. Is it not so?"

Megaphon assented.

"Then let us speak of the matter in this fashion," I said. "Suppose you had an acquaintance who came to visit you every day in the year, and was admitted not only to yourself, but freely to your wife and your sons and

[1] The theological terminology of antiquity clings to the narrator's language.

daughters. On entering, he first makes a great show of importance and a great deal of noise by calling out in an exceedingly loud voice that a cruel murder has been done, or a savage battle has been fought, or a shocking accident has happened, or a great robbery has been attempted, and comes up quite close to all of you and points out in every detail just how the accident or the crime took place. After this, he tells you of lesser crimes and mishaps — of thefts, adulteries, and murders among the poor and vicious, and the like; and then he tells with great exactness of many brutal contests — of the pancration,[1] of boxing with the cestus,[2] and of the fights of cocks and dogs. He tells you also of the life of the idle, who do nothing but eat and drink, passing the nights in waking and the days in sleep, consuming in pleasures they do not need the substance they have not earned. And suppose he counsels you to hate not only them, but all who possess greater store of goods than you. And then suppose he will tell you of various things which he says you should not lack, now screaming loudly that these goods will be sold for less than they cost, and now whispering other things of the sort with equal earnestness, and with equal intent to deceive you. Suppose he not only tried to sell you good and necessary wares, but that which he knew you did not need, or was worthless. And suppose he told you much that was true of your neighbors but was no concern of his, and repeated much that was false and harmful. And suppose his words were often vulgar and many times profane, and that his jests were coarse, and even obscene, and you should come upon him murmuring to your wife and children such things as the tongue should in no wise repeat."[3]

Megaphon seemed not quite content with my words.

"Suppose," I said, "that he did and said such things in your house, not twice or thrice in the year, but daily,

[1] Now called "rough-and-tumble", or "catch-as-catch-can".
[2] Meaning the hard glove.
[3] Socrates is in striking agreement with Fred Newton Scott, The Undefended Gate, *English Journal*, January, 1914, p. 5.

ever boasting of his virtues, and telling you all that he was your true and faithful friend. Would you not think the advantage of his presence doubtful?"

"I should," said Megaphon, "if he were all you say he would be; and I should not let him remain, but kick him out of doors without delay, and forbid him to enter again. But surely there are other matters he would relate, such as we should be glad to hear of, and we should not need to listen to all he said, nor buy all he would have us buy."

"No," I said, "doubtless not; but his company would be unpleasant, even if you neither bought nor heeded. For he would offend you often, and waste your time."

"And the *Republic*, I think, is not wholly like the acquaintance you describe," Megaphon said. For he bore ill what I said.

"But it will be so in no long time," I said.

"Will you tell us why?" he asked.

V. "I will, assuredly," I said. "Let us inquire farther. Just now I paid for the *Republic* one obol, did I not? and heretofore it cost two? The price is now but half, and soon it will be still less. For so at least they promise. Is it not true?"

"It is," Megaphon said. "And justly, as I think. For the demos should be encouraged to read."

"Very well," I said, "when the former price is cut in half, will it not be impossible to gain as much? For gain is the purpose of the newspaper, and its owners will not publish it unless they receive gain, and the greatest possible amount. If they cut the price in half, they will of a surety use other means to bring them the money thus lost. Will it not be so?"

"But more people will buy and read," he said.

"Yes," I said, "they will. But more men and better machines will be needed, and the paper will be much larger, as you already see. Without doubt, they will not be able to give for so small a sum a paper so large."

"You seem to speak truly," he said.

"Then whence will come the gain I speak of?" I said. "Will it not come perforce from advertisements? At least, so I have read, for you see I know what is being talked. And how shall they increase the number of those who advertise, and make the price greater? For both, I think, will be necessary. Will it not be by having more who purchase and read? For those who buy and sell goods will pay a higher price only if more are to read their advertisements. Do you think I am right, Megaphon?"

"So it appears to me," he said.

"Then," I said, "is it not clear that we shall have a change in the newspaper's ways? Until now, the newspaper has had its gains mostly from those who read, and but little from those who advertise; but henceforth it will be contrariwise. It will not enrich itself from readers — except as their number brings more and better-paying advertisements."

"And there is another thing," Chærephon said. "The character of the readers will also change. There will henceforth be more of them untaught and unthinking than before, because of the cheapness of the paper. Will it not be so?"

"Most certainly," I said; "you have anticipated my thought."

VI. "Then," I continued, "if this is as I say, will it not of necessity follow that henceforth the paper will be so ordered as to suit the tastes of the many rather than of the few?"

"I do not disagree," said Megaphon.

"For," Chærephon said, "you cannot suit at once the tastes of both the ignorant and the intelligent."

"And what are the tastes of the demos?" I said. "Does not the demos like excitement, and will not the newspaper set forth in detail every manner of accident and crime and gossip? Doubtless you have seen the demos, how it behaves when the dead are to be seen, or when the wedding of some rich person takes place, or evildoers are being led by the Eleven to be punished."

"Yes," he said, "I have. The demos has but poor taste in many matters. The demos likes above all to be entertained, and it delights in things that are strange and horrible."

"True," I answered, "and the demos does not like to think; for that is a difficult sort of labor. It will be necessary to omit that which would please the few, and put in its place that which is amusing and easy to understand. And there will doubtless also be much that is unseemly and shameful to read."

I took up the *Republic* from Megaphon's side.

"Indeed," I said, "that of which I speak has already begun. I will read you what stands written here:

'An important witness against Bloombury Bright, Priest of the Pericles Avenue Temple of Zeus, in Bright's trial before fifteen priests of the State Synodos, was Theodora wife of Diodoros Ploutocrates. She charged that in the month Anthesterion the priest embraced and kissed her twice. On a second visit, when he found her wearing a chiton,[1] she says, he was more violent in his attentions.'"

"Do you not think this very vile, O Megaphon?" I asked.

"Most vile indeed," he said.

"And would you like to have your daughter read it?"

"No, by Zeus!" he cried. "For there is no good in it, but only evil. It would befoul her mind."

VII. "And there will be another consequence," I said. "Will not the makers of the paper think they must make it attractive to the demos at all costs, and will not the gatherers and arrangers of the news learn to do this by

---

[1] Socrates altered several terms as he read, probably for the sake of humor. An examination of the original shows "kimono" for "chiton."

adding to or taking from the truth, or even by inventing news; so that we shall not be able to distinguish between the true and the false?"

"It will be," he said, "as you say; at least in the case of the paper that tries above all to please the demos."

"There will thus be deception in two ways," I said: "they will omit, and they will invent and add. But this is not the only evil from which we shall suffer. For consider the editor's page. The newspaper has always been, it says, the moulder of the demos's thoughts; and so, indeed, it was, so long as its editors were leaders of great causes, and thought strongly, and were masters of their own words. But how, when it must make its gains from those who buy and sell, and not from the followers of truth, shall it be able to attack or to favor whatsoever and whomsoever it please? How shall it be free to attack evil rich men whose advertisements it must have, or oppose a party or a movement cherished by them? And how in turn shall it be free to attack the inconstant demos itself, by whom it must be purchased? For it will not be conducted on principle, and look for its gains to those who read, but commercially, and look to those who advertise."

"I do not see," Megaphon said, "how it can avoid these evils."

VIII. "Does it not seem clear, then," I said, "that the editor's page will be secretly open to purchase, and no longer truthful? For 'We must live,' the owners will say."

"Yes," Chærephon replied; "and I have another thought. I am thinking that much harm may come because we shall have news confused with advertisement, or with secret attempts of various kinds."

"You think rightly," I said. "We shall have persons or groups of persons making deceitful use of the news in advertising their products, or in courting the favor of the demos for some project. Indeed, I think that something might occur like this: those who sell goods for our triremes and hoplites might pay out great sums for the secret aid of the newspapers in rousing the passions of the demos by appeal to its natural hatred and fear of the barbarians. For then the State would increase the number of ships and soldiers of every kind, and thus they would sell more goods, and make greater gains. Or a maker of some food or medicine, or a false follower of Asklepias, might do the like; and the demos, which is ever seeking after cures for real and fancied ills, would soon enrich him. Can you not think that this could happen?"

"I can indeed," Megaphon said.

"Then," I said, "have we not proved that the newspaper will be used to educate the demos wrongly — I mean by giving too much news of one kind, and not enough of another, and exaggerating, coloring, and otherwise falsifying the truth, and pretending to be a friend when it is an enemy, and selling itself, whenever it safely can, to him who will give most?"

"I will admit what you say," Megaphon said; "for I am eager to hear whither your discussion will lead."

IX. "It appears, then," I said, "that there is some doubt as to this education of the demos you rely upon, as to whether it will be as nearly perfect as you think. But let us go farther. I have spoken until now of matters of fact. Shall I now say something of matters of taste? — if you will yield to me in this, that taste has much to do with the worth of nations."

"I will concede it," he said.

"Consider, then," I began, "the language which the newspaper will employ in its effort to please the demos. Will it not be of necessity untaught and rough, and often coarse, like the speech of the demos itself? For if it is to attract the demos, it must be easy to read, and of spicy savor, thus to say, and must not speak after the manner of the few. For the demos will have nothing superior to itself. We shall thus find ourselves at cross purposes; our didaskaloi will be trying to teach our epheboi to speak and write purely, and the newspaper will teach them to speak and write like the demos. Of a truth, men who write purely and well will not be employed, but only those whose manner is of the demos. And again, they will cost the owners less. Do you think I am right?"

"I grant it," Megaphon said.

"And consider not only the news and the manner in which it is written, but the advertisements also, of what nature they will be. Will not many worthless things be advertised in a bold and shameless manner? and will not the effect of this be to confirm bad taste on the part of the demos, and beget and encourage it among the few who are better taught? Let me see your paper again."

Megaphon gave me the paper.

I opened it, and, having searched some moments, "Listen," I said:

'Oh, say boys, don't forget that sore, sweating, tired feet often have a wonderful penetrating and terrific odor which is very unpleasant in the home or with company. Asklepian's Antiseptic cures all the trouble. Pharmakopoles Pharmakopolides.'

Pharmakopoles moves in our best society, as the saying is, and is foremost amongst those who sacrifice to Zeus. Does it not seem to you that we have here an example of that which must be expected?"

"Undoubtedly," said Megaphon and Chærephon together.

"And will not also the art of the newspaper often be vulgar? For it will be used to entertain the demos."

"We agree with you," they said.

"And they will try to amuse the children, too," I said. "Our young ones will be taught many things they should not know, and the ugly will seem fair to them, and the fair ugly.[1] For that which is vulgar will seem to have power when seen in print."

---

[1] He evidently foresees the comic Sunday supplement.

X. "And I think we shall have something still worse," I said. "For I fear our morals, too, will stand in some danger. Consider the advertisements of those who would sell the barbarian potion,[1] and the weed of Lethe,[2] and other like doubtful wares, and among them books professing to tell of such mysteries as only sires should tell their sons, and mothers their daughters. Will not our epheboi be constantly assured how harmless these things are, and how pleasant to have, and thus become convinced that they are good rather than evil? For the printed word is a power, as I said, and we fear less the dangers we see most often."

"At least," said Chærephon, "there will be danger if we do not guard ourselves."

XI. "You speak truly," I said; "there will. But I bethink me of still another danger now, and one that will affect not individuals, but classes. Shall I speak of it?"

"Go on," Chærephon said.

"Very well," I said. "The demos is composed of men and women, and is but human. The demos likes sympathy, and the demos is also vain, and likes to be talked of, and to see its own name in print. If, then, the newspaper would make friends with the demos, it will need to tell of the demos and what it does — of its leaders, and of its virtues, and in like manner of its vanities; for it is no less vain than those it rails at. It will thus flatter the demos by making it feel as important as its betters, and teaching it to think it knows as much as they, about not a few things, but many. It will speak much of the demos's sufferings, and of the demos's worth, and of the demos's rights, and it will make much use of sentimentality, and little of real sentiment, reason, and fact; for reason is a

---

[1] This means lager beer, which has never appealed to the Hellenes, either now or in antiquity. The celebrated potologist Symposiastes records his conviction (Opera XL, 3, 2) that barbarian, barley (from which beer is made), bar (where it is sold), barrel, baron, and baroque are all etymologically related.
[2] Can this mean tobacco?

troublesome thing. Will not this be an excellent way for the newspaper to win friends in great numbers, O Megaphon?"

"It cannot be denied," he said.

"And if this is true, will it not increase its favor with the demos if it also assails those who have store of goods, or gifts bestowed by the Muses, and makes it appear that their riches are due to accidents of fortune or unjust workings of the law, that their talents are not above the ordinary, and that the gifts of the Muses have no value whatsoever? For it will be among the demos that the greatest number of the paper's friends must be won."

"Yes," Megaphon said, "in that manner it would surely make friends."

"It appears, then," I said, "that flattery of the demos and fault-finding with the few will be an excellent means for the newspaper to become rich. And consider the evil this will work among us. For the newspaper will make the few seem to the many richer and prouder and more selfish than they are, and the many seem to themselves poorer and more humble and virtuous than they are; besides making them wise in their own conceit, so that they will become meddlesome by trying to do many things of which they know nothing, and by doing them all awry. For the demos is a many-headed beast, lighter and more fickle than

> 'the moon, th' inconstant moon,
> That monthly changes in her circled orb,'

as one of our poets saith."

"And consider," I said, "the newspapers of the few — for some will not enslave themselves wholly to Hermes, the God of Gain — how they will be misunderstood, and blamed without desert. The demos will be told by its leaders and its newspapers that the papers of the few pretend to know more than other folk, and that they are against the poor and secretly in favor of the rich. And they will not receive them into their homes, and will take little account of them. And that will make the task of these papers difficult, and they will lose hope, and will be inclined to counsel the few to distrust overmuch the many, just as the papers of the many will counsel the many to distrust the few. So that the many and the few will be encouraged to suspect, distrust, and hate each other. Will they not?"

"Yes," Megaphon said. "At least, so you make it appear."

"And this will be very harmful to the State?"

"I agree," he said.

XII. "Then," I said, "we seem to be at this point in our discussion: that there will be danger that the newspaper will not speak the truth impartially and thus educate the many, but will give them only phases of the truth, deceitful news, and interested opinions, misleading instead of educating them; and instead of forming their opinions for the better, it will rather follow their opinions, and often encourage them in thinking that which they should not think; and instead of improving their taste, it will confirm it, and degrade the taste of those who should know better; and it will counsel men to think ill one of another, and thus work damage to the State. Does this seem to sum up our conclusions?"

"It does," Megaphon said.

"And does not this seem to you quite the opposite of what a short time ago you said was to be expected?"

"So it seems," he said.

XIII. "And still," I said, "I do not think that this is the worst that may befall. I have another matter in mind. Shall we discuss that also, O Megaphon and Chærephon?"

"Yes, by Zeus," they said, "by all means."

"Very well, then. What," I said, "do you think will be the effect on the mind of the demos when it shall read daily of so much murder, violence, stealing, and deceit, and so many mishaps caused by carelessness? Will it not surely conceive that mankind is wholly selfish and lawless and not to be trusted, and hopelessly bad? You are aware, are you not, that men judge of the world by what part of it they see and read of, and that this they cannot help? And in the case whereof we speak, what they read will be mostly bad, and will have greater weight than what they see about them. For all evil things seem dreadful at a distance."

"I see the force of your argument," Megaphon said.

"Doubtless," I said, "you have been told of the man without sight who was made acquainted with the great African beast.[1] Having been led to the animal, he was permitted to grasp only its tail; whereupon, 'This animal,' he said, 'is very like a rope.' Now I think that one who had touched another part would have made a different answer. Would he not?"

"You speak truly," Chærephon said. "It would be according to the part he touched."

"Then let us continue," I said. "The followers of Zeus and Athena, what will they think when they shall have been told again and again, sometimes with truth and sometimes falsely, of priests or worshippers that have loved not wisely but basely, or have stolen, or cheated, or misbehaved in any other wise? Will they not soon distrust all who sacrifice to Zeus and Athena and the other blessed gods, and will they not of necessity disbelieve in them? For they will think that the gods have failed to make their worshippers good men. And thus the demos will become skeptical of all religion, and our temples will be empty. What do you think?"

"I think it will be as you say," he said; "for indeed, I have already seen it happen with men as you describe."

"And what will be the effect if the demos is told from early youth to manhood, not once in a while but every

[1] The elephant.

day, of the lies of those who would be rulers of the State, the knavery of those who buy and sell, the baseness of those entrusted with their neighbors' money, and the unseemly means employed by men of every class to circumvent their enemies? Will it not be to convince the demos that all men are to be won by gain, and that no one may be trusted? Will it not suspect, after so many deeds of baseness, on the part of its leaders as well as others, that no law is proposed, no deed performed, however fair in its seeming, that has not an unworthy purpose at its root, and that no pleasant word is spoken and no fair promise given but with intent to deceive?"

"You seem to speak truly," Megaphon said.

"And will it not become skeptical of all men of any calling whatsoever, in even greater measure than of our priests and our religion?"

"In even greater measure," he said; "for men are loath to give up their faith in the gods."

"And will it not say that to know the truth is impossible, inasmuch as every man obscures the face of truth for his own advantage? And is it not plain as regards the State, in what condition it then will be?"

"What?" said Chærephon and Megaphon.

"Every citizen," I said, "will be convinced that many of his fellows are rascals, and that all are selfish and deceitful, and will say in his heart: 'What boots it for me alone to speak the truth, or to do for Zeus and my neighbor that which brings travail to me?' And he will conclude by doing as he has been taught that all men do. And this is the very worst of ill fortune for the State, for its citizens to be filled with suspicion and distrust and hopelessness, and to think they should act for no one's welfare but their own. This is evil thinking at its worst.[1] Is it not, O Chærephon and Megaphon?"

"It is, in very truth," Chærephon said.

[1] He means pessimism, which is known to have existed before the term came into use.

XIV. But Megaphon was silent.

"What is it, O Megaphon?" I asked.

"You do not seem to me wholly just, O Socrates," he answered. "And I have been thinking that if I should ask and you should answer, or if you should ask in a different way, the matter might not appear the same, but otherwise."

"Then will you ask?" I inquired.

"I will ask but this, O Socrates," he said: "for in most things I think you speak truth. But are we, then, to hear naught of what our citizens do except that which is good, and are we never to know the evil they commit? Is not darkness the friend of evil, and light its enemy? And will it be well with the demos if it have no friend to cry out its wrongs?"

"I will answer briefly," I said; "for He of the Far-darts is already high in the heavens. If there were no guilty men, and no foolish, doubtless the newspapers would not tell the demos of their deeds. Nor do I think that guilt and folly and every manner of intemperance should be let thrive in darkness, and not be brought forth for men to scorn and punish. But I will tell you in what manner I think. Suppose, O Megaphon, that it were allowed to you to look into some dark and unknown chamber, through only one narrow chink, and that through this chink your guide should let enter strong rays to light up but one little corner, and that an ill-ordered one with crawling vermin. Would you not become convinced, from seeing that only, and not the rest, that all the chamber was awry and foul? And if you looked into many chambers, and saw all in the same condition, would you not become convinced that all chambers were awry and foul, and that to strive for cleanliness and order were in vain?"

"I think I should," he said, "if I saw as you describe."

"That," I said, "is what I think about the use of light in these matters. I think 'twould be far better to use a candle and explore more thoroughly; and best of all to open the chamber to the light of the sun, which is the light of truth. Then we should see the entire chamber, and I think we should say: 'This is a goodly chamber, but hath a foul spot,' and fall to and set it in order, and sacrifice to Zeus for his goodness to mortal men."

"But the wrongs of the demos," he said; "must it not have champions to right them?"

"Truth is the champion that will best right wrongs, both for the many and the few," I replied. "But truth ill told for selfish and evil purposes will set men one against another, and we shall have no peace. Do you think I speak words of reason?"

"Yes, by Zeus and Athena!" said Megaphon and Chærephon.

"Then," I said, "let us pray to Athena, Giver of Wisdom, beseeching that she will make men love that which is true, and hate that which is false. For thus they will learn justice, and our State will be one people, and not two."

"Let us indeed," they said.

Chærephon and I then took our leave.

THE CURSE OF ADAM AND THE CURSE
OF EVE

I

"THE wide-spread change in thought and attitude of my sex towards yours," which Anastasia Beauchamp announced to Adrain Savage in "Lucas Malet's" novel of the latter name, affects marriage, of course, primarily. And it appears from Ida M. Tarbell, *Making a Man of Herself* (*The American Magazine*, February, 1912) that the leaders of Feminism have been trying for many years to dissuade their younger sisters from matrimony:

Man and marriage are a trap — that is the essence the young woman draws from the campaign for woman's rights. . . . She will be a "free" individual, not one "tied" to a man. The "drudgery" of the household she will exchange for what she conceives to be the broad and inspiring work which men are doing. From the narrow life of the family she will escape to the excitement and triumph of a "career." The Business of Being a Woman becomes something to be ashamed of, to be apologized for. All over the land there are women with children clamoring about them, apologizing for never having *done* anything. Women whose days are spent in trades and professions complacently congratulate themselves that they at least have *lived*. There were girls in the early days of the movement, as there no doubt are today, that prayed on their knees that they might escape the frightful isolation of marriage; might be free to "live," and to "know," and to "do."

In another article she says:

"Celibacy is the aristocracy of the future," is the preaching of one European Feminist. . . . The ranks of the women celibates are not full. Many a candidate falls out by the way, confronted by something she had not reckoned with — the eternal command that she be a woman. She compromises — grudgingly. She will be a woman on condition that she is

266

guaranteed economic freedom, opportunity for self-expressive work, political recognition. What this amounts to is that she does not see in the woman's life a satisfying and permanent end.

Naturally, this attitude does not tend toward domestic contentment, peace and happiness. The woman who marries in this frame of mind already has her face set toward Reno.

Yet the instinct for maternity is a force. Therefore the great desideratum in the opinion of George Bernard Shaw and Ellen Key is the satisfaction of the instinct without the inconvenience of a husband. But when he comes to deal with the facts Shaw's courage fails him, and he turns tail and flees. In *Getting Married* he confesses that, in spite of all its horrors, he can invent no substitute for marriage. Ellen Key, on the other hand, in *Love and Marriage*, has the courage of her convictions.

And yet her relations to man cannot be entirely without satisfactions to woman. She cannot be quite the slave that the Feminists describe. Anna A. Rogers, in *Why American Marriages Fail* (*Atlantic Monthly*, September, 1907) speaks of

the present false and demoralizing deification of women, especially in this country, an idolatry of which we as a people are so inordinately proud. One of the evil effects of this attitude is shown in the intolerance and selfishness of young wives, which is largely responsible for the scandalous slackening of marriage ties in the United States. . . . Our women as a whole are spoiled, extremely idle, and curiously undeserving of the maudlin worship that they demand from our hard-working men. . . . The hair-dressers, the manicurists, the cafes at lunch time, are full to overflowing with women — extravagant, idle, self-centred. . . . She has not merged her fate with her husband's, if married, nor with her father's if not: she does not properly supplement their lives; she is striving for a detached, profitless, individuality. . . . The sacredness and mystery of womanhood are fast passing away from among us.

A successful woman dramatist, an interview with whom

was published in *The New York Times* a few months ago, said:

The American man is a great deal more unselfish and chivalrous than is good for the woman. He often bears his own burden, and part of the woman's. This is very excellent discipline for him, but it is hard on the woman. She doesn't have a chance to learn sacrifice.

Miss Tarbell recognized that the Feminist was in revolt against the drudgery of the household. Edna Kenton, for the militants, is even more explicit. She says in *Militant Women — and Women* (*The Century Magazine*, November, 1913):

There is rising revolt among women against the unspeakable dullness of unvaried home life. It has been a long, deadly routine, a life servitude imposed on her for ages in a man-made world. . . . There is nothing in the home alone to satisfy woman's longing for variety, adventure, romance.

How many men have any means of satisfying their longings for variety, adventure and romance? Miss Kenton's notion that "the restrictions on men's free-willing are comparatively few," is mere silliness. In the business and professional classes woman's opportunities of disposing of her time and cultivating her tastes are vastly greater than man's, and among the less fortunate classes, the care of a three-room flat or a five-room house is a lighter servitude than that by which the man gets the bread for his wife and babies. There is more companionship in the children and the neighbors than there is in digging, in tending the lathe, and operating the loom. There is more social life in hanging out the clothes in the back yard, and talking to the woman who is doing the same thing in the next yard, than there is in making entries in a ledger, and adding up columns of figures. The kitchen utensils are as interesting as the saw and the monkey-wrench.

Ninety-five per cent of the work of men is drudgery, and

few men have any choice in the selection of their drudgery. They do what as boys they were set at, or what they can get a chance at. A very small proportion of men have variety, adventure, romance, and no one who looks at our shopping streets and places of amusement will be in any doubt that women are less tied to their galley oars than men. Olive Schreiner, in *Woman and Labor*, ungenerously says that men have always been willing that women should do the coarse and ill-paid work; it is only when women demand admission to the higher and more intellectual occupations that men admonish them to keep within their sphere. Yet to women of genius the world of literature and art and music has long been open, and within recent years a multitude of occupations have been opened to women, with little if any objection from men; perhaps in consistency the Feminists should approve the many men who have been glad enough to shirk the support of their womankind and let their sisters and daughters take care of themselves.

But these are for the most part the unmarried women, very many of whom marry and "lapse with their marriage into the old parasitism," in the agreeable phrase of Edna Kenton. One remedy for this that has been proposed is that men shall pay wages to their wives. This, however, besides commercializing the union of men and women, is open to the further objection that if a man hires a woman to be his wife, he must have the right to discharge her when he finds some one else that would suit him better, for a time. This is admittedly a makeshift. A more "thorough" remedy offered is "paid motherhood," the men supporting the state and the state supporting the women and children. In such a case the state would naturally decide what mothers to pay, and what men to mate them with. Nothing that is now recognized as a home could survive such an arrangement, and the Feminists don't wish it to survive.

And even so, the house work has got to be done by somebody. If it is done by a hired charwoman she would be economically justifying her existence, while if it is done by a wife and mother, she would be a parasite, in the language of Olive Schreiner, and would be earning her living by the exercise of her sex functions, in the chaste words of Charlotte Perkins Gilman in *Women and Economics*, and Edna Kenton. And in any case the men must go on with their drudgery, which comprises overwhelmingly the greater part of all the work that is done in the world.

II

On the one hand, we are assured by Feminists that women do not differ from men, and therefore should not be confined to a "sphere." On the other hand, we are no less confidently assured by them that politics and industry are in pressing need of qualities which men do not possess, and cannot acquire, because they are distinctively feminine. Olive Schreiner has carefully studied the male and female dog, and reaches the conclusion that there is no difference between them to justify different treatment and different occupations. She does not expect woman suffrage to effect any political changes, except in one or two matters where she believes women have interests which men have not, or do not recognize. For example, war. Woman in politics will put an end to war because she knows how much it costs to produce each human life. This is mere rhetoric. What are the facts? The Teutonic women, whose status she would re-establish, went to the wars with their husbands, and fought by their sides. From the Spartan mother who charged her son to return with his shield or on it, to Mlle. Juliette Habay, of Brussels, who wrote: "We are learning to shoot with rifles. Here in Brussels great numbers of young girls have joined rifle corps, and a professor of arms is teaching us to shoot," when has woman ever failed to gird the sword upon her man? Socially there is assuredly no discrimination against the red coat in England, or the blue coat in the United States.

Very recently *Femina*, the woman's newspaper in Paris, addressed to i.s readers the question, "If not a woman, what man would you have wished to be?" We are told in a news despatch that "Napoleon won easily."

But Mrs. Schreiner is substantially correct. Biology may know something of male and female temperaments, but in their general characters and habits and adaptability to employments, there is no great difference between her male and female dog, or the male and female of other animals. If the path of progress leads downward by all means let us learn our sociology and domestic economy from the beasts of the field and the fowls of the air. If human progress has been retrogression, let us get back by way of primitive man and the missing link, to the animals and birds whose social economy commends itself strongly to Feminist and socialist.

The differentiation of men and women is the most valuable product of ages of gradually developing civilization. The world does not need twice as many diggers in the earth, and workers in metals, as it has now, but it does need homes. If the beasts merely have dens from which they go forth at night for their prey, and in which they produce their young, which they care for only till the young can catch their own game, Mrs. Gilman sees no reason why men and women should have homes, except as places for sleeping, from which they go out every morning to secure subsistence for themselves and for their young. But the latter, in her system, would soon be removed to training institutions conducted by the state, and managed by experts in child-culture; for Mrs. Gilman does not credit women with ability to rear their own offspring (however well she thinks they can rear those of other women), though the world is perishing for lack of their greater participation in industries and politics.

The prolonged association of parents with children, the

protraction of mother-love beyond the infancy of offspring, the association of men and women intimately, but
not entirely for the perpetuation of the race; the instinct of
exclusiveness in the relations of man and woman, and their
refinement by sentiments of romance; the development of
chivalry and accountability for others in man, and of
modesty in woman; the separation of one part of the race
from much that the other part must often be in close
contact with; the creation of a domestic atmosphere which
is not like that of the shop or the field — the essential
features of the home and the family — these are the best
results of civilization, and against them the Feminist
storms. Yet they are more important, if possible, to
woman than to man.

Women are different from men as the result of ages of
segregation, and that is above all things else the object of
Feminist attack. The whole purpose of Feminism is to
make the conditions of life the same for men and women.
Women are more chaste than men, and the Feminists may
be right when they say that this has been forced upon
woman by man, but they are mistaken when they treat
this not as a gain, but as a grievance. It need not be
disputed that men ought to be as pure as women, but it is
at least a great gain to hold one sex to a high standard of
purity. In the course of time something may be achieved
by the other — much has been already, or mixed society
would be impossible — but it will not be effected by the
Feminists who complain of servitude to man-made standards of morals, and demand for women the freedom
practiced surreptitiously by some men.

The common notion of the innate moral superiority
of woman is due to fond recollections of happy childhood,
to the warm language of poets, to the romance of the
male when in the springtime of life his fancies lightly turn
to thoughts of love, and to actual differences which are the
result of the segregation of women. Feminism is breaking
that down, and we are already getting some of the results.

In *The Vanishing Lady*, *The Atlantic Monthly*, December, 1911, Mrs. Comer finds that the contrast between the people in the novels of Howells and in those of David Graham Phillips suggests something like a submergence of Christian civilization under a wave of materialism and paganism. The interval between these two writers is the period during which Feminism has been spreading like an epidemic. Women have not saved society from the change. The advanced women have not tried to. Like their clothes, they have been entirely up-to-date, and the materialism and paganism of the day are quite as apparent among women as among men.

This is Mrs. Comer's description of the type of woman who is being evolved by Feminism:

One cannot travel far in these days without being filled with wonder at the vast numbers of these women roaming the continent. They are usually of a willful fatness, with flesh kept firm by the masseuse; their brows are lowering, and there is the perpetual hint of hardness in their faces; their apparel is exceedingly good, but their manners are ungentle, their voices harsh and discontented; there is no light in their eyes, no charm or softness in their presence. They are fitting mates, perhaps, for the able-bodied pagans who are overrunning the earth, but hardly suitable nurses for a generation which must redeem us from materialism, if, indeed, we are to be so redeemed. Facing them, one wonders if race-suicide is not one of nature's merciful devices?

In a period of rapidly acquired fortunes women have accepted the dollar as the unit of individual worth quite as readily as men have, and have applied it more relentlessly, for men are more democratic than women; rich and poor wear the same costumes, and in their friendships they do not draw the financial line so closely as their wives do. During the spread of Feminism manners have coarsened, modesty is disappearing, the fiction and drama of the day familiarize the young with vice under the thin pretext of fortifying virtue. If it be true, as is sometimes charged, that women are taking to alcohol and tobacco, it is merely one additional evidence that in breaking down the distinctions between men and women, the standards of the former are not raised, but those of the latter are lowered.

Two women have lately suggested the assimilation of the figures of the male and female of the species. Ellen Key refers to the flattening of woman's bosom as the result of the growing use of artificial means of nourishing infants, and "Lucas Malet" speaks of "large-boned, athletic, sexless persons, petticoated, yet conspicuously deficient in haunches and busts."

III

As the garb of male and female in the lower animals does not differ radically, and seldom varies much except in the brighter hues of the male, so the socialist who seeks to assimilate the human sexes, objects to radical differences in their costume, and many essays toward the adoption of the costume of men have been made by advanced women. Morris and Bax, in *Socialism, Its Growth and Outcome*, deplore differences of costume, saying: "Another fault may be noted in all bad periods (as in the present), that an extreme difference is made between the garments of the sexes." Since that was written the skirts of women have been reduced to a point suggestive of a single trouser instead of a pair, and the divided skirt, the harem skirt and the riding costume for the cross saddle indicate a movement that Morris and Bax would welcome.

There are history and politics in clothes. Trousers are described as a product of democracy, because they conceal the material of the stocking, whether silk or wool. Not so very long ago men wore laces, and ribbons, and jewels, and delicate tints. With the gradual breaking down of the caste system, the spread of democracy in politics, and of the brotherhood of man in philanthropy and religion, men have reduced their costumes to the present inartistic, but very serviceable standard. There has been no lasting change in that direction in the costume of women. If the determination of some women to "make men of themselves" had coincided with the severe simplicity of the tailor-made suit there would have been, as there has been in some cases, a certain measure of harmony between the inner and the outer woman. But the period of aggressive Feminism coincides with decrees of fashion that are designed to expose as much of the female figure as the police will permit. The paucity of garments, and their thinness and scantiness are suggestive of Vivien, upon whom

> A robe
> Of samite without price, that more exprest
> Than hid her, clung about her lissome limbs.

The pageants and tableaux which afford women an opportunity to appear in the garb of statues, leave one somewhat in doubt whether Feminism relies chiefly upon arson and malicious mischief, or upon the arts Vivien practiced upon Merlin, for the accomplishment of its ends. Salome is dancing before Herod in the confident expectation that he will give her the half of his kingdom. But it is idle for women in the Western world, in the Twentieth Century, to pretend that they are odalisques, compelled by their helplessness to appeal to the sensuous side of men. They exhibit themselves for their own pleasure, and they dance the whole list of modern dances, with their vulgar names, because they enjoy them.

The extreme of fashion, in this day when Feminism is demanding larger opportunities to refine, purify and uplift the world, is fast reaching the point of

> One Pan
> Ready to twitch the Nymph's last garment off,

and on the Paris stage this has already been done, with the approbation of the audience, until the Nymph came forward to the footlights to bow her acknowledgment of the applause, when the audience intimated plainly that she was overdoing her part.

In Berlin, in Chicago, and in Washington, very recently opposition to distinctive titles for married and single women has broken out. It is asked indignantly why women, and not men, should be tagged with their conjugal condition. One woman remarks, not without force, that it is more important to know whether men are married, than to know whether women are wives or maidens.

But men have so far been the more public, and therefore the better known of the two. General information about their status is more probable. Perhaps the conjugal status of men ought to be indicated in their titles, but they do not change their names in marriage, and therefore it is less convenient to change their titles. At any rate, it is better that the conjugal condition of one sex should be indicated than that that of neither should be. The distinctive titles for married and single women go back in England, France and Germany, rather less than 250 years, and they constitute a part of the differentiation of women from men which the Feminist resents, but which is really one of the most valuable products of civilization. It is a necessary feature of a society based upon the family as the unit, but in which women are free to move about without guards, and without the supervision of their men.

Intimately connected with the title is the last name the woman is to bear. The Feminist resents being "branded" upon marriage by her husband's name. Certainly under Ellen Key's system it would be folly to change the name for each association. One distinguished Feminist in Boston retained her maiden name after marriage, and her daughter uses the names of both parents. But this does not solve, it only evades, the real problem. What is the mother's name? It is the name of her father. There is no reason to the Feminist or the socialist why she should bear the name of her father, any more than that her daughter should bear her father's name.

There are no family names now except the names of the men, and in a Feminist society there can be no family names; which will not matter, for there will be no family. The Feminist is less frank in admitting this than the socialist is, but their programs are equally destructive of it. Each person will select his, or her, own name. To this social individualism leads. In no other way will the Feminist woman be satisfied that her identity is not merged in a man, and her ownership by a man indicated for public information.

IV

Feminism is a declaration of sex war, Edna Kenton proclaims. Yet the havoc involved in this might well give advanced women pause. Miss Tarbell (*The Uneasy Woman, The American Magazine*, January, 1912) does not believe that "Man is a conscious tyrant, holding woman an unwilling captive — cutting her off from the things in life that really matter — education, freedom of speech, the ballot." She asks:

Is man the calculating tyrant the modern uneasy woman charges? . . . Is not man a victim as well as she — caught in the same trap? Moreover, is woman never a tyrant? That a man's life may not be altogether satisfactory, she declines to believe. The uneasy woman has always taken it for granted that man is happier than woman.

Mrs. Rogers recognizes that man, not woman, is the idealist. The unselfishness of woman, beyond her willingness to sacrifice herself for her offspring, is poetic license. She is often unselfish; so is man. In a small material way it may be worth noticing that the amount of ordinary life insurance in this country, nearly all of which is paid for by men for the benefit of women, is thirteen times the amount of the national debt. Man and woman have been happy together, or miserable together. There have been times when a man pounded his wife, but she in turn pounded the children, and he in his turn was pounded by men higher than he in the social scale. With an improvement in manners and morals, man ceased submitting to pounding on the one side, and inflicting it on the other. When force was the rule in all social relations, both suffered from it. Since force ceased to be the rule, woman has had very much the better of man; for she cares less about his comfort than he does about hers; and while he will give up a good deal for the sake of peace, there is little that she will not give up peace for the sake of. "It is the perseverance which conquers," says Thackeray, "the daily return to the object desired. Take my advice, my dear sir, when you see your womankind resolute about a matter, give up at once and have a quiet life."

The common interests of men and women, subserved by co-operation and certain to be destroyed by competition, should avert sex war. The bonds of matrimony, which gall so many women, are mainly restraints upon men, and protections of women. Their dissolution would be cheerfully submitted to by very many men, but it ought not to be necessary to refer to the condition women would find themselves in after a few years. The condition of the greater part of the women who have achieved economic independence in the mills and shops is not such as to commend economic independence to all the others, disregarding for a moment the certain destruction of the domestic life, the home, and the family, that would result from the universal economic independence of married women.

The answer to both Feminist and Socialist is that of The Lords of Their Hands, in Kipling's, *An Imperial Rescript*. They were on the point of signing the pact which would put an end to all struggle in the industrial world —

When — the laugh of a blue-eyed maiden rang clear through the
    council hall,
And each one heard Her laughing, as each one saw Her plain —
Saidie, Mimi, or Olga, Gretchen, or Mary Jane.

After several delegates had expressed themselves ener-
getically in regard to their plans for themselves and the
Eternal Feminine, who was untouched by the Feminist
movement —

They passed one resolution: "Your sub-committee believe
You can lighten the curse of Adam when you've lightened the
    curse of Eve.
But till we are built like angels — with hammer and chisel and
    pen
We will work for ourself and a woman, forever and ever. Amen."

TABU AND TEMPERAMENT

WHEN, I wonder, did the word "temperament" come into fashion with us? We can hardly have got it from the French, for the French mean by it something very different from what we do; though it is just possible that we did get it from them, and have merely Bowdlerized the term. At all events, whatever it stands for, it long since became a great social asset for women, and a great social excuse for men. Perhaps it came in when we discovered that artists were human beings. At least, for many years, we never praised an artist without using the word. It does not necessarily imply "charm," for people have charm irrespective of temperament, and temperament irrespective of charm. It is something that the Philistine never has: that we know. But what, by all the gods of clarity, does it mean?

It means, I fancy, in one degree or another, the personal revolt against convention. The individual who was "different," who did not let his inhibitions interfere with his epigrams, who was not afraid to express himself, who hated *clichés* of every kind — how well we know that figure in motley, who turned every occasion into a fancy-dress ball! All the inconvenient things he did were forgiven him, for the sake of the amusing things he said. Indeed, we hardly stopped to realize that his fascination was largely a matter of vocabulary. Now it is one thing to sow your wild oats in talk, and quite another to live by your own kaleidoscopic paradoxes. The people who frowned on the manifestations of "temperament" were merely those logical creatures who believed that if you expressed your opinions regardless of other people's feelings, you probably meant what you said. They did not know the pathology of epigram: the basic truth of which is that word-intoxicated people express an opinion long before they dream of holding it. They say what they think, whether they think it or not. Only, if you talk with incessant variety about what ought to be done, and then never do any of the wild things you recommend, you become in the end perfectly powerless as a foe of convention.

This tactical fact the unconventional folk have at last become aware of; and, accordingly, hostility to convention is ceasing somewhat to take itself out in phrases. Conventions, at the present moment, are really menaced. The most striking sign of this is that people are now making unconventionality a social virtue, instead of an unsocial vice. The switches have been opened, and the laden trains must take their chance of a destination.

The praise of temperament, I verily believe, was the entering wedge. But whatever the first cause, "conventional" is certainly in bad odor as an epithet. And this is really an interesting phenomenon, worth investigating. What is it that makes it a term of reproach? Why must you never say it about your dearest friend? Why must you contradict, in a shocked tone, if your dearest friend is said to be conventional? Most of my best friends are conventional, I am glad to say; but even I should never think of describing them to others thus.

Conventional people are supposed to lack intelligence — the power to think for themselves. (It seems to be pretty well taken for granted that you cannot think for yourself, and decide to think what the majority of your kind thinks. If you agree with the majority, it must be because you have no mental processes.) They are felt to lack charm: to have nothing unexpected and delightful to give you. And, nowadays, they are (paradoxes are popular) supposed to be perilous to society, because they are immovable, because they do not march with the times, because they cling to conservative conceptions while the parties of progress are re-making the world. All these reproaches are, at present, conveyed in the one word.

Now it is a great mistake to confound conventionality with simplicity — with that simplicity which indicates a brain inadequate to dealing with subtleties; or to confound "temperament" and unconventionality with a highly organized nature. The anthropologists have exploded all that. I have looked warily at anthropologists ever since the day when I went to hear a great Greek scholar lecture on the Iliad, and listened for an hour to talk about bull-roarers and leopard-societies. I doubt if the anthropologists have any more perspective than other scientists. I am as near being an old Augustan as any twentieth-century observer can be: "nihil humani," *etc.* But, for God's sake, let it be human! Palæontology is a poor substitute for history. No: I do not love any scientists, even the anthropologists. But I do think we ought to be grateful to them for proving to us that primitive people are a hundred times as conventional as we; and that their codes are almost too complicated for European minds to master. If anyone is still under the dominance of Rousseau, Chateaubriand *et Cie.*, I wish he would sit down impartially before Messrs. Spencer and Gillen's exposition of group-marriage among the Australian aborigines. If, in three hours, he knows whom, supposing he were a Matthurie of the dingo totem, he could marry without incurring punishment, or even the death penalty, he had better take his subtlety into Central Australia: he is quite wasted on civilization. Or he might go over and reform Yuan-Shi'h-Kai's administration: the Chinese would take to him enormously.

Someone may retort that I am not exactly making out a shining case for *tabu*, in citing the very nasty natives of Australia as notable examples of what *tabu* can do for society. My point is only this: that it is folly to chide conventional people for simplicity, since convention is a very complicated thing; or for dulness, since it takes a good deal of intelligence and a great many inhibitions to follow a social code. To be different from everyone else, you have only to shut your eyes and stop your ears, and act as your nervous system dictates. By that uncommonly easy means, you could cause a tremendous sensation in any drawing-room, while your brain went quite to sleep. The natives of Central Australia are not nice; but they are certainly nicer than they would be if they practised free love all the year round, instead of on rigidly specified occasions. Their conventions are the only morality they have. Some day, perhaps, they will do better. But it will not be by forsaking conventions altogether. For surely, in order to be attractive, we must have some ideals, and above all some restraints. Civilization is merely an advance in taste: accepting, all the time, nicer things, and rejecting nasty ones.

When the temperamental and unconventional people are not mere plagiarists of dead eccentrics, they lack, in almost every case, the historic sense. I am far from saying that all conventional folk have it; but they have at least the merit of conforming. If they do not live by their own intelligence, it is because they live by something that they modestly value a good deal more. It is better that a dull person should follow the herd: his initiatives would probably be very painful to himself and everyone else. No convention gets to be a convention at all except by grace of a lot of clever and powerful people first inventing it, and then imposing it on others. You can be pretty sure, if you are strictly conventional, that you are following genius — a long way off. And unless you are a genius yourself, that is a good thing to do. Unless we are geniuses, the lone hunt is not worth while: we had better hunt with the pack. Unless we are geniuses, there is much more fun in playing the game; there is much more fun in caste and class and clan. Unconventional people are apt to be Whistlers who cannot paint. Of course there is something very dull about the person who cannot give his reasons for his social creed. But if it is all a question of instinct, better a trained instinct than an untrained one.

I am inclined to think that the mid-Victorian prejudice against — let us say — actors and actresses, was well founded. Under Victoria (or should one say under mid-Victoria?) stock companies were not chaperoned, and ladies and gentlemen went on the stage very infrequently. What is the point of admitting to your house someone who will be very uncomfortable there himself, and who will make everyone else even more uncomfortable? It is not that we are afraid he will eat with his knife: that is a detail we might put up with. But eating or not eating with your knife is merely one of the little signs by which we infer other things. In this mad world, anyone may do or be anything; but the man who has been brought up to eat with his knife is the less likely to have been brought up by people who would teach him to respect a woman or not to break a confidence. It is a stupid rule of thumb; but, after all, until you know a person intimately, how are you going to judge except by such fallible means? I have nothing in the world against Nature's noblemen; but the burden of proof is, of practical necessity, on their shoulders. Manners are not morals — precisely; yet, socially speaking, both have the same basis, namely, the Golden Rule. No one must be made more uncomfortable or more unhappy because he has been with you. Now, in spite of Oscar, it is worse to be unhappy than to be bored; and I would rather be the heroine of a not very clever comedy of manners than of a first-class tragedy. Most of us, when we are once over twenty, are no more histrionic, really, than that. The conventional person may bore you (though it is by no means certain that he will) but he will never, of his own volition, make you unhappy unless by way of justified retort. He will never put you, verbally or practically, into a nasty hole. Perhaps he will never give you the positive scarlet joys of shock and thrill. But, dear me! that brings us to another point.

Conventional folk are often accused of being dull and valueless because they have no original opinions. (How

we all love original opinions!) Well: very few people have
any original opinions. Originality usually amounts only
to plagiarizing something unfamiliar. "The wildest
dreams of Kew are the facts of Khatmandhu"; and dead
sages, if there were only retroactive copyrights, could sue
most of our modern wits for their best things. What is
even Jean-Jacques but Prometheus-and-water, if it comes
to that? Very few people since Aristotle have said anything new. What passes for an original opinion is, generally, merely an original phrase. Old lamps for new —
yes; but it is always the same oil in the lamp. Some
people — like G. B. S. and Mr. Chesterton — seem to
think that you can be original by contradicting other
people — as if even the person who states a proposition
did not know that you could make the verb negative if
you chose! Often, they are so hard up that they have
to contradict themselves. But they are supposed to
be violently — subversively — enchantingly — original.
Even the militant suffragettes have not "gone the whole
hog": they have stopped short of Aristophanes. What
is the use of congratulating ourselves on our unprecedented
courage in packing the house solemnly for *Damaged Goods*,
when we have expurgated the *Lysistrata* — and had the
barest *succès d'estime*, at that? No: our vaunted unconventionality is usually a matter of words. I have tracked
more than one delightful vocabulary through the jungle,
only to find that it brought up at the literal inspiration of
the Old Testament; and I have inwardly yawned away an
afternoon with a person who talked in *clichés*, to discover
perhaps, at twilight, that on some point or other he was
startlingly revolutionary. The fact is that we are the
soft prey of the phrase; and the rhetoricians, whether we
know it or not, will always have their way with us. Even
the demagogue is only the rhetorician of the gutter.
"Take care of the sounds and the sense will take care of
itself" — as the Duchess in *Alice* did *not* say. Dulness
is a matter of vocabulary; but there are no more dull

people among the conventional than among the unconventional. And if a person is to be unconventional, he
must be amusing or he is intolerable: for, in the nature of
the case, he guarantees you nothing but amusement. He
does not guarantee you any of the little amenities by
which society has assured itself that, if it must go to
sleep, it will at least sleep in a comfortable chair.

I was arguing at luncheon one day, with three clever
women, the advantages and disadvantages of unconventionality. They were all perfectly conventional in a
worldly sense, and perfectly convinced of the charms of
unconventionality. (That is always the way: we sigh for
the paradises that are not ours, like good Christians spurn-
ing the Apocalypse and coveting the Mohammedan
heaven.) They cited to me a very amusing person — a
priestess of intellectual revolt. Yes: she walked thirty
blocks to lunch in a pouring rain, and when she came in
she took off her wet hat, put it in her chair, and sat on it.
The fact that my guest, did she choose, could afford to
crown herself with pearls, would not make up to me for
the consciousness that she was sitting on an oozing hat
throughout luncheon. In spite of epigrams, I should feel,
myself, perfectly wet through. Surely it is the essence.of
good manners not to make other people uncomfortable.
Society, by insisting on conventions, has merely insisted
on certain convenient signs by which we may know that
a man is considering, in daily life, the comfort of other
people. No one except a reformer has a right to batten
on other people's discomfort. And who would ever have
wanted John Knox to dinner? To be sure, we are all a
little by way of being reformers now — too much, I fear,
as people went to see the same *Damaged Goods*, under
shelter of its sponsorship, who cared for nothing whatever
except being able to see a *risqué* play without being looked
at askance. But we shall come to that aspect of it later.

Now "temperament," again, has often been confused
with charm; and conventional folk — who are, by def-

inition, dull and unoriginal, all baked in the same archaic mould — are supposed to lack charm. They are at best like inferior prints of a Hokusai from worn-out blocks. The "justification" is bad. Their original may have been all very well; but they themselves are hopelessly *manqués*, and besides, there are too many of them. How can they have charm — that virtue of the individual, unmatchable, unpredicable creature?

It is not against the acutest critics, the real "collectors" and connoisseurs of human masterpieces, that I am inveighing. I am objecting to the stupid criticisms of the stupid; to the presence of "conventional" as a legitimate curse on the lips of people who do not know what they are talking about. One often hears it — "I find him" (or "her") "so difficult to talk to: he" (or "she") "is so conventional." Good heavens! As if the conventional person were not always at least easy to talk to! He may be dull, but he knows his cues, and will play the game as long as manners require. It is the wild man on a rock, with a code that you cannot be expected to know, because it is his own peerless secret, who is hard to talk to. The people who say that conventional folk lack charm, often mean by "conventional" not wearing your heart on your sleeve. Now I positively like the sense, when I dine out, and stoop to rescue a falling handkerchief, that I am not going to rub my shoulder against a heart. What are hearts doing on sleeves? Am I a daw, that I should enjoy pecking at them? And who has any right to assume that, because they are not worn there, they are non-existent? It is of the essence of human nature to long for the unattainable. If you do not believe me, look at all the love-poetry in the world. As Mr. Chesterton says, "the coldness of Chloe" has been responsible for most of it. Certainly, if Chloe had worn her heart on her sleeve, the anthologies would have suffered. And with woman the case is the same. Let not the modern hero flatter himself that he will ever arouse the same kind of ardor in the female heart that the heroes of old did: those seared and saddened and magnificent creatures who bore hearts of flame within their granite breasts — but whose breasts were granite, all the same. No, gentlemen, women may marry you, but it is with a diminished thrill. We want — men and women both — to be intrigued; and I venture to say that for purposes of life, not of mere irresponsible conversation, it is the conventional person who intrigues us, since it is only the conventional person who creates the illusion of inaccessibility. He may be accessible, in reality; and the unconventional, temperamental person may be an impregnable fortress. That is the dizzy chance of life. But since all relations must have a beginning, the initial impression is the thing that counts. Of course one wants to know that the Queen of Spain has legs; but then we can be pretty sure that she has. We do not need a slit skirt to reassure us. One wants to know that there is a human face behind the mask; but who shall say that the mask does not heighten such beauty as there is? The conventional manner is a kind of domino: the accepted costume that all civilized people adopt for a time before unmasking. I do not suggest that we should disguise ourselves to the end; but that we should talk a little before we do unmask.

For there must be some ground on which to meet the person we do not know; and why may not the majority decide what grounds are the most convenient for all concerned? There must be some simplification of life: we cannot afford to have as many social codes as we have acquaintances. Imagine knowing five hundred people, and having to greet each with a different formula! Language would not run to it. And would it, in any case, constitute charm? Charm, as we all know, is a rare and treasurable thing; and no one can say where it will be found. But, as far as we can analyze it at all, its elements seem very likely to flourish in conventional air. Of course there may be a fearful joy in watching the man of whom you say: "One can never tell what he is going to do next."

But you do not want him about, except on very special occasions. For the honest truth is that the unconventional person is almost never just unconventional enough. He is pretty sure to take you by surprise at some moment when you do not feel like being taken by surprise. Then you have to invent the proper way to meet the situation, which is a bore. It is not strange that some of our *révoltés* preach trial marriage: for the only safe way to marry them at all would be on trial. Until you had definitely experienced all the human situations with them, you would have no means of knowing how, in any given situation, they would behave. They might conform about evening-dress, and throw plates between courses; they might be charming to your friends, and ask the waiter to sit down and finish dinner with you. Or they might in all things, little and big, be irreproachable. The point is that you would never *know*. You could never take your ease in your inn, for nothing discoverable in earth or heaven would determine or indicate their code. Conventional manners are a kind of literacy test for the alien who comes among us. Not a fundamentally safe one? Perhaps not. But some test there must be; and this, on the whole, is the easiest to pass for those whom we are likely to want for intimates. That is really the social use of conventions.

And as for charm: your most charming people are those who constantly find new and unexpected ways of delighting us. Are such often to be found among people who are constantly finding new and unexpected ways of shocking us? I wonder. It seems to me doubtful, at the least. For shock — even the superficial social shock, the sensation that does not get far beneath the skin — is not delight. If you have ever really been shocked, you know that it is a disagreeable business. Of course, if some wonderful creature discovers the golden mean, the perfect note: to satisfy in all conventional ways, and still to be possessed of infinite variety in speech and mood — that wonderful creature is to be prized above the phœnix. But you cannot

give rein to your own rich temperament in the matter,
let us say, of auction bridge. The rules you invent as you
go alone may be more shatteringly amusing than anything
Hoyle ever thought of; but you cannot call it auction, and
you must not expect other people to know how to return
your leads. And usually it only means breaking rules
without substituting anything better — revoking for a
whim. Life is as coöperative a business as football; and
we all know what becomes of the team of crack players
when it faces a crack team. Only across the footlights are
we apt to feel the charm of the Ibsen heroine; and even
then we are apt to want supper and some irrelevant talk
before we go to a dream-haunted couch.

Now this matter of charm is not really an arguable one;
for charm will win where it stands, whether it be conventional or unconventional. Everyone knows about the
young man who falls in love with the chorus-girl because
she can kick his hat off, and his sister's friends can't or
won't. But the youth who marries her, expecting that
all her departures from convention will be as agile or as
delightful to him as that, is still the classic example of
folly. It is not senseless to bring marriage into the question, for when we advisedly call a man or a woman charming, we mean that that man or that woman would apparently be a good person with whom to form an intimate
and lasting relation — not for us, ourselves, perhaps, but
for someone else of our sort, in whom he or she contrives,
by the alchemy of passion, to inspire the "sacred terror."
To amuse for half an hour during which you incur no
further responsibilities, to delight, in a relation which has
no conceivable future, does not constitute charm; for it is
of the essence of charm that it pulls the people who feel
it, — pulls, without ceasing. Charm magnetizes at long
range. I contend only that conventional people are as
apt to have it as anyone else, for they have the requisites,
as far as requisites can be named.

As for the charm actually resident in conventionality

per se: how should anyone who does not feel it be converted
to it by words of mine? For it is a beauty of form: not so
much of good form as opposed to bad form, as of form opposed to formlessness. The foe of convention enters into
the social plan, if at all, as a wild, Wagnerian *motif*. And
the truly unconventional person has not even a *motif;*
for he disdains repetition. He scorns to stand for anything whatever, and you are insulting his "temperament"
if you suppose that it is capable of only one reaction on
any given thing. The temperamental critic of literature —
like Jules Lemaître in his salad days, before the Church
had reclaimed him — prides himself on never thinking the
same thing twice about any one masterpiece. Your temperamental creature will not twice hold the same opinion of
any one person. If he has ever been notably pleased with a
fellow-guest at dinner, it is safest never to repeat the combination. For the honor of his temperament, he must be
disgusted the next time. It is his great gift not to be
predicable, from day to day, from hour to hour. But a
pattern is always predicable; and what you learn about a
conventional person goes into the sum of knowledge: you
do not have to unlearn it over night. Psychology becomes
a lost art, a discredited science, when you deal with the
temperamental person. You might as well have recourse
to astrology. His very frankness is misleading. He can
afford to give himself away, because he gives away nothing
but the momentary mood. Never attempt to hold him to
anything he has said: for his whole virtuosity consists in
never saying the same thing twice, and never necessarily
meaning it at all. He does very well for the idle hour, the
box at the play; but for the business of life — oh!

And to some of us there is charm in the code itself —
charm, that is, in any code, so long as it has behind it an
idea, though an antique one, and is adhered to with faith.
The right word must always seem "inevitable"; and so
must, after all, the right act. An improvisation may be —
must be, if it is to succeed — brilliant; but acts, like words,

are best if they are in the grand style. Whether in speech
or in manners, the grand style is never a mere magnificent
idiosyncrasy; for the essence of the grand style is to carry
with it the weight of the world.

And conventionality is now said to be subversive of the
moral order! At least, most avowedly unconventional
people are now treating themselves as reformers. Conventions did not fall, in spite of the neo-pagans; so the
neo-Puritans must come in to make them totter. And
with the neo-Puritans, it must be admitted (Cromwell did
not live in vain) most of the charm of unconventionality
has gone. It has become a brutal business. The neo-
pagans realized that, to be endured at all, they must make
us smile. If they told a *risqué* story, it must be a really
funny one. At the present moment, we may not go in for
risqué remarks in the interests of humor, but we may make
them in the interests of morality. We may say anything
we like at a dinner-party, so long as we put no wit into
saying it. We must not quote eighteenth-century *mots*,
but we may discuss prostitution with someone we have
never seen before. Anything is forgiven us, so long as we
are not amusing. If we only draw long faces, we may even
descend to anecdote. And when people are asked to break
with conventions in the interests of morality, they may
feel that they have to do it. It has always been permitted
to make the individual uncomfortable for the good of the
community. So we cannot snub the philanthropists as
we would once have snubbed the underbred: for thereby
we somehow damn ourselves. If you refuse to discuss
the white slave traffic, you are guilty of civic indifference;
and that is the one form of immorality for which now there
is no sympathy going. I may have no ideas and no information about the white slave traffic, but I ought to be
interested in it — interested to the point of hearing the
ideas, and gathering the information, of the person whom
I have never seen before. It is the "Shakespeare and the
musical glasses" of the present day. Vain to take refuge

in plays or books: for what play or book is well known at all unless it deals with the social evil?

Now it has already been pointed out that Vice Commission reports have done as much harm as good. The discussion of them is not limited to the immune, "highbrow" caste. I know of one quite unimperilled stenographer who was frightened by them into the psychopathic ward at Bellevue; and we have all read instructive comments in the daily papers which reiterate that virtue is ten dollars a week. A much lower figure than Becky Sharp's, but the principle is the same. Out of her weekly wage, we may be sure the shopgirl (it is always the shopgirl!) buys the paper — and therewith her Indulgence for future faults, much cheaper than Tetzel ever sold one. For Purgatory now is replaced by Public Opinion. Even my own small town is not free from the prophylactic "movie." One small boy nudges another, as they pass the placarded entrance, exclaiming debonairly, "Oh, this 'ere white slave traffic, y'know!" And the child, I have been given to understand, is the father of the man. The unconventional reformers quote to themselves, I suppose:

"Vice is a monster of such frightful mien," *etc.*

It never occurs to them to finish the sentence:

" We first endure, then pity, then embrace."

The fact is that Anglo-Saxon society has got beyond the enduring stage, and is largely occupied in pitying. There is a general sense that the people at large, in all moral matters, know better than the specialists. We will take our creed not from the theologians, but from Mr. Winston Churchill; and we will take our pathology not from medical treatises, but from Brieux. We will discuss the underworld at dinner because, between the fish and the entrée, the thin lady with the pearls may say something valuable about it. If we are made uncomfortable by the discussion, it only shows that we are selfish pigs.

Now I see no reason why decent-minded people should not discuss with their intimate friends anything they please. If you are really intimate with anyone, you are not likely to discuss things unless you both please. But I do see, still, a beautiful result of the old order that the new order does not tend to produce. The conventional avoidance as a general subject of conversation of sex in all its phases was a safeguard to sensibilities. You cannot, in one sense, discuss sex quite impersonally, for everyone is of one sex or the other. The people who cry out against the segregation of the negro in government offices have hardly realized that non-segregation is objected to, not because of itself, but because of miscegenation. There is a little logic left in the world; and there are some people who perceive that sequence, whether they phrase it or not. Social distinctions concern themselves ultimately with whom you may and whom you may not marry. You do not bring people together in society who are *tabu* to each other. Not that you necessarily expect, out of a hundred dinner-parties, any one marriage to result; but you assume social equality in the people seated about your board. Is not, in the last analysis, the only sense in such a phrase as "social equality," the sense of marriageability? Even conventions are not so superficial as they seem; and they have that perfectly good human basis. It is vitally important to the welfare and the continuance of the civilized race that sex-sensibilities should be preserved. Otherwise you will not get the romantic mating; and the unromantic mating, once well established in society, will give rise to a perfectly transmissible (whether by heredity or environment, O shade of Mendel!) brutality. It is brutalizing to talk promiscuously of things that are essentially private to the individual; just as it is brutalizing (I believe no one questions that) for a family and eight boarders to sleep in one room — even a large room. All violations of essential privacy are brutalizing. We do not take our tooth-brushes with us when we go out to dinner, and if we did, and did not mind (very soon we should not), the practice, I am sure, would have a brutalizing effect. A certain amount of plain speaking is, perhaps, a good thing; but there is no doubt that at present we have far too much of it to suit most of us, and I cannot see why we should be made to endure it just because a few people who are by way of calling themselves moralists cannot get on with society on its own terms.

It has long been a convention among people who are not cynical that bodily matters are not spoken of in mixed and unfamiliar gatherings. Of course, our great-grandmothers were prudes. The reason why they talked so much about their souls, I fancy, is that there was hardly a limb or a feature of the human body that they thought it proper to mention. They were driven back on religion because they held that the soul really had nothing to do with the body at all. The psychiatrists have done their best to take away from us that (on the whole) comforting belief. In America, at least, we are finding it harder and harder to get out of the laboratory. It is the serious and patriotic American in *The Madras House* who asks the astonished Huxtable, "But are you the mean sensual man?" In *The Madras House* the question is screamingly funny; but I cannot imagine any man's liking, in his own house, to have the question put to him by a total stranger. The fact is that we have dragged our Ibsen and our Strindberg and our Sudermann lovingly across the footlights, and are hugging them to our hearts in the privacy of our boxes. We have decided that manners shall consist entirely of morals. It is just possible that, in the days when morals consisted largely of manners, fewer people were contaminated. You cannot shock a person practically whom you are totally unwilling to shock verbally; and if you are perfectly willing to shock an individual verbally, the next thing you will be doing is to shock him practically. Above all, when we become incapable of the shock verbal, there will be nothing left for the unconventional people but the shock practical. And that, I imagine, is what we are coming to — all in the interests of morality, be it understood. At no time in history, perhaps, have the people who are not fit for society had such a glorious opportunity to pretend that society is not fit for them. Knowledge of the slums is at present a passport to society — so much the parlor philanthropists have achieved — and all they have to do is to prove that they know their subject. It is an odd qualification to have pitched on; but gentlemen and ladies are always credulous, especially if you tell them that they are not doing their duty.

Moreover, when you make it a moral necessity for the young to dabble in all the subjects that the books on the top shelf are written about, you kill two very large birds with one stone: you satisfy precocious curiosities, and you make them believe that they know as much about life as people who really know something. If college boys are solemnly advised to listen to lectures on prostitution, they will listen; and who is to blame if some time, in a less moral moment, they profit by their information? If we discuss the pathology of divorce with the first-comer, what is to prevent divorce from becoming, in the end, as natural as daily bread? And if nothing is to be *tabu* in talk, how many things will remain *tabu* in practice? The human race is, in the end, as relentlessly logical as that. Even the aborigines that we have occasionally mentioned turn scandals over to the medicine-man, and keep a few delicate silences themselves. Perhaps we are "returning to Nature," as the Rousseauists wanted us to; with characteristic Anglo-Saxon thoroughness, going the savages one better. But it is a pity to forget how to blush; for though in the ideal society a blush would never be forced to a cheek, it would not be because nothing was considered (as our German friends might say) blushworthy. Each man's private conscience ought to be a nice little self-registering thermometer: he ought to carry his moral code incorruptibly and explicitly within himself, and not care what the world thinks. The mass of human beings, however, are not made that way; and many people have been saved from crime or sin by the simple dislike of doing things they would not like to confess to people with a code. I do not contend that that is a high form of morality; but it has certainly saved society a good many practical unpleasantnesses. And we are clearly courting the danger of essentially undiscussable actions when we admit every action to discussion.

I saw it seriously contended in some journal or other, not long ago, that, whether any other women were enfranchised or not, prostitutes ought undoubtedly to have the vote, because only thus could the social evil be effectively dealt with. Incredible enough; but there it was. Not many people, perhaps, would agree with that particular reformer; but undoubtedly there is a mania at present, in the classes that used to be conventional, for getting one's information from the other camp. It is valuable to know the prostitute's opinion — facts never come amiss; but why assume that we have only to know it to hold it? Is it not conceivable that other generations than our own have known her opinions, and that lines of demarcation have been drawn because a lot of people, as intelligent as we, did not agree with her? The present tendency, however, is to consider everyone's opinion important, in social and ethical matters, except that of respectable folk. My own pessimistic notion is, as I have hinted, that the philanthropic assault on the conventional code has come primarily from people who were too ignorant, or too lazy, or too undisciplined, to submit to the code; and that the success of the assault results from the sheer defenceless niceness — the mingled altruism and humility — of the people accused of conventionality. At all events, the fact is that our reticences have somehow become cases of cowardice, and our rejections forms of brutality. We are all a little pathetic in our credulity, and we are very like Moses Primrose at the fair. Well: let us buy green spectaeles if we must; but let us, as long as we can, refuse to look through them!

It may seem a far cry from "temperament" to social service. I have known a great many people who went in for social service, and I do not think it is. The motives of the heterogeneous foes of convention may lie as far apart as the Poles (one Pole is very like the other, by the way, as far as we can make out from Peary and Amundsen) but the object is the same: to destroy the complicated fabric which the centuries have lovingly built up. (Even if you call it "restoration," it is apt to amount to the same thing, as any good architect knows.) At the bar of Heaven, sober Roundheads and drunken rioters will probably be differently dealt with; but here on earth, both have been given to smashing stained-glass windows. Many of us do not believe in capital punishment, because thus society takes from a man what society cannot give. The iconoclasts do the same thing; for civilization, whether it be perfect or not, is a fruit of time. Conventions are easy to come by, if you are willing to take conventions like those of the Central Australians. The difference between a perfected and a barbaric convention is a difference of refinement, in the old alchemical sense. A lot of the *tabu* business is too stupid and meaningless for words. Civilization has been a weeding-out process, controlled and directed by increasing knowledge. We have infinitely more conventions than the aborigines: we simply have not such silly ones. The foes of modern convention are not suggesting anything wiser, or better, or more subtle: they are only attacking all convention blindly, as if the very notion of *tabu* were wrong. The very notion of *tabu* is one of the rightest notions in the world. Better any old *tabu* than none: for a man cannot be said to be "on the side of the stars" at all, unless he makes refusals. What the foes of convention want is to have all *tabu* overthrown. It is very dull of them: for even if a cataclysm came and helped them out — even if we were all turned, over night, into poten-

tial fossils for the delight of future scientists — the next
beginnings of society would be founded on *tabu*. We shudder at the Central Australians: we should hate life on their
terms. But I would rather live among the Warramunga
than among the twentieth-century anarchists, for I cannot
conceive a more odious society than one where nothing is
considered indecent or impious. We may think that the
mental agility of the Warramunga could be better applied.
Well: in time, it will be. But they are lifted above the
brute just in so far as they develop mental agility in the
framing of a moral law, however absurd a one. I said that
their conventions were almost too complicated for us to
master. That, I fancy, is because any mind they have,
they give to their conventions. It is the natural consequence of giving your mind to science and history and
philology and art, that you simplify where you can; also,
that your conventions become purified by knowledge.
Even the iconoclasts of the present day do not want us to
throw away such text-book learning as we have achieved.
They do ask us, though, to throw away the racial inhibitions that we have been so long acquiring. Is it possible
that they do not realize what a slow and difficult business
it is to get any particular opinion into the instincts of a
race? Only the "evolution" they are so fond of talking
about, can do that. Perhaps we ought to take comfort
from the reflection. But it is easier to destroy than to
build up; and they are quite capable of wasting a few
thousand years of our time.

No: they want to bring us, if possible, lower than the
Warramunga. Some of them might be shocked at the
allegation, for some of them, no doubt, are idealists —
after the fashion of Jean-Jacques, be it understood. These
are merely, one may say respectfully, mistaken: for they
do not reckon with human nature any more than do the
Socialists. But the majority, I incline to believe, are
merely the natural foes of dignity, of spiritual hierarchy, of
wisdom perceived and followed. They object to guarded

speech and action, because they themselves find self-control a nuisance. So, often, it is; but if the moral experience of mankind has taught us anything, it has taught us that, without self-control, you get no decent society at all. When the mistress of Lowood School told Mr. Brocklehurst that the girl's hair curled naturally, he retorted: "Yes, but we are not to conform to nature; I wish these girls to become children of grace." We do not sympathize with Mr. Brocklehurst's choice of what was to be objected to in nature; we do not, indeed, sympathize with him in any way, for he was a hypocrite. But none the less, it is better to be, in the right sense, a child of grace than a child of nature. Attila did not think so; and Attila sacked Rome. We may be sacked — the planet is used to these *débâcles* — but let us not, either as a matter of mistaken humility or by way of low strategy, pretend that the Huns were Crusaders!

ON HAVING THE BLUES

THE letters of Charles Eliot Norton have lately been published, and the time is opportune for a lesson from that good man's life. Though always physically frail, he lived to be over eighty, and got more out of his life, and gave more from it, than do most robust men, even when they have his rare degree of intellect. Some who knew him well, say that one great secret of his long life of helpfulness and happiness was that he never had the blues.

While men like Norton make cheerfulness a religion, many other people of very good intentions do not even recognize it as a duty, but grope, and drag others, through clouded lives, while the clouds are generally of their own permitting, and not seldom of their own making. They are often thoughtful people, but not thoughtful enough to realize how much happiness and usefulness are wasted by the habit of the blues, or how easily that habit can be overcome. They sometimes even indulge it from a notion that depression of spirit is synonymous with depth of spirit, not realizing how often black waters set up a very abysmal appearance in a chasm so shallow that if a man clinging to the edge would only let go, he could touch bottom without submerging his chin. But if he delights in what he assumes to be the gloomy depths of his soul, he does not want to let go: he wants to believe his own puddle deep, and hates nothing worse than the possibility that it may be shallow, just as nothing so enrages the insane as the suggestion that they are insane.

Really superior persons (without capitals or quotation marks) are sometimes superior because of superior sensibility, though oftener, I suspect, in spite of it; and sometimes because of superior morality. Upon such people the shortcomings of life—especially of human nature, weigh harder than upon common folks. It was by no means Carlyle's dyspepsia alone that kept him grumbling all the while, and that, but for his sense of humor, would have killed him long before his time. Then, too, superior people often have superior imaginations, and often abuse them by imagining horrible things, and suffering more from them than the clod suffers from realities.

Moreover, people with sensibilities and imaginations are apt to be queer in their morals: they may have too few, because sensitiveness and imagination breed passions, and are inimical to the philosophy, as well as the plain common-sense, that regulate passions; or they may have too many morals, because sensitiveness makes them hate the ugly consequences of immorality worse than the rest of us can, and also because, where Hell is in fashion, if it still is anywhere, they imagine it so much more vividly, and shrink from it so much more vigorously than the rest of us can, that they get New England consciences. Worse still, that kind of superior person with too few morals to do business with, or too many, is subject to insufficient food and clothing, and to poor quarters and inefficient medical care — to being sick, in short; and deprivation and sickness very naturally bring on the blues; and last of all, sensitiveness and imagination and too many morals and too few comforts, and sickness do not develop a sense of humor. The poet or the tragedian in the black frock-coat buttoned up to hide the absence of the shirt, is not half so funny to himself as to us.

In giving so many of the reasons why people who make great and beautiful things are apt to have the blues, I have run along the edge of platitude, and occasionally, I fear, slipped over, because I want to emphasize the fact that there is no warrant for the fallacy nursed by so many would-be troubled souls, that having the blues will enable them to make great and beautiful things, and that because Carlyle and Poe had the blues, your or my having them is evidence that ours have the same causes as theirs or will be accompanied by the same results.

And there are several other things tending the same way which we had better put an end to. Depression of spirits is not as often the result of vanity, or over-sensibility or any other form of weak wits, as it is of weak nerves or weak liver. And yet all these weaknesses are generally inextricably mixed as cause and effect. If without any real cause of worry, you wake up two or three consecutive mornings feeling that the world is an unsatisfactory place, probably you had better go to the doctor. He won't be apt to give you anything worse than rhubarb and soda. You might even try them before going; and if it is a sunny day, try to glory in it, out of doors if possible; and if it is a rainy day, try to think how cozy it will be by the fire, or if you have to go to an office, how good it will be to have a day for steady work, when clients and customers are not apt to come in.

I wish I felt sure that the doctor would make you realize that we need healthy emotional pickers and stealers just as much as we need healthy physical ones. Overstrain and undersleep will make the world appear an empty place, simply because the nerves won't pick up the good things in it. Hence the listlessness apt to follow happiness, when happiness is great enough to fatigue. Hence people on honeymoons sometimes having entirely baseless suspicions that they don't love as much as they supposed they did. Hence, too, no end of texts for temperance.

The bacteria of the blues of course always seize on a favorable culture medium. Probably the best of such media is a settled and exaggerated consciousness of the possibility of disaster, which soon becomes magnified into a probability. Some people feel as if they were always treading on a thin crust over a volcano. Your doctor can do a good deal for one cause of that. The other cause

is what Bacon called defective enumeration — generalizing
from the remarkable, instead of the usual — the most frequent of all fallacies. Hundreds of people can be killed
in automobiling without your considering it more **dangerous** than other sports, but as soon as somebody very
near to you is killed, you think the sport dangerous. Now
as to danger in general, think of the facts. At any moment, perhaps one person in five hundred actually is in
danger of disease or other misfortune. But the remaining
four hundred and ninety-nine are not, except in the dis-
torted imagination of far too large a proportion of them.
There's a big chance — perhaps one in three or four, that
you who read these lines, being a person who lives not
merely on the surface of things, are in the habit of letting
your imagination play too much with what is under **the**
surface. Now stop it! You *may* of course be actually
the victim of ill fortune; but even if you are, there's a
chance that, in compensation, you have been made a
saint by it, and that you really get more out of life than
do most people more happily situated: for that's the way
of saints, as you can tell by looking at their serene expression.

True, a few terrible disasters must be expected, but
they are generally so much like surgical operations that,
unless they are fatal, the character recovers with some
of its evil elements removed. And most strange to say,
outside of character, and merely in relations to the **ex-**
ternal world — to wealth, opportunity, friendship, -- the
very worst disasters are often blessings in disguise. It
pays as well to seek for the bright side of our miseries,
as it does to count our mercies. "Count yo' mahcies,
Honey, count yo' mahcies!" recommended the old colored
auntie. You will remember it in that shape.

I have heard one of my ink-diffusing friends confess
that having had an infirmity that interfered with his
sleep, he long grieved over it as lessening his production.
But at last he realized that the sleeplessness had enforced

economy of time, in which, before the infirmity, he had been sadly lacking, and that his waking hours, in the undisturbed night, had bred the best of the thoughts which have contributed to his share of fame and fortune, and to the philosophy which secures his happiness.

But the realization of hidden blessings in misfortunes to ourselves generally requires a long experience: so let us take a case concerning everybody. It is not long since the civilized world experienced from the earthquakes in Sicily and Calabria, a thrill of moral stimulus probably the most intense it ever knew.

At first, on reading of such widespread and merciless destruction — maiming, killing, starving, roasting of children to death before the eyes of pinioned mothers, mothers pinioned before strong sons also pinioned from helping; large communities destroyed, and the survivors driven mad; horror piled on horror until the mere reader suffers, the imagination shrinks back miserable and incapable, and the mind loses faith in a beneficent cause and control of the universe. But after the first intense revolt of feeling has spent itself, and the reason attempts calmly to estimate the evil and what there may be of resultant good, the preponderance of the good, even in such an extreme case, may not seem impossible. The disaster evoked a universal burst of charity that turned fleets of battleships into engines of mercy. The moral advantage to humanity was colossal — nothing less than a distinct injection of kindness into all the relations of men.

It involved the death of but one in hundreds of thousands of the inhabitants of the civilized world. Most of the survivors received distinct moral benefits, not to speak of the advantage to future generations from the effect on the moral quality of the race.

Moreover, the case cannot be justly put without noting that the sufferers were of a people notoriously lawless (the Northern Italians are reported to have said: "After all, they're nothing but Calabrians and Sicilians"), and that the survivors received a powerful call to righteousness.

But reason on them as we may, and get from them what moral good we can, great tragedies tend to breed a terrible uncertainty regarding the stability and goodness of life — and indeed of the universe and the moral law. Yet though much uncertainty is very apt to start from great troubles, it is by no means sure to wait for them. This skepticism is the bottom horror. I have wondered if Sill was thinking of it when, in his poem "Truth at Last" about the Alpine guide hurled down by the snow slide, he asks:

> Did he for just one heart-throb — did he indeed
> Know with certainty, as they swept onward,
> There was the end. . .
>   'Tis something if at last,
> Though only for a flash, a man may see
> Clear-eyed the future as he sees the past,
> From doubt, or fear, or hope's illusion free.

Did Sill mean that even death may be preferable to that haunting uncertainty which is the worst of the blues? Early in life he had more than his share of it, but he lived it down.

If any man can look on birds and flowers and most women and children and some men, and upon the manifold beauties of earth and sea and sky, from dawn on to dawn, if any man can realize that we might have been driven by pain more effectively than even attracted by pleasure, to feed ourselves and reproduce ourselves — if any man can see these things, and not be certain that behind the universe there is intention, and effective intention, to produce happiness, that man simply has, at least temporarily, an abnormal mind. But he is the very kind of man who gets the blues. All that can be done for him is to help him see the other side of the shield. As for mere argument, sometimes one might almost as well use it against paresis as against pessimism.

Neither can much be done for fools. But there are degrees and kinds of fools. The worst are probably those who, having committed a folly of lasting consequences, sulk over it instead of facing it cheerfully and trying to make the best of it. When we can't get happiness, we can at least get discipline. But the hopeless thing about a fool is that he can never be convinced that he is one: his follies are always in the past tense.

Next to doubting too much, is expecting too much. Aside from the few great disasters of a lifetime, the worst things are proverbially those that never happen. This paper has not much to say about things that *do* happen. They may involve feelings not to be remonstrated against, or even mentioned lightly. But still those feelings, often very sacred, should, like everything else, be limited to their proper range. The chief cause (and the chief consequence) of the blues are *borrowed* troubles. One of the most effective ways of borrowing them is to take for granted that a bad situation will not right itself, and then, instead of merely taking care of the immediate issue, letting the imagination work at all possible issues, and devising means of taking care of them. This is often promoted by a mistaken notion that such constant thought over the matter is a duty — that if the worst comes, one will at least have done one's best. Generally one's best really is to drop the subject. But that is not so easy. Just as the tongue always seeks the uneasy tooth, so the mind always seeks the uneasy question. But the tooth is not always under control, and the question generally is, or ought to be. Rigid discipline will develop a habit of leaving it alone except as something can be done about it. The true method generally is to decide what the moment admits of, and then to await the next real occasion for decision, and meanwhile to keep the mind occupied with other things. Usually thought between times is worse than wasted. An occasion when it is not, is usually not between times, but one of the times. Of course one does not want to be taken unawares, but not a tithe of the imagined situations ever occur, and those actually to be met are often not foreseen at all: so most of the devising is wasted, attention is distracted from the immediate requirements of life, and time is spent in a continuous overshadowing of the blues. All this takes tissue, and when the next issue comes, the power to meet it is dulled. The strength of the great fighters — generals, lawyers, parliamentarians, depends largely on temperaments which preserve them from such waste of their powers. "The coward dies a thousand deaths, the brave man dies but one," and exaggerated anticipation of evil is simply cowardice.

Akin to doing work that never is called for, is over-refinement in needed work. True, "perfection consists in trifles," but don't forget that "trifles can't make perfection." There comes a point beyond which the most conscientious workman can really do no more. Part of the equipment of a true artist is the capacity to recognize that point. After every essential thing is done, there remain non-essentials which may as well go one way as the other. They raise the hardest questions, if they are permitted to raise any, because they are as nearly balanced as the load of Burridon's ass. Moiling over them is threshing straw: it leads to no result but fatigue and monomania. Monomania is generally the first step in insanity, and nearly every step in insanity is attended by the blues.

But objections to superfluous work and over-refined work, are not objections to hard work, especially when one is in trouble. Carlyle says (I quote from memory): "To him who can earnestly and truly work, there is no need for despair." But that advice is generally superfluous for an American. He is more apt to need advice to play hard — to mount his hobby or get hold of a new one, and ride it hard.

It is especially bad to let the mind run on worries at night; and to take them to bed with one is madness. This is a special reason for seeking society or the theatre: other people, in real life or on the stage (better in real life, of course, because there one has to talk back) can best pull one out of oneself when one's own powers are utterly inadequate. When actual causes of anxiety seem overwhelming, if one can be made to forget them for a time, hope comes into the ascendant.

One most important point is that worries are apt to settle themselves during sleep. There may be a subconcious mental action, or one may wake up with the thinking powers invigorated; but whatever the reason may be, people go to bed in perplexity, and soon after waking, do certainly often find that all the considerations have slipped into their relative places, and that the perplexity has cleared.

The best of all remedies is perhaps the most difficult, though not impossible. It is to "rise superior" to your troubles — to convince yourself, lift yourself, force yourself into the feeling of directorship — of competent and confident directorship of all your affairs. Add "with God's help" if you want to: for that may back up our worthy intentions more even than our ancestors began to realize — whatever they professed to believe. This feeling of calm adequacy does much to *secure* adequacy, and what is of perhaps more importance, compels peace.

But adequacy is only adequacy to do the best that circumstances permit. To attempt more than circumstances permit is at once inadequacy — to put yourself on the weak side of a false equation. Attempt only what you can do, and you never need fail. Yet unless you attempt the best you can do, you do fail — fail just so far as the difference between the actual and the best possible. But if you are reasonably brave and wise, that difference will be slight; and the healthy conscience, like the law, takes no account of trifles.

Shoot your arrow at the sun, and hitch your wagon to a star, all you want to — as religious exercise; but in your daily work shoot only when game is within range, and hitch only to something which will hold tight, and is reasonably sure to draw.

And don't be misled by shrewd Yankees who make divine phrases, but who regulate their actions in daily life as cannily as other Yankees who never make phrases at all.

Absence of work, and no less absence of play, — the mere opportunity to brood, is dangerous to those subject to the blues. When we are in the busy haunts of men, their activity inspires ours, and keeps our thoughts away from introspection and baleful notions; but if we are alone, even with Nature in her loveliest aspects, the mind is apt to seek the profundities, and to drag the spirits with it.

Interest in this subject has brought me some confidences. I knew a man beyond middle life, who had long longed for more opportunities of study and meditation. At last he obtained the cherished desire in the most desired way — in a lovely home amid the loveliest scenery. He took three solid months of it, and found himself low-spirited, ailing, and in need of tonics. But when he was called to the city, the first time he walked down Fifth Avenue, he felt that he didn't need any other tonic. Yet the habit of years had put him, all unconsciously, in chronic need of that one. He took it at monthly intervals, and it did its work. But it cost time. As he approached old age, he realized in himself a tendency to melancholy, that, in spite of the city life that had been efficacious for himself, had given the declining years of one of his parents much unhappiness. He was frightened: he felt that external aid, like all tonics, must lose its effect in time; and so he worked hard to develop powers in himself that would put him above the need of it. After a few years, circumstances led again to three months away from the city, and so effectually had he enlightened and trained himself that it was a period of greater cheerfulness, health and fruitfulness than he had ever known.

His bottom principle was: "Kill the thing at the start. Watch! As soon as the serpent's head shows itself through the egg, scotch it. If you don't, your mind will become the abode of monsters."

Of course to those who believe in immortality, a faith in the ultimate goodness of the universe is almost unescapable. Beliefs cannot be made to order, but looked at in the most Philistine way, this one fills so many otherwise apparent gaps in the order of the universe, saves so many apparent wastes, changes so much chaos into kosmos, that, when relieved of some of its absurd accompaniments from the past, the belief seems, in the broadest view, almost a matter of course; and the narrowing of one's view of existence by physical death appears absurd. The belief in immortality is such a simple and inexpensive machine for settling bad problems that, as in the case of any simple and inexpensive machine that throws out good results, there is a presumption in favor of investing in it. This, I suppose, is what they call Pragmatism. It has its dangers: for its principle is apt to be misconstrued, and Hope tells such flattering tales! But apparently Pragmatism has no direct business with hopes, but only with cold hypotheses; and if one must choose between hypotheses, the preferable one is that which strings the facts into the most orderly coherence; and certainly without immortality, the universe is much nearer chaos than with it.

Most of our upsets come from lack of health, or money or friends. Now if the universe holds for us ultimately an existence where we shan't have to bother with such vile bodies, or such demands as they make for money, and where we may recover all the friends we have lost here, and if our troubles here aid in our development, as they certainly do, the universe appears much more orderly, and our worst problems are fairly settled. Perhaps a strong proud effective soul might not care much for a future existence that, in such brief outline, seems so easy; but I don't know that our wide and exact knowledge of that existence contains anything to indicate that in it one will not have at least as good a chance as here to make his own way, or the way of those he cares for; and while doing this, to make his own additions to the gayety of nations, or their celestial equivalent. I don't see, either, any indication warranting any shameless, weak and impotent soul — one like yours and mine when we have the blues — in refraining from doing its little best here, on the ground that everything will be made straight there, and that therefore it is just as well to wait. For there appear more and more weaknesses in the demonstration that even shining garments and harps and halos are to be passed around free, or indeed that anybody will start there with anything more than he takes with him. There does not seem, however, aught to negative the guess already hazarded regarding health and fortune and friends — that what capacity for winning them one does take, may have a better chance for activity there than it has here. And as capacity improves by practice, all this plain paragraph is an argument for doing one's best here, and not sitting around indulging in the blues.

I freely admit, however — most freely — that such views, especially regarding the gayety, have not the sanction of very old or very wide acceptance; but with the decay of Puritanism, they seem on the way to more.

Before we leave old-fashioned remedies, under however new-fashioned aspects, it may be well to consider another one that greatly helped our ancestors — the belief in an over-ruling Providence that really does help those who help themselves. In the form the belief was known to them, it is not known to many of us; but we may have it in a better form. For the narrow conception of an anthropomorphic god constantly tinkering at the universe, we can substitute the idea of an intelligence so great that it does not need to watch each act, and specifically adjust each result; but has established a law so comprehensive as to give each of our motives its legitimate consequences — a law that in some ways rewards each of our good intentions, even when it seems to fail, and punishes each of our evil ones, even when it seems to succeed. Faith in such a law makes us feel secure in spite of the haunting anxiety lest we break through the volcano's crust. The sparrow's flight may be free if compensation awaits its fall. And we may know a higher freedom and a fuller meaning, even a creative joy, in the feeling that when we shape our acts toward the best ends we know, we can leave the rest to a benign law that goes deeper into motive than human gropings can, gives rewards better than we can devise, and punishments that do not merely afflict but tend to cure.

But all these faiths are another story. Faiths are good when they are not counter to reason, and the most matter-of-fact of us act on them every hour. But the big ones won't come at mere bidding. What I have been principally trying to get you to do, in case you are subject to the blues, is to take hold and keep hold of the actual prosaic fact that in our year and place of grace, life has reached a fairly substantial foundation, and that throwing oneself open to every possible attack of the blues, through a chronic feeling that life is on a very ticklish basis, not only permits a great many needless attacks, but goes counter to the facts — is mathematically absurd. When you are scared, it is not because the universe is going to turn turtle, but because you are confusing its center of gravity with your own, and developing too much of a wrong sort of gravity above your own. Hopefulness is really the only reasonable attitude; at worst you lose nothing by it, unless it makes you careless.

Life is fairly reliable, and death at worst is simply
nothing, while there are growing reasons to believe that
it is better than life. And yet it is the one unfailing subject
of abnormal brooding. It is possible at any moment, inevitable at some moment; and for that very reason it is,
from most aspects, as a subject of worry, absurd at any
moment. One of the sanest and sweetest men I ever knew,
who lived to be nearly ninety, told me that he never
thought of it.

Of all the humbugs of priestcraft, it is the greatest.
The priests, who once owned a third of England, and
probably more than a third of Italy, made more money
out of death and its accessories than out of all the rest of
the paraphernalia in their kit. Hell and purgatory and
poor dear Dante's scenery and properties were all part
of the machinery. How shocked Dante would have been
if he had realized how he was furnishing such ammunition!
(A friend, on reading this, was surprised at my calling
Dante "dear," because he is generally regarded as so
austere a man. To me he is not only dear, but like nearly
all great geniuses, "as a little child.") And some four
centuries later, how shocked would have been another
poet — not so poor or quite so dear, if he could have
realized what a part he was playing in the same loathsome
game! With them, one thinks of the geniuses who wrote
the *Dies Irae* and those other wonderful hymns, and questions what they too might have felt if they had realized
all they were doing. Then come to mind some other contributors to the humbug, who as a rule were not poor, and
were not dear at all, and who stole the sheet-iron thunder
and resin lightning — John Calvin and Cotton Mather,
and so on down to some poor dear men even so late as
when the older of us were in college, who made us get up
before daylight in winter, and go and hear them pray,
because they feared that if they didn't, and we didn't,
we should all go to Dante's or Milton's or some other man's
Hell.

Well, perhaps we who have a new century to play with, especially the younger of us, fancy among its fresh attractions a thorough emancipation from these old superstitions. But they are in the very blood our fathers transmitted to us. Many have had all the anti-toxic serum needed for immunity from serious attacks, but we are all liable to twinges — hours, perhaps days, of discomfort from that identical disease, when we don't know what's the matter with us.

Fear of pain is part of the equipment of self-defense evolved in the higher animals, but whether those below man fear death, is, I suppose, open to question. I believe horses and sheep, at least, show fear or aversion from the dead of their own kind. I have known it instantly shown by a child supposed too young to know anything of the subject. But be all that as it may, you can get far above the mere animal instinct, up into the tender human affections like those of my dear old friend, and find it probably true that normal creatures do not think about death, unless some external circumstance leads them to. Yet my old friend, with intelligence enough for the ordinary demands of life and the most delicate of its courtesies, would not have been called a thoughtful or imaginative man. But another dear old friend who was both (I don't know why I shouldn't say that I'm thinking of Stedman), I don't believe ever thought much about death, except in the abstract, unless some distinct external circumstance led him to. And he was a very unusually normal man. On the whole, I don't believe normal people do think about it, in the concrete, unless they have to. Well then, most of the thought about it in the concrete is abnormal, and in more senses than even the priests made it, death is a humbug.

Don't let us get the blues about it then. If we want an excuse for them, let's find it reasonably, in being obliged to survive when we prefer to follow. But there are few such cases, and Time takes care of them; and, as reasoning beings, let us realize that it is sweet and normal that he should, and let us no more resist Time in our perverse ways, than we would in the ways of the Egyptians.

And our ways are very perverse when they make us cling to some of the most absurd fashions from older civilizations, and neglect the wise ones. How long will it take us to put the Greek symbol of the lovely youth with the inverted torch, in place of the skull and cross-bones on the Puritan tombs? But we are coming on well when we bring forward the symbols of love to cover grief, and put flowers with the crape outside the door, and over the coffin. But we are not doing equally well when, after we let a woman have a veil, or a man slink down a side street, because they don't want to recognize people, we, after they have got beyond that, still compel them to keep away from people, and even from music and the theatre, when they most need them. We can generally count on mourners suffering enough without any aid from such fashions.

But leaving out our relations to other people, in the deepest part of our very selves — the part that gets the blues, why have them over the certainty of death? When we were boys, wasn't it a good way to avoid them before going back to school, to make the most of the last days? Today may be the last day.

If the best way out of worry is work, don't sit around moping about that journey, but work. Pack up. You can't take too much baggage — of the right kind. There are some reasons to suspect that in the new country you'll find more use than you had here for all that you can get together of learning and wisdom and aspirations and af-fections: love is giving rather than receiving, you know — even to the point of giving unrecognized. Why not there as well as here? True, your constitution may not be up to that one-sided kind forever, but you may not have to wait so long as that.

And even if you're lost, baggage and all, it will not have

been wasted: for it will have done its service here, and it will not need to be renewed. And you can't be sure now that you won't want it. And how ineffably silly it is to worry over the possibility of oblivion! That surely can't hurt. But if anybody believes that consciousness continues, shut up in a Pozzi-like darkness, deprived of an opportunity to enjoy this beautiful universe or any other, *that's* something to worry over. But did anybody ever invent such a Hell as that, or if anybody did, has anybody now any justification for having the blues over it? If you are worried by Scripture, probably you know that of the three uses of "outer darkness" in Matthew, two plainly refer to earthly conditions, and the third may fairly be taken in the same sense.

If you get tired packing, and need more work in view of departure, don't go back to moping, but get right up and put things in shape for those you're going to leave behind. But don't bother them, or do foolish things. One of the best things about that journey is that nearly all the wise preparations for staying here are equally wise for going. So you would be foolish to make very many *specific* preparations for going. In fact specific preparations for that journey have involved more of the waste and tomfoolery of the world than almost anything else — perhaps more than even war or fashion.

But be ready to go when you're called.

Meantime circumstances may be so against you that you can't have a happy life; but probably you can, if you so will, have at least a cheerful one, and those who have had the experience say that it's pretty hard to tell the difference — that they amount to about the same thing, except that, on the whole, the cheerful life is the more effective; and that, at best, happiness is but a by-product.

All this simple advice may be easier to follow than you think, and if you do follow it, probably you won't have the blues.

THE PRINCIPLES AND PRACTICE OF
KICKING

NOW, at this present moment, and for the next two months, twenty million American youth, — turning from syndicalism, the new morality, forgotten virtues, capitalism, psychical research, sociology, trust-busting, fly-swatting, preventive medicine, the evils of alcohol and tobacco, and other of the million burning questions of the day, — are and will be chiefly occupied with the important historical problem as to whether Mr. Charles Brickley, captain of and kicker-in-extraordinary to the Harvard football team, is a mightier man than the ancient heroes of the kicking game, — Moffatt, Bull, Brooke, Trafford, O'Dea, Poe, Sharpe, Eckershall, — and with this discussion they will couple the practical ambition and personal hope of joining the great galaxy.

But why bother about such matters? We cannot all, dear brother sports, become members of the firm of Brickley and Company. There is no use in trying. Besides, satisfaction for disappointment is ready at hand. As is common in human affairs, when we cannot do a thing literally, we may always turn to a metaphor. The turn has this advantage: whereas actual kicking is the prerogative of a few favored mortals, its practice, under the metaphor, may become the pastime of any person, however humble. For this use of the word there is the highest possible authority: the heavenly vision that appeared to Saul of Tarsus on the road to Damascus, was accompanied by a voice which said, "It is hard for thee to kick against the pricks." It is interesting to note, by the way, that these words were the only ones uttered in that famous conversation which bear any suggestion of rationality,

318

and it is not unlikely that the great and able apostle, perceiving the hard-headed and common-sense quality of the advice, made haste to adopt a less futile pursuit than that of persecuting new movements.

Now this metaphor stands for an operation far more common than most of us are usually aware. Figuratively, we are all kickers, at least nearly all of us, in one way or another, at one time or another, for one cause or another. Illustrations are as common as football associations or earth worms. Thus that oracular Englishman, Mr. G. K. Chesterton, has all Victorian literature the outcome of various reactions against the "Victorian Compromise," but, in less elegant phrase and from the point of view of the aforesaid "V. C.," all Victorian literature might be said to have arisen from the *Stossenslust*, or desire to kick. And, whereas that desire, literally considered, is surging in the breast of every manly young American at this very moment, — the metaphorical function may be administered by young and old, male and female, alike. An extra strong cup of coffee, too many buckwheat cakes, too prolonged indulgence in prayer-meetings, will often do the trick, without those long years of patient practice which make certain of our football heroes distinguished above their kind.

Personally I like the easy way, and therefore I may, at the outset, and with all due modesty, lay a not-to-be-denied claim to some share in the function that I am describing. I admire the motives, and occasionally the works, of my colleagues in the noble art which we profess, the art of setting the world, the whole world, or the particular world, right, — perhaps of setting some parts of the world by the ears, who knows? I greatly admire such periodicals as are instruments and vehicles for the "registering of kicks" that will take the offender and the offence squarely and forcibly and leave the remains to be carted away by the scavengers of reform. I enjoy nothing more than a blithe, personally conducted "muck-rake"; I hope sometime to offer a Nobel kicking prize. Whatever makes against the crudeness, the carelessness, the complacency especially, and the contentment with mediocrity that so pervade some of the aspects of our modern civilization charms me. Doubtless we in America are eaten up with the heir-to-all-the-ages, we-can-do-as-we-like, America-for-the-Americans sort of feeling and sentiment. Though Mr. Wells is probably right in saying that "the United States of America remains the greatest country in the world, and the living hope of mankind," yet anything that checks our bumptiousness is surely a good thing. But I do not halt here; far be it from me to delight solely in the advantages of my own land. I love to read about Ministerial and Opposition struggles, and the Austrian parliament and the French strikes are very merry spectacles. Kicking is really the most sacred tradition handed down to us from our puritan ancestors, themselves most accomplished in the art. Why should not one love it? But I dislike clumsy workers. As Matthew Arnold might have said, we want real kicking, real criticism, real objection. The vital question is as to the nature of good kicking and of bad kicking. What are the "pricks" to be shunned? for, as we have said, the advice of the heavenly voice would, in general, seem to be as sound as the Elizabethan semi-slang is lively. Into the answer enter considerations of motive, of object, of method, and of technic. In the interests of sound thinking, I am going to register my own demurrer against certain abuses of the noble pastime.

First as to the motive. Generally speaking this is dissatisfaction with the *status quo* and a desire to alter it. Altering may evidently be about anything one pleases. Hence the motive for kicking may be anything from crude envy to lofty altruism; it may be a simple reaction, scarcely more noble than the electrically stimulated kick of the frog's leg in the classical experiment, or it may be quite rational and untemperamental. It is obvious that the artist, the *Stossenskunstmeister*, should avail himself of the high motive; and no matter how much he may personally pine, should at least assume the altruistic virtue. Skilful mammas customarily observe this principle when they spank their children, saying, with greater reference to an ideal than an actual world, "This hurts me more than it hurts you," or "I do this for your own good," or other equally convincing remarks. In contrast with this amiable and ambi-flagellatory or bipenal practice, may be placed the character and instance of the unjust judge who frankly admitted boredom as his motive for action.

It would seem as if the present generation, in America, at least, besides losing the old fashioned virtues of tact and reticence, had also to some degree lost the artistic sense of the selection of the proper motive, and in so far have become unskilful kickers. Perhaps the growth of democracy has engendered obtuseness to the more delicate arts, but what could be cruder, for example, than the motives of many suffragettes, of many trade unions, of many socialists. It is crude raw envy: "You have something that I haven't got; I want it or something just as good." Intellectually and morally this position is about as far advanced as that of a group of infants, whose conception of play seems to be the snatching of those toys that are for the moment most desired by their companions. "What is the city doing for women to make up for the money that has been stolen from the treasury to found a man's college?" cries one, and another exclaims: "What is it all worth so long as we haven't the vote?"

> "What are all these kissings worth
> If thou kiss not me?"

says Shelley, and the child in proportion to his infancy will not be happy until he gets the star, the watch, the rattle, or the cake of soap.

One may believe in Votes for Women, rejoice over the improvement of the position of workingmen, and hope to see many of the ideals of socialism prevail, — and yet lament clumsiness and maladroitness in the use of motive. For all causes need the aid of the judiciously selected method, the appeal to high expediency, whereas they have to some degree fallen into the hands of extremely clumsy operators, the Pankhursts, the Carons, the Tannenbaums, who recall Newman's words: "Others are so intemperate and intractable that there is no greater calamity for a good cause than that they should get hold of it." They also recall Shakespeare's version of the words of Antony, which may be regarded as the epitome of good form in kicking, so far as motive is concerned:

"This was the noblest Roman of them all:
All the conspirators, save only he,
Did that they did in envy of great Caesar;
He only, in a general honest thought
And common good of all, made one of them."

Even more various, important and interesting than the motive of kicking is the object of the kick, *l'objet d'appui*, *das Stossensstoff*. Judging from some specimens and examples still to be found among us, we may imagine that the primitive man always objected to specific and tangible things; if an acquaintance impinged too violently upon the person of the primitive, the latter replied by "handing out," or footing out, a good "swift" blow. So too, now-a-days, the wise and simple person is not likely to go too far afield to kick, there being plenty of objects in the immediate neighborhood on which he can break his toes, such as little eccentricities in his neighbor's or his own *ménage*. If he is wise, really wise, he takes exception to these things from the high impersonal motives that we have been examining, and only where he is pretty sure of success. But if he have a disinterested mind, a philanthropic temperament, a broad philosophical outlook on life, he will see a very large assortment of objects that are by no means those of his special field of activity. These are the generalized *objets d'appui*, and it may be said to the credit of our civilization that we have accumulated them in larger numbers than any of our predecessors. The fact is, indeed, that the primitive had none of them, or, if in his later aeons he recognized some of them, his attitude was religious, terrorful, abject. They apparently grow in number quite as rapidly as other inventions of the human mind; and as each of these latter has been devised and recognized, so its accompanying kick has been engendered, thereafter never quite to leave it; just as the louse of the dead Filipino accompanies him to the nether world. Thus the general recognition of something called Life, brings a kick at Life by those who are hard hit by it. This is on the whole the most idle of the manifestations of the *Stossenslust*. The most evident thing about life, for the individual, is that it apparently begins somewhere, through no fault whatever of the individual's own, and ends for the individual in some way that he cannot specifically forecast. Evidently to object to the most hard and fast fact of the world, the time-honored premise that all men are mortal, is a most futile proceeding; and yet it has been made not only the subject of the most varied and legitimate inquiries, but also of wailings and gnashings of teeth, of religious terror, fervor and abnegation. So far as the subject of this paper is concerned, the reasonable kick at life is the kick at conditions that lie along the way; and it is a healthy sign of the times that our energies are being directed rather to improvement of affairs in this world than to a too active calculation about the compensations that the next one affords.

Another almost equally futile aim of the *Stossenskunst* lies in a kind of objection to alleged tendencies. With the advance of civilization, to use Macaulay's phrase, new tendencies and movements are thought to appear; and these naturally develop their own special crop of kickings. The decay of modern manners, the growing corruption of the English tongue, the growing impudence of modern youth, the encroachments of scepticism upon the domain of religion, the antagonism of classes, the sentimentality of democratic life, the general increase of foolishness, — these and a thousand other alleged tendencies, are really futile matter for fretting about. Here, indeed, the operation is something like this: the kicker goes forth to kick. He mistakes a balloon for a football and with an inflator proceeds to blow the balloon up, puffing it into enormous size with air (at 99F) from his own lungs. Then he paints on it the sign, "Degeneracy of modern times," and kicks it a mile or two into the air in about any direction, except toward a goal. Meanwhile really skilful kickers are trying to score by accurate judicious kicks over a cross-bar.

The recognition of real tendencies, of movements, of purposes, of motives, on the other hand, is of course indispensable if the art of objecting is to be successfully practiced. If I were oblivious to the tendency of my neighbor to absorb small portions of my estate, of harum-scarum pictures and statues to oust a more sober art, of armaments to go on increasing, I should find myself bunkoed in a minute; I should be as inept as Piggy Moore in the story, who did not know one goal from another. If one looks up only when his toes are trod on, he will see little. Tendencies must be recognized; without them we could have no such thing as the anticipatory, the preparative, the restraining, the stimulating kick. But it is evident that little except by way of suggestion can come through treating these matters in general; the effective kick has a specific objective. And unless one's criticism of tendency be based on facts, one does as the protagonists of the last paragraph, booting the self-blown air of vituperation or aspiration.

It is a pastime to kick at institutions as well as at tendencies. I once knew a man who for a whole long year never ceased to complain of the Subway; it was noisy, ill-ventilated, ill-mannered. The kick was very inapposite: I was not the president of the Metropolitan, and moreover I liked the Subway, in spite of some drawbacks. But the correct attitude is quite simple: one is under no undeniable compulsion to ride in the Subway; but even if one cannot escape, to destroy it is inconvenient and impossible; and therefore the only sensible course is to attack the abuses, by writing about them to the management, or to some benignant newspaper. In like manner many of us find a peculiar joy in attacking modern journalism, flats, pianolas, victrolas, automobiles, the modern drama, the study of rhetoric, the management of asylums, city life and many institutions of many descriptions. Whereas the judicious kicker usually aims only at the abuses that such institutions bring with them, — unless the evils are inherent and colossal, as possibly in Tammany Hall and war and the corner saloon. But even here kicking must be piecemeal.

If for a moment a practical application of the foregoing principles and kinds of kicking be made to contemporary American life, it is evident that we do not, on the whole, frown sufficiently at the varied assortment of specific objects at our feet. That is the charge often brought against us by observant foreigners. Whether in our eager individual pursuit of the main chance we neglect the details that lie along the way, or whether we do not like to interfere with what is not our own particular business, it is certain that we put up with abuses and impositions that would not be tolerated in other lands. Every country, to be sure, has its special crop of abuses, which are more apparent to the foreigner than to the native, and there can be no harm in the visitor's indulging in the very common pastime of plucking them out if the act helps him to consider the beam in his own eye. Yet our attitude is seldom so correct as that of the old deacon who said, "When you see a fault in me, mend it in yourselves,

brethren." It is really much easier, — and quite as futile, — to rail at what we don't like in other lands — the
lack of hot bread and ice-water in England, of swift and
slaughterous railways in Germany and France, of public
control of beggars in Italy and Spain — than to set our own
house in order. But kicking, like charity, should begin at
home. It ought to be the duty of everybody at home to
object, persistently and effectively, to the specific overcrowded street-car, the badly paved road, the encroaching
door-step, the neglected yard, the malodorous cesspool,
the irresponsible automobile, and the reckless railroad —
especially if he have any personal part in the maintenance
of similar abuses. If the tendency of these evils were
rightly apprehended, if a part only of the effort that is
expended, presumably, in objecting to generalized, foreign
and futile subjects, were bestowed on specific and tangible
details, if we would forego the emotional pleasure of the
impersonal "muck-rake," to assail the evil at our very
feet, — especially if each one of us were careful to avoid
offence in matters of the same kind — our country would
surely be a much fairer one.

If we are to distinguish good kicking from bad the
matter remains to be looked at from a somewhat different
point of view, that of method and technic. The matter
is important enough to run some risk of repetition. I am
far from following a school of thinkers who seem to imply
that when the method of a subject, — as of teaching,
brick-laying, railroading, etc., — is properly apprehended,
the learner may ride gaily away on a successful career
without reference to the facts of his business. Nor is
method easy to define; all that I know is that it is very
important. In addition to the inspiration and animus of
a good, or at least a plausible, motive and to a judicious
choice of object, good kicking should also be in the right
direction. Let us see what is actually in vogue.

A common kind of kick might be called conservative.

Under the loose figure of the "gridiron" we may imagine certain more spirited and adventurous souls who wish to propel the game toward a more or less distant and obscure goal; they have some idea of tendency. In their efforts they are constantly hampered, checked, and tripped by an equally numerous body of players, who desire to keep the game where it is, alleging that there is no fairer prospect than the fields that have already been played over, that every advance is sure to lead to the bog and the morass. Life has nothing better to offer than what it has already offered; their efforts are to keep the ball in the middle of the field; no score games are best. Now this conservative kick certainly has manifest advantages; it may be used, for example, with great effect against the common cry that we are better than anybody else, or against rash and hasty innovation. But in its extreme form it is peculiarly irritating. This extreme form may be called the reactionary kick, a favorite pastime in all the ages. Let me take an example that I happened to come across a day or two ago. In *The School of Abuse*, Stephen Gosson said among many other things of like reasonable tenor and sense of fact, —

"Consider with thy selfe (gentle reader) the olde discipline of Englande, mark what we were before, and what we are now: Leave *Rome* a while and cast thine eye backe to thy Predecessors, and tell mee howe wonderfully wee have been chaunged, since wee were schooled in these abuses. *Dion* saith, that english men could suffer watching and labor, hunger and thirst, and beare of al stormes with hed and shoulders, they used slender weapons, went naked, and were good soldiours, they fed uppon rootes and barkes of trees, they would stand up to the chin many dayes in marishes without victualles: and they had a kind of sustenaunce in time of neede, of which if they had taken but the quantitie of a beane, or the weight of a pease, they did neyther gape after meate, nor long for the cuppe, a great while after. The men in valure not yeelding to *Scithia*, the women in courage passing the *Amazons*. The exercise of both was shootyng and darting, running and wrestling, and trying such maisteries, as eyther consisted in swiftnesse of feete, agilitie of body, strength of armes, or Martiall discipline. But the exercise that is now among us, is banqueting, playing, pipyng, and dauncing, and all such delightes as may win us to pleasure, or rocke us a sleepe."

This is amusing; we are so far from Gosson's time that we are not afraid to laugh at it; we recognize its absurdity, as we recognize the humor of the quack medicine vendor in *Punch* (Dec. 24, 1913): "Here you are, gents, sixpence a bottle. Founded on the researches of modern science. Where should we be without science? Look at the hancient Britons. They hadn't no science, and where are they? Dead and buried, every one of 'em." But, *mutatis mutandis*, Gosson's words are a reactionary formula of all the ages: we find it, more persuasively and more subtly, in the *Past and Present* of Carlyle, in some of the criticism of Arnold, in many of the denunciations of Ruskin, and it is even betting that one will not find an example of it any day in the pages of our more staid journals. It objects to most modern enterprises, to imperialism, to the increase of foreign trade, to modern science, to psychical research, to the Ph.D. degree, to children's courts, to scientific philanthropy, to eugenics, to the Panama Canal, to a thousand other things, not because there may be a reasonable and conservative scepticism regarding the outcome of these matters and the facts on which they are alleged to rest, but because they were not recognized by the pre-Baconian philosophers, and fail to be specifically commented on by Aristotle or Marcus Aurelius or St. Paul.

Whereas it must, of course, be evident to common sense that the enterprises of an age may be properly criticised, for the most part, only in terms of the age. One's own age is usually regarded as a particularly enterprising one, and an enterprising age is one full of experiment. All that experience has to teach us about new enterprises in the main is that they have never been tried before, and that we were best not to be over sanguine of their success. But that is merely reasonable caution, — such as doubtless mingled with the loftier spirit of a Themistocles, a Pericles, a Michael Angelo, a Raleigh, a Bismarck, a Wilbur Wright, a Scott, in the ages that we are accustomed to think of as great. The enterprising age has always tried to find better houses, better ships, better laws, — to find its north pole, — and it is good much in proportion as it tries to find these things. Many of the attempts are failures, and the way to success is strewn with bones of men, but they are failures because they do not attain the goal for which they are striving, because they do not win the satisfactions of their own times; not because they do not conform to the achieved success or to the reactionary formula of a past age.

The reactionary kick is not without virtue; it is usually a gentleman's instrument. It may even be charming, as with those dear ladies in *Cranford* who never used any word "not sanctioned by Johnson." The charm may arise from the fact that the reactionary kick really requires no thought at all; a fair acquaintance with the literature of past ages, of one past age in particular, — the Periclean, the Medicean, the Spenserian, the Johnsonian, — is all that is necessary. Therefore one can put one's effort on manner and style, and may produce the effect of great suavity and wisdom. The reactionary kick is really terribly easy, possibly the easiest of all intellectual exercises, — indeed, it barely merits the name of intellectual; for it really consists in putting some standard on ice, and taking it off from time to time whenever a warm modern idea is thought to be in need of cooling. Whereas, on the other hand, the man in the thick of an active enterprise must work and think with all his might, and etiquette and style are of minor moment.

Yes, on the whole, the reactionary kick must in turn

react on the intellectual and moral quality of its operator and cause his fibre to degenerate through easefulness. But this we seldom notice. The poet says:

"The crown of olive let another wear;
It is my crown to mock the runner's feet
With gentle wonder and with laughter sweet."

and we scorn him, calling him hedonist, epicurean, indifferentist, "quitter;" but he is really less bad than the reactionary kicker who, when he has energy enough to get into the game, still hugs the side lines or keeps trotting back to the bleachers to shout needless warnings to players who know quite as much as he. Or again, we usually reckon it doubtful ethics to quarrel with another man's job, and can see the absurdity in lack of harmony between the pot and the kettle; for we are fundamentally of the opinion that live and let live is ordinarily a good public and private motto. And yet, the strife that sometimes arises between the representatives of various activities is no more absurd than the attempt to pry down from its various pedestals the enterprise of modern times, with the levers and pulleys of past generations. The reactionary kick is, on the whole, as useful as plowing with wooden plowshares, battling with the pilum, crushing flies with a steam-hammer, repudiating the typewriter and the locomotive, or giving one's days and nights to the volumes of Thomas Aquinas.

A word as to technic, which is in a comparatively crude state and leaves much to be desired. That is perhaps inevitable, since really skilful kicking, no matter in what direction, does not really proclaim itself as such, and is consequently not likely to be thought of at all as anything more than advice or persuasion, whereas the unskilful technician is too likely to call names to be really effective. Some of the phrases in vogue will show the crudeness of the technic: the white man's burden, the strenuous life, a tendency toward socialism, this is an age of transition, simplified spelling is an entering wedge, let us sweep anarchy into the sea, we are up against it in life, home is the girl's prison and the woman's workhouse, I fear that I am too old-fashioned, we must uplift the masses, what are home and children and country if we have not the vote, America for the Americans, destroy the very foundations of our faith, threaten to overwhelm our fairest institutions beneath a wave of ignorance and despotism, to crucify mankind on a cross of gold,

> "Why be this juice the growth of God, who dare
> Blaspheme the twisted tendril as a snare?
> A blessing, we should use it, should we not?
> And if a curse, why then, who set it there?"

etc., etc., etc., etc.

Nor is the pantomime of kicking more advanced: the melancholy air of grave concern at the state of scholarship in America; the tears in the voice lamenting the decay of our dear mother tongue; the placid large-eyed sorrow at the spectacle of corruption, of reckless automobiles, or of unkempt pavements; the firm and elevated chin and stretching neck of her who presses into the service of the Cause; the slow and silent tread, albeit in public places, of him who goes about in meditation on the misery of mankind (*eheu miser!*); — all these methods were the object for the satire of a Swift or the sweet rationality of a Montaigne; but they must be content with this sketchy cataloguing from a humbler pen.

One school of kickers only, so far as I am aware, has paid much attention to the technic of the great art. Their names will presently appear (for should they not be named with honor?), but the essence of their method is this, that they side-step every move in the game and, as the play goes rushing by, plant a skilful kick where they think it will be effective. In this game they do somewhat imitate the methods of the reactionary kicker, who as we have seen, retreats to the rear of the field, bidding the play come to him on the ground where it was played by St. Thomas, Samuel and Noah. That is to say, the method consists in assuming a point of view different from the current one. There the resemblance ceases, for these modern masters of technic rarely retreat to the rear, but keep alongside the game or even ahead of it, and even mingle in it with jest and laughter. And thus Mr. Shaw, from his coign of vantage just ahead of the player, is constantly thrusting things between his legs to trip him up if he run awkwardly; and Mr. Wells is making diagrams of how badly the game has been played in the past, and showing how it is bound to improve when we divest it of old and ragged toggery, which somehow holds together; and Mr. Chesterton is engaged in proving that nobody but himself knows anything about sport anyway; while Mr. Galsworthy, Mr. Belloc, and a host of others are kicking away brilliantly, imagining that they also have discovered something quite new in the annals of the sport. Meanwhile hosts of good quiet people are lending a helping hand or are, like skilful guards or backs, actively but unostentatiously pushing the good cause through the opponents' line and towards the goal.

If, by way of summary, one were asked to draw a brief sketch of the ideal kicker, much as Herbert Spencer drew the character of the ideal writer, the answer would be something like this. The ideal kicker is he who would improve his own condition or the condition of the town, community, age, and atmosphere in which he lives, mainly according to the light of his own generation. His attack is against the particular and the immediate; for he knows that for the purposes of his art, life is made up of an infinite number of small and specific acts. The larger abuse he recognizes to be assailable chiefly in its detail, and hence the pursuit of it, except in rare circumstances, — as when a whole community is like minded with himself, — is likely to be a sort of guerilla warfare and a kind of pot-hunting. But it is guerilla warfare and pot-hunting directed to as large ends as can be compassed by the limits of one's imagination and practical common sense. The adroit kicker knows that many sad objects will in the usual course of events be left behind, by a sort of common consent, just as we discard certain clothes, less by deliberate pursuit of the ragman than by forgetting the old suit in the delightful possession of the new. He therefore spends his strength in calling attention to the new and beautiful attire of civilization. Nor is he likely to be seduced into the belief, that the armor of old days, or the stately shoe buckles and flowered waistcoats and well-curled wigs of the eighteenth century, are a better costume for our light running modern world and our warm climate than the flexible jersey and springy stockings of the contemporary athlete.

Do you ask if such an ideal kicker actually exists? I am forced to admit that I know no such one, any more than Spencer could have pointed to the actual embodiment of his deduction. And if it be further objected that the foregoing pages do by no means wholly exemplify the doctrine that they attempt to expound, in that they kick at what is essentially unkickable, the *Stossenslust* of humanity, I can merely register a mild and dainty kick to the effect that it is unreasonable to expect me, more than any other reformer or *censor morum*, to abide quite exactly by the doctrine that I would inculcate. Does it at all matter? Not very much one way or the other.

THE GENTLEMAN–SPORTSMAN

HERE upon the opening of the shooting season, I am reminded of the impression made on me some time ago by an article on hunting lions in Africa written by a very well-known author. I remember being much struck by his admirably expressed and lucid explanation of his reason for engaging in that pursuit. Being a native of Vermont I had never devoted much thought to the ethics of lion-hunting and was interested to read that the author of the article felt justified in killing lions because there is really no place for them in the modern world; because they are anachronistic and objectionable survivals from another phase of the world's history; because they are obstacles in the advancing tide of colonization. This very obvious line of reasoning had never chanced to occur to me before. I stopped a moment to savor the pleasure one always feels at having hazy ideas clarified and set in order, and before I went on with the article I reflected that the world owes a debt of gratitude to the highly educated men of trained minds who undertake out-of-the-way enterprises, because with their habit of searching and logical analysis they bring out the philosophy underlying any occupation they may set themselves.

Then I read on further through some most entertaining descriptions of African scenery till I came to an eloquently written paragraph denouncing in spirited terms those men who hunted lions in "an unsportsmanlike manner." My curiosity was aroused. I wondered what this objectionable method could be — probably one which involved the escape of many of these undesirable lions, or possibly more suffering to them. My astonishment was great, therefore, when I read that this pernicious manner of

334

hunting lions consisted in going after them with dogs and horses, and that the author objected to it because it is practically sure to secure every lion hunted. He put it with an evident distaste, that the lion became so worn out with running and so dazed with the barking of the dogs that the hunter could walk up to him and put the rifle-barrel in his ear. If you really want to kill a lion, my sportsman-author went on disdainfully, the thing to do is to shoot a zebra, cut holes in the carcass, put strychnine in the holes, and leave the carcass where the lions can get at it. The ringing accent of scorn in which this whole passage was written cast me into the greatest bewilderment. Had I not just read that the author considered it a laudable thing to put lions out of the world? I must have mistaken his meaning. Feeling greatly perplexed, I hastily turned back over the pages until I encountered that first passage again, and found that I had not in the least mistaken his meaning. He had said in so many words that lions ought to be killed because they were an anachronistic survival, etc., etc. Putting the two statements side by side I looked from one to the other in the first of the seizures of complete perplexity which marked my attempt to understand his ideal of sportsmanship. I read on into the article with the liveliest curiosity, hoping that the author would throw more light on the subject of what constituted a really sportsmanlike method of killing an objectionable animal, and from the sum total of his remarks I made out quite clearly why he objected to the zebra-strychnine method. It was not after all because it was sure, for his own avowed aim was to kill every lion he encountered, and to look up all he possibly could, whether they evidenced any desire to encounter him or not. It was because it "did not give the lion a chance."

In varying forms he repeated this sportsman's ideal of "giving the game a chance," but from the context it was clear, even to my inexperienced eye, that he did not mean to be |taken literally. It was not a real chance the lion had "when the sportsman could arrange matters to his taste — it was a hypothetical, metaphysical chance. The aim was to give the animal, the illusion of having a chance, and when, acting on that idea, he had furnished the hunter with sufficient excitement in frustrating his desperate attempts to escape, the sportsman was to kill him in the end, thus proving his own skill and ingenuity. Yes, it was all quite clearly set forth in the same lucid style which had aroused my admiration at first.

With the repetition of these manœuvres in the case of every lion killed in the author's gentlemanly advance across Africa, I had a stronger and stronger impression that somewhere else I had encountered this sort of reasoning. Somewhere I had heard it all before; or if I had not heard it, I had seen it. But how could I, a Vermont rustic, ever have seen anything which might remind me of lion-hunting according to these impeccably sportsmanlike rules? I laid down the book, trying to bring up the haunting memory more clearly, and in a moment it had flashed up vivid and clear-cut. Why yes, the sportsmanlike method of killing lions reminded me of something with which I had been familiar all my life, — of a cat playing with a live mouse before eating it. It was now more evident that, in comparison with the brutally direct methods of the pot-hunting dog, the cat is actuated by the finest devotion to the ideals of sportsmanship. Not for her the quick pounce and avid crunch of Rover. She "gives the mouse a chance," and only kills him after she has extracted the most deliciously titillating excitement out of his frenzied dashes for liberty. The facts that he never does get away from the cat, and that the lion does sometimes get away from the man only prove how infinitely more clever in this game of sportsmanship, is the cat than the man, since the open purpose of both cat and man is to kill the other animal in the end.

Now nothing can be more unphilosophical in one's attitude towards the world than to blame creatures for acting according to their natures, and I have never felt in the least inclined to censure the cat, although I always put her out of the room with some violence if she brings in a live mouse and begins her sportsmanlike tactics with him. This is not because I think the cat is a wicked animal and ought to be punished, but merely because the sight of the frantic mental sufferings of the mouse happens to be very disagreeable to me. I have no illusions about pussy. I know that if I kicked her out of the room a thousand times ten thousand, I could never inculcate in her any genuine conception of the idea that it may be wrong to get her fun out of another's extreme pain. That is the way cats are. Her virtues lie in other directions. If she keeps herself and her kittens clean, and does not steal my beef-steak, I can ask no more from her.

But now as I meditated on her character, for which I felt a contemptuous tolerance founded on a knowledge of her limitations, I was most disagreeably struck by the close resemblance between her nature and that of the gentleman-sportsman. It is all very well to make the best of the cat's shortcomings, to refrain from expressing, in the only way she can understand, my disgust at a trait she cannot alter, but it is quite another thing to resign myself to the presence of the same trait in the character of many human beings for whom I should like to feel nothing but admiration and respect.

I recognize of course that the lion-hunter may shift his ground, admit that he hunts more for the excitement of the chase than to protect poor colonists from marauding lions, yet still protest against my criticism. "It is unfair," he may urge, "to assume that human nature is all mind and spirit. Flesh and blood exist and have their claim for consideration. Killing animals might be unworthy for a seraph, but I am a man, and for me it is a harmless method of exercising my age-old inherited battle-lust.

I as well as the cat am linked to the past. Is it fair for you to censure in me what you pass over in her?"

Such a plea will hardly answer. Human nature is not animal nature, and though dogs and cats may possibly have their own standards of right and wrong, based on the needs and possibilities of their species, man with his different needs and possibilities has no ethical point of contact with them. But in his own case he is and always has been convinced of the spark disturbing his clod. He is not content to regard himself as a highly intelligent primate, destined to make over the material world for his own uses; whatever his practice may be, he cannot free himself from the belief that he must be good, and must become better. Nor has this conviction wasted itself in impotent speculation. Throughout his history, he has continued to set up standards of conduct so lofty that no age has come near to living up to its profession of right living. Nevertheless aspiration has induced development: for the standard of its ancestors has seemed inadequate to every generation. What the grandfather considered a matter of course, and the father condoned as a peccadillo, the son and his contemporaries proclaim a vice. They may themselves indulge in the vice, but they do so with a feeling of guilt, and they hail with rejoicing the moments when they resolve to improve their lives: such wishes are everything: the rest is merely a matter of time.

No man, therefore, can regard himself solely as the son of an earthy family: for with the lusts of the flesh he has also inherited the aspirations of the spirit; and he is bound by this mental heredity to hold himself responsible as the father of a posterity always advancing toward perfection. Unless he is willing to confess himself either an imbecile or a criminal, he is not justified in yielding to an impulse which he recognizes as unworthy.

Again, the gentleman-lion-hunter may object that I am stating the matter with too much heat. Even though forced to admit that hunting is neither really useful (since lions can be exterminated more easily and surely without it) nor an ineradicable heritage from man's savage past (since men have outgrown so many other supposedly ingrained instincts) he may make a stand on the contention that hunting is a blameless pastime, and that if a gentleman chooses to spend his vacation shooting lions, instead of climbing mountains, neither he, nor society, nor posterity will ever be a penny the worse for it.

I cannot agree with the Gentleman-sportsman. His contention that lion shooting is an obviously blameless recreation for civilized men does not appear to me self-evident. Among the difficulties which beset us in our great campaign to keep the higher elements in human nature, and to discard the lower ones, there is no more puzzling problem than the question of our relation to the animal-world. On this problem there is a great difference of opinion between the older and the younger branches of the Aryan family. The Hindus elaborated their merciful and elevated theory of life at a time when, so to speak, we were still tearing meat from the bones and eating it raw. When, at a much later period, we ourselves came to face the problem, the discoveries of science had so widened the horizon of our knowledge that we were unable to accept the Hindu doctrine of never taking animal life because the principle of life is sacred. Aware that life is not only animal, but exists in everything, we perceived that to eat a dish of oatmeal is to destroy life as truly as to butcher an ox. It is apparent to us that one of the dark mysteries of the world is that we can avoid taking life only by refusing to live ourselves.

Confronted with this problem, when we began to question our habits, we have, after a fashion, worked it out on logical grounds, and have decided that we have a right to take life which is necessary to ours, or which is injurious to ours; but we have tempered this high-handed decision by the feeling, based on all that is best and highest in our natures, that to take life is a serious business, should be undertaken in a serious spirit, for some evident purpose, and should be accomplished in the most painless fashion possible. All the nation-wide campaign against flies has not lessened by a jot our horror at the child who amuses himself by tearing off their wings. Moderns think of themselves as the legal executioners of those animals which they elect must die; and the essence of the executioner's duty is to be merciful, quick, competent in the accomplishment of his task. Most of us would not care to work in a slaughter-house, but that is not because we think the butcher a wicked man. Neither would we choose of our own accord to care for the insane, or clean out the sewers in a city, but that is not because those are shameful acts. They are necessary but uncomely parts of the world's economy, to be performed with a decent reticence and as quickly and economically as possible.

This theory of the entire subservience of the animal world to our human needs can certainly not be criticized for being too ethereally exalted. In fact its best friends cannot claim that it is very elevated doctrine; but at least it is an honest acknowledgment of apparent necessity, it is tempered by all the mercy possible under the circumstances, it is fairly consistent, and it has been accepted by the majority of the inhabitants of the civilized world as a working theory. But how can the curious institution of the good sportsman be fitted into this frank and open modern attitude about a sombre mystery in the intertwined interests of the world? As a matter of fact modern ideas and the good sportsman cannot possibly be reconciled, and whenever society has cast a glance at sportsmanship, that institution, dreading a real scrutiny and a resulting question concerning its right to existence, has hastily thrown out a sop of concession, muttering angrily under its breath about the demagogic modern mob which undertakes to restrict the freedom of gentlemen. In this way, some hundred years ago, the institution of bear-baiting was conceded to be not precisely a sport to inculcate fine qualities in its human spectators; many years later, the contention that prize-fighting was good fodder for the younger generation was given up, and very recently, with a pettish protest that really the world is becoming *too* emasculated, the fine, virile joys of trap-pigeon-shooting have been grudgingly abandoned. But for the most part society is busy about more important matters, and no one except a few unheeded sentimentalists pays any attention to the conflicting claims of man and the animals. During such tranquil periods, the sportsman revises his code according to his own ideas, for, having long outlived the days when its contribution to the food supply gave it actual value, hunting has reached the critical, codified stage common to the senility of all institutions. To an outsider it is rather entertaining to see the unanimity with which each succeeding generation of sportsmen looks back with scorn on its predecessors as a parcel of muckers with no true idea of gentlemanly restraint in sport; a mild diversion is to be extracted from the elaborate platforms in which they set forth the latest rules, — that artificial flies are noble, — that bait is an abomination, — that a magazine shot-gun is fit only for the pot-hunter, — that men need precisely the exercise for their wit, courage, foresight, perseverance and skill which is to be found in hunting animals according to whatever rules chance to be in vogue in the sporting world of their day.

It is true that hunting animals trains a man to use his brains and perseverance in overcoming obstacles. It is also true that everything worth while is achieved against obstacles, so that we do well to train ourselves to overcome them in our play as well as our work. And it is true that a man playing a trout with light tackle enjoys the delight of exercising his own wit, ingenuity, and perseverance in the battle against obstacles; but so would he if, without tying the animal, he should set himself to the difficult undertaking of skinning a dog alive. The fact that he causes more pain in one case than in the other, differentiates the two pursuits only in the matter of degree. How shall the line be drawn? How much pain, in what manner, to what sort of animal, may a man cause for the sole purpose of enjoying the exercise of his wit, ingenuity and perseverance?

As to the exercise of courage in hunting, it is difficult to take seriously this claim on the part of huntsmen, who for the most part are quite unable to travel far enough to encounter any animals more ferocious than a trout, a fox (whose cowardice is proverbial), or at most a deer, who asks nothing better than to be allowed to run away as long as breath lasts. But there are exceptions. There is, for example, the gentleman-sportsman in Africa, who by the expenditure of a great amount of time, effort, and money has succeeded in getting to a country inhabited by an animal which, if sufficiently annoyed would undeniably eat up a gentleman-sportsman if he could get at him. This is exciting no doubt, this undoubtedly calls for physical courage. Courage is a virtue, and excitement is certainly a need of the human heart. No observer of human nature can deny that we need excitement as much as we do bread. But the modern world does not consider even this great desire to justify every and any mode of gratifying it. The man who hunts lions according to the code of the gentleman-sportsman gets his excitement out of the fact that the animal he is attempting to kill may possibly be able to turn the tables and kill him. It would be even more exciting and dangerous, and would call for even more courage, to attempt to track down and kill a man fully armed like the hunter. But the conscience of the world, insensitive as it is to some of the finer points of conduct, would not for a moment countenance turning loose even the lowest of convicted criminals for the purpose of allowing other men to extract excitement out of his chase, — no! not though all the most delicate distinctions of the most modern and fastidious code of gentlemanly hunting were thrown around this most inimitably thrilling of sports. The fact is that the world is becoming more and more squeamish about the way in which its inhabitants are to secure their excitement. There was a time when all the gentlemen-sportsmen supplied themselves with excitement by sitting in comfortable seats about an arena and watching wild animals tear human beings to pieces. There is still a modern nation which allows its gentlemen to vary the monotony of their lives by watching bulls gore horses and even men, to death. There is even a considerable amount of excitement to be extracted from a whiskey-bottle if administered to that end. But there are some ingenious moderns who manage to escape from boredom by seeking for rare and valuable new plants in remotest Thibet, or in risking their lives in the pursuit of the microbe which causes cancer, or (if these pursuits are too costly for their means) there is the profession of fireman in a great city, or coastguard on a dangerous shore, or surveying engineer in a new country. All of these occupations call for a reasonable amount of physical courage, and supply a change from the dull routine of humdrum life.

To return to our lions; although to hunt them by the sportsman's code undoubtedly takes courage, does it not seem rather a pity to waste in the destruction of animals admitted vermin, a human quality so fine, so inspiriting, so necessary as physical courage, sanctified as it is by a thousand struggles of men against disease, against wrong and violence, against the inert forces of Nature? Lions interfere with the peaceable occupation of the world by humanity: therefore we believe we have a right to kill them. Formerly the only way in which they could be killed was by the exercise of physical courage on the part of men. But that is not in the least necessary, now that a powerful drug has been discovered which will do the unsavory but necessary task for us and leave us free to use our courage for more valuable purposes. Why not let this unimportant and unpleasant detail of the world's work be attended to in the most competent way possible, without the unseemly attempt to make it at the same time an entertaining spectacle for human beings? And why not apply the same principle to the killing of other animals for whose destruction we feel we have a fair warrant of execution signed by our reasonable needs. Rabbits and foxes injure our crops, and propagate so fast that they are a menace to our husbandry. If they are to be killed, and everyone except an occasional zoölater grants that the world is not large enough now both for them and for us, let us kill as many as we need to put out of the way, as quickly and surely as may be, with no quaint discrimination against ferrets in the case of rabbits, or rifles in the case of foxes. If we need fish as a variety in our diet, let us go honestly about the business of securing it, and not quibble about the great ethical elevation of light tackle as opposed to nets. And if a man is trying to kill a bird for food, let him forget the grotesque reasoning that it is not fair to shoot it sitting on a bough where he can almost certainly kill it at one shot, but must let it fly so that there are ten chances to one that the shot will only maim or mutilate it.

Now it is certainly true that there are among our twentieth century men, a good many individuals from whom no help in the upward movement of the race can be expected, and whose fondness for hunting, undoubtedly is based upon the survival in them of the paleolithic liking to kill. They prefer to hunt rabbits rather than shoot at a mark, because a target cannot shed blood. If they make no pretence about this taste being the basis of their liking for hunting, it would be showing no due sense of the proportion of things to visit them with too serious a reprobation. It is possible that this sort of man, if he were not allowed to amuse himself by tormenting animals might react from the humane régime of his time by committing deeds of violence against human beings.

Only let this outlet for non-eliminated pre-historic instincts be frankly a drainage-pipe for the purpose of moral sanitation only. Let there be no attempt to fool our noses as to its true scent, by the use of the musk of pseudo-gentlemanliness. If hunters will but be open about it, theirs is not a very heinous survival of what was a most necessary, though now superseded instinct in humanity. There are many worse things than having fun out of the dying struggles of a trout or a rabbit. Hunting in the open air is certainly better than the opium habit. Animals nearly always die a violent death anyhow, and it does not, I daresay, make a vital difference to them whether it is a fox or a man, or a bigger fish which finally dispatches them.

The number of human beings unleavened by humanity appears larger than it really is, because most children as they live rapidly through their personal reproduction of the history of mankind, pass through the cave man's phase of frank, thoughtless, and unconscious cruelty; and some of them are slow to pass out of it. But cases of prolonged atavism are few, and though disagreeable, need be little more regretted than the occasional outcropping survival in a modern of the tremendous jaw and beetling brows of our neolithic grandsires. Left to themselves, these anachronistic and objectionable traits will vanish as the race ascends the slow spiral of its upward way. Already most twentieth-century boys and girls (if their development be not arrested by perverted public opinion) tend to outgrow this relic of savagery, as they outgrow their exaggerated gregariousness, their slavish conformity to the ideas of others, and the rest of the primitive phases of their development. The process needs no special attention from their instructors: good example and encouragement to clear thinking about habitual actions will almost always do the work.

But few young brains are vigorous enough to continue clear thinking under the narcotic influence of a generally accepted social hypocrisy. It is not acquaintance with the grim necessity of killing as the butcher practises it which is dangerous to young consciences, it is the sight of the sportsman killing without necessity. What stupifies the moral sense in this connection is the pretence that to take one's pleasure at the cost of another's suffering is a commendable, highly respectable, nay, even very aristocratic amusement for grown men of brains and education. The most gentlemanly restrictions cast about hunting animals for fun, cannot mask the fact that its essence is enjoyment taken consciously at the expense of another's pain, an enjoyment against which the conscience of the world has pronounced a righteous verdict of total condemnation. The butcher kills, the pot-hunter kills, the sportsman kills; but only the last openly finds entertainment in the act.

TRADE UNIONISM IN A UNIVERSITY

THE so-called strike of the Wisconsin Student Workers' Union has much of instruction for those who have been watching the trend of University development during the past few years and are inclined critically to examine the effect upon the student of modern educational methods.

The strike occurred in an institution that is recognized as the leader in progressive education; that has given extraordinary liberties to the student body; that is probably working more directly for the material interests of the people than is any other American university; and it occurred in a State that is convinced of the expediency of generously maintaining an institution of higher education, and is levying taxes therefor which during ten years have increased more than threefold.

Largely under the initiative of the University, but with faith, often fully justified, in the practical value of the instruction therein given, the State has adopted many of the principles enunciated in the class room, and has accepted as advisors, or taken over and appointed on its commissions, practically every professor and instructor whose counsel might be of direct service in its legislative and executive efforts, or of indirect service to the people at large. The professional staff of the University, and the legislative and executive staff of the State, have thus organized what might be called a beneficent interlocking directorate, which is expressed more or less truthfully in the local aphorism: "The State University is destined to produce a University State."

During the past decade, influenced by and participating in the political and social changes that have made Wisconsin conspicuous, and encouraged by the large enrollment in the so-called social and political sciences — an

347

enrollment of nearly two thousand students, containing a generous representation from the congested districts of American cities, from the oppressed people of Europe and from formative governments generally — the University has added to its staff of professors and instructors, until these departments are not surpassed in attractiveness by any institution in America or indeed in Europe.

There is, then, among the student body a liberal admixture of those whose social and political convictions, so far as they are definitely formed, are not in entire accord with prevailing conventions. Some of the more restless have organized a Socialists Club, and affiliations have been established with Socialist organizations at Milwaukee and elsewhere, and speakers of advanced anarchistic views, such as Emma Goldman, on coming to Madison, draw large and not entirely unsympathetic student audiences.

Within the University, and justified under the plea for a more perfect democracy, the presence of strong class distinction and party feeling often introduces an earnestness and bitterness into student gatherings which is much more intense than in our older institutions of the east. Moreover, the discussion of party differences is not confined to the campus. The contestants, even though students, are accustomed to air their views in the public press; and the state legislature — in which there is a liberal admixture of representatives of all political parties — is occasionally called upon to adjust real or imaginary student wrongs.

To the Wisconsin student there is no mystery about the making or unmaking of law; to him the capitol is a place of recreation, and the legislators, many of them alumni, are his companions. The freshman comes under the control of a student legislative body that defines his privileges and attempts to control his liberties. This elective body not only assumes jurisdiction over the student as an individual, but, like an interstate commerce commis sion, it regulates the activities of various student organizations, particularly those alleged to have aristocratic tendencies. It fixes penalties for the infraction of student laws, authorizes arrests, and sees that culprits are brought before the Student Court, where they are tried and sentenced. This student legislative body, through its representation on student publications, and in other ways, is an active agency in making and molding student opinion, and the faculty has already recognized its jurisdiction. The Regents have agreed not to alter or abridge the control of Student Self-Government, except through process of conference. The student body has thus assumed, in certain respects at least, the same attitude toward the administration of the University that the University is accused of having assumed toward the administration of the State; or, to paraphrase the aphorism already given, "The University Student is destined to produce a Student University."

The student labor trouble, therefore, is not to be looked upon as the result of a justifiable grievance between a handful of waiters, and the Steward in control of the University Commons. The relations between the student workers and the Steward had been cordial, and the reduction in the number of student employees was an economic necessity, and ordinarily would have excited no particular opposition. But under the peculiar conditions existing at Madison, where there are students who do not believe in the present order of things, where it is thought, by not a few, that legislation by labor will bring better social conditions, where machinery for organized resistance is fabricated as a pastime, where the tactics of "collective bargaining" are thoroughly understood, and where there are impulsive students anxious to assume leadership, the temptation to translate static into kinetic energy became irresistible.

It seems that about one hundred and thirty students had been given positions in the University as waiters, kitchen helpers, etc., receiving in compensation a substantial meal for each hour or fraction thereof of service. There was no dispute concerning the amount of service or the value of the compensation. The students admitted that the work was light, the board excellent; and the positions were considered the most desirable of their kind in the city. The body waited upon some two hundred and fifty men students, and upon nearly three hundred women students. (Thirteen women student waiters and helpers, employed in one of the dormitories, did not join the Union, and took no active part in the agitation.)

The completion of a new central kitchen had led to economies, and a few weeks before the end of the semester — it was thought in ample time for the young men to find employment elsewhere — preliminary announcement was made that the staff of student employees would be reduced, and twenty students out of a total of one hundred and thirty were individually so informed. Since it was perfectly obvious that their services were in fact not needed, the waiters received the announcement in good spirit and without serious question.

It was at this point, however, that certain other students, who were not employed by the University, but were generally interested in organized agitation, called a mass meeting of the student workers both of the University and of the city, and through the vigorous application of well-known forensic excitants, brought about a condition of hysteria, which affected a large proportion of the student employees, although the general student body remained immune.

The waiters and helpers found themselves organizing a Union, subscribing to extragavant declarations, and electing as their officers representatives from the most violent of the agitators. It was alleged that the organization had more than four hundred members. The president of the Union, a student in Law, was not a University worker. The secretary was the president of the local Socialist Club, and originally registered at the University as from New York City.

The leaders of the "strike" (a strike was only threatened) took the position that they would protect the student waiters, that the number of waiters should not be reduced, that economies, if necessary, should be effected in some other way, and that dire consequences would result if the plans of the University administration were carried into effect. In any event, nothing should be done until the organization was duly recognized by the University authorities, until proposed changes in the method of conducting the business of the Commons had been submitted to the Student Union for its approval, and until it was agreed that all present and future grievances and difficulties should be submitted to a board of arbitration satisfactory to the Union.

At Madison it is customary to adjust differences through conferences, or a series of conferences, but here was a case that affected the business management of the University, and where delay would involve loss to the State. The situation was also extremely amusing, because of the fact that the longer a settlement could be deferred, the longer the student waiters would continue to be fed at the expense of the University. It resembled some of the difficulties our government experienced in the neighborhood of the Rio Grande.

As a coercive measure, the leaders submitted a document to the effect that if the original plans of the administration were not altered there would be a sympathetic "walkout" on the part of a hundred or more boarders.

Startling articles appeared in the press, syndicalism and sabotage were academically discussed, and there were threats that unless "justice" were shown the students, every dining room in Madison would be closed.

As time went on, the general disturbance had its effect upon the regular kitchen staff of the University, composed of paid employees, who saw, or thought they saw, in the rising power of the student body, their own impending extinction.   At this time, a strike or walkout on the part of the regular paid force would have been serious: for the University was practically under contract to house and feed approximately three hundred women students, enrolled residents of the dormitories.

Hearings were held before the Regents, but all efforts on the part of the management to change the attitude of the leaders were futile, and the appetites of the aggrieved seemed to increase with the vigor of the agitation.

At a critical moment the cooks sent in their ultimatum, calling the Steward to declare allegiance either to the insurgents or to the regulars; or in default of such declaration, operations in the kitchen would abruptly terminate. This announcement was decisive: for

We may live without friends; we may live without books;
But civilized man cannot live without cooks.

The administration ordered the doors of the dining halls closed, locked, and guarded; service within the women's dormitories was conducted as is customary in convents, and the debarred student waiters, boarders, and guests gathered without on the campus, dumfounded that a public institution should close its doors to the populace.   It certainly looked like a "lockout," and it was alleged that the plant was being operated by "scabs."

All the stage machinery that accompanies a real strike and lockout was brought into requisition — circulars were issued appealing for the sympathy of the public, and implying that poor students had been discharged for no other reason than that they had belonged to the "Union," and stating that girls working their way through college had been dismissed because they had expressed sympathy. Mass meetings were called, speakers were imported, inflammatory addresses were delivered, additional resolutions adopted, and appeals made to the Federation of

Labor, to the State Industrial Commission, and to the Governor.

But in due time the members of the Student Workers' Union found that their services were not indispensable, that State institutions do not invariably yield to the pressure of organized resistance, and as chastened individuals they applied for such positions as remained vacant, and went back to work.

The recital of these occurrences as a trivial circumstance has no place in a publication of this kind, but the significance, so far as it may throw light upon the general path of university development, and may help to determine the kind of mind and men that universities are producing or may produce, justifies serious contemplation.

It is generally admitted that universities are destined to become something different from what they now are. University men have a duty to perform, not only in watching the trend of this inevitable drift, and determining its probable course, but they are in a measure responsible for the course.

Not all institutions move with the same rapidity. Some possess a power that takes them away from their companions and into new territory. The records of their movements and the attendant results are generally looked upon as public property. It thus becomes possible for the conservative university, or the university that is not inclined, or does not have the means, to go into expensive experimentation, to learn much through the inexpensive process of observation.

What have we to learn from the conditions and occurrences above outlined?

Are we really getting all of the good things out of our institutions of higher culture that we think we are getting?

When the citizens of a commonwealth tax themselves in order to give university instruction to their children, does it necessarily follow that the university life will develop the highest citizenship? Does it develop a feeling of pride in the State and of loyalty to it? Is the position of the State as an instrument of modern civilization strengthened or weakened thereby?

Does university training tend to produce an accelerated or a deferred maturity of the judicial sense — the power to distinguish between what is reasonable and what is unreasonable, what is genuine and what is false; and to distinguish promptly between the man that is frankly striving for principle, and the one who is falsely striving for position?

If any considerable number of college graduates should be of the opinion that the State, in addition to providing some twenty-five years of free instruction, should also provide free board, is it not obvious that difficulties akin to those that surround the issue of fiat money would quickly arise on the issue of fiat food?

If graduates on becoming citizens believe that they are entitled to anything and everything that can be extracted from the State, and if their lives are to be spent under this obsession, ought not the community to prepare itself for a long series of constitutional amendments?

Is a university graduate sufficiently prepared to meet the strife of adult life if he leaves his institution wise with facts, emotional to the spell of the professional agitator, and innocent of the craft of the publicity agent?

Our institutions may teach what is right, but what is being done to develop the moral fibre and personal independence that will put the right into operation? What forces are at work to encourage open and vigorous opposition to social doctrines that are generally considered damaging to the State?

Does free and excessive opportunity engender a feeling of gratitude on the part of the recipient, or are such feelings inconsistent with modern conventions?

When the lust for individual gain and personal possession on the part of the few, is legitimatized at the expense of many, are the results more reprehensible when the process has been conducted by the aristocratic adult, than when conducted by the proletariat youth?

When students have listened to and communed with the most eminent instructors in social and political science that the State can furnish, why should they believe that labor, when organized, has inherent rights that labor individualized does not possess?

Are the cardinal principles of our form of constitutional government being upheld when it becomes necessary for the individual to declare allegiance to some party or organization before he can enjoy the ordinary privileges of citizenship?

Why should a body of university students — men that have enjoyed the privileges of education — take the position that unless the prerogative of the few is promptly recognized and implicitly followed, the innocent will be harassed, and the entire community made to suffer?

Is it not possible that in our effort strictly to maintain the principles of academic freedom, we are giving instruction with such impartial neutrality that those who have worthy views conclude that their convictions are subject to question, and those who have ulterior motives are encouraged to believe themselves justified?

What the State really needs at the present time is some agency that will develop the powers of discrimination, that will enable its citizens to arrive at conclusions independent of plausible presentations.

MONARCHY AND DEMOCRACY IN EDUCATION

I T is a truism that since the day of Plato's *Republic* no subject has had such widespread discussion as has that of the proper form of government. It is equally a truism that if imitation is the sincerest flattery, the hundreds of written constitutions that have sprung up since 1789 attest the belief that America has successfully put into practical form the theories of democracy. Yet a minority has always questioned whether democracy is after all the panacea for political evils, and recent writers like Mr. Lecky, have but given expression to a somewhat widespread feeling of uncertainty as to the permanent success of democratic institutions.

It is noteworthy, however, that the discussion of democracy has been confined to the field of politics, and that its adaptation to educational institutions, where presumably a high grade of intelligence, education, opportunity and experience seem to offer the greatest promise of success, is never publicly discussed, much less in this country practiced.[1]

It is equally anomalous that in Europe, with its tendency to monarchy in the state, there is found absolute democracy in the government of educational institutions, while America, democratic in the state, furnishes the

[1] The only important exception to this statement is the University of Virginia. The feeling of college faculties evoked by its change from democratic to monarchical organization is probably expressed by a contemporaneous editorial. "The thirteenth of June is to be an important date in the history of the American college. On that day the democratic system of government by the entire body of professors, which has marked out the University of Virginia from almost all other institutions of learning in the country, is to come to an end. This system, in spite of all that can properly be said on the other side, has good features which it is a pity to see extinguished." — *The Nation*, June 11, 1903.
It is evidently the college president who speaks in an editorial some weeks later in the same publication. "We believe that the president should be something of an autocrat in his proper domain and that faculty government would be bad government." — *The Nation*, Sept. 24, 1903.

most extreme illustration of absolute monarchy in the government of its educational institutions. It seems, if possible, even more strange that American college students have for years been going to European universities, and yet apparently have paid no attention to questions of educational organization. It can only be explained by the general lack of information and interest in the management of educational institutions.

The UNPOPULAR REVIEW is not a fitting place for the discussion of questions concerning the college, if frequent discussion means popularity: for the fashionable question in the serious periodical of the day is "What's the matter with the colleges?" But while there is absolute agreement that *something* is the matter, every diagnostician has his own explanation. Athletics, the curriculum, the classics, vocational training, and every part of the educational system unable to speak for itself, have been held responsible for the existing evils. It may, however, be sufficiently unpopular for a mere college professor to say that in his humble opinion at least one thing the matter with the college is its form of government, and that here is an interesting place in which to test democracy before abandoning it as hopeless. Certainly these opinions have been so unpopular as to lead many who honestly hold them to hesitate to state them. When they are stated, it is generally by those not within the academic pale.

One of the most serious evils in the situation is that it is impossible for those most concerned to meet and discuss it openly. More than one important article has come from a college professor, but it has been anonymous because it is out of the question for him to write freely of the position in which he is placed. If he openly questions the present system, he is called "a sorehead," "a knocker," and "a kicker." Every discussion of the administrative department of the university is interpreted as "an attack on the president." To publish a doubt of the wisdom of concentrating all authority in him, is regarded as "attacking the administration." It is at least significant that in the great work on *University Control*[1] the opinions of two hundred and ninety-nine members of college faculties are anonymous, while a bare half-dozen are published under the names of men holding academic positions at the time of writing. Academic freedom is usually interpreted as meaning the right of speaking freely about matters and things in general, including the trusts, anarchy, socialism, prohibition, the control of public utilities by municipal, state, or federal agencies, and kindred subjects, but never about academic organization. That freedom of expression for which Wycliffe and the Lollard movement stood in England, Luther in Germany, Calvin in France — albeit his ecclesiastical followers in this country may have wandered far from his ideas — that movement for freedom led in Europe by great university men, when it comes to discussion of educational organization has, by the irony of fate, been denied to their heirs in America to-day.

It is easy to trace the path by which monarchy in education has been reached. When education was largely controlled by the Church, students were educated by the Church, and for the Church. Educational institutions, as a part of the Church, were governed as the Church was governed. Implicit obedience was given superiors, not as educators, but as members of the Church. We have inherited from mediæval times a condition of educational organization that was the natural outgrowth of this organization, but we have perpetuated it in an age when education is controlled by the State, which has itself become democratic. The result is a tug-o'-war between the monarchical organization of education, and the democratic spirit that permeates the vast body of educators and educated.

It is also easy to see the immediate steps by which we have arrived at the present situation. The institution with which the writer is connected had fewer than two

[1] J. McKeen Cattell, *University Control*, Science Press, 1913.

hundred regular college students when he first became a member of the faculty. It has shared in the enormous development of such institutions all over the country, and its students now number more than a thousand. Yet in all this time, the method of government has not changed. In the early days it was convenient for the president to decide every question, and this system has been continued, even though the student body has increased more than five fold, and the instructing body in the same proportion. In spite of changed conditions everywhere, this plan has been perpetuated, and has often been legalized by boards of trustees.

Thus, by both remote and immediate inheritance, education, in its organization, has arrived at absolute monarchy, with all its attending evils, — evils that affect the university as a whole and all of its separate and individual parts.

One obvious evil is the confusion everywhere found in the academic world between legislation and administration. The normal plan in a political democracy — an administrative body that carries out the wishes of the legislative body — is reversed in education. The legislative and the executive departments may be combined, and the executive made responsible to the legislative, as in England, or they may be independent, as in America; but it is only in an absolute monarchy that the administrative body both legislates and administers its own legislation. The university has thus allied itself with absolute monarchy rather than with democracy.

Another element of confusion is found in the anomalous conditions of citizenship. Educational citizenship within a faculty, attaches to the position, not to the individual. A man is appointed to a professorship in a faculty, and *ipso facto* he acquires full citizenship in that body, with power to vote immediately on every question submitted to it. Yet the faculty may list as "instructors" no small proportion of its members who have been connected with

it many years, yet they have no share in the government
of the institution. They are in a state of indeterminate
probation, and are often never admitted to the privileges
of full citizenship in the governing body.

Confusion also grows out of the application to the government of the university, of the unit vote long ago abandoned in the federal government. In the New England
Confederation, the experiment was tried of giving equal
representation to each colony, regardless of its population.
This proved unsatisfactory, and subsequent plans of union
attempted to square the circle by increasing the number
of representatives, but giving each colony only one vote.
After this in its turn proved ill-advised, the whole system
was thrown overboard, and a "one man, one vote" principle adopted. In college legislation has either theory or
experience shown any necessity for reverting to an antiquated political custom, and requiring that the unit rule
shall prevail and each department have one vote but only
one vote?

The most disturbing factor in the situation is that all
questions concerning the actual government in a university are decided, not by the faculty itself, but by an external board of trustees; that this body, rather than the
faculty, is ultimately and legally responsible for all legislation affecting the university; and that it transfers this
responsibility to the president of the institution whom it
itself appoints. If it is suggested that the faculty is the
natural legislative body in an educational institution, and
that this body should determine all matters of educational
policy, objections are immediately interposed.

The first objection is the alleged incompetence of a
faculty to legislate. But it may well be asked how often
matters of genuine legislation are even submitted to it.
Some years ago a university president was elected, and the
special correspondent of a great metropolitan daily sent
it a two-column account of his probable policy. "All over
America," he writes, "the question is being asked: 'What

are President X's views? What is he likely to do with the elective courses? What with requirements for admission? What with the different departments of the University, re-modelling the scheme which now runs through each in a confused way? What with university extension? The compulsory chapel, and the college pastorate questions, and the complicated problems of undergraduate and general intercollegiate athletics?'" Yet every one of these questions represented as being asked "all over America" concerns not the administrative office of a university president, but the legislative department of the institution. Whether a faculty is or is not a failure as a legislative body, can be only a matter of conjecture until the experiment has had a fair trial.

A variant of this objection is that "college faculties can not do business." To this it may be said parenthetically that a faculty has little opportunity except to fritter away its time, when a college president refuses to submit an agenda to it, and thus enable it to do its business in a business-like way. But every great university numbers among its faculty those who have from time to time been asked to render service to the state or to the community, and this service has been rendered in an acceptable, even a distinguished, manner. In the fields of diplomacy, finance, organized philanthropy, municipal affairs, the college professor is everywhere being requisitioned by the state as a consulting expert, or asked to render it temporary active service. Yet many of these prophets are without honor in their own country, in that no opportunity is ever given them to suggest improvements in the business administration of their own institutions, or to confer officially on educational. policy with the representatives of other faculties. Thus the powers of the faculty are being atrophied through lack of use, while the college, in the midst of abundance, suffers from poverty of nourishment.

It is also urged that faculties are not interested in gen-

eral educational policies, since each member is primarily
concerned with his own special department. This too is a
matter of conjecture until the statement has been tested
by experience. It may, however, readily be granted that
not all members of every faculty are interested in educational legislation. But this is true in the state, and yet
it is not used as an argument either for disfranchising
voters, or for refusing them the franchise. Rather, is every
voter urged to do his political duty, and vote, and every
alien urged to take out his naturalization papers, and as
speedily as may be become a voting citizen.

The fear has also been expressed that if faculties were
given increased legislative powers, the result would be confusion in the consideration of educational problems. This
fear in its turn seems certainly not well grounded. It is
seldom expressed with reference to the political system,
yet if danger exists anywhere, it is assuredly there, and
not in the college world. What education needs above
everything else, is all the wisdom that can be contributed
to it by the experience, intelligence, observation, and
theory of every person connected with it. The result
would assuredly be, not confusion, but enlightenment. A
recent examination of the academic career of the members
of a single college faculty, shows that they have been connected either as students or officers with nearly two hundred different institutions in this country or in Europe.
This history is doubtless repeated in every other institution, showing what a wealth of academic experience and
knowledge the college has never yet turned to account. It
is generally believed that the great work of the trained
mind is to utilize the forces of nature, and make them do
its bidding, to harness fire, water, air, electricity, and to
reap the advantages of the power multiplied by these
means. But no effort is made to utilize the educational
forces that lie dormant in a college faculty, and to multiply
a hundred fold the educational forces now used. The
question may at least be raised whether some fraction of

the confusion found in the educational system may not be due to the failure to bring to bear upon it the clarifying power of college and university faculties. Investigation has found an outlet in every field except that of education itself.

The fear was once expressed by Edward Thring lest in any scheme for the organization of education "the skilled workman engaged in the highest kind of skilled work should be deliberately and securely put under the amateur in perpetuity." [1] This fear is not unwarranted in its application to America. As long as college and university trustees are for the most part chosen from business interests, they naturally assume that college officers must "want something" in the way of personal advantage when they discuss the disadvantages of the present system of academic government. They do not understand that what college officers wish is not personal gain, but simply freedom of opportunity to serve the college to the limit of their powers, and that this opportunity must include a controlling voice in the educational legislation of the institutions with which they are connected, and in the formulation of the laws governing their own actions as legislating bodies. The members of college faculties seem justified in thinking that they are now deprived of all the broadening and deepening influences that come from sharing the responsibilities of the larger affairs of education. They are parts of a machine irresponsible for its final results: the planning, the direction, the thinking are all done by the administrative head. Were the duties of a college professor such as those of a letter carrier, a policeman, a snow shoveler, a brick layer, or a day laborer, it would be a simple thing to regulate his hours of work, his pay, his vacation, and his uniform. But the more complex the duties of any person, the more difficult the regulation of them by an external authority. The more serviceable

[1] *The Schoolmaster's Year Book*, 1904, p. 4.

any person to any organization, the more must he have freedom of thought, judgment, and action.

The further questions also arise — Does a university officer sustain the same relation to the president, or the board of trustees, that a minister does to the ministry, or that a diplomatic officer does to his government, or to the government to which he is accredited? Are college officers to be paid employees, or to be co-operators in the government of the college? If the former, then certainly military discipline must prevail. Men in high business or financial circles do not allow their employees to go about openly discussing or criticizing the way they conduct their business. But if college officers are to be co-operators in determining the educational policy of the institution with which they are connected, what is needed is not keeping them under army discipline, but the encouragement of frank discussion with them and by them of all matters pertaining to the welfare of the institution, and of education in all its largest aspects.

The situation may be confused by the custom of choosing the college president from the ranks of the clergy; the clergyman-president naturally believes that since his relations to his congregation have been those of an expert in theology to those who are ignorant of it, his relations to a college faculty must be similar. He forgets that he has to deal with those who are themselves experts, each in his own field, and that they are also presumably interested in the general field of education, and acquainted with it.

It may be that college authorities intend to encourage college faculties to discuss with them questions of educational policy; but if so, the intention has not been made with sufficient emphasis to be clearly understood. "We are clerks in a dry goods store, the dean is the floor walker and the president is the proprietor," is the way the situation has been put by a well-known university professor. The college professor sometimes feels that while, before the law, a man is innocent until he is proved guilty, in the college world faculties are guilty until they can prove themselves innocent, and their normal attitude thus becomes one of defense against an unseen power.

The results of all this confusion between the legislative and the administrative departments in academic government are unfortunate for all concerned. Destructive criticism will always prevail, and will sap the vitality of any institution that denies to its members the right of constructive action, while external government leads to the spirit and attitude of externalism, — the members of the teaching body of a college rarely say "we," but refer politely to the institution with which they are connected as "the college." The impression is sometimes carried away from an educational assembly, that the profession of teaching has not attracted many brilliant college graduates. Will mediocre men continue to seek the teaching profession, while men of independence of judgment and character continue to shun a profession which offers little scope for their abilities? "What science and practical life alike need, is not narrow men, but broad men sharpened to a point," writes President Butler, and this admirably expresses the great need in education, — a need difficult to be met as long as present conditions remain. It is a grave question whether the college professor is to continue an automaton, or to become an initial force.

The chief administrative officer of the college has come to be considered the college; in his own eyes, and in the eye of the public, he *is* the college; he is the only person considered competent or authorized to represent it; and it is his view that is to prevail in all matters of educational policy.

Now with the college president as an individual, the college professor has no quarrel. He often counts him among his warmest friends, and his personal relations with him are often cordial, and even intimate. But this is quite compatible with a strong and conscientious belief based on a study of facts and conditions, that the organ-

ization of the college presidency is an anomaly in a demo_
cratic state.   The college professor may perhaps recognize
the justice of the administration of the president *per se*,
even when it takes such extreme form as regulations that
members of a faculty are not permitted to invite anyone
to speak to their classes without authorization from the
president; that they cannot be absent from a class without
getting permission from the president; that sudden illness,
accident, or unforeseen emergency that has involved
absence, must be reported; when the president gives permission to accept an invitation to lecture at another university but with the proviso that it does not involve
absence from class, or that the request be not repeated during the academic year, or with the reminder that a professor's first duty is to his own college; when it is the president
who passes on the propriety of a professor's wearing a golf
suit in the lecture room, and who sometimes decides the
question of wearing caps and gowns on commencement
day.   The objection of the college professor lies less in the
nature of the rules and regulations prescribed than in the
manner of the prescription.   He sometimes wonders why
he could not be trusted to legislate on some of these questions, and why it is so difficult for the president to realize
that a professor may take an active interest in educational
affairs, without having his eye on the presidency.

The professor realizes that the president is not always
to be blamed for present conditions, — often he is himself
the victim of a system he has had no part in creating, and
forces that he cannot control apparently compel him to
perpetuate it.   Yet blame must be attached to him for
defending it, and for refusing to discuss with his colleagues
the possibility of modifying it.   He seems equally remiss
in not presenting the whole question of college government
to the board of trustees, and pointing out to them the in-
congruities and anomalies of the present situation.   The
professor realizes that the president has a hard time of
it — Does he not hear it at every educational conven-

tion? — but he always wonders if it is inevitable. He sometimes remembers an illustrated lecture given by the representative of a great manufacturing company, showing its organization and workings. One slide represented in graphic form its early organization; it was a pyramid trying to maintain stable equilibrium on its apex, and the apex was the president supporting on his shoulders the solid mass of the employees. Another slide represented the same pyramid on its base, and the apex, in its natural position, was the smiling face of the president. Underneath was the legend "It pays." If the organization of a great business enterprise has gained in strength and stability, and has found that "it pays" in dollars and cents as well as in comfort and peace of mind, to have the responsibility for conducting it shared by all connected with it, would not a similar organization "pay" the college? As a result of recent outbreaks on Blackwell's Island, the Commissioner of Corrections went among the inmates to learn the causes of their grievances, and with the same end in view called to the office a half-dozen of the most intelligent convicts, and invited them to state all their complaints. It is not on record that a college president or board of trustees has talked over causes of dissatisfaction with educational conditions, or has invited the members of the faculty to state their views. Is it possible that some pointers on academic government may be gained from a method employed in a modern penal institution?

It is conceivable that such a plan might also pay in dollars and cents. In one college it took nine years to get a requisition signed for a small improvement needed to relieve the officers working in the building from undue anxiety for the care of the property; and the total cost involved was six dollars. During these nine years the college treasurer was on record as saying that it cost three thousand dollars a year to enforce the compulsory attendance at chapel prescribed by the board of trustees. Would some conference between trustees, president, and faculty have resulted in a better showing on the treasurer's books?

If the present system has entailed endless confusion in the relations between the legislative and the administrative departments of the college, it has resulted in equally anomalous conditions in the administrative department itself. Some years ago, when a gentleman distinguished in the educational field was chosen president of a university, a member of another faculty remarked, "It seems a great misfortune, does it not, that he should be made president: he has done so much for education, and now of course he will have to give up all that work."

Nor are members of college faculties alone in thinking that the office of president is overweighted. At the time of the election of a certain university president, the alumni of the institution put themselves on record as believing "that the presidential prerogative has increased, is increasing, and ought to be diminished." In this opinion, probably the majority of every faculty in every college and university in the country would concur.

Many college professors are restive not only because "the presidential prerogative has increased," but also because they are called on to expend much mental and physical energy in preserving the prerogative. The offense of *lèse-majesté* has become almost as criminal in the educational as in the political world. They are restive because the presidential office is overweighted, and the result as regards the administration, is to develop that most pernicious of all forms of government, — a bureaucracy. They are restive because of their inability to remedy conditions not of their own making. Some of these are financial, and a college instructor once put the matter thus: "Our president has created conditions whereby we have an annual deficit of about $20,000. This deficit is met by the chairman of the board of trustees, and the president must stand in with him. The faculty are in a hole, — they must hang on to the president, and he must hang on to the board of trustees, and they must hang on to their chairman, and trust him to pull everybody out." Some of these conditions are educational. Wisdom seems to be attached to the office of president, rather than to the individual filling it. A man may be made president because he is known to be a good business man and an able executive officer, and *ipso facto* he becomes an expert on all educational questions. Progress in all educational matter must be halted while the excellent executive is familiarizing himself with the A B C of education, and perhaps in time learning how large the subject is.

Many professors are discouraged because, while the same tendency towards autocratic government has been seen in the political world, the reaction against it is already noted. The power of the speaker of the House of Representatives that gained the title of "czar" for one incumbent, has already been modified by the rules of the House. But the college professor sees nothing on the educational horizon that portends a change for the better. Every week he reads somewhere the well-known account of the first official meeting between a president of Harvard University and his faculty. When changes were proposed, and some of the faculty reasoned why these things must be, the president replied, "Because, gentlemen, you have a new president." The professor always wonders if anything like it ever happens when a university acquires a new member of the faculty; he wonders why this vivid description of professors rubbing their eyes in amazement at the statement of their new master, should give such pleasure to the press and to the public; and he wonders if the spirit of it has not blossomed in the most recent authoritative statement of the place of the university president as it is understood by the president himself.[1]

The professor is discouraged because, although, in the present organization of the educational system, a president

---

[1] Charles W. Eliot, "The University President in the American Commonwealth," *Educational Review*, December, 1911.

is considered necessary, the supply of presidents never equals the demand. So varied and numerous are the qualifications insisted upon, that when a person is found approaching the desired standard, he is sought for every vacancy. Several well-known professors have for a number of years been "mentioned" in connection with every presidency vacant, and as a society belle is said to boast of the number of desirable offers of marriage she has refused, so the professor, or more often his wife, makes known the number of presidencies that he has declined. The professor wonders why one or more of our great universities, in this age of vocational training, does not establish a training school for presidents. But this in its turn leads to the query how the supply of students in such a school could be maintained.

The professor is discouraged because of the difficulty of "getting at things." The question of college government involves the relation of the boards of control to the president and the faculty, the relation of the president to the faculty, on the one hand, and to the student body on the other, with the result that the president becomes the official medium of communication between the governing body and the faculty. This triangular arrangement can but be productive of lack of harmony, and of constant misunderstandings; and its evils fall upon trustees, president, faculty, students, and alumni. The trustees nominally exercise an authority that is virtually given over to the president, the office of president is overweighted, the faculty are left without responsibility, as are the students in their turn, and the alumni are often in ignorance of what the policy of the college is, while everybody is exhorted to be "loyal to the college" without any clear understanding of what loyalty to the college means, or even indeed just what "the college" means. He sometimes wonders if the Duke of York's gardener was anticipating present academic conditions in America, when he instructed his servants,

"Go, bind thou up yond dangling apricocks,
Which, like unruly children, make their sire
Stoop with oppression of their prodigal weight;
Give some supportance to the bending twigs.
Go thou, and like an executioner
Cut off the heads of too-fast growing sprays,
That look too lofty in our commonwealth;
All must be even in our government."

Yet after all 'tis a good world, my masters! The professor is not wholly downcast. If he does not know by name, without consulting the catalogue, a third of the members of the board of trustees that controls his academic destiny; if he does not know by sight a fourth of them, and if he has never exchanged comments on the weather with more than a fifth of them, he at least hopes that the sixth of the board who may chance, through the college catalogue, to know of his connection with the institution, may not feel unkindly toward him. He can only plead in extenuation of his rashness in suggesting a more democratic form of academic government, his strong conviction that only as *all* parts of the educational structure are strengthened, can the structure approach perfection, and serve the end for which it has been erected.

OUR DEBT TO PSYCHICAL RESEARCH

I

EARLY in the history of the Society for Psychical Research, Von Helmholtz speaking to Professor Barrett, of telepathy, said, "Neither the testimony of all the Fellows of the Royal Society, nor even the evidence of my own senses, could lead me to believe in the transmission of thought from one person to another independently of the recognized channels of sensation. It is clearly impossible." Many have followed the example of the psychologist Wundt, in holding that "no man of science, truly independent and without *parti pris*, could be interested in occult phenomena." Stranger still, as reported by William James, "An illustrious biologist told me one day that even if telepathy were proved to be true, the savants ought to band together to suppress and conceal it, because such facts would upset the uniformity of nature, and all sorts of other things without which the scientists cannot carry on their pursuits." Dogmatic skepticism, veiled or overt contempt, and an unreasoning aversion — such was the attitude of the scientific world in general toward the men who, in the early eighties of last century, first seriously grappled with the problems of the weird and the uncanny; while the great majority of educated laymen, almost equally under the spell of the preponderating materialism of the age, heartily endorsed the verdict of the scientists.

Things have not much changed in the years that have passed. It is true that there have been numerous accessions to the ranks of the "psychical researchers" from the scientific world itself. Many men of science — some among them even eminent men of science — have scandalized their fellows by adopting Newton's ridiculous point of view — "To myself I seem to have been as a child playing on the seashore, while the immense ocean of Truth lay unexplored before me" — and by deeming psychical research not unworthy their personal participation. Crookes, Lodge, James, Richet, Flammarion, Flournoy, Bergson, Lombroso, Morselli, are a few names that instantly flash into mind. And from some great thinkers of non-scientific training, but justly esteemed for their intellectual powers, has come an endorsement of Gladstone's appreciation: "Psychical research is the most important work which is being done in the world — by far the most important." But scientists and laymen, so far as concerns the great mass, are still over-eager to deride and belittle the delvers into the occult — who, so their critics say, have been laboring all these years to no purpose whatever, and whose labors, no matter how long continued, can have only futile or mischievous results.

This widespread conviction of the futility of psychical research is evinced in many ways. It is seen in the jesting or scornful comments of writers in the periodical press; it is continually cropping out in the half-contemptuous, half-pitying smile that greets any sympathetic reference to "ghosts" or "telepathy"; it manifests in petulant outbursts from "orthodox" scientists, akin to the outburst of Von Helmholtz, as when our genial friend, the excellent Professor Münsterberg, heatedly proclaims, "As to spirit communications, there are none, and there never will be any." Perhaps most striking of all is the almost complete indifference with which the published reports of the various psychical research organizations now in existence are regarded by instructors and students alike in many, if not all, institutions for higher education. In one great American university, to the writer's personal knowledge, the many volumes of the *Proceedings* and *Journal* of the English Society for Psychical Research, and of the younger American Society for Psychical Research, are seldom removed from the library shelves except to be dusted. Truth-seekers in this university, it would seem, have no time to waste on the "bosh," "rot," and "rubbish" which these silly publications contain.

Now, it may be true — though a number of really learned men believe otherwise — that those engaged in psychical research have not as yet demonstrated scientifically either telepathy or survival; and it may be true that they have set themselves a hopeless task in endeavoring to establish communication between this world and the next. But it decidedly is not true that their investigations have been entirely fruitless. On the contrary, it is safe to say that no other scientific movement ever set on foot has, in the same length of time, contributed so much toward the advancement of knowledge as has psychical research.

Few will dispute that psychology today is the most conspicuous and most promising of the "recognized" sciences. Its marvellous growth during the past quarter of a century is quite generally attributed to the increasing application of the laboratory methods devised by Wundt and his pupils. In reality a large part of the credit — perhaps the larger part — must be given to those "dabblers in the occult," who, like Sidgwick, Myers, and Gurney, in England, and Janet and Richet in France, thought it not beneath their dignity to study table-tipping, alleged telepathy, and the disputed phenomena of the hypnotic trance. To them, incontrovertibly, we owe the foundation-laying of abnormal psychology, with its manifold practical implications to the physician, the criminologist, and the educator; to them, as will hereinafter be shown, we chiefly owe the opening up of vistas of progress undreamed in the days before scientific psychical research began.

The men who enrolled under Sidgwick in 1882 to form the English Society for Psychical Research, were not the fanatical, credulous "ghost-hunters" they are commonly supposed to have been. Their first task, they saw clearly, was to determine whether the alleged facts adduced in support of the soul doctrine were really facts; and, if facts, whether they were not susceptible of adequate explanation on a wholly naturalistic basis. In the words of Frank Podmore, one of the earliest and most active members of the Society (*The Naturalization of the Supernatural*, p. 2):

The title which I have chosen for the present book, *The Naturalization of the Supernatural*, describes in popular language the object aimed at. The facts which the Society proposed to investigate stood, and some still stand, as aliens, outside the realm of organized knowledge. It proposed to examine their claim to be admitted within the pale. And it is important to recognize that whether we found ourselves able to accept the credentials of these postulants for recognition, or whether we felt ourselves compelled to reject them as undesirables, the aim which the Society set before itself would equally be fulfilled. In undertaking the inquiry we did not assume to express any opinion beforehand on the value of the evidence to be examined. Whatever the present bias of individual members toward belief or disbelief, it will not, I think, be charged against us, by any one who dispassionately studies the results . . . that any private prepossessions were allowed to pervert the methods of the inquiry. To ascertain the facts of the case, at whatever cost to established opinions and prejudices, has been the consistent aim of the Society and its workers.

In this spirit the Society for Psychical Research attacked the whole strange medley of occult phenomena, from hypnotism to premonitions and hauntings. To most readers of these pages it may seem almost incredible that so short a time ago hypnotism was still outside the pale of science, and was pretty generally regarded as imaginary or supernatural, according to one's temperament and training. But, prior to the founding of the Society for Psychical Research, only a few inquirers of established reputation — such as Esdaile, Braid, Liébeault, and Charcot — had deemed it a proper and desirable subject of investigation; the scientific brotherhood would have none of it, and frowned on its exponents as self-deluded simpletons or impudent charlatans. As late as 1875 a writer in the *Grand Dictionnaire Encyclopédique des Sciences Medi-*

cales, summing up in a few words all that was to be said about hypnotism, brushed it aside as non-existent. It was because they questioned dogmatic utterances like this, and because they hoped through hypnotism to gain fresh light on the problem of the soul, that the members of the English Society for Psychical Research listed the study of hypnotism among their principal activities.

The result was not merely the confirmation and correction of much that Esdaile and other earlier inquirers had noted, but also an impressive, and in some respects startling, extension of knowledge concerning the processes of the human mind. Bearing out these discoveries, moreover, came the findings of sundry French savants — Janet, Binet, Féré, etc. — who, about the same time as the English investigators, and in the same spirit of open-minded research, sought to ascertain the true inwardness of hypnotism. On the one hand, the work of the Englishmen and the Frenchmen, between the years 1882 and 1890, made it certain that in hypnotism psychology possessed a wonderful instrument for experimentation. And, on the other hand, their own experiments with hypnotism revealed the various mental faculties — perception, attention, memory, and the rest — in entirely new aspects; paved the way to a correct understanding of hitherto obscure and baffling maladies; nay, even made necessary a radical readjustment of the scientific concept of human personality itself.

In this productive study of the phenomena of hypnotism two names stand supreme — the names of Pierre Janet and Edmund Gurney. Janet, who still is with us, deservedly enjoys today a worldwide fame for the part he has played in the inception and development of psychopathology, or medical psychology. Gurney to most people is not even a name. Yet in the brief period of experimentation that preceded his untimely death, he achieved so much as to suggest that had he lived he would probably have won a place in contemporary science fully as high as that held by Janet. More than one medical psychologist, in all likelihood, has been inspired by Gurney's researches to specialize in that fascinating and important branch of the healing art — as was Morton Prince, on his own statement to the writer. It was not for medical purposes, however, that Gurney himself experimented with hypnotism: medical psychology was then in embryo, and Gurney was only secondarily interested in its possibilities. His great aim was to ascertain the nature of the hypnotic state, and the condition of the mind during hypnosis.

To review adequately the ingenious methods he adopted and the results he obtained, would delay us unduly. Enough to stress the salient fact that, through a brilliant series of experiments full of interest to modern psychology, he demonstrated the existence of a great undercurrent of mental life, in which the most complex processes are carried on without the individual's conscious knowledge. Already, to be sure, several students of personality — Hamilton and Carpenter, for instance — had recognized the necessity of postulating something of the sort as the only means of rationally explaining certain anomalies and mysteries of human behavior. But to take it for granted was one thing, to demonstrate it was obviously quite another. And it remained for Gurney's experiments — together with the concurrent experiments of Janet and his French colleagues — to effect the work of demonstration, and, still more, to trace the operations of this mental undercurrent in channels, and with consequences, formerly unsuspected.

Not until Gurney's and Janet's time, to be more explicit, had experimental proof been forthcoming of the far-reaching influence of "subconscious ideas" in affecting human conduct, and of the possibility of initiating trains of thought completely cut off, or "dissociated," from the field of conscious mentation. This was first convincingly revealed by experiments based on the discovery of the fact that commands "suggested" to a hypnotized person would be faithfully executed at a stated moment after the awakening from hypnosis, and this despite the absence, in the normal waking state, of any conscious recollection of the commands in question. That this actually involved mentation beneath the threshold of consciousness was shown by Gurney in a number of experiments made possible by the further discovery that there are some people who can write "automatically" — that is, without conscious control of the words they put on paper, and even without knowing that they are writing anything. Thus Gurney records, in the course of his detailed record of these experiments (*Proceedings of the Society for Psychical Research*, vol. iv, pp. 268–323):

On April 20 [P—ll] was told [while hypnotized] that half an hour after his next arrival he was to wind up a ball of string, and to let me know how the time was going. He arrived next evening at 8.30, and was set to the planchette [an instrument then often used to obtain automatic writing] at 8.43. He wrote, "13 minett has passed, and 17 more minetts to pass." Some more experiments followed, and it so happened that at 9, the exact time when the fulfillment was due, he was in the trance. He suddenly said "Oh!" as if recollecting something, but did not move; he was then woke, and at 9.2 he walked across the room to where some string was lying, and wound it up. . . .

Another day the same "subject" was told that when I coughed for the sixth time he was to look out of the window. He was woke, and I gave at intervals five coughs — one of which, however, was a failure, owing to its obvious artificiality. He was set to the planchette, and the words produced were, "When Mr. Gurney cough 6 times I am to look out." At this point I read his writing and stopped it. I asked if he had noticed my coughing, and he said, "No, sir"; but this, of course, showed no more than [that] he had heard without attending. He was now hypnotized, told that I wanted to know how often I had coughed, and at once woke. The writing recommenced, "4 times he has cough, and 2 times more he has to cough." I coughed twice more, and he went to the window, drew aside the blind, and looked out. Two minutes afterward I asked him what sort of a night it was. He said, "Fine when I came in." I said I thought I had seen him looking out just now, but he absolutely denied it.

Any doubt that the memory oblivion in the waking state

was genuine was removed by the interesting circumstance that though the "subjects" — men to whom even small sums of money meant much — were repeatedly offered substantial rewards if they could state what had been said to them during hypnosis, they were invariably unable to do so. Stranger still, Gurney demonstrated that it was entirely possible to develop, in the hypnotic state itself, different sets of memories, each completely independent of the others; so that, so far as concerned the contents of his consciousness, the hypnotized "subject" seemed to possess two or more personalities, each with its own distinct set of memory-images (*Proceedings of the Society for Psychical Research*, vol. iv, pp. 515–521). This may be made clearer by giving a sample of the many curious conversations between one of the "subjects" and G. A. Smith (known in the published reports as S.), a hypnotist often employed by Gurney to assist him in his experiments:

A young man named S—t . . . after being hypnotized was told in state A that the pier-head had been washed away, and in state B that an engine-boiler had burst at Brighton station and killed several people. He was then roused to state A, when he proved to recollect about the accident to the pier; after which a few passes brought him again to state B.

S. "But I suppose they'll soon be able to build a new one."

Had the pier been now present in S—t's mind, this remark would have been naturally understood to refer to it, as it had formed the subject of conversation a few seconds before. But he at once replied, "Oh, there are plenty on the line" — meaning plenty of engines.

S. "The pile-driving takes time, though."

S—t. "Pile-driving? Well, I don't know anything about engines myself."

A few upward passes were now made, and it at once became clear that the memory had shifted.

S. "If they have plenty more, it doesn't matter much."

S—t. "Oh, they can't put it on in a day; it was a splendid place."

S. "Why, I'm talking about the engine."

S—t. "Engine! What, on the pier? I never noticed one there."

Again, the same "subject" was told in state A that a balloon had been seen passing over the King's-road. Some passes were made which carried him into state B, when S. said, "But I didn't see it myself."

S—t. "What was that?"

He was now told that two large dogs had been having a fight in the Western-road; and a few upward passes roused him to state A.

S. "But it was a good long time in sight."

S—t. "The balloon?"

S. "No, the dog."

S—t. "Dog? Why, was there one on it? A dog on a balloon!"

The "subject" is brought down again to state B.

S. "But it didn't remain in sight long; it soon went up."

S—t. "What didn't? What went up?"

S. "Weren't we talking about balloons?"

S—t. "No; but one of them dogs looked like a busted balloon when he was down."

A few upward passes, and S. says, "Which one?"

S—t. "Why, there was only one."

S. "One what?"

S—t. "Balloon."

S. "I was talking about dogs."

S—t. "I don't know nothing of dogs."

Three days afterward S—t was again hypnotized, and S. said, "What was that you said about the pier?"

S—t. "Oh, about the head being washed away."

This, it will be seen, was the memory appropriate to state A. Some downward passes were made, and S. said, "A good thing that things don't often happen like that."

S—t. "No, they don't at Brighton; they do on the Northern lines."

Here we have the engine accident again — the memory appropriate to state B. The balloon over the King's-road was now strongly suggested to S; but that idea belonging to state A, it could not be recalled in state B.

In all these conversations, in short, it was exactly as if the hypnotist, S., when talking to his subject in state A, and talking to him in state B, were talking to two different persons, each ignorant of facts known to the other. (The profound significance of this, from a practical as well as a theoretical standpoint will be made evident later.) On the other hand, and in sharp contrast, Gurney, in common with the Continental investigators, also demonstrated through hypnotic experimentation that the memory process as a regular thing is almost incredibly retentive, so that under appropriate conditions it is possible to recall happenings, it may be of earliest childhood, which have long since dropped out of conscious recollection — happenings, even, of which one has never had conscious knowledge. But, indeed, credit for the experimental demonstration of this twofold principle of subconscious perception and subconscious memory — which lies at the very root of abnormal psychology — by no means belongs wholly to Gurney and the French hypnotists. Many other pioneers in the systematic study of the "phenomena outside science" had a hand in proving and elucidating it, notably those who made a special study of crystal-gazing.

The average scientist of that time — perhaps it would be true to say the same of the average scientist of today — had about as much interest in the phenomena of crystal-gazing as he had in the "ravings" of the entranced spiritistic "medium." He well knew that from time immemorial it had been a practice among the mystically minded to employ crystals, mirrors, or other objects with a reflecting surface, for purposes of divination; and that it had been insistently claimed that, by gazing steadily into such objects, hallucinatory pictures often became visible, imparting useful knowledge about people and events outside the crystal-gazer's ken. But the scientist dismissed this as merely another evidence of the invincible superstitiousness of mankind. It never occurred to him to try crystal-gazing on his own account; or if it did, he shudderingly repelled the idea. The founders of the Society for Psychical Research were not so squeamish; crystal-gazing was approved by them as a fitting subject for investigation; and ere long, their decision was abundantly vindicated.

One member of the society, Miss Goodrich-Freer, finding that she possessed the crystal-gazer's "gift," sedulously cultivated it for experimental purposes, and made as careful and detailed a record of what she observed as would any scientist employed in the vitally important task of watching and recording the wriggles of a tadpole. A fact which soon made itself evident to her was the frequency with which her crystal-visions represented incidents in her own past life, sometimes incidents dating back to early childhood. On one occasion, she notes, somebody was speaking in her presence, though not to her, of Palissy ware. She happened at the moment to be staring aimlessly at a dark green scent-bottle. At once there appeared in it a picture of a man furiously tearing up garden palings. She was wondering what this meant, when it was followed by a second picture showing, with the greatest distinctness, the library where as a child she had kept her books. Among these, Miss Goodrich-Freer now remembered, was one she had not seen for many years called *The Provocations of Madame Palissy*. Then she also remembered that one of this lady's provocations was a bad habit her husband had of using the first material that came to hand as fuel for his furnace; and immediately the meaning of the first picture became clear to her.

Similarly one of her earliest experiences in crystal-vision was a picture of "a quaint oak chair, an old hand, a worn black coat-sleeve resting on the back of the chair — slowly recognized as a recollection of a room in a country vicarage, which I had not entered, and had seldom recalled, since I was a child of ten." Again, looking in her crystal she saw a copy of a medical prescription for which, a few hours before, she had been vainly hunting. On further inspection she perceived, without being able to read the words, that it was in the handwriting, not of her physician, but of a friend. Acting on the hint she searched through her friend's letters, and found the medical prescription folded in one of them, where, she had reason to believe, it had been for more than four years. It could have been put there only accidentally, yet it was clear that she must have subconsciously perceived what she was doing when she slipped the prescription into the letter, and that the mechanism of memory had registered an image of her absent-minded act. Many other examples of the memory registration of subconscious percepts are given in Miss Goodrich-Freer's reports to the Society (*Proceedings of the Society for Psychical Research*, vol. v, pp. 486–521; vol. viii, pp. 484–495). For example:

I find in the crystal a bit of dark wall, covered with white jessamine, and I ask myself, "Where have I walked today?" I have no recollection of such a sight, not a common one in the London streets but tomorrow I will repeat my walk of this morning, with careful regard for creeper-covered walls. Tomorrow solves the mystery. I find the very spot, and the sight brings with it the further recollection that at the moment we passed this spot I was engaged in absorbing conversation with my companion, and my voluntary attention was pre-occupied.

To take another example. I had been occupied with accounts; I opened a drawer to take out my banking-book. My hand came in contact with the crystal, and I welcomed the suggestion of a change in occupation. However, figures were still uppermost, and the crystal had nothing more attractive to show me than the combination 7694. Dismissing this as probably the number of the cab I had driven in that day, or a chance grouping of the figures with which I had been occupied, I laid aside the crystal and took up my banking-book, which I certainly had not seen for some months, and found, to my surprise, that the number on the cover was 7694. Had I wished to recall the figures I should, without doubt, have failed and could not even have guessed at the number of digits or the value of the first figure. Certainly, one result of crystal-gazing is to teach one to abjure the verb "to forget," in all its moods and tenses. . . .

I saw in the crystal a young girl, an intimate friend, waving to me from her carriage. I observed that her hair, which had hung down her back when I last saw her, was now put up in young-lady fashion. Most certainly I had not consciously seen even the carriage, the look of which I knew very well. But next day I called on my friend; was reproached by her for not observing her as she passed; and perceived that she had altered her hair in the way which the crystal had shown.

Next as to sounds not attended to. . . . A relative of mine

was talking one day with a caller in the room next to that in which I was reading, and beyond wishing that they were *further* I paid no attention to anything they said, and certainly could have declared positively that I did not hear a word. Next day I saw in a polished mahogany table, "1, [Earl's] -square, Notting Hill." I had no idea whose this address might be. But some days later my relative remarked, "H. (the caller aforesaid) has left Kensington. She told me her address the other day, but I did not write it down." It occurred to me to ask, "Was it 1, [Earl's] -square?" and this turned out to be the case.

From investigators in other departments of psychical research came — and still comes — evidence no less impressively testifying to the marvellous power of the human memory, with its subconscious awareness even for sights and sounds not consciously perceived. It was further discovered that memory-images not infrequently emerge above the threshold of consciousness in the form of spontaneously externalized visual and auditory hallucinations, sometimes of a striking sort. The discovery was also made that, in persons of a peculiar temperament, subconscious memories might be so completely switched off, or "dissociated," from the field of consciousness that on coming into it again they would be unrecognized, and would give rise to the conviction that they related to matters which could not possibly have been within the range of previous knowledge, conscious or subconscious. Perhaps the best illustration of this curious and important psychological fact is found in a case reported quite recently by Mr. Lowes Dickinson.

Among his friends was a young lady who developed a form of "trance mediumship," in which she claimed to visit another world and meet and talk with people there, particularly a certain Blanche Poynings, described as an earth-dweller in the time of Richard II. This "spirit," speaking through the voice of the entranced "medium," gave as proof of her identity many interesting particulars regarding her sojourn on earth. She had been, it seemed, an intimate friend of Maud, Countess of Salisbury, and much of her talk had to do with that lady, and with the Earl of Salisbury. Odd little incidents in the latter's life were vivaciously recounted — such as his throwing an image out of his chapel into a ditch, where it was found by a wayfarer, who repainted it and set it up in a bake-house. "Blanche" also commented in an amusing way on the appearance of Joan, "The Fair Maid of Kent," and other historical personages; told about her own exile from Court; and gave much information respecting the customs and manners of the period.

All this interested and puzzled Mr. Dickinson, because his friend, whose veracity he could not doubt, assured him that she had never made a study of the events of King Richard's reign, and had not so much as read anything about it. Yet, as he ascertained by patient research among old chronicles, the alleged "spirit" unquestionably possessed accurate and extensive knowledge of the men and women who had been prominent at King Richard's Court, and of happenings which in some instances were barely mentioned by the annalists. The only logical explanation seemed to be that this was a genuine case of "spirit communication." But one day, taking tea with his friend and her aunt, Mr. Dickinson made a discovery that placed the affair in an entirely different light.

The subject of automatic writing chanced to come up, and it developed that the "medium" owned a planchette, and often experimented with it. At her investigator's request it was brought out, she placed her hands on it, and questions were put to it concerning the Blanche Poynings statements. These questions elicited the unexpected announcement, by the automatic writing, that corroboration of every statement made by "Blanche" would be found in a book called *Countess Maud*, written by Emily Holt. So soon as planchette wrote the name of this book, the "medium" exclaimed that she believed there was a novel with that title, and that she had once read it. Her aunt confirmed this, but neither she nor her aunt could recall anything about its plot or characters, nor even the period with which it dealt. Following the clue thus strangely given Mr. Dickinson soon had *Countess Maud* in his hands, and found mentioned in it, with corresponding detail, almost every person and every incident given by the "spirit" of Blanche, who, in the novel, was of quite secondary importance. Even then his mediumistic friend could not recall anything about the book, except a vague impression that she had read it as a child.

He now caused her to be hypnotized, and questioned her anew, when he learned to his surprise that she had never actually read *Countess Maud* herself, but had heard her aunt read it aloud. "I looked at it, and painted a picture in the beginning. I used to turn over the pages. I didn't read it, because it was dull. Blanche Poynings was in the book; not much about her." And, in response to a question as to how the Blanche Poynings impersonation really originated, she made the reply, of great interest psychologically, "There was a real person named Blanche Poynings that I met, and I think her name started the memory, and I got the two mixed up."

These, then, were some of the first-fruits of systematic psychical research: Proof that percepts may be subconsciously, as well as consciously acquired, and that, as Pierre Janet so tersely put it, "Whatever has gone into the mind may come out of the mind"; proof that the emergence of subconscious memories may be in the form of self-induced hallucinations; proof that such memories sometimes develop a dynamic force, impelling the individual to seemingly inexplicable conduct; proof that the personality itself may be artificially dislocated, so that whole areas of memory sink temporarily below the threshold of consciousness; proof that, even below the threshold, intelligent mentation continues in a fashion similar to the mentation consciously directed by the waking will; and, finally, proof that in hypnotism, crystal-gazing, and automatic writing, invaluable means are available for exploring the remotest nooks and corners of "the subconscious." From one point of view their establishment of such facts as these was, indeed, disconcerting to the "psychical researchers," for it obviously made increasingly difficult the demonstration of the survival of the soul on evidence afforded by phenomena like apparitions, hauntings, and mediumistic utterances. But it also marked an enormous advance in man's knowledge of himself, and in his control of his development here on earth.

The first to appreciate this — at any rate, the first to turn it to practical account — were the Frenchmen who, like Gurney, had attacked with special vigor the problems raised by hypnotism. Sharing to the full the belief of their English colleagues that here was a subject which science ought to have investigated long before — many of them, in fact, expressing their sympathy with the general purposes of the Society for Psychical Research by becoming members of it — the French savants' motive in invading the realm of the occult had in most cases been intellectual curiosity rather than any ardent desire to prove life after death. They were not so much concerned with the possible bearing of hypnotic phenomena on the soul problem, as with their possible bearing on man's earthly welfare. And no sooner was it borne in on them that hypnotism did have practical uses, than the majority concentrated their efforts on ascertaining what these uses were, and to what extent, and with what consequences, the phenomena of the hypnotic state were paralleled in everyday life.

The leader in this movement — which, with Gurney's experiments in England, may be said to constitute the beginning of abnormal psychology — was Pierre Janet, who, in 1881, at the early age of twenty-two, had been appointed professor of philosophy in the college of Chateauroux, and soon afterward received a similar appointment in the College of Havre. At Havre, Janet took up in earnest the investigation of things psychical, studying mediumistic phenomena, and making a series of experiments in hypnotic telepathy that brought him into mutually helpful relations with Gurney, Myers, and other active workers in the Society for Psychical Research. But from the first he was specially interested in the peculiarities of the mind in hypnosis, and his interest in this particular problem became all-absorbing when he observed that even the most bizarre hypnotic phenomena were sometimes spontaneously produced. Perhaps most influential in determining the future course of his life-activities was his discovery that hypnotization was not always necessary to effect the strange dissociation of personality evinced in, for instance, the case of Gurney's "subject," S—t, cited above.

Janet himself, experimenting with Madame B., the peasant wife of a charcoal-burner, had been astonished to find that when hypnotized she developed a personality markedly different from that of her normal waking life. The waking Madame B. was a timid, dull, ignorant woman; the hypnotized Madame B. (who called herself Léontine) was bright, vivacious, even inclined to be mischievous. Between the two personalities, again, there was an absolute cleavage of memory; each knew nothing of the other's thoughts and actions. And after a time, to Janet's profound astonishment, the Léontine personality began to manifest spontaneously. In an article contributed to the *Revue Philosophique*, for March, 1888, he records (translation by Frederic Myers):

She had left Havre more than two months when I received from her a very curious letter. She was unwell, she said, worse on some days than on others, and she signed her true name, Madame B. But over the page began another letter in a very different style, and which I may quote as a curiosity, "My dear good sir, I must tell you that B. really, really makes me suffer very much; she cannot sleep, she spits blood, she hurts me; I am going to demolish her, she bores me, I am ill also, this is from your devoted Léontine." When Madame B. returned to Havre I naturally questioned her about this singular missive. She remembered the *first* letter very distinctly . . . but had not the slightest recollection of the second. . . . I at first thought that there must have been an attack of spontaneous somnambulism between the moment when she finished the first letter and the moment when she closed the envelope. . . . But afterward these unconscious, spontaneous letters became common, and I was better able to study their mode of production. I was fortunately able to watch Madame B. on one occasion while she went through this curious performance. She was seated at a table, and held in her left hand the piece of knitting at which she had been working. Her face was calm, her eyes looked into space with a certain fixity, but she was not cataleptic, for she was humming a rustic air; her right hand wrote quickly, and, as it were, surreptitiously. I removed the paper without her noticing me, and then spoke to her; she turned round, wide awake, but surprised to see me, for in her state of abstraction she had not noticed my approach. Of the letter which she was writing she knew nothing whatever.

To Janet this strange occurrence, when viewed in conjunction with phenomena manifested by two or three other of his "subjects," was chiefly significant as hinting at the possibility that the same mechanism which produced the various phenomena of the hypnotic state — from hallucinations, loss of memory, and automatic execution of "suggestions" given during hypnosis, to the production of blisters, paralyses, and other physical effects of hypnotic suggestion — might be operant in, and responsible for, the protean manifestations of that baffling disease hysteria, with which Madame B. and the other subjects were known to be afflicted. On this theory, hysteria — which until then had been generally assumed to have a physical basis — would be essentially a mental malady; and its fundamental characteristic would be some degree of dissociation of personality.

Already, as Janet was aware, Charcot had demonstrated the inadequacy and downright error of the prevalent medical notions concerning hysteria, and had also rendered a splendid service to humanity by compelling recognition of the fact that sufferers from hysteria often develop symptoms — paralyses, growths, etc. — all too easily mistaken for the symptoms of some really organic disease perhaps incurable, or curable only by the aid of the surgeon's knife. But while he had thus revealed the wholly functional character of hysteria, and had saved countless sufferers from useless and unnecessary operations, Charcot had thrown little or no light on its causation and mechanism, and this was the problem which Janet now undertook to solve, removing from Havre to Paris, and associating himself with Charcot in the latter's clinic at the Salpêtrière Hospital.

Observing, experimenting, recording — with a truly catholic mind profiting from the observations and experiments of other workers, including his fellow-members in the Society for Psychical Research — he gradually achieved his epoch-marking demonstration of the rôle played by "dissociated memories" in the causation, not alone of hysteria, but of all functional nervous and mental troubles. He showed that severe emotional shocks — frights, griefs, worries — might be, and frequently were, completely effaced from conscious recollection, while continuing to be vividly remembered in the depths of the subconscious; he showed that thence they might, and frequently did, exercise a baneful effect on the whole organism giving rise to disease-symptoms, the particular types of which were determined by the victim's "self-suggestions" (just as Mr. Dickinson's "medium" suggested to herself the Blanche Poynings impersonation); and he showed how important it was, as a preliminary to effecting a permanent cure, to get at these dissociated memories and drag them back to the full light of conscious recollection.

To get at them he made use, as medical psychologists all over the civilized world are today making use, of hypnotism, of automatic writing, even of the "mystical" crystal-gazing, the use of which for medical purposes was directly suggested to him by the experiments of Miss Goodrich-Freer. Janet himself, it should perhaps be added, would be the last to disavow the assistance he received in one way or another from the "psychical researchers" of England; indeed, he has not forgotten that everything he has accomplished is the outgrowth of his early studies in the "occult" phenomena of hypnotism. It is to be regretted that many of his present-day fellow-workers in the domain of scientific psychotherapy are not equally appreciative of the fact that every "cure" they put to their credit — every hysteric, neurasthenic, or psychasthenic patient whom they send on his or her way rejoicing in a restoration to health — is a living witness to the beneficial results that have flowed from the patient labors of the courageous pioneers, who, at the risk of their scientific reputations, so boldly adventured into the psychical thirty years ago.

We shall have more to say in a later article on what society owes to psychical research.

THE WAR

BY A HISTORIAN

WHEN for slight reason a continent shakes with the tread of marching battalions, it is easy to fall into moral despair. We seem to confront a world-order that limits the sway of reason between nations, and gives full scope only to the hatreds and destructive ingenuities of mankind. In the wholesale deliberate slaughter of multitudes of men of good will, workers, lovers, husbands, fathers suddenly dedicated to systematic homicide of their fellows, piling up in blood and travail grievous burdens for their own children's children — in such a spectacle the thoughtful mind at first finds only nightmare. And nightmare intolerable it is, if to the end of time a few out of pride or fear or sheer incapacity shall thus be able to decree the last sacrifice and swift death to the many.

In such moments of natural dejection, the mind must rally to its own defence. We live after all in a moral world. Intelligence has persisted and grown through worse occultations. The future may hold out hopes of a world-order in which the nightmare of the present cannot repeat itself. Meanwhile if we face the thing steadily in the light of its underlying causes, considering the moral issues involved, looking forward to the just retributions that the world will surely require of those who have shattered its peace, we may reëstablish in ourselves the sense of an overruling moral order, toward which we may each in his degree work. Such an inquiry into the responsibility for the war will lift the obsession of universal, insensate violence. Even the offenders are obeying race loyalty, and responding to certain obsolete ideals which yet are deeply grounded in history, while the defenders are vindicating the cause of the world's peace by the only course left open to them. Against the brute law of strongest bat-

talions, they have been forced to fight, that ideals of forbearance, comity, and honor may still be held among
nations.

On the broader moral issue of the war, mankind has
already spoken. The military isolation of Austria and
Germany is no more marked than their moral isolation.
In the history of warfare, has there ever been so uniform
a verdict of the human race? Though instinctive and
rapid, the sentiment may also be rationally grounded.
Let us test it by an examination of the causes of the war.

What made the war possible is the fixed antipathy
between impatient, ruling Germans and restless, subject
Slavs. Such racial discord is naturally most acute in
Austria, where a domineering Teuton minority holds in
uneasy subordination the Slavs of Bohemia, Austrian
Poland, and the Balkan and Adriatic range; but it is a
distinct factor also in Prussia, where an embittered and
losing campaign against Polish national feeling in the
Posen region has long been waged. These disharmonies
are an inevitable incident of expansion without the consent of the annexed peoples. The part of wise statesmanship is to bear much of this sort of opposition, trusting to
healing process of just government and time. In Austria
and Germany, however, these antipathies, were deliberately fomented by the war clique. The surest way of
getting huge army appropriations is to show a foe or a
rebel in being. In 1908 the unrest of all the Balkan Slavs
was increased by Austria's assuming permanent tenure of
Bosnia and Herzegovina, where by treaty she had been
exercising a temporary, police jurisdiction. The annexation
extinguished national hopes, and while it undoubtedly established order, did so in arbitrary and oppressive fashion.
The fact that Germany supported the annexation, intimi-
dating the natural ally of the Balkan Slavs, Russia, ac-
centuated the racial feud. The recent heroic struggle in
the Balkans, which resulted in the aggrandizement of the
Slavic powers of Servia, Bulgaria, and Montenegro, nat-

urally excited the Slavs under Austrian domination. Austria, on the other hand, had maintained a persistent hostility to her southern neighbors, and after the war, had by diplomatic means, and again aided by Germany, frustrated many of the legitimate hopes of Servia and Montenegro. An illogical and already derelict Albania, is the chief result of Austria's dog in the manger policy. Her smouldering resentment against Servia was raised to an intense pitch by the deplorable assassination of the Crown Prince and his wife. It was an act as foolish as heinous, but it was also a natural product of arrogant and oppressive rule. Though the deed was done on Austrian soil, the assassins were Slavs, and the plot traceable to Belgrade, and this gave Austria the chance to hold Servia nationally responsible for the crime. She issued an ultimatum in which Servia was virtually required to avow responsibility for the outrage, to investigate and punish anti-Austrian agitators, and in such proceedings to admit Austrian officials. In effect, Servia was asked to plead guilty, on penalty of invasion, and to place her case in the hands of Austria as both prosecutor and judge.

The ultimatum of July 23, was outrageous, such as no state ever dreams of issuing to an equal. Weakened by two wars and apparently menaced by overwhelming force, Servia drank the cup, hesitating only at the last dregs. With the bulk of the Austrian demands she complied, demurring only to the waiver of her own national estate implied in alien interference with her police. Even this humiliating stipulation she offered to arbitrate. The reply of Austria was to set 300,000 troops across the Danube, and to shell the undefended city of Belgrade. The history of war has shown few more baseless aggressions. Austria had reckoned on Servia's weakness, and on the willingness and ability of Germany, as in 1908, to hold off Russia. Austria unwittingly reckoned with forces to which Russia and Germany are small. The analogy of the Bosnian annexation was false. There the deed had been carefully prepared and delay had blunted the effect of the final move. This time Austria suddenly and without preparation outraged the moral sense of the world. The official plea is that in some mysterious way the Austro-Hungarian Empire was threatened in its very existence by the machinations of the Serbs at home and in the newly annexed Austrian provinces. That plea is hollow. Austria was neither more nor less in peril than she has been for sixty years; she was merely enduring a slight, however sensational, exaggeration of the chronic difficulties of dominion over alien and unwilling races. The reality is that Austria was incensed by the prosperity of the new Slavic nations in possessions that she had prospectively marked out as her own. To confuse ulterior ambitions with immediate rights is characteristic of the mentality of neo-Imperialism.

So far, for convenience, I have spoken of Austria and other powers as units, and with the usual rhetorical personification. The practice is misleading. When we say Austria, in the political sense, we mean a mere handful of high administrative and military officers, a few diplomats and journalists, a portion of a small and exclusive aristocracy, a pack of manufacturers of arms and military contractors, a rabble of speculators hoping out of troubled waters to fish extraordinary profits — that is political Austria, that with slight differences is the permanent war party in every nation. The peace of the world ultimately hangs on the nod of a few hundred individuals — men at best of intense, narrow, and backward-looking vision; at worst basely interested in the destruction of their fellow beings, accustomed to regard carnage as normal business. The problem of insuring the world's peace is that of putting such men out of control, and replacing them by men who think the thoughts and feel the feelings of modern civilization. Incapacity to grasp the modern man, is the defect of the war caste everywhere. It indulges mediæval alarms, appeals to factitious loyalties, speaks an obsolete tongue. Politically Austria is still very much where Met-

ternich left her. A crafty balancing off of the aspirations
of new nationalities has been the method of consolidating
the artificial sway of the Emperor. There has been a constant disregard, perhaps ignorance, of the generous motives
that move in modern society. The aged and afflicted Emperor has many times shown himself to have an insight
superior to that of his counsellors. Had the present emergency not caught him infirm in body and spirit, I believe
the event would have been very different. Free from his
controlling hand, the war machine has worked almost
automatically its fitting product.

When we say Austria and Germany, we must distinguish
clearly between the peasants of many tongues, the thrifty
tradesmen, the ingenious manufacturers and hardy artisans, the scientists and scholars, the keen students of public betterment, the artists and musicians, — between these
socially useful people with their women and children, upon
whom falls the actual burden of this war, — and a little,
complacent, opinionated minority, miseducated, aloof from
the generous instincts of humanity, dead to the kindling
enthusiasms of the new century, — a little complacent,
pitiful, minority which from any outcome of the worst war
reaps its private harvest of profit, promotion, and prestige.
Any genuine representation of the real Austria and Germany would have made this war impossible, any adjustment looking to permanent peace must include the
elimination of the misrepresentative administrators who
have frivolously plunged a continent into war.

In a moral analysis of the causes of the war, the single
ambiguous term is Russia. On the face of it she promptly
rallied to the support of her fellow Slavs in Servia, by
diplomatic protests at Berlin and Vienna and by mobiliz-
ing on the Austrian border. Humanitarian and political
motives combined to force some kind of intervention.
Without denying the bond of race, Russia could not permit any Slavic nation to be ruthlessly overborne. Honor
in the highest sense and policy combined to dictate some

such course as Russia actually took. The official statements of Austria and Germany waver between two at-
titudes. On the whole, the Austrian apologists condemn
the Russian move as merely defective and unhappy in
form. Had Russia not mobilized, the Servian situation
might have been adjusted diplomatically. As things went,
the provocative moves of Russia, forced similar precautions first on Austria, then on Germany, with the unforeseen result of a general war. The speech of the German
Chancellor, however, echoes that of the Kaiser, in charging Russia with deliberately provoking Germany and
Austria into war.

To me the issue, though evidently a crucial one, — for if
Russia is deliberately making a war, most of the European
world is being dragged into devil's work, — is set in such
technical fashion by the German manifestoes, that their
own sincerity is open to doubt. It remains a somewhat
interesting academic question what a Russian protest
without mobilization might have effected. The obduracy
of Germany in the face of more formidable military preparations by France and England, seems to indicate that
a wholly pacific intervention by Russia would have effected little. On an alternative theory, Germany and
Austria are fighting solely on a point of technical honor.
They couldn't " take a dare " from a threatening neighbor.
Doubtless some of the arbiters of war in Germany and
Austria did honestly so feel. But in so feeling they were
parrotting the phrases and indulging the alarms of forty
years ago.

The figment of a ruthlessly expansive Russia has today
little reality behind it, but for militaristic ends it is still a
most useful bugbear. Twice in a generation Russia has
tasted the bitter fruits of heedless aggression. Today she
is overtaxed, not merely by the arrears of these wars, but
also by the great task of assimilating her present subjects.
Her political situation at home is one of instability. Direct gain from venturing to support Servia, Russia had

none to hope for. Twice she has stood aside while her sphere of influence in the Balkans was being repartitioned. In short, there is no conceivable reason why Russia should have invited war at this time, and every reason why she should have desired peace. Her mobilization must be interpreted in that light. Ostensibly it was done *pari passu* with similar preparations in Austria and Germany, but suppose she began first. Mobilization means just what those who order it mean. It is not *per se* an offence, much less a cause of war. Russia made most solemn protestations that she would fight only in the last resort. All the world except the Germans and Austrians believed these assurances.

What weakens the Austrian case is the unduly spectacular demonstration she made on the Danube. Ostensibly she was engaged in a punitive expedition which might have been satisfied with the occupation of the offending capital, and an indemnity. It is probable that Russia and the world, rather than hazard a general war, would have tolerated a reprisal, which however inherently excessive, did not transcend the usual bounds of such enterprises. But Austria hurled half her effective force into Servian territory. Surely she had given ground for the inference that no argument unaccompanied by show of force would deter her. In our day we shall probably not know what Austria actually intended towards Servia, but it is plain enough that, granting the whole thing was a merely punitive move, it was exaggerated with the insolent thickheadedness characteristic of military bureaucracies. At best it can only be said that Austria needlessly blundered into a demonstration that must be alarming to Europe and most offensive to Russia, without correctly calculating either the moral reaction of Europe or the limits of Russia's forbearance. It must be conceded, however, that the Austrian militarists had been grievously exasperated by the murder of their Prince, and the impulse to seek somewhere some sort of vengeance was, however mistaken, entirely natural.

So much cannot be said for the conduct of Germany. Her grievance was remote and indirect, her public sentiment relatively calm and tractable. A word from her would have checked Austria at any time. Accordingly upon Germany falls the heaviest responsibility for the war. From her power and detachment she was doubly in a position to play the peacemaker. There are those who think that the Kaiser and his counsellors foresaw the whole outcome and deliberately hastened it. I am unwilling to think such baseness of any human being, and find the evidence for such a suspicion as yet lacking; the whole transaction seems to show a blundering from step to step, making each decision not on principles of common sense, but under some esoteric code of military honor, honor soon being forgotten in the pursuit of military success. Germany's official attitude, as voiced by her Chancellor, is that she was forced to mobilize under menace at her Russian and French borders. This is the best construction that can be put on her case. Whether one accepts this plea or not, will depend on his view of the motives that prompted the Russian and French mobilization. Would France and Russia have waited quietly during long negotiations, or were they awaiting the favorable moment for an invasion? did they want peace or war? Considering the little advantage and the certain sacrifice that each nation finds in this war, the answer can hardly be in doubt. There is not the slightest indication that either had any intention of invading Germany, or anything to gain by it. But the militaristic mind is trained to see in every movement of foreign troops a direct threat, and it is credible enough that the Kaiser's counsellors were intellectually incapable of grasping the idea of a mobilization in the interest of peace. For years they have propounded the axiom that to negotiate without show of force, is fruitless waste of time, and now they add the paradoxical corollary, "But Germany will not treat with any nation that makes a show of force." Obviously Germany could have mobilized while continuing to treat. There were evidences that Austria, had her face been saved, would have reconsidered her rash move. From the British "White Paper" it is plain that, had Germany effected any slight modification of the Austrian demands, England would have stood out of the war. The fact that three weeks after the declaration of war Russia was hardly ready for an advance shows that Germany was not immediately menaced by the Russian mobilization. The German ultimatum which cut short both the direct negotiations between Vienna and St. Petersburg and Lord Grey's promising plan of mediation was a crime against civilization — and stupid military policy as well.

The German attitude may again and most simply be construed as blindly loyal support of an ally right or wrong. It is a purely technical duty that Italy very sensibly repudiated. In the sense that Germany had unquestionably countenanced the ultimatum to Servia, she would seem committed. But such committals are subject, after all, to humanity and common sense, and to the conduct of the ally to whom support has been engaged. No nation is bound to risk its very existence for a rash ally. Yet on the theory of *pundonor*, that is where Germany finds herself today. The stern unreasoning maxims of a military caste must have counted for much in Germany's obduracy. No motive of interest, immediate or remote, would at all justify or account for the assumption of a hazard involving the continuance and integrity of the Empire itself.

It is certain that Germany underestimated the hazard. A dynastic war with Russia she was willing to accept and almost courted. The contingent hostility of France she apparently did not fear. For securing the neutrality of England she had a most plausible programme. The explicit warnings from London she believed to be bluff. She probably counted on a servile Belgium. How badly she had misconceived her world, the event promptly proved. England and France were as ready to make the last sacrifice for ideals of international moderation and good faith as Germany for mediæval punctilio; industrial Belgium was capable of heroic resistance.

All the official statements of Germany abound in technicalities which to common sense are negligible. The precise amount and chronology of French and Russian provocation at the border, the amount of infraction of Belgian neutrality implied in the secret presence of French officers — all these matters are weighed with the solemnity and exactness of the seven degrees of the lie. The very language is that of the tiltyard or fencing floor. Such a move implies another; to the thrusts of Russia and France, Germany always parries in the forms. This was throughout the temper of the Wilhelmstrasse and of the German ambassadors at the danger points, Vienna and St. Petersburg. Had the Germans wanted the war, they could not have acted a whit otherwise. It is entirely possible that the secret memoirs of the future, will show that the whole clumsy transaction was merely the Kaiser's parody of the astute machinations of Bismarck in 1870.

The position of France was in all main regards a defensive one, although she was bound as well by treaty to support Russia. Against unavowed German military movements, France openly reinforced her frontier, meanwhile seeking a diplomatic solution. Germany once more took the ground that she would not negotiate with a foe in process of mobilization, and precipitated the rupture by an ultimatum. In a larger sense France is defending her own civilization and her own influence among nations against the pretension of Teutonic preponderancy in Europe.

England's participation in the war was required, first, by her naval agreement with France; next, by her determination to maintain the neutrality of the small nations Luxembourg and Belgium. For several years the English in the North Sea and Channel and the French in the

Mediterranean, have mutually engaged to defend each other's interests in those respective waters. This meant that imminent war found the French fleet in southern waters, and her northern and western coast open to Germany's attack. Sir Edward Grey in his first statement before Parliament promised that England would live up to her bargain, and if necessary undertake the naval defense of the French coast. This was the frank acknowledgment of a minimum obligation, to break which, Mr. Asquith later justly remarked, would have utterly discredited a private individual. England's next move was determined by the appeal for aid of neutralized Belgium. England demanded a statement of Germany's intentions as regards Belgium and the other neutralized powers, and when the note was answered by the hastening of the invasion of Belgium, declared war.

Sound national policy as well as honor forced the decision. England could not take the risk of Germany at Antwerp. And German assurances to respect the sovereignty of Belgium had been proved worthless in advance by Germany's violating the neutrality she was pledged to maintain. It is significant that the bullying sophisms with which Germany had confronted her Continental neighbors were not even hinted at in the case of England. There was no longer any disinclination to confer with a power in a state of martial preparation. There were numerous suggestions by which England might defend France passively, there was even a hint that the violated neutralities would be respected, for a consideration. In any case the evident preparedness of the British fleet was not regarded as disqualifying England as a negotiatory power, though as a matter of fact the bounds of Germany were never more effectively attacked than when sealed orders were issued to Admiral Jellicoe. Germany could, when she wished, deal with a potential foe in arms, — deal patiently and at length. The point of honor raised against France and Russia should be interpreted in the light of the repeated offers to buy off England.

England had the good fortune to take the clearest and most disinterested stand of all the embroiled powers. She was bound by a special obligation, which she could not dishonor, but which, had the Germans engaged not to attack France or her colonies by sea, might have left England a neutral. She was driven to arms by the ruthless molestation of neutral Belgium. It was the cause of civilization. In no particular have international law and world peace been more developed than in the neutralization of states. To attack this is to attack in perhaps its most vital spot the progress of the world. It is at best the act of a barbarian and an outlaw, and when committed upon a people who have offended in nothing but in asserting the right that the aggressor himself has guaranteed, it is the act of a savage. That there is a penalty for violating a neutralized state, the presence of England in this war is most exemplary evidence. She has truly taken up arms in the cause of peace.

Reviewing the motives of the combatants, Austria and Germany are fighting for the prerogatives and ideals of a politico-military hierarchy; Russia is fighting for a little nation of kindred blood and identical faith which had been outrageously attacked; France is fighting in self defense and for her treaty obligations; England is explicitly fighting for the principle of neutralization. In a larger sense the various motives of the powers embattled against Austria and Germany merge in the need of a gigantic police enterprise. We have on a tremendous scale the attempt to chastise two criminally aggressive powers, which Mr. Norman Angell proposed, on a smaller and less ruinous scale, as a means towards securing peace. The spirit that animates the European coalition against the two central Empires is that a small nation should not be brutally entreated by a stronger by reason of its greater strength, nor a neutralized nation be molested by violation of its soil and slaying of its citizens. If we hold clearly in mind this police aspect of the war, we are in a position to weigh some of the possibilities.

The success of Austria and Germany would mean the extinction of what little international law and morality has been painfully built up through the centuries, the impact of the mailed fist throughout Europe, the rigid rule of a pedantic and tyrannical bureaucracy, the diminution of the variety and vitality of western civilization, the clamping upon the world for an indefinite future the most unendurable bonds of militarism. Fortunately there is small reason to dread so dire a disaster for humanity. The stars fight in their courses against those who would undo the work of time.

The success of the *Triple Entente*, may, as it is directed, take us far towards permanent peace, or once more establish a military tension that in its turn must produce new wars. What is all important is that the police character of this war should not be lost sight of. It is always easy for the most generous causes to sink to a level of immediate small interests — the Crusaders forgetting the Holy Sepulchre while Constantinople is being looted. Such temptations will beset the *Triple Entente* in the event of a triumph. Meanwhile, it may be the part of France and England to restrain the bitterness of Russia, who is engaged in a war essentially racial. It is necessary that the lesson administered to Germany and Austria be complete and convincing. Their best wishers can only desire for them a prompt and sharp chastisement. The peace of the world requires either the reduction of Germany to military impotence or a change in the arrogant temper of her ruling class.

Since the war has been occasioned by the stubborn folly of a military and diplomatic caste, the minimum of reform, is that that caste should be deposed in Austria and Germany. France set an example over forty years ago. Such deposition to be effective would apparently involve such constitutional changes that it is difficult to see how either the Hapsburg or Hohenzollern dynasty could logically survive the revolution. In the light of history neither would be missed.

Historically, the notion of a central European Empire has meant nothing but harm. Through the Middle Ages the cheap parodists of the Cæsars trafficked when they might, and fought when they must, claiming territory at large, setting race against race, and pontiff against king, raiding and looting rich neighboring lands rather than waging war, fomenting religious persecution, opposing by trickery and force the development of the new races and nationalities. Such was for centuries the record of the Holy Roman Empire. For Europe its legend has ever been baleful. Everybody knows that the House of Hapsburg inherits by direct descent this tradition, and Austria with its loose hold over many races is today a simulacrum of the Mediæval Empire, owing her new lease of life, after the Imperial idea had discredited itself, to the suppression of Hungary with the aid of Imperial Russia. In the Emperor Franz Josef we have an individual superior to his origins, but he inevitably inherited the diplomatic and military caste of advisors and administrators who have brought Austria to the present pass. The mentality of this hierarchy was fixed after the Napoleonic wars, at the moment when reaction was exaggerated, and has not changed with changing times.

At least the Austrian Empire and its ruling caste had the warrant of tradition. In Germany the tradition was recently made to order by the genius of Bismarck. The mediæval caste which Austria inherited, Germany deliberately created for herself. The Empire rose out of no instinctive need of the race, from no demand of the numerous small states and free cities, but as the clever utilization of a brilliant military triumph. What war gave, war could take away. The Empire that was proclaimed at Versailles might be terminated at Potsdam. The offence of

the Empire is not its title and form but in the changing for
the worse of the German character. Governments are
worth just what they produce in national character. The
German temper is naturally genial, thrifty, deliberate,
patient, scholarly and musical. Official Germany has
developed an intolerable arrogance that threatens the
whole world. The Kaiser has mediævalized Germany's
ruling caste, and is the symbol of that process.

Personally I do not believe that the *Triple Entente* will
be called upon to dispose of the Hapsburg and Hohenzollern dynasties, any more than in 1871, Germany was
burdened with the disposition of Napoleon III. Like
causes produce like effects, and when Austria and Germany shall have awakened from red dreams of conquest,
to the gray reality of defeat, they may be trusted to call
to account these responsible for their humiliation.

With an Imperial Austria and Germany, the *Triple
Entente* could only deal most sternly, always along those
modern lines of penology which do not avenge the offence,
but see to it that the offender be not allowed to repeat it.
On the theory that the present administration of Germany
and Austria is to be perpetuated, nothing less than the
crippling of those powers could guarantee even a few years
of peace. With a reorganized Germany and Austria, the
allies could and should deal far more generously than
Germany did with the bantling French Republic. Belgium, for violated neutrality should obviously be made
Germany's preferred creditor.

Into more speculative matters I will only briefly inquire. There will naturally be some readjustment of the
central European map to make political and racial lines
more nearly coincident. Many of the historic states which
have been whipped or cajoled into the two Empires may
reëmerge. A number of small neutralized states in central
Europe is among the possibilities. How much of such a
process the loosely articulated Austrian Empire can stand
is problematical. Some kind of a coherent Germany

should emerge from the disaster, and all that is most certainly and valuably German will be preserved. German victory would overwhelm it under militarism. The intellectual primacy of Germany has never depended on the legend of the Empire. It was acknowledged before the Empire was dreamed of, and would survive if the Empire were only an unblest memory. The real Germany has today only friends in the world. To many of us she is an intellectual foster mother and very dear. We hope to see her relieved of disguising mediæval frippery, and once more her radiant and edifying self. In the Kaiser's proclamation he protests against world wide jealousy and hatred of Germany. Without mincing words, it may be admitted that the world is justly hostile to him and what he represents. He identifies himself and what he represents with Germany. When she shall have set that misunderstanding straight, she will find in the world only friends and sympathizers.

Looking to the future, and especially to the cause of peace, the war suggests certain reflections. If the war results only in a consciously suppressed Germany and Austria kept in order by the armies of the *Triple Entente*, nothing much will have been done. If the ruffian temper of German officialdom persists, Europe will merely have lavished once more her treasure, tears and blood in the old inconclusive way. The hope lies in a solution so just that the defeated nations may accept it, so wise that it may safely include a general reduction of armaments. The cause of peace is already the gainer by a sensational demonstration of the fallacy of the stock sophism that the only guarantee of peace is competitive arming. The way in which the little spark struck on the Danube overran Europe proves that competitive arming is not merely the ready occasion of war, but of war on the most costly and disastrous terms.

But pacificists should not press their momentary advantage beyond the bounds of common sense. There is already a fanatical tendency to denounce war as such, instead of seeking out and denouncing those who have made war without just cause. Of course war abstractly is just as much and just as little moral or immoral as a cyclone. It would be quite as logical to meet and pass resolutions against the earthquake that filled peaceful Messina with human carrion, as to denounce wholesale this or any war. The case of Belgium suggests that it is not the moment for any sensible person to waste his time in working for complete disarmament. Had she trusted solely to the treaties that protected her, how complete would have been her humiliation! Belgium also shows most instructively that the maintenance of an effective military *morale* does not imply militarism. None of the Belgian officers who held the cordon of Liege had been taught that his honor as a soldier might at any moment require him to sabre an unarmed civilian. Yet the Belgian officers gave a sufficiently good account of themselves against those who had been trained in the bullying tradition. With Belgium still in view, and recalling what would have been her fate had she trusted solely in the treaties that protected her, no sensible person could now advise any nation to disarm below the reasonable requirements of defense. It is possible however that these limits may be greatly reduced by right thinking among nations. Already the individual is measurably free to criticise his own country when engaged in a war that he deems unjust. How great a liberty that is few of us realize. The next step is freedom for large bodies of individuals to refuse to serve their country in a war waged without popular consent and palpably unjust. A people thus minded would be the greatest check on that interested bureaucracy that any military establishment, however, moderate, involves. How far we still are from that, the rallying of the socialists to all the colors shows plainly.

Perhaps the most fertile notion arising from the situation is that of an international police function to be exer-

cised by the most enlightened nations. Something of
this there was, though motives were badly mixed, in the
Spanish-American war; the notion has plainly governed
President Wilson's Mexican policy. Indeed this police
right has at all times been pretty freely claimed by strong
powers against weak. It is a tremendous moral gain to
see the principle asserted against strong powers who are
imperilling the good order of the world, — and this irrespective of the outcome of the war.

A most valuable demonstration has been made of the
validity of the principle of neutralization. Since small
neutralized states are not for the future to be abandoned
to any strong aggressor, they may safely be multiplied.
Here may be a solution of the problem of racially varied
central Europe. Everything depends upon England and
France holding their representative function loyally to the
end, and avoiding the national egotism that war in the
past has usually aroused. If they are faithful to the
charge they have explicitly undertaken, a new era may
open for humanity.

The part of pacificists is to avoid phrases, and deal with
facts. In the long run there can be no peace so long as
individuals put their lives at the disposal of any kind of
leader who waves the flag in any kind of cause. So long
as nations are unreasoning mobs the moment the trumpet
sounds, it will be idle to depose military castes; others
will promptly form, and in their turn prevail. Accordingly the educational campaign of the pacificists must
continue, — continue, however, with the frank admission
that the sword has often in the past been drawn for ulterior
righteousness and peace, and that if the time ever comes
when from mere horror of war men decline to draw the
sword in a clearly righteous cause, so exanimate a world
will enjoy precisely the peace it deserves. We must be-
ware of considering peace and war as respectively *bonum*
and *malum in se*. In the present case, to have yielded to
Germany would, in the lowering of the moral tone of

Europe, have been more disastrous than the unhappy war that has resulted from a single outrageous move: for submission would have meant that the world was content to continue in the twentieth century the ethics of Metternich and Bismarck, while the fact of the war means that the twentieth century world is prepared, at whatever cost, to repudiate the neo-mediævalism that paradoxically imposed itself upon the international politics of the nineteenth century — prepared to work out a better ethics and politics, looking to a more peaceful future. Meanwhile the present task of civilization is to avert an imminent Prussian Peril, and to humble the new Tamerlane who has thrust a continent into war. Should he win, no nation is safe.

THE WAR

BY AN ECONOMIST

IT is early to hold inquest upon European civilization. But to attempt to forecast the findings of the
historian-crowners of the next period of peace, is neither
presumptuous nor premature. Experience has taught
us much of the evolution of the written record of a
war. After our Civil War we had two distinct historical
traditions, Northern and Southern. Nearest the event,
personalities, deified and damned, loomed portentously.
"If Lincoln's character had been different — if Jeff Davis
had been more forceful" — why, perhaps there might have
been no war, or its issue might have been other than it
was. In a later stage, Civil War history, though still
sectional, accepted the obligation to set forth and make
plausible the motives animating either side. Finally,
sectionalism is fading from Civil War history, at least in so
far as the work of the trained writer is concerned. Whether
we are Northerners or Southerners, we see in the great war
the natural outcome of the irreconcilable conflict between
two economic and social systems, each seeking expansion
to the detriment of the other. A particular personality
may have worked to bring some of the contending forces
to a focus; a particular political movement may have
hastened, another may have retarded, the final appeal to
arms. Given, however, the underlying social economic
situation, given, too the existing limitations upon the
political intelligence, North and South, and the appeal
to arms was inevitable. Neither party, to be sure, can be
absolved from the charge of wrong-doing, or even of crime.
But it is not now so important to strike a balance of guilt
as it is to determine the conditions that made wrong seem
right in the eyes of otherwise moral men.

When the present war is over there will be a flood of

nationalistic histories. The literary representatives of each party will endeavor to roll the whole blame upon the enemy. Vast significance will be attached to personalities; emperors and kings, statesmen, prelates, journalists, will stand forth in light supernal or infernal, according to the point of view. Were the Servian authorities in league with the assassins of the Archduke? Did the German emperor dictate the terms of the Austrian ultimatum? Was the Czar preparing war while pretending peace? Was Sir Edward Grey watching for an opportunity to crush the German fleet? In a later stage impersonal political forces will assert their claim to the foreground of history: the expansive tendencies of Russia; the fatal pride of armed Germany; the pretensions of England to the empire of the seas. Ancient antagonisms of race and nationality, of culture and religion, will aid in explaining what would otherwise remain inexplicable.

No one will dispute the fact that certain individuals in positions of power worked actively to bring on the present crisis, nor that acts were committed that deserve the execration of mankind. It will not be denied that ancient political and cultural antagonisms essentially conditioned the present war; but for such antagonisms the peace would have remained unbroken. Still, these forces are, in a sense, static, and hence not adequate to explain change. The Russian is not more aggressive, the German is not more arrogant, nor the Englishman more intent upon naval dominance, than they were twenty years ago. Pride of race and intolerance of religion have been with us always, and there is no evidence of their recent intensification. What chiefly needs explanation is that for a generation the consciousness of Europe has been filling up with fighting concepts. The fact has been noted by all serious students of European international relations. It is forcibly demonstrated by the enthusiasm with which the several nations, each with a reason of its own, has entered the present conflict. Desperate efforts have been making, for years, to prepare for the struggle that was regarded as inevitable.

Accordingly we can impute to the acts of particular persons little more than the choice of time and occasion for the outbreak of hostilities. The time may have been inauspicious; the occasion may have been one that will not look well in history. For the underlying forces working cumulatively toward an issue, we must, however, look elsewhere than to personal volition.

The greed of the armament industries and the incessant playing upon popular opinion by their subsidized organs have often been assigned to a chief rôle in the drama of international discord. Competitive military preparations, drawing to themselves an increasing share of the intellectual energies of a nation, have long been regarded as a menace to the peace of the world. Every organ seeks to exercise a function. The Crown Prince of Germany, in his panegyric of militarism, expresses poignant regret that all the splendid military forces of the Empire should be expended futilely, in peaceful show. Professional warriors want war, and will work to bring it about.

The future historian will doubtless give weight to the above mentioned forces, as well as to many others that can not here be touched upon. But he will assign vastly more importance than we of today, to the national antipathies engendered by the scramble for colonial possessions, and to the motives giving rise to it. It may be worth our while, even now, to fix our attention upon this aspect of the question. Not only for the light that may be thrown upon the fundamental causes of the present conflict, but also for the grounds we may discern for conjectures as to the international relations of the future.

II

Every one at all familiar with recent German literature will recall frequent references to the *Drang nach Morgenland*. The "impulse toward the Land of the Morning" —

fit inspiration for a sentimental nation. It has been pointed out, again and again, that the open road to German expansion lies in the direction of Anatolia, Syria and Mesopotamia. Indeed, the expansion has been actually taking place, by a process of infiltration, as it were. Recall the Bagdad Railway, the German incursions into Ottoman finance, the German reorganization of the Turkish army. All that lay between the Germans and their dream of the Morgenland was a group of petty states, easily to be subjugated or overleaped, and the decaying Turkish political organization.

But there was an irreconcilable Russian dream of Constantinople and the Eastern Mediterranean, and a British dream of a sub-tropic zone, all the way to India, taking laws, if from any power, from Britain.

For years, as every one knows, these dreams have played at cards with the Balkans. Not to go beyond the present century, did we not see Russian influence steadily advancing there, until rudely checked by Austrian annexation of Bosnia and Herzegovina? Again, the insidious development of Russian influence, culminating in the humiliation of Bulgaria in the Second Balkan War, but checked by the creation of an independent Albania under a German prince. Russian influence encroaching once more, stimulated by the Albanian fiasco and the intensification of Pan-Serbism, to be checked — for no doubt so it was intended — by the utter humiliation of Servia. Probably it was not believed that Russia would trump the Austrian ace. But who could suppose that, in such a game, the trumps would not, sooner or later, be drawn out?

It would be interesting to know why the ace was led just now, and why it was trumped at this precise moment. What is of more importance, however, is to know why the game was set. What did Germany want with the Land of the Morning? What does the Eastern Mediterranean mean to Russia? And what would it signify to England if either dream were realized? Is it matter of sentiment, of "historic mission," or is it matter of practical interest? And if matter of practical interest, whose interest weighs so heavily that it must be bought with cities in ruins and provinces devastated, with hundreds of thousands of the best and most useful lives sent down to dusty death?

Manifestly, not the interest of the mass of humanity.

III

The Morgenland, be it understood, is only one of the rotten stones in the arch of civilization. Mexico is another. India, China, Africa are of similar character. But the Morgenland may serve as type for our study, and we may profitably confine our analysis to the German yearnings for the Morgenland, not because they are in any way unique, but because they are typical.

There are political scientists who tell us that Germany is forced by her teeming population to seek this outlet to the East. This would imply that the impulse toward expansion is similar to that which carried the Anglo-Saxons to England and the Lombards to Italy. Let us consider whether this is really the case.

It is admitted, of course, that never before was the population within the present borders of the German Empire so great as it is today. Mere physical density of population is, however, a fact of no direct political significance. The important question is, whether the population is too dense to be comfortably maintained. Now, there is undoubtedly much privation in Germany, but it appears to be almost the unanimous verdict of economists and statisticians that the standard of welfare in Germany is constantly rising. Of this fact we have indirect evidence in our own immigration statistics. In the early eighties Germany sent us 200,000 immigrants a year; now she sends less than 40,000. Why have the numbers dwindled? Not because our free land is gone: for the Germans never were distinctively pioneers. In so far as they turned to agriculture, they settled in the older communities, and by superior thrift and industry, took the land away from the native born. This was never easier to do than today. Such of the Germans as remained in our cities occupied themselves with small business, the mechanical trades and the professions. The demand for such services is greater today than ever. The costs and hardships of oversea migration are less now than formerly. If the Germans stay at home, it must be because Germany, in spite of its great population, offers better opportunities for life and work than formerly.

It is not the land area of a nation that determines the magnitude of the population that can be supported in comfort. Rather, it is the organized intelligence of the people; and this, as every one knows, has been steadily advancing in Germany. There are, of course, ultimate limits beyond which organized intelligence can not provide for an increasing population under the handicap of restricted natural resources. Was it perhaps a recognition of this fact that led the statesmen to seek new territories for the Germans of the future?

The birth rate in Germany is declining, as in every other modern state. Conservative statisticians have estimated that, unless the tendency to decline is checked, the German population will come to a standstill within a generation. Germany has now no excess of population wherewith to plant colonies, and will probably never have such excess. Accordingly, it can have been no part of the *Morgenland* dream that the mongrel population of Turks and Armenians, Syrians and Arabs, was to be supplanted by German *Biedermänner*. It can not have been imagined that Antioch and Bagdad were to become German cities, the seats of German universities; that Gothic spires were to rise among the ruins of Palmyra, and over the redeemed wastes of Bassorah. The life of the *Morgenland* will pursue its dark and furtive ways, whether under German rule or the rule of any other Power of the light or of the darkness.

IV

It will be said that the standard of wellbeing of the German Empire has advanced *pari passu* with her foreign trade, and that trade needs a secure market. Hence the requirement of a rich colonial domain, from which the German trader can not be excluded by hostile customs laws. Perhaps we have here an adequate justification for Germany's Morning Land aspirations. Germany is an industrial nation; so also are England and the United States and France, and Russia will soon become one. Now, is it not inevitable that the trade of the industrial nations shall be directed toward the non-industrial? That is, towards the tropics and the subtropical belts? The argument is trite, but it looks reasonable enough to deserve consideration.

Germany is indeed an industrial nation, and so are we. But the German industries are not the same as ours, nor can they ever be the same, so long as the German genius and natural environment continue to differ from ours. So long as difference exists, some German goods will command our markets, whether we pursue protectionist policies or not. Germany need not write our laws for us in order to control our markets; she has an indefeasible title to those markets so long as she maintains superiority in supplying our needs. And the same thing is true of the markets of England and France and Russia. They take German goods eagerly, in vast quantities. Wipe out Germany's trade with industrial states, and her commerce is practically at an end.

The trade between nations of rich and varied industries is alone capable of indefinite expansion. Yet the delusion persists that a nation's closed trade with a subject state is somehow of superior importance. Such trade is admittedly incapable of great development. Only semi-barbarous peoples will submit to foreign control of their trade; and such peoples produce little beyond the requirements of home consumption, and therefore, having hardly anything to sell, can buy but little. But colonial trade, meagre as it is, may be monopolized and made to yield large profits. The trade between industrial nations, since it is essentially competitive, diffuses its benefits throughout the trading nations. Hence these benefits are easily overlooked. The rapid enrichment of a few houses engaged in the colonial trade gives visible evidence of national gain.

Out of the overestimation of the value of the colonial trade arises, unquestionably, some part of the international jealousies now working out their nature upon the field of battle. Control of the trade of the Levant would advance the general welfare of the German people in very limited measure; but it would greatly enrich a small number of traders, and this very fact of the concentration of the gains gives them added potency in determining political relations.

V

The colonial trader was once the chief cause of wars, and he still contributes his quota to international misunderstanding and hostility. But there is another interest that has grown to far greater importance in the colonial domain. This we may describe as the concessionary interest. Vast fortunes have been accumulated, in the semi-barbarous belt, by the exploitation of natural resources and works of public utility. The Land of the Morning would be exceptionally rich in concessions to the nationals of any imperial state. There are oil fields and mines to open, railways and irrigation works to construct. Some of these opportunities are already in German possession; their security, however, depends upon continued exercise, by Germany, of influence upon the Ottoman government. That government is notoriously shifty, and the interests involved will never be wholly safe until the Levant is a German colony.

The concessionary interest, like the colonial trading interest, offers chances of sudden wealth. The former, however, is far more vulnerable than the latter. The fixed investment of the concessionary is far greater than that of the trader. Hence, while the colonial trading interest thrives best with the support of the home government, to the concessionary interest such support is indispensable. Politics is a necessary part of the concessionary business.

How far is the concessionary interest identical with the national interest? Let us consider what difference it makes to you and me whether the Pearson interests, or the Waters-Pierce interests, control the oil fields of Mexico. If the Pearson interests, several great fortunes will be constituted in England; if the Waters-Pierce, similar fortunes will be constituted here. In either case the money will lie at an infinite distance from you and me. Still, we are patriots, and would rather have it here than in England.

Patriotism aside, the great fortune here will pay income tax to our own treasury. Its spending will afford many golden crumbs to fellow citizens of ours. The exploitation of the oil fields will require much machinery, for which, under Waters-Pierce control, the first bid would be offered to our own industry. Many young men of our nationality would find employment as engineers, foremen, superintendents. Undoubtedly, it is better for the national interest to have the concession in national hands.

But what is the magnitude of the concessionary interest, and how many votes should it have on questions of peace and war? Of the whole capital of Great Britain, not one-fifth consists in foreign investments; and of that fifth scarcely a quarter can be concessionary. One-tenth of Germany's capital is invested abroad; probably not a fifth of that is concessionary. Of our own capital one part in a hundred is in foreign investments, of which one-half is in Mexico. Not nearly all of that half is concessionary. It did not prove to be enough to go to war over.

VI

From the foregoing review it might appear to be the natural conclusion that the economic element in the present war is practically negligible. By far the greater proportion of the trade relations of the world — and the relations most significant to the general welfare — obtain between the very nations that are now endeavoring to destroy one another. The opportunities for concessionary capital that could be secured by any nation, if completely victorious, can hardly be equivalent to the losses of the far more important industrial capital at home. It is certain that if all capital had been conscious of its interest, and the question of peace or war had been left to capital, each hundred dollars having one vote, there would have been no war. There is a war: costly demonstration to the Socialists that capital does not, as alleged, enjoy control of modern political society.

Before we accept this view, however, let us look somewhat more closely upon the structure of capital as a social economic force. We shall find that it is not homogeneous, but embraces two elements differing widely in character. The one, which we may denominate capital proper, is characterized by cautious calculation, by a preference for sure if small gains, to dazzling winnings. The other, which we may call speculative enterprise, is characterized by a readiness to take risks, a thirst for brilliant gains. The relative political power of the two elements, as we shall see, is not proportioned to their respective pecuniary volumes. Accordingly, altho it may easily enough be demonstrated that the majority interest of European capital has been seriously prejudiced by the present war, it does not follow that a large share of the responsibility for the war may not be fixed upon capital. The minority interest may have determined a majority vote.

Capital proper thrives best in a settled order of society,

where the risks of loss are at a minimum. It accepts favors from government, to be sure, but politics is no part of its game; peace, and freedom from disturbing innovations, are its great desiderata. Speculative enterprise, on the other hand, thrives best in the midst of disorder. Its favorite field of operations is the fringe of change, economic or political. It delights in the realm where laws ought to be, but have not yet made their appearance. To control the course of legal evolution, to retard it or divert it, are its favorite devices for prolonging the period of rich gains. Politics, thus, is an essential part of the game of speculative enterprise.

At the outset of the modern era, speculative enterprise quite overshadowed capital proper. Colonial trade, government contracts, domestic monopolies were the chief sources of middle class fortunes. But with the progress of industry, slow, plodding capital has been able steadily to encroach upon the field of enterprise, or to create new fields of its own. In our own society the promoter of railway, and public utilities, the exploiter of public lands, the trust organizer, are as prominent, relatively, as in any modern nation. Quantitatively their interests are, however, greatly inferior to those of the trader, manufacturer, banker, the small investor and the farmer, to whom a ten per cent return is a golden dream, and twenty per cent a temptation sent by the Evil One.

But quantitatively inferior as the speculative capitalist really is, his hold upon the popular imagination is vastly more powerful than that of his slow-going colleague. Say that an employer of this type prefers to spend money on machine guns to repress strikes rather than in better wages: instantly it is declared by all the radicals of the earth that such is the general spirit of capitalism. No radical is able to keep clearly in mind that the overwhelming majority of employers are doing their best to keep their working forces contented, and are succeeding fairly well. The radicals, however, are not the only persons whose minds are overcrowded with the doings of the speculative capitalist. You and I read eagerly the lives of Jay Gould, Oakes Ames, Harriman and Morgan, feeling that somehow we are thereby brought nearer to the spirit of modern life. We find it impossible to sustain an interest in the account of the life of James Metzger, grocer, who set out in life worth ten thousand, and by faithful attendance upon his customers, without ever once taking a risk, ended life with an estate of one hundred thousand. James Metzger is a type of the thousands making up the ranks of capital proper. His story is told in statistics, which you and I won't read.

We may love or we may hate the speculative capitalist, but at all events we admire him. We admire him when he works for the public interest, and we admire him when his efforts are subversive of the public good. We admired Harriman when he built the Salt Lake cut-off, and we admired him when he cut the Alton melon. Now, is it to be supposed that the speculative capitalist does not turn this popular admiration to use as a political force, since politics is a part of his game? Inconceivable! As compared with his brother of the small profits and quick return, he enjoys a plural vote in our political scheme.

VII

In a new country of vast natural resources, especially if it is not too well governed, there is sufficient scope for both speculative enterprise and capital proper. The United States has been such a country, at least down to a very recent date. There was easy money enough for all men of shrewdness and resolution possessed of the necessary initial stake — public forests to be leveled, railways to be built or wrecked, trusts to be organized, cities to be provided with public utilities. But all this easy money now appears to be in danger of being locked up. We have a conservation movement in full swing, and a civic reform tendency that is no longer a mere cloak for the insatiable appetite of plunderers out of power. The popular attitude toward monopolistic combinations is growing ominously serious; if old and strong combinations do not dissolve in fear before it, yet those who would organize new combinations are deeply discouraged. We have an Interstate Commerce Commission with the will and the power to choke all railways when some are believed to have stealings in their gorge. Already we are beginning to hear murmurs about town, that in view of the popular hostility to wealth, it will be necessary for American capital to look to foreign investments. Not foreign investments in England and France and Germany, where government is efficient and capital proper prevails. But foreign investments in the undeveloped countries, in a Land of the Morning, "east of Suez."

In England the domestic field for capitalistic speculation has long been restricted. For generations the British citizen has been taught to look to Asia, Africa, America, for the opportunities for sudden wealth. Germany, more recently launched upon an industrial career, might have offered many rich opportunities at home. But Germany has been well governed. The early nationalization of railways closed one lucrative field; the cities, with their excellent business governments, have taken control of their own utilities, or have driven hard bargains with private enterprise. Industrial combinations have been as numerous as with us; but they have assumed the form of the Kartell — a legally binding agreement between independent producers, fixing prices and volume of production. Such a form of organization, like our former "pools," distributes the profits of combination fairly equitably among all the producers, and therefore has offered little opportunity for such promoter's gains as we are familiar with in American trust finance. Some opening there was, of course, for speculative enterprise. The launching of new industrial companies, dealings in real estate, the military and naval industries, laid the basis for many astounding mushroom fortunes. But the progress of governmental effectiveness has been steadily encroaching upon these fields. The German internal situation, then, has been such as to recommend the *Ausland* to those who wish to risk large stakes on the chance of brilliant returns.

The progress of modern industrial society, with its parallel development in the art of government, tends to the extrusion of speculative capital, and its concentration in the tropical and subtropical belts. In the older societies the process has been in operation for a considerable time; with us it is just beginning. But in a generation, we may be sure, much of our own speculative capital, like that of the older countries, will be engaged in colonial exploitation.

VIII

Capital, it is often said, is cosmopolitan; capital knows no such thing as patriotism. This may be true of the cautious, colorless capital of ordinary finance and industry. It is not true of the capital upon which speculative enterprise is based. It was an intense patriotism that was avowed by Jay Gould and Harriman; intense is the patriotism of J. J. Hill, of the DuPonts and the Guggenheims. Even Mellen is, or was, patriotic in his feelings toward New England. But most intense of all is the patriotism of the capitalist whose interests lie in the twilight zone of the barbaric belt. Purer expressions of devotion to America, of deep concern for her future, than those issuing from the lips of American concessionaries in Mexico, you never hear. We were all moved by the grandiose African dream of Cecil Rhodes. "All red" — i. e. British — a British heart within every black skin, from the Cape to Cairo. The case is typical of the capitalist speculator abroad. He is a patriot through thick and thin, not a white-blooded "cit" like you and me, who before volunteering support for our country's acts would presume to pass judgment upon them. He is a patriot who would knock a chip off the shoulder of the meanest upstart of a barbarian dictator — without regard to the cost of doing it: not a calculator, like you and me.

By interest, the concessionary capitalist is a patriot. He needs his country in his business. But this is by no means the whole explanation of his patriotism. His type is reckless, and therefore generous and idealistic. He must love and admire great things, and what thing is greater than the imperial dominion of his country? One must have a mean opinion of human nature to suspect the purity of the motives of Cecil Rhodes. Doubtless Rhodes began with selfish motives, but his private interests were soon submerged in his imperial ambitions. We may not be justified in assuming that selfish interest operates, to the utter exclusion of all patriotic motives. It does not necessarily follow that because Mr. William Randolph Hearst, for example, has mines in Mexico, his motives are determined by them. His Mexican interests would be advanced if the American boundary were extended to include all on this side of Panama. Is this, however, the whole tale of his aggressive Americanism? Patriotism has always burned more brightly in border provinces than in the heart of the national territory. It is natural, then, that patriotism should be still more intense in those extensions of the national domain represented by permanent interests abroad.

In an ideal scheme of things, love of one's own country would not involve hatred and contempt for other countries. But patriotism compounded with financial interest does usually produce detestation for the corresponding alien compound. We who meet the Germans in America, in England, in Germany, engaged in the common labor of advancing man's control over nature, respect them, and if we see much of them, love them. Our capitalist speculators in South America and in the Orient, meeting their similars of German nationality, hate them heartily. Those speculators are the nerve ends of modern industrial nationalism, and they are specialized to the work of conveying sensations of hate. For the present we have few nerves of the kind, and all they have succeeded in conveying to us is a vague feeling of uneasiness over the German advance in the colonial field. Far more powerful must have been the reaction upon nations like England and France that are serious competitors in the same field. And German capitalist speculators, thwarted in their designs by the English and the French, have contributed to the popular feeling that Germany must fight for what she gets.

The capitalistic speculator, even when operating at home where his action may be directed against us, enjoys a power over the popular imagination, and a political influence quite incommensurate with the extent of his interests. When the seat of his operations is a foreign territory, whence flow back reports of his great achievements — achievements that cost us nothing, and that bring home fortunes to be taxed and spent among us — his social and political influence attains even more exaggerated proportions. And this is the more significant in view of the fact that his relations with government — now even a more important part of his business — are concentrated upon that most sensitive of governmental organs, the foreign office.

When diplomatic questions concerning the non-industrial belt arise, and most modern diplomatic questions concern this belt, the voice of the concessionaries is heard in the councils of state. This voice is the more convincing because of the patriotism that colors its expression of interest. What is perhaps more important, the ordinary conduct of exploitative business in an undeveloped state keeps the concessionary in constant relation with the consular and diplomatic officers established there. In a sense, such officers are the concessionary's agents, yet their communications to the home office are the material out of which diplomatic situations are created.

It is accordingly idle to suppose that exploitative capital in foreign investments weighs in foreign policy only as an equal capital at home. When we consider the personality of the director of colonial enterprise, the conditions in which he meets competitors of foreign nations, and his relations with the foreign service of his home government, we can readily understand how a very small investment may prove a great menace to the peace of nations. For years the popular consciousness, in the several nations, has been steadily absorbing conceptions of rivalry of interest that have no meaning except to the category of concessionary capital. Germany, Russia, England and France have been brought to the belief that something very vital turns upon the control of the Land of the Morning. Indeed the whole civilized world has been seduced into accepting the view that something very vital turns upon the control of the tropics. Yes, something very vital for exploitative capital. Indirectly vital for the rest of society: for from such delusions spring wars that sow the unwilling fields with the shattered limbs of the best of our youth.

IX

It is the interest of exploitative capital that makes the Morning Land, Mexico, China and Africa rotten stones in the arch of civilization. But for exploitative capital, those regions might remain backward, socially and politically: this would not greatly concern any industrial nation, except in so far as it responded to a missionary impulse. The backward states afford, however, possibilities of sudden wealth; and since this is the case, they must attract exploiters, who must seek, and obtain, the backing of their home governments, with resultant international rivalry, hostility, war.

If we could confidently predict the industrialization of the backward countries, we should be able to foresee an end of this one most fruitful of all sources of international

strife. But China will not be industrialized for a generation, at least; and many generations must elapse before
the tropics are concession proof. Accordingly the one hope
for universal peace would appear to lie in the possibility
of divorcing, in the popular consciousness, the concessionary interest from the national interest.

For the present war will settle nothing. When it is
over, the skeleton titles thrown about the undeveloped
lands may have undergone change; but underneath the
new order, the struggle of exploitative capital will emerge
as before. Diplomatic squabbles will again arise; popular
envy will be wrought upon; international hostility will be
fomented; military and naval rivalry will again crush out
progress. The minor interest will once more drag the
major interest to ruin.

There will, however, be in the situation one element
new, at any rate, to us. In a generation we shall not be, as
now, a nation with almost all its capital secure within its
own boundaries. Our strong men of speculative finance
will be established in the undeveloped countries; concessions will figure conspicuously among the items of our
national wealth. The foreign contingent of our capital
will join battle with that of the group of nations destined
to fare best in the present struggle: if Germany and Austria, in South America; if Russia and Japan, in the Orient.
And who shall say that our country may not be a protagonist in the next great war? One half of one per cent of our
capital just failed of forcing us to subjugate Mexico.

The concession and the closed trade are the fault lines
in the crust of civilization. Solve the problems of the concession and the closed trade, the earth hunger will have
lost its strongest stimulus, and peace, when restored, may
abide throughout the world.

THE WAR

BY A MAN IN THE STREET

THAT a kindly old man having his nature temporarily reversed by a passion for revenge for the murder of two relatives, should have the power to waste a large portion of the lives and treasure of the civilized world, is so counter to everything that civilized men ordinarily consider reasonable, that it is perhaps the sharpest evidence yet given of the tyranny of the past over the present.

Perhaps the strangest thing about such a circumstance is that, while it is counter to the deliberate reason of nearly all sane and civilized men, millions of sane and civilized men are contributing to its occurrence, not only with devoted self-sacrifice, but with enthusiasm.

The conflict between these two utterly opposing conditions is, in the last analysis, simply the conflict between the jungle and the railroad, between the lion and the savage, between the savage and the civilized man.

And the same conflict is in each man's soul. Behind the man of today, who reasons, is his savage ancestor who merely felt; behind the gentleman in evening dress who goes to the boxing match is his ancestor who turned his thumb down over the arena; behind the jurist who arbitrates at The Hague, is his ancestor who commanded a pirate ship in the neighboring sea; behind the German who, less than a generation ago, was leading civilization, is the barbarian who attacked Rome, and who now has come out to attack Belgium.

Now absolute power is old fashioned, alliances are old fashioned, even violence and revenge are old fashioned, and among civilized nations they are "not done," except through the madness or the imbecility of crowds. Nobody really wants to do either of them, except the rulers and soldiers who see a chance of gain.

Of the hosts of men sacrificing, fighting, suffering, dyin℮.
not one in twenty wants to do it, or even knows why he
is doing it, or what is to be gained by doing it, and not
one in fifty thousand was consulted about doing it. Mr.
Lowes Dickinson after expressing himself in the *London
Nation* somewhat to the foregoing effect, adds:

We are sane people. But our acts are mad. Why? Because
we are all in the hands of some score of individuals called Governments. . . . These men have willed this thing for us over
our heads. No nation has had the choice of saying no. The
Russian peasants march because the Czar and the priest tell
them to. That of course. But equally the German socialists
march; equally the French socialists. These men know what
war means. . . . They hate it. But they march. Business
men, knowing too, hating too, watch them march. Workingmen watch them march, and wait for starvation. All are powerless. The die has been cast for them. The crowned gamblers
cast it, and the cast was death.

But "some score of individuals" is too many. The *New
York Nation* puts that better:

Whatever happens, Europe — humanity — will not settle
back again into a position enabling three Emperors — one of
them senile, another subject to melancholia, and the third often
showing signs of disturbed mental balance — to give, on their
individual choice or whim, the signal for destruction and mas-
sacre.

The German tradition of 1870, so strongly in favor of
getting in the first blow, made it impossible for a spreading
of the war to be seriously threatened without Germany
striking that blow, and so turning any possibility of a
general war into the reality.

In fights between individuals, the wrong has usually
been laid to the one who struck first. There is equal
reason for so laying it between nations.

When to the tradition in favor of the first blow is added
the military habit diffused through the nation to a degree
absolutely strange to modern times; when over a nation

thus accustomed to arms, there is a ruling class whose only ambition and only hope is in War, and when at the head of this class is a ruler with a megalomaniac ambition and conceit, the wonder is not that such a nation has gone to war with virtually all its neighbors, but that it has so long been at peace with them.

This war is probably the world's greatest illustration that a condition of "preparation for defence" is apt to lead to war. Forty years of such preparation has developed in the peaceful scholarly German nation an oligarchy of swashbucklers who crowd women off the sidewalk and cherish an ambition to conquer the world.

More specific causes of the low condition of Germany are not far to seek. If a hundred portraits of each of the rulers of, say, the ten leading nations were culled at random from the leading illustrated publications, a due proportion being kept of the various functions in which the rulers were engaged when the pictures were taken, there is no reasonable doubt that the absolute rulers would be represented the greatest number of times in military dress — like savages in war paint, and that William of Germany's proportion would be larger than that of any other ruler. The presidents of republican France and the United States would not appear in war paint at all, and the king of democratic England would so appear less often than the head of any other dynasty.

Of all alleged civilized rulers, William II has alone borne the barbarous title of "The War Lord," yet before last August he never saw a battle. He was "The War Lord" simply because it was his delight to pose as such, and what a man poses, he wishes to become. Since 1870, and to some extent before, the Kaiser's country has been, to a degree approached by no other in Europe, an armed camp. In Germany, gentleman and army-officer have been almost synonymous terms: no amount of learning, genius or eminence in any other direction has brought a man as high social consideration as eminence in the army. The army has been the dominant interest of the Emperor, and, despite the enormous industries, the dominant power in the eyes of the people — a power more recognized than the legislature and the courts. Among the aristocratic and would-be aristocratic classes, it has been the one career, and the one avenue to eminence. But in times of peace, promotion is slow: it is liveliest only when war kills off or wears out superiors. Hence in the German army the chief yearning — all the stronger for being suppressed for nearly half a century — has been for war: the daily toast at the officers' messes has been for many years "Zum Tag!" Of such conditions as these, the natural outcome has been the barbarities in Brussels, Antwerp, and Louvain.

For these conditions of course neither the German people nor their Kaiser has been entirely to blame: everybody knows how, at the start, the conditions were forced upon them. But what pains have been taken to keep at the lowest terms their barbarizing influence, not to speak of doing away with it altogether? What has been the general attitude of Germany, under the Kaiser's influence, toward the proposals instituted by the Tzar — sovereign of a far inferior people — for the development of machinery for international peace?

This war, in its murders and destructions, is probably the worst calamity the world has ever known. Yet it is doubtful whether the murders and destructions are the worst things about it: for it has, for the time being, turned a people long among the most admirable and lovable and peaceable in the world, into a nation of destroyers, and made some of their admirable qualities — their coolness, their patience, their energy, their system, their ingenuity, their coöperation, their patriotism, all of which were long among the chief agencies of the world's progress, into the chief agencies for its misery and debasement.

But, with all the German's old-time merits, there is no blinking the fact that the current of civilization which came through Mesopotamia, Egypt, Greece and Rome does not flow through his veins. He came into civilization late, and he shows it despite the virtues Tacitus saw him bringing with him: he still holds the barbarities of a highly inflected speech, a highly centralized government, and a ruthless disregard of the finer amenities of both peace and war. But we repeat that, except as his barbarian warlike passions have been trained since the fifties, and now been specially aroused, the great virtues which he had evolved even when History first knew him, made him admirable and lovable, and when he has felt the consequences of his mistakes, will make him so again.

The obvious conditions would suggest, even to the visitor from another planet, that there must be two Germanys; and so there are — the Germany of industry and peace, and the Germany of idleness and war. The higher Germany — not the higher in the army or the state, but the higher in intellect and morals, even less than a generation ago was among the greatest examples of mankind. The lower Germany — baser though more brilliant — nurtures a nest of microbes, and they have entered into the blood of the higher, and made it mad.

One thing that has made possible this great tragedy is the survival of old ideas of high and low, which, like many other ideas, were once true, and in the progress of evolution have now become false — more destructively false in Germany than anywhere else in civilization. In all savage communities, the ruling class is apt to be the best. Evolution approaches equilibration — the beam of the scale approaches the level — by the arbitrary power of the upper class going down, and the capacity of the lower class rising up, until at last, we may hope all classes will be on a level. The scale of course oscillates until, if ever, equilibration shall be reached: the revolutionary movements at times place the lower classes in the ascendant, even make them for brief moments the rulers, — often very ridiculous and even destructive rulers, as in the French revolution, and the ascendancy of the silverites in the American congress.   But the mistakes of the temporary rulers from the ignorant classes have been nothing beside the excesses of a Zenghis Khan, a Tamerlane, an Alexander, a Nero, a Henry the Eighth, a Napoleon, and a William II of Germany.

The claim that Germany is waging a war of defence is too thin to justify attention. The Kaiser's responsibility for spreading the conflict is of course disputed by him and his supporters; but the thing has been brewing from the day the young Emperor, imitating the pirates and stage villains, pasted up his moustache farther than any other man's to make himself look fierce. No man of peace or modesty ever hung out such a sign.

He has hardly ever made a speech without showing his megalomania, and placing his army first among his many interests; in agreements proposed for the promotion of peace, from the first meeting at The Hague, he has been the one to hang back; and he refused the arbitration suggested by Sir Edward Grey, which the other nations seemed ready to accept.

But his responsibility for spreading the war is of little consequence beside his conduct since it began. His first step was to trample under foot his own nation's contract with Civilization itself; to violate the rules that, with infinite labor and through infinite suffering, had been slowly built up in aid of international peace and justice; to begin murdering an unoffending people whose peace his own country had solemnly pledged itself to maintain — devastating their country and robbing them of millions on millions, all because they had defended rights which, as already said, were pledged by his own country.

He had prepared for this by debauching his own peaceful, industrious, scholarly and harmony-loving people into such familiarity with the apparatus and drill and idea of war, that they have been taking on the army ways, ideas, ambitions and megalomania at a progressive rate that has saddened the former admirers who have visited them at sufficient intervals to notice the change. Even among the scholars, not only has the army influence spread, but the old allegiance to the simple life is gone. Our exchange professors report the deterioration. Says one: "They have been bought by court favors."

And they, like us, have been corrupted by their prosperity; their patriotism has become perverted into greed; and the vast industry, the vast wealth, even the vast population that this once exemplary people had built up in spite of the Emperor's colossal military waste, he is destroying to feed his own lust of power, and he has impregnated them with that lust, and the trade which his people have made worldwide by their industry, he is, for most fallacious and insignificant reasons, seeking to extend by their blood.

He is widely believed to be insane. However that may be, I do not see how any candid and unbiased judgment can find him other than a man forsworn, a robber, a murderer of the innocent — of his own people no less than of other peoples, a destroyer of civilization, an enemy of mankind.

Perhaps the worst tragedy in the whole awful drama is this man's militarism rotting out the morality of the people of Luther, Kant and Fichte. His ministers now talk of the highest moral stand a nation ever took, in England's defence of Belgium's neutrality, as the absurdity of going to war over a little piece of paper. It is also a large part of the present German philosophy that force and cunning are essential agents in evolution. The pity and tragedy of it! — that the German race, long the moral leaders of the world, should have sunk to a Machiavelism below Machiavelli — one not even, like his, superficially intelligent and refined, but throughout stupid and brutal.

This German military philosophy that reckons only with itself, carries the elements of its own destruction. It is already actually at war with most of civilized Europe. It may not be destroyed this year or even next, but destroyed it will be; and until it is destroyed, civilization stops and stands at bay.

If necessary, its every resource must be called into play. Even those of remote Japan are already in action. If the need becomes greater, inaction on the part of nearer nations will become disgraceful. The wisdom that ignored the comparatively petty issues in Mexico, will become folly if it ignores anything so colossal as the present issues may become, especially as they already deeply concern our own blood.

If the outcome of the battles shall be the Kaiser's victory, it will be for us only to reflect that the end is not yet, and that the Power which works out our good, often does it by ways that appear to our limited vision strangely devious. But if the battles shall destroy his dynasty, and dismember the artificial and cruel Austrian empire which ostensibly initiated all these horrors, and lead to a concord of the nations against such disasters in future, the justice of the Power above all empires will, despite all the misery, again be made plain.

It must no longer be possible for any madman who happens to sit upon a throne to wreak worldwide destruction. Whatever the cost, the peace of the world demands that Germany shall not hereafter be left in a condition to strike the first blow — that she shall not be permitted to keep an army large enough to give the military class the control of the nation, and that for her crimes against International Law she shall be made to bear proper penalties.

The next step to the limitation of her armies will be the limitation of all, and the uniting of them ostensibly, as they are now in reality, as the police force of the world.

It may be a relief to turn from the barbarity of the war to its absurdity. All its conditions are of course heritages from the barbarous past, and the only process of doing away with them is the slow complexity of human progress. Not the least element of that progress is the development of a sense of humor. If everybody felt the supreme ridiculousness of these conditions, they could not stand a year.

Another ridiculous element in the situation is the shortsightedness of capital. The force of the fighting world is in its wealth — directed by its brains. An army is proverbially a monster that crawls upon its belly. Now how long are the brains of the world going to permit its wealth to feed this monster, and leave industry and exchange paralyzed? Yet though those in control of the world's wealth have not prevented the war, they must have learned that it will pay to devote a good percentage of the wealth to perfecting the machinery for peace which centers at The Hague. That the capitalists have not already taken hold of those agencies, is as little creditable to their sense of their own interests as to their sense of the interests of mankind — and of the ridiculous.

The nations are still in the stage of civilization that individuals were when every man carried a sword, and impromptu fights were matters of course. The first step out of that stage was the organization of the premeditated duel, with its "code of honor." The next stage was the leaving of quarrels to arbitration and the courts, and the prohibition of individual fights and of carrying weapons to facilitate them.

The nations have lately made rapid progress toward the second stage. Yet International Law, though rapidly growing before Germany's attack on it, is, so far, nothing but a "code of honor." It prescribes rules for the conduct of international duels, both for the principals and for neutrals, but, like the code of the duello, it has no sanctions to enforce the rules but public opinion.

Among the most important of these rules is respect of combatants for the peace and independence of neutral states, especially when the neutrality has been specifically guaranteed by the warring states. Another very important rule is that unfortified towns shall not be bombarded, and that to fortified towns twenty-four hours' notice shall be given, to permit the removal of non-combatants. The military oligarchy who have corrupted and misrepresented the German people, have not attained to, or have fallen from, the stage of civilization needed for the observance of these rules. They invaded Belgium and Luxemburg, and dropped bombs into Antwerp without notice.

In these acts, the Germans have done what they could to destroy the International Law which has been one of the most laborious and most hopeful products of civilization.

All law, local and international, has been made by the most advanced people, and must be guarded by them against the less advanced. Each civilized nation has a police force to guard its national law, but International Law has not yet progressed so far. Yet whatever may have been the origins of the present war, the Germans' conduct of it has made them international outlaws, and constituted the nations fighting them a police to maintain the law.

Whatever the time and sacrifice involved, whatever other nations may be needed to strengthen the police force, the law must be vindicated, or civilization must go backward generations, and build the law up again.

That a union to develop and enforce International Law may result from the present war, seems among the possible compensations of the waste and misery. The world will have had enough of war, and more than enough, to a degree never before concentrated in as brief a period. In the early and long wars, men had not outgrown the stolid conviction that war was the inevitable and normal condition of the race; and at that stage of the race's evolu-

tion, so it was. But evolution has progressed, men's —
many men's — ideas are different, and during this unpar-
alleled tragic absurdity, they are going to become still
more different, and at an unprecedented rate. Never
before did a nation go to war as England now has done,
to vindicate, enforce, and preserve what had been evolved
of International Law. The German barbarities have
made all England's allies warriors in the same cause, and
have opened the eyes of the world, as never before, to its
value, its dignity, and, the blood flowing for it is going to
add, its sacredness. To the seed planted at The Hague,
this blood will be a fertilizing stream, and a growth may
be expected that will be a shade and a defence to the
nations.

EN CASSEROLE

Special to Our Readers

IN this number, we have put the war articles last, giving them the place of second emphasis, and at the cost of cutting into the Casserole, because at the time the table of contents was made up, we considered the topic of our first article, Free Speech, of more consequence than any War possible among civilized nations. But we did not then suppose that one of the nations we considered civilized was capable of stamping on treaties, violating neutralities, dropping unnotified bombs on cities, and, if late reports are true, guiding the Turk in another assault on civilization.

Resistance to such infamies we regard as of more pressing importance than even the main object to which our leading articles have been heretofore devoted, namely, the elevation of the humbler man. We even regard that as, in the long run, the most effective agency toward Peace. But sometimes in emergencies, the long run has to be disregarded. Thus, not the least of the bad effects of the war is its diversion of effort from the social and political amelioration to which, for a generation, the world has given a degree of interest without precedent in all previous history. From this cause, where we would have our peculiar function the saving one of a brake, even our own humble efforts must be considerably diverted by an emergency so overwhelming; and we know that our readers, despite their inclination for the still air of delightful studies, can not fail to respond to so general and poignant an interest.

Buzzing around this subject, one of our most valued contributors writes: "Please don't print a *peace article.*

There are only two possible kinds of peace in this world, while man is man: the peace of exhaustion and the *pax romana.*"

How prophecy does rage on this subject — on both sides!

Which peace with each other did the chief European nations enjoy from 1871 to 1914, and the English speaking nations from 1814 to 1914? And we seem abundantly justified in hoping that it may be permanent.

"While man is man." Which man — Homer's, — butchering unarmed foes whom he finds in bathing; or today's, — arbitrating most of his quarrels, and busying himself over schemes for the automatic settlement of the rest? Any one who fails to recognize the change in man, may well fail, especially at a time like this, to recognize the increasing peace and aids to peace among the nations. Between civilized peoples, war comes now mainly because of one decaying institution — autocratic government, and of one vanishing human peculiarity — the madness of the crowd — the readiness of men to do in mass what they scorn to do as individuals — to get excited over foolish causes, or no cause at all, and to find glory in doing at wholesale, work which, at retail, they shrink from as robbery and murder.

Academic Courtesy

A CERTAIN college professor was asked by a lawyer for technical information needed in a property case. The professor spent half a day in disentangling the material and putting it into practicable shape. With it he presented a bill for $25.00.

Was this sensible or shocking? — business or betrayal? The lawyer, who seems in no way to have begrudged the money, told the tale as an instance of vulgar commercialism worming its ugly way into the fair ethics of the academic profession. And with him doubtless most college professors themselves would agree, even in the face of his confession that for any scraps of legal information formally sought by the professor a lawyer would charge a fee.

To a layman the case for the defence seems simple. Here is no shining opportunity for the idealism of the scientist who, preferring to give to humanity the fruit of his works, refuses to patent discoveries made in the university laboratory. Nor is there in such an instance any question of aid to a disinterested "seeker after truth." A professor of Greek will gravely spend several hours in answering a village clergyman's question about the New Testament "baptism." The historian himself will take the free hours of several days to make out reading lists for a woman's club. But why should one man who is making his living give time and work freely to another man who is going to use them to increase his earnings? The professor's salary, unadorned by inherited capital or wife's dower or extra work, is not a living wage. He has to endure the annual appeal to humanitarian alumni to consider his needs, the reiterated disclosures of his poor economies and poorer expenditures. Why should he not take from a lawyer's pocket, rather than from a "donor's," in return for desirable goods, money which will pay part of his expenses to the next meeting of that learned society before which he is to read an unmarketable paper?

Why, indeed? we seem to hear the college professor echo. There is no reason save that he likes learning without courtesy, as little as religion without charity — and courtesy, like charity, makes no exceptions.

Simplified Spelling

While Germany is fighting in disregard of International Law, and the allies fighting in its defence, it is a good time to impress a very powerful consideration for simplifying English spelling.

Probably the strongest reason why International Law has developed so much more slowly than law in the separate nations, has been the greater difficulty of the nations understanding each other, and this is rapidly disappearing under increased facilities of intercommunication. Apparently there is no agency in sight which would promote this as much as an international language. Many considerations nominate English for the place: not only do more people speak it already than speak any other civilized language; but quite probably more people not born to it, speak it. Of all civilized languages, it is by far the simplest in its inflections and the richest in its vocabulary, and contains most words already contained in other languages. As a possible world-language, it far surpasses them all, except in the difficult inconsistencies of its spelling; and many devoted men, including virtually all the leading authorities, are now working hard to remedy these, perhaps their strongest motive being, as it is that of their most generous supporter, the interests of peace.

And now for a few words regarding some details of the simplification, which wil contain a few examples of mildly impruuvd forms, insted of the most outrageusly inconsistent of the uzual wons. Those we uze wil be inconsistent enuf in all consience.

Of experienses discuraging to those who favor the reform, the worst we hav encounterd has been in the letrs from members of the Simplified Spelling Board which hav bin evoked by our articls. Probably not one in five of those letrs has contain any new forms whatever, or at least enuf to be notist. If the anointed aposls of the reform don't bac it up any betr than that, those who oppose it hav occasion to rejoise. On the other hand, the letrs from som of the faithful who really wer faithful, wer deliberately impruuvd until they wer very funny, tho very probably our grandchildren woud not find anything funny in them.

If the reform ever coms, it now seems most likely to com thru peepl getting so familiar with the milder impruuvd forms in correspondence, advertisments, and prospectuses, that they wil be reddy to giv their children a consistent scooling.

In such ways, and thru argument and right reson, probably there may gro up, in time, approval enuf to start the better forms in som scools, and when that is don, the spred and establishment of such forms seems inevitabl.

But there wil be som difficultys that ar obvius even now. Inevitably at this stage, experts ar qarreling among themselvs, tho qarreling is hardly the term: for the differenses ar in the best of temper. It is a question whether enuf new forms ar yet agreed upon, even by those who attemt thurro and consistent reform, to make possibl a scool-bouk that woud succeed. The foregoing sentence givs som illustrations. The word we spel as *thurro* is spelt by the S. S. B. as *thoro,* and by the S. S. S. as *thuro.* The word we spel *woud* is spelt by the S. S. S. as *wood,* and the S. S. B. leavs it alone, after som tentativ votes that resulted in *wud. Wood* is excellent if identity with present practis wer desirabl, but if *wood* is right (*riit?*), how about *food* and *door,* and how, in any case, about using *o* to express a *u* sound? The S. S. S. setls part of the difficulty by keeping *wood* as now, and making *food = fuud,* and *door = doer.* The present *doer* (won who duz) it makes *duer.* With *fuud* and *duer* we agree; but with *doer* for *door* we don't: we think *door* as it is, is as good as possibl, and think that *coast, ghost, globe, lore,* etc., would be vastly impruuvd if they wer made uniform and to agree with door, thus: *coost, goost, gloob, loor.*

It is a question wether reform had betr wait for a betr agrement of experts, or wether there is now enuf agrement to justify anybody's going ahed with his share of it, and such personal extras as his consience reqires (*reqiirs?*) him to ad; and letting everybody's personal extras fight (*fiit?*) it out to a survival of the fittest.

INDEX

THE UNPOPULAR REVIEW

Vol. II

[*Titles of Articles are printed in heavier type. The names of authors of articles are printed in italics*]

A., Miss, 160–162.
Academic Courtesy, 441.
Academic Donors, A Post Graduate School for, 213.
Academic Leadership, 132—uneasiness of mind among thoughtful men; its significance and character, 132–133—present small regard for scholarship, 134—education and society, 135—need of discipline; failure of language and science courses, 135–137—superior discipline of classical studies, 137—"efficiency," 138—lack of academic solidarity, 138–139—value of common background of the classics for social efficiency, 140—Elyot's *Boke Named the Governour* quoted, 141–142—the Magna Charta of education, 142–143—intellectual aristocracy the basis of English education, 143–145—the aristocratic principle embodied in Greek and Latin literature, 145–146—liberty and distinction, 147–148—real service of the classics in education, 148–149—duty of the college to mould character and foster leadership, 150–151.
Addams, Jane, 5–6.
Advertisement, 216.
Advertising, 246.
Agriculture, 240.
Allinson, Mrs. F. G., 'Academic Courtesy,' 441; 'The Muses on the Hearth,' 189.
Americanism, 128.
Anarchists, 231.
Angell, Norman, 403.
Arbitration in New Zealand, 29.
Asquith, H. H., 402.
Associated Press, 230.
Austria. *See* War.

B., Madame, 388–389.
Balkans. *See* War.
Bartlett, Geo. C., 153–156.

Bax. *See* Morris and Bax.
Beer, 259.
Belgium. *See* War.
Belloc, Hilaire, 332.
Bergson, Henri, 184.
Bernhardi, General, 201.
Bismarck, 405.
Blues, On Having the, 301—gloomy persons, 301—superior persons and the blues, 301–302—a fallacy, 302–303—depression a result of weak nerves, 303—folly of fearing disaster, 303–304—blessings in disguise, 304–305—moral benefits of the Sicilian and Calabrian earthquakes, 305—worst blues, 306—uncertainty as to the goodness of nature, 306—borrowed troubles, how to avoid, 307–308—over-refinement in work, 308—value of sleep, 309—on "rising superior," 309–311—keeping busy, 310—faith in immortality, 311–312—the Providence that helps, 312–313—have reasonable since life is reliable, 313—brooding on death, 314—the normal feeling toward it, 315—mourning customs, 316—proper preparation for the end, 316–317.
Bosnia and Herzegovina. *See* War.
Brewster, William T., 'The Principles and Practice of Kicking,' 318.
Bruce, H. Addington, 'Our Debt to Psychical Research,' 372.
Bumpus, H. C., 'Trade Unionism in a University,' 347.
Burrows, C. W., 207.
Butler, Nicholas M., 365.

Cattell, J. M., 358.
Charcot, J. M., 389–390.
Chautauqua, Lecturing at, 116—personal point of view, 116—sudden summons, 116—arrival, reception and hotel, 117—early swim, Hall of Philosophy, lecture on Poe, 118—

445